Metonymy in Language, Thought and Brain

Bogusław Bierwiaczonek

SHEFFIELD UK   BRISTOL CT

Published by Equinox Publishing Ltd.

UK: Unit S3, Kelham House, 3 Lancaster Street, Sheffield, South Yorkshire, S3 8AF
USA: DBBC, 28 Main Street, Oakville, CT 06779

www.equinoxpub.com

First published 2013

British Library Cataloguing-in-Publication Data
A catalogue record for this book is available from the British Library.

ISBN   978-1-908049-34-6   (hardback)

Library of Congress Cataloging-in-Publication Data
Bierwiaczonek, Bogusław.
Metonymy in language, thought and brain / Bogusław Bierwiaczonek.
   p. cm.
Includes bibliographical references and index.
ISBN 978-1-908049-34-6 (hardback)
1. Metonyms. 2. Cognitive grammar. I. Title.
P301.5.M49B54 2012
401'.43—dc23
                                   2011030664

Typeset by S.J.I. Services, New Delhi
Printed and bound by Latimer Trend & Company Ltd, Plymouth, U.K.

Contents

Acknowledgements   iv

Introduction   1

1   A short history of the concept of metonymy   3

2   Formal metonymy   61

3   Metonymy in morphology   109

4   Metonymy in pragmatics   153

5   Metonymy in semantics   187

6   Metonymy in the embodied mind   231

7   Summary and prospects for future research   267

References   271

Index   289

Acknowledgements

This work would never had eventuated if it had not been for the support and encouragement of a great number of people. They are all too numerous to name, so I will confine myself to a few most important ones. As mentors, friends and inspirations I must certainly mention Barbara Lewandowska-Tomaszczyk, Linda Thornburg and Klaus-Uwe Panther, Antonio Barcelona, Mario Brdar, Roman Kalisz, Henryk Kardela, Peter Koch, Tomasz Krzeszowski, Günter Radden, and Francisco Ruiz de Mendoza. Some of them do not even know how important they were for the development of the ideas presented in this book.

As for friends and colleagues from Bielsko-Biała and Częstochowa, I wish to thank Ania Turula, Marysia Korusiewicz, Tomek Markiewka, Roman Ociepa, and Magda Czader-Wiśniowska for simply being there and trusting in me.

Furthermore, I am extremely grateful to Professor Iwona Nowakowska-Kempna and Professor Piotr Fast for their understanding and generosity as I was incessantly approaching them, as their humble employee, for money for books and conferences.

I also wish to thank Christine Frank-Szarecka for her patience with the first draft of my manuscript, which she tirelessly proof-read and improved.

Last but by no means least, I must express my deepest gratitude to Frances Byrnes and Sandra Margolies, my Equinox editors, for their extremely helpful comments and stylistic improvements. Thank you, Fran and Sandra.

Bogusław Bierwiaczonek

Introduction

If there was one single important change brought about in linguistics by the publication of Lakoff and Johnson's *Metaphors We Live By* at the beginning of the 1980s, it was a sudden interest in figurative language. Lakoff and Johnson's main focus in their book was metaphor and the ensuing years witnessed an unprecedented number of publications dealing with metaphoric aspects of language. However, it soon became clear that metonymy deserves at least as much attention as its more renowned sister. This realisation could already be seen in Lakoff's *Women, Fire and Dangerous Things* (1987) and Lakoff and Turner's *More Than Cool Reason* (1989), and was most emphatically voiced by John Taylor in his *Linguistic Categorization* with his now famous observation that "metonymy turns out to be one of the most fundamental processes of meaning extension, more basic, perhaps, even than metaphor" (1995: 124). As a result, the 1990s saw a whole wave of studies of metonymy, particularly in Europe, which culminated in 1999 in the volume *Metonymy in Language and Thought* edited by Klaus-Uwe Panther and Günter Radden, followed by a number of other collections of papers such as Antonio Barcelona *Metaphor and Metonymy at the Crossroads* (2000), René Dirven and Ralf Pörings *Metaphor and Metonymy in Comparison and Contrast* (2003), Krzysztof Kosecki *Perspectives on Metonymy* and the most recent Klaus-Uwe Panther, Linda L. Thornburg and Antonio Barcelona *Metonymy and Metaphor in Grammar* (2009), to name just a few. At the same time and perhaps because of this increasing interest in metonymy, the scope of the concept of metonymy itself and its relevance to a growing number of traditional linguistic problems has grown as well. Consequently, rather than a purely referential device, it is now construed as a major conceptual tool of both form and meaning construction not only in semantics but also in morphology, syntax and discourse. In pragmatics, it has been extended from reference to the theory of speech acts and inferencing.

The main aim of this work is to survey the studies which demonstrate how metonymy works in various aspects of language. Although in general I subscribe to the cognitive linguistic view that language is an inventory of symbolic units which form a continuum from single morphemes to large constructions of arbitrary length, nevertheless, for the reader's convenience and ease of reference, the whole body of the book is divided along traditional lines into chapters such as 'Metonymy in morphology', 'Metonymy in pragmatics' and 'Metonymy in semantics'. Metonymy in syntax is discussed in Chapter 2, which is devoted to what I call 'formal metonymy'. In many cases I discuss the contributions of other authors and researchers, but on a number of occasions I propose my own original solutions. I hope that my Polish perspective and data will make my presentation interesting to those who, like me and many others, consider metonymy as a universal conceptual phenomenon.

In addition, in the last chapter I attempt to shed some light on the possible biological or, rather, neural and evolutionary reasons why metonymy is so ubiquitous. Thus, another important aim of this study is to address the problem of the embodiment of metonymy. Comparable attempts have already been made regarding metaphor (e.g. by Lakoff 2005, and Rohrer 2007) and I believe the time has come for a serious study of the neural underpinnings of metonymy. As a non neuro-scientist, in this chapter I rely on the data, experimental results and theories that can be found in the available neuro-scientific and neuro-linguistic literature. As a set of first, extremely tentative suggestions, I hope this work will inspire other linguists, particularly neuro-linguists and neuro-scientists, to test these hypotheses in their experimental research and pursue these questions further. I have no doubt the hypotheses deserve attention because without metonymy our thinking and our communication would not be what they are.

1 A short history of the concept of metonymy

1.1 Classical views on metonymy

As with many other ideas in the field of rhetoric, the origins of the concept of metonymy can be found in the writings of Greek philosophers. Before we consider these classical ideas, however, let us recall that the term *metonymy* is derived from the Greek *meta*, a prefix indicating 'change' and *onoma*, meaning 'name'. This etymology may be misleading for the modern reader insofar as the meanings of metonymic expressions often do not, in fact, change at all. They often retain their prototypical meaning, but, in particular contexts, they may be used to designate entities different from their basic designations.

1.1.1 Democritus and Aristotle

One of the first philosophers who used and discussed the term *metonymy* was Democritus, quoted in Proclus' commentary on *Cratylus 16*, where he gives four arguments for the arbitrariness of the sound-meaning relation (cf. Householder 1995:93):

(a) 'homonymy' or 'polysemy' (i.e. the fact that one form may be associated with two or more unrelated meanings)
(b) 'polyonymy' or 'isorrophy' – Democritus' term for synonymy (i.e. the fact that some forms have the same meaning)
(c) 'metonymy' (i.e. the fact that words and meanings of words change)
(d) 'nonymy' (i.e. the fact that there are no words for certain simple ideas).

Clearly, for Democritus, metonymy was not so much a relation between senses as a process of motivated change of meaning, in agreement with the original meaning of the term. Another well-known attempt to define the change in meaning characteristic of metonymy was made by Aristotle. In particular, in the famous passage of Chapter 21 of his *Poetics*, where he distinguishes four kinds of metaphor:

> Metaphor is the application of a strange term either transferred from the genus and applied to the species, or from the species to the genus, or from one species to another, or else by analogy.

If metaphor is understood in its original sense as 'to carry over' one sense of a word to another sense, then it is difficult to understand why Aristotle included in his classification the first two cases, which clearly involve different levels of specificity and thus basically hyponymic relations. In the first case, a more general term (hyperonym) is used to denote a more specific term (hyponym), such as *boat* for *rowing boat*, while in the second case the situation is reversed and it is the hyponym (or at least a term with narrower scope) which is used instead of the hyperonym, for example *Adidas* instead of trainers or *Mercedes* for good cars.[1] As we shall see later, some researchers consider such relations as synecdoche (Seto 1999; Nerlich and Clarke 1999; Al-Sharafi 2004) and we shall adopt this position as well (cf. §1.6).

Unfortunately, Aristotle discusses the third case also in terms of class-inclusion relations, which renders his concept of metonymy extremely narrow, and would generate cases where an armchair is referred to as *a sofa* (on account of them both being 'species' of the same 'genus' of FURNITURE) and the word *cat* is used to denote a dog (on account of them both being MAMMALS). I will argue that such denotational or referential shifts are not impossible but they require a degree of analogy and a semantic 'leap' typical of metaphor, (i.e. a speaker may call a dog *a cat*, or an armchair *a sofa*, providing she perceives some analogy between the target referent and the source category). On lower levels of categorisation, however, such shifts seem to work differently and require what is fundamental for metonymy, namely conceptual contiguity. At the same time, however, they are linked by considerable conceptual overlap, for example among different kinds of sofa or cats, which makes them similar to the hyponymic relations Aristotle refers to in his account.

We may thus conclude that although Aristotle's discussion of metaphor has been historically important, it did little to elucidate the essential aspects of metonymy. Nevertheless, it does not mean that he was not aware of the importance of conceptual contiguity. He used it, however, only in his analysis of memory and failed to link it with language (cf. Koch 1999; Al-Sharafi 2004: ch.1.3). The metaphor 'proper', as we understand it, is indicated in the fourth type of metaphor discussed by Aristotle, i.e. the metaphor based on analogy.

1.1.2 Latin and later traditions

In Latin metonymy was usually referred to as *denominatio* or *transnominatio*. According to Koch (1999), the first full definition of metonymy can be found in a work attributed by some to Cicero, *Rhetorica ad Herennium* (86–82 BCE). The definition is as follows: *denominatio est quae ab rebus propinquis et finitimis trahit orationem, qua possit intellegi res quae non suo vocabulo sit appellata,* that is "denominatio [i.e. metonymy – BB] is a trope that takes its expression from near and close things and by which we can comprehend a thing that is not denominated by its proper word".[2] The reason why the above definition can be regarded as the first full definition of metonymy is that it highlights two of its crucial aspects: proximity and substitution. Although the criterion of substitution must be taken with care, as we shall see later (cf. §1.8 and 'An alternative'), the criterion of proximity (or, in a slightly later, but equally metaphoric terminology – contiguity) is probably the most distinctive of all properties of metonymy. It should be noted, however, that it was not immediately recognised as such. For instance, Quintilian (first century CE) seems to have overlooked it and defined metonymy as a trope which "consists in the substitution of one name for another, and as Cicero tells us, is called hypallage by the rhetoricians".[3] On the other hand, it is precisely proximity, on a remarkably abstract, conceptual level of signification, that lies at the center of Sacerdos's (third century CE) definition "speech descending from a proper signification to an improper [one] through an interpretation of proximity" (after Al-Sharafi 2004: 18). Other scholars belonging to Sacerdos's tradition of interpreting metonymy in terms of a process of signification were Charisius, Diomedes and Isidore of Seville. The subsequent analyses of metonymy remained largely unchanged and followed the classical accounts (cf. Ziomek 1990 for details). However, in the twentieth century two other approaches emerged, which I shall refer to respectively as formal and conceptual.

1.2   A formal approach to metonymy

In the 1950s Roman Jakobson made his famous attempt to reconcile the two key 'metaphoric and metonymic poles' of language with the fundamental paradigmatic and syntagmatic relations between linguistic units.[4] Accordingly, Jakobson (1956) proposed that while metaphor should be defined in terms of paradigmatic relations, metonymy is based on syntagmatic relations, which are by definition structural, hence formal. In that way Jakobson initiated what might be called a 'formal' approach to metonymy, although it should be remembered that Jakobson himself made it clear that metonymic links "combine and contrast the positional similarity with semantic contiguity" (in Dirven and Pörings 2003: 43). This formal approach is still very much alive and was quite recently emphatically expressed by Karolak, who claims that in the case of metonymy

> there is a transfer along the syntagmatic axis. ... [metonymy] arises when a syntactic position is not filled by an expression which is semantically compatible with the expression which opens this position, and, instead, another expression, which would otherwise be in syntagmatic relation with the missing expression, is moved to this position. ... The expression moved to the unoccupied slot in the

> semantic structure does not of course replace only the missing expression but the whole syntagm of which it constitutes a part. (Karolak in Polański 1993: 364; transl. mine – BB)

More recently, a similar though more balanced view has been expressed by Warren (1999, 2003), who distinguishes propositional metonymy (which is of a conceptual nature and does not violate truth conditions) from referential metonymy (which is based on modifier-head, hence formal, relations). Consequently, Warren argues that in the sentence *She married money*, *money* is used instead of the whole noun phrase *someone who has money*. As we shall see (§2.3 and 2.4 below) this 'syntactic recoverability' of metonymy must be restricted to formal metonymies. As Kalisz (1983) has shown, it is often impossible to formulate any single, predictable 'underlying structure' for most metonymies.

Finally, we should also recall an important account by Dirven, who also attempts to reduce metonymy to syntagmatic relations, but at the cost of considerably extending the scope of the notion of syntagm. As a result, Dirven distinguishes three kinds of syntagm: a purely linear syntagm, as in a phrase or sentence, a sociocultural syntagm, as in knowledge structures defined as a "combination of different elements or referents into a functionally ordered set" (2003:81), and an inclusive, figurative syntagm, which involves two different sub-domains of a single concept as well as metonymic chains relating the vehicle and the target concepts. The three kinds of syntagm give rise to three different kinds of metonymy:

(a) linear metonymy (e.g. *different parts of the country* for *people in different parts of the country*)
(b) conjunctive metonymy (*tea* denoting 'a light meal eaten in the afternoon')
(c) figurative metonymy (the expression *to have a good head* meaning 'to be intelligent').

Although Dirven seems reluctant to interpret linear metonymy in purely formal terms, a lot of examples of what he calls 'linear metonymy' could also be regarded as cases of formal metonymy as I use the term in the present study, that is cases where a part of the formal representation of a linguistic unit stands for the whole formal representation of this unit. (See Chapter 2.) I prefer the latter term, however, because *i)* it avoids the ambiguities of the term 'syntagm', which we have discussed above and *ii),* and more importantly, there are aspects of formal metonymy which could be straightforwardly analysed in terms of syntagm only if the term 'syntagm' was even further broadened, for example to cover spelling conventions, which is not necessary if the modifier 'formal' is chosen.

The fact that the new formal account of metonymy dominated in linguistic accounts for at least thirty years (from the publication of Jakobson and Halle's *Fundamentals of Language* till the end of the 1970s) does not mean that all linguists subscribed to it. One outstanding exception was certainly Ullmann, who remained on the lexical-objectivist level and defined metonymy as a figure of speech based on the relationship between words denoting objectively existing contiguities (Ullmann 1972: 218ff).

In the 1980s and 1990s the formal approach to metonymy gave way to the cognitive-conceptual approach (see below) but to some extent was resurrected in the work of Kövecses and Radden (1998), who discussed abbreviations such as *UN* for United Nations as cases of FORM$_A$-CONCEPT$_A$ FOR FORM$_B$-CONCEPT$_A$ metonymy (i.e. a sign metonymy). They also distinguished PART OF A FORM FOR THE WHOLE FORM metonymy (Kövecses and Radden 1998: 36), such as *crude* for *crude oil*, or *tgif* for *Thank God, it's Friday*), as well as two other formal metonymies, namely MODIFIED FORM FOR ORIGINAL FORM (*ibid.*: 43) such as *effing* for *fucking*) and SUBSTITUTE FORM FOR ORIGINAL FORM (*ibid.*: 36) such as *Do you still love me? – Yes, I do*. Thus they discussed a number of formal 'metonymy-producing relationships' but did not in fact set off formal metonymy as a distinct category. Therefore, in section 2 on ontological realms in which metonymy occurs they distinguish only Sign, Reference and Concept metonymies. A distinct category of formal metonymy was first proposed by Bierwiaczonek (2007a), details of which are discussed in Chapter 2.

1.3   Conceptual view on metonymy

The modern conceptual theory of metonymy stems from the work of Nunberg (1978), Lakoff and Johnson (1980) and Norrick (1981). Nunberg was probably the first to discover the referential aspects of metonymy and to suggest that what enables metonymic reference is a referential function, which, for example, links authors with their work, as in a common case such as *Plato is on the top shelf*. The same function may also link a customer with the dish he ordered in a restaurant, as in *The ham sandwich has spilled beer all over himself*. In their well-known book on metaphor, Lakoff and Johnson admit that "metonymy (…) has primarily a referential function, that is, it allows us to use one entity to stand for another"; at the same time, however, they point out that it also has "the function of providing understanding" (1980: 36). In their words:

> in the case of the metonymy THE PART FOR THE WHOLE there are many parts that can stand for the whole. Which part we pick out determines which aspect of the whole we are focusing on. When we say that we need some good heads on the project, we are using good heads to refer to 'intelligent people'. The point is not

just to use a part (head) to stand for a whole (person) but rather to pick out a particular characteristic of the person, namely, intelligence, which is associated with the head. The same is true of other kinds of metonymies.

(Lakoff and Johnson 1980: 36)

It should be remembered that Lakoff and Johnson distinguished a number of different types of metonymic relationships. In particular, they mentioned the following types (metonymic expressions are shown in italics in the examples):

(a) THE PART FOR THE WHOLE – 'Get *your butt* over here!'
(b) PRODUCER FOR PRODUCT – 'He bought a *Ford.*'
(c) OBJECT USED FOR USER – 'The *sax* has the flu today.'
(d) CONTROLLER FOR CONTROLLED – '*Nixon* bombed Hanoi.'
(e) INSTITUTIONS FOR PEOPLE RESPONSIBLE –'*Exxon* has raised its prices again.'
(f) THE PLACE FOR THE INSTITUTION – 'The *White House* isn't saying anything.'
(g) THE PLACE FOR THE EVENT – 'Let's not let Thailand become another *Vietnam.*'

This list was not meant to be exhaustive and it was not. We shall consider the problem of categorising metonymy in greater detail later in this chapter.

The last important work that formed the basis for the modern account of metonymy was Norrick (1981). What was special about Norrick's approach was that metonymy was regarded as one of the semantic relations whose properties followed from more general semiotic principles, specifically that "regular semantic relational principles instantiate special cases of more general semiotic principles of motivation" (Norrick 1981: 75). Thus, strictly speaking, Norrick's approach should be considered 'semiotic' rather than 'conceptual'. However, Norrick does refer to conceptualisation on a number of occasions, and his work apparently inspired a more consistently conceptual approach, which also included semiotic relations. Consequently, Norrick should be regarded as one of the forerunners of the theory of metonymy formulated by Kövecses and Radden (1998).

One of Norrick's most important contributions was a taxonomy of metonymy, recently adopted by Nerlich, Clarke and Todd (1999), who distinguish the following major metonymy-generating relationships and their particular kinds:[5]

I.   CAUSE – EFFECT
     CAUSE – EFFECT: *black – blacken, chilly – chill, dry*$_{Adj.}$ *– dry*$_{Verb}$*, kill the fatted calf – prepare a meal from the fatted calf*
     PRODUCER – ARTIFACT: *pot – potter, wheel – wheelwright, bread – baker, book – author*
     NATURAL SOURCE – NATURAL PRODUCT: *chicken* (meat or animal), *wood* (lumber or forest), *grape* (grape vine or grape juice)

INSTRUMENT OR PROCESS – PRODUCT: *copier – copy, toaster – toast, oven – bread, drill – hole, weaving – basket.*

II. ACTS – MAJOR PARTICIPANTS

ACT – OBJECT: *drink* (act or object), *nail* (object or act), *draw – drawing*
ACT – INSTRUMENT: *hammer* (instrument or act), *filter* (instrument or act), *house*$_{Noun}$ *– house*$_{Verb}$, *sit – seat, open – opener, gun*$_{Noun}$ *– gun*$_{Verb}$ (down)
ACT – AGENT: *baker – baking, bigot – bigotry, tailor – sewing, barber – cutting hair*
AGENT – INSTRUMENT: *farmer – plough, sailor – ship, trucker – truck.*

III. PART – WHOLE

PART – WHOLE: *sail – ship, blade – sword, head – animal, go to the bathroom – urinate, go to bed with someone – have sex with someone*
CRUCIAL ACT – COMPLEX OF ACTS or PROCESSES: *bring home the bacon – provide sustenance for the family*
CENTRAL FACTOR – INSTITUTION: *the press, the steel, education, medicine, furniture.*

IV. CONTAINER – CONTENT

CONTAINER – CONTENT: *teaspoon, cup, bottle, the eighteenth century* (people living in the eighteenth century)
LOCALITY – OCCUPANT: *the White House, the Kremlin, city hall*
COSTUME – WEARER: *crown* (monarch), *red cap* (porter), *black belt* (advanced karate fighter), *pantaloon* (old man).

V. EXPERIENCE – CONVENTION

PHENOMENON MEASURED – PHENOMENON EXPERIENCED: *warm* (cf. the ambiguity of *this sweater is warm*), *old and new* (the period of time a thing has existed or the period of time a person has been involved with it)
MANIFESTATION – DEFINITION: *fast* (current speed or permanent property), *happy* (temporary state or permanent trait).

VI. POSSESSOR – POSSESSION

POSSESSOR – POSSESSION: *That's Harry* (Harry's possession)
OFFICE HOLDER – OFFICE: *the director* (particular person or function).[6]

Although Norrick's taxonomy looks impressive, it raises a number of doubts. For instance, is killing a calf indeed the CAUSE of preparing a meal from a calf? Why should COSTUME–WEARER be set apart from POSSESSOR–POSSESSION, or even PART–WHOLE? What is meant by Central factor in Type III? Why should 'crucial acts' in Type III belong to a different type than other acts, as in the euphemistic expressions *go to bed* or *go to the bathroom,* included in the PART-WHOLE relationship? Moreover, some relationships are conspicuously missing, such as TIME – EVENT (e.g. *Sept. 11, 1939*), PROPERTY – ENTITY EXHIBITING THE PROPERTY (e.g. *turquoise, ruby* as stones and colors), SUBSTANCE – DEFINITE AMOUNT /PIECE OF SUBSTANCE (*beer – a beer, gold – a gold*).

As for the semiotic basis of Norrick's list, it is beyond the scope of this study to compare in detail the semiotic and cognitive approaches to meaning, but there is little doubt that one of the main differences lies in the differing perspectives of semioticians and cognitive linguists. Semioticians believe in the theoretical usefulness of the triangle of signification and, consequently, in the objectively existing referents (which/who can be represented without resorting to conceptualisation). Cognitive linguists, on the other hand, believe that the triangle reduces to a symbolic combination of form and conceptualisation (cf. Langacker 1987; Taylor 1995); therefore all semiotic principles are ultimately conceptual. If there is a third apex to this relationship, it is not the referents but rather neural assemblies/circuits and processes underlying the emergence of concepts and conceptualisations (cf. Lakoff and Johnson 1999; Fauconnier and Turner 2002). It is therefore possible to view semantic relationships and processes as linguistic manifestations of more basic neural and conceptual structures (cf. Bierwiaczonek 2005, 2007d; and Chapter 6).

1.4   Modern theories of metonymy

The increasingly deeper understanding of cognitive processes involved in linguistic phenomena, and the resultant theoretical proposals put forward by cognitive linguists in the 1980s, had their impact on the theory of metonymy too. The three related key concepts were *frame, Idealized Cognitive Model* (Lakoff, 1987) and *domain*.

1.4.1 Metonymy in frames

The concept of frame (cf. Fillmore 1982, 1985) plays a crucial role in the theory of metonymy developed by Peter Koch (1999, 2002). On the basis of diachronic semantic data, Koch (1999) shows convincingly that metonymy must not be reduced to purely lexical and/or semantic relations, since such analysis, Koch argues, would excessively complicate semantic representations. For instance, the semantic representation of the French word *feu* (fire) would still have to contain a semantic component or feature indicating its link with FIREPLACE (because this was the original sense of the classical Latin word *focus*, from which the word, via vulgar French, metonymically developed). Providing that the distinction between semantic and conceptual levels of analysis can be retained, contiguity must then be defined in conceptual, not semantic, terms. On the other hand, Koch agrees with those authors who point out that the term 'contiguity' itself is too metaphorical to serve as a defining term of metonymy. Therefore, in order to constrain it, Koch suggests that it should be restricted to components of individual frames. It will be remembered that frames were first used by Minsky (1977) in his work on representations of knowledge in artificial intelligence and were subsequently introduced into linguistic theory by Fillmore to represent non-linguistic, conceptual Gestalts providing the basis for linguistic meaning. Since frames are usually represented graphically, and hence spatially, the spatial term 'contiguity' seems suitable and may be retained. Accordingly, in Koch's approach, contiguity is defined as "the relation that exists between elements of a frame or between the frame as a whole and its elements" (Koch 1999: 146). For instance, since one of the senses of *bar* is COUNTER in the PUBLIC HOUSE frame, the word *bar* developed a metonymically motivated sense PUBLIC HOUSE (cf. Figure 1.1). This metonymy is of course based on a typical PART-WHOLE relation. A slightly different case is represented by the extension of the Old French *prison*, meaning ACT OF SEIZING through CAPTIVITY to PRISON as a LOCATION (cf. Figure 1.2). Thus the whole development is an elegant illustration of the PART-FOR-PART metonymy.

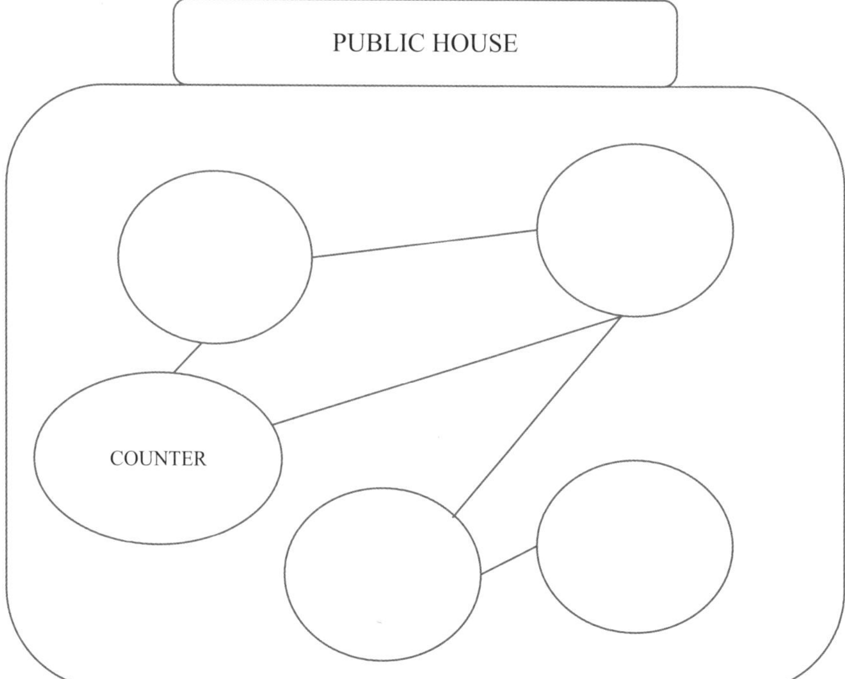

Figure 1.1 PUBLIC HOUSE frame according to Koch (1999: 146).

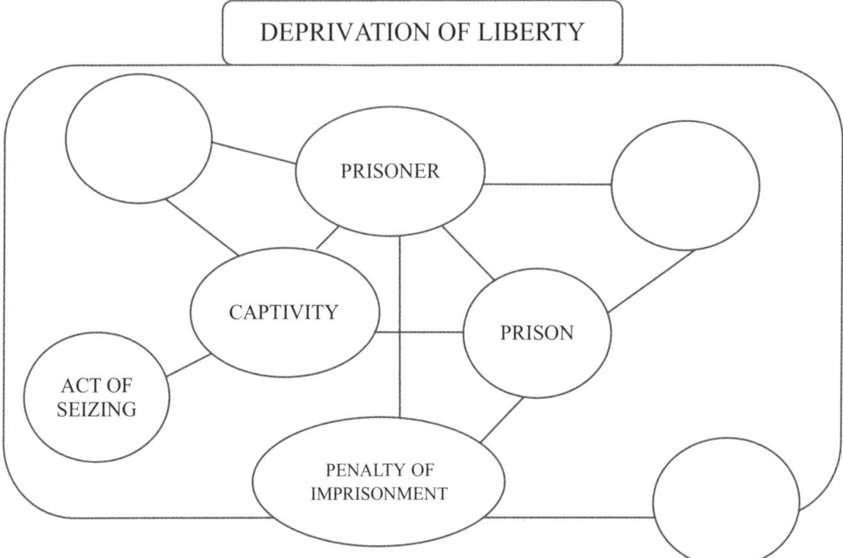

Figure 1.2 Deprivation of liberty frame according to Koch (1999: 147).

Koch's analysis is interesting and consistent; however, it still leaves us with the question of which elements belong to a given frame. For instance, does the PAVEMENT before the public house belong to the frame of the public house or not? Is EXECUTION or the JUDGE part of the DEPRIVATION OF LIBERTY frame? Koch tries to resolve this difficulty by stipulating that "frames and the continuity relations constituting them have 'prototypical' character" (Koch 1999: 150). Nevertheless, the question of the delimitation of frames remains and it seems that it can be answered either by resorting to a rather vague criterion of encyclopedic knowledge or by using empirical tests we shall discuss briefly in Chapter 6.

Furthermore, Koch claims that, if analysed in terms of frames, "metonymy turns out to be a 'figure/ground' effect" (Koch 1999: 151, 2001: 202ff). I find this claim rather controversial for two reasons. Firstly, Koch's analyses suggest that he views the figure-ground relationship in a binary fashion. For instance, Koch (2001: 204) proposes that the two senses of the verb *chasser* in French result from the change in the figure–ground alignment shown in Figure 1.3.

Details aside, Koch's analysis seems inaccurate as it fails to account for the fact that MAKE RUN AWAY is just a fraction of the whole ground of the HUNTING-frame and, in addition, it wrongly implies that sense B also has the component TRY TO CATCH, albeit backgrounded, in its semantic structure, whereas in fact the opposite is the case (e.g. if shooting is involved in sense A, it is meant to

Fr. *Chasser*		... try to catch	...make run away
Sense A	*Nous irons* chasser *du gibier* (= We will go to hunt game)	figure	ground
Sense B	*Nous avons* chassé *les chiens de notre cuisine* (= We chased the dogs from our kitchen)	> ground	> figure

Figure 1.3 Change in the basic and metonymically derived senses of the verb **chasser** in French, according to Koch (2001).

kill the game; while if it is involved in sense B, it is meant NOT to kill it). It seems then that the semantic transition from sense A to sense B cannot be reduced to the simple figure-ground shift, but instead must be represented in terms of a more complex difference in the construal of the frame, including utter obliteration of some of its parts in sense B. Consequently, Figure 1.4 (a) shows an approximate, simplified version of the prototypical construal of sense A of *chasser*, while Figure 1.4 (b) shows its metonymically derived

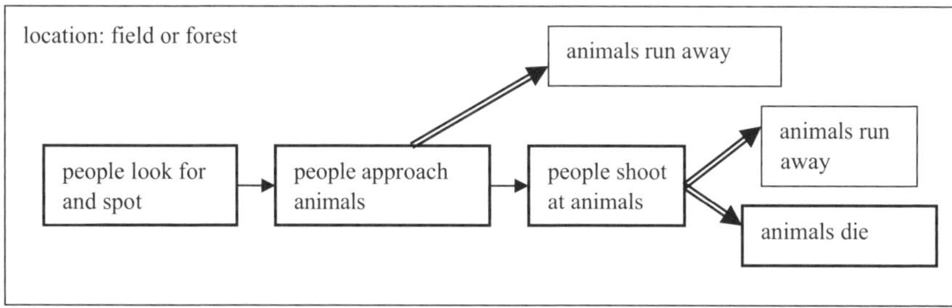

1.4 (a)

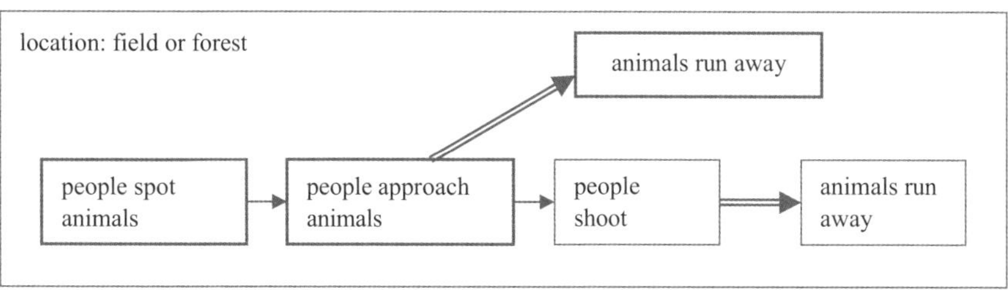

1.4 (b)

Figure 1.4 Schematic representation of the scenario of: (a) the prototypical meaning of **chasser** = 'to hunt'; (b) the non-prototypical meaning of **chasser** = 'to chase away'.

sense B. In the figures the bold boxes indicate activated components of the frame, single arrows indicate temporal sequencing, while double arrows indicate causal relations (which are often temporal as well).

As can be seen, the basic sense A of *chasser* perspectivises the sequence of events, including looking for animals, which lead to the death of some animals with the components of the animals running away backgrounded. In the metonymic sense B, it is the component ANIMALS RUN AWAY (caused by people approaching them) that becomes salient (although, as indicated, the running away may also be caused by people firing their guns), while the components of shooting at animals and animals dying are completely suppressed.

The other reason for rejecting Koch's proposal is that in order for some part of a frame to be selected as a metonymic vehicle it must already be much more salient than other parts of the frame or ground. In Chapter 6 I shall suggest that this aspect of metonymy can be explained if metonymy is considered to be based on salience within the image space (i.e. the mental space representing the actual perceptual content of the speaker's mind).

1.4.2 Kövecses and Radden (1998)

It seems that the most comprehensive and in many ways the most satisfying account of metonymy to date is the one proposed by Kövecses and Radden (1998), who have defined it as *a cognitive process in which one conceptual entity, the vehicle, provides mental access to another conceptual entity, the target, within the same domain, or ICM.*[7] This broad processual definition enables Kövecses and Radden to include in their account both semiotic and conceptual and formal aspects of language. The picture they propose is one in which metonymy is a basic cognitive process which underlies the emergence of meaning in almost all compartments of language because ultimately all 'realms' of signification, i.e. reference, form and concept, can only contribute to the meaning of expressions to the extent they can be conceptualised. As for typological distinctions, Kövecses and Radden consistently propose to classify various kinds of metonymy, firstly, in terms of ontological realms and, secondly, in terms of the ICMs they operate on. Accordingly, they distinguish 'sign metonymies', based on the sign ICM linking form and concept, 'reference metonymies', linking form and/or concept with a real-world thing or event, and 'concept metonymies', linking concepts with concepts. In terms of structural relations within ICMs, predictably, Kövecses and Radden propose two basic kinds: relations between the whole ICM and its parts, and relations between various parts of an ICM. Furthermore, they enrich the typology suggested by Norrick by adding to it another thirty-one kinds of metonymy-producing relations, and thus reaching the total number

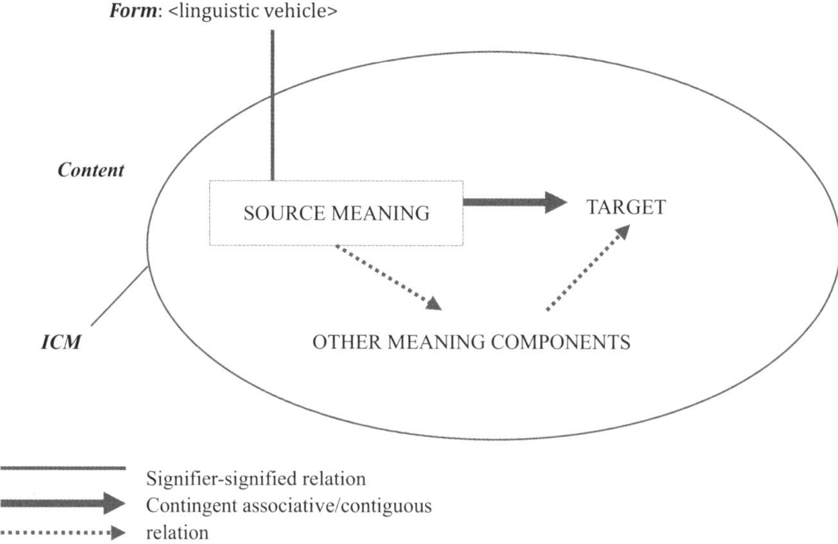

Figure 1.5 A semiotic view of metonymy, based on Panther and Thornburg (2005: 42).

of forty-nine. Some of the categories they have added were first introduced by Lakoff and Johnson (1980) and Lakoff (1987), for example metonymies based on the ICMs of scale, control and perception. They have also included in their list those metonymies which Norrick regarded as elements of the iconic code, such as OBJECT – REPRESENTATION. Panther and Thornburg (2005: 42) present Kövecses and Radden's idea in the form of the graphic representation shown in Figure 1.5.[8]

The only serious doubt I have about the proposals of Kövecses and Radden and Panther and Thornburg is that restricting metonymy to a single domain (or domain matrix) or ICM would exclude from its scope those cases that are based on novel on-line conceptualisations, as in the case of *The pork chop is waiting for his check*, where the customer and the food constitute two parts of a single integrated whole, which corresponds to Damasio's notion of image space, but which, by definition, is not as entrenched as domain matrices or ICMs (see Chapter 6). As a cover term that includes both fairly constant, well-entrenched ICMs and image spaces based on the on-line representations of current perceptual data I suggest the term 'single integrated conceptualisation'. Thus I follow the logic of Dirven's (2003) and Feyearts' (1999) argument that "the restriction of a metonymic extension to a single domain matrix is to be considered an inherent effect of construing two conceptual entities as contiguous" (Feyearts 1999: 320), although, for reasons to be explained later (see Section 1.8), I prefer the term 'association' to 'contiguity'.

This implies that for one concept X to be used as a metonymic vehicle for another concept Y, the two concepts must be conceptually associated. Thus, according to this modified Kövecses and Radden's definition, metonymy is *a cognitive process in which one conceptual entity, the vehicle, provides mental access to another conceptual entity, the target, associated with it within the same single integrated conceptualisation.*

1.4.3 How can metonymy be constrained?

Given the number of types of metonymy and its all-encompassing scope, it might seem that in the realm of metonymy simply 'anything goes'; therefore, it comes as no surprise that Kövecses and Radden also devoted a considerable part of their work to the principles governing the selection of cognitively appropriate vehicles. They divided the principles into two big groups: cognitive principles and communicative principles:

Cognitive principles

    (a) *human experience*
- human over non-human
- subjective over objective
- concrete over abstract
- bodily over mental
- interactional over non-interactional
- functional over non-functional

    (b) *perceptual selectivity*
- immediate over non-immediate
- occurrent over non-occurrent
- more over less
- dominant over less dominant
- good Gestalt over poor Gestalt
- bounded over unbounded
- specific over generic

    (c) *cultural preferences*
- stereotypical over non-stereotypical
- ideal over non-ideal
- typical over non-typical
- central over peripheral
- initial or final over middle
- basic over non-basic
- important over less important

Communicative principles

(a) the principle of clarity
(b) the principle of relevance

It is important to bear in mind that the above principles suggested by Kövecses and Radden should not be treated as absolute. Rather, they represent general tendencies motivating the use of particular metonymic expressions governed by a meta-principle which Kövecses and Radden formulate as follows: "the more cognitive principles apply to a particular metonymic expression, the greater the cognitive motivation" (1998: 71). They function as optimality principles which are not always necessarily satisfied and which at times conflict with one another. Accordingly, what Kövecses and Radden call a 'natural' or 'default' metonymy, and which might as well be called 'prototypical' metonymy, is one in which all the relevant principles are at work. As an illustration they cite the example *to read Shakespeare* (meaning 'to read one of Shakespeare's works'), as motivated by a whole set of principles, such as HUMAN OVER NON-HUMAN, CONCRETE OVER ABSTRACT, GOOD GESTALT OVER POOR GESTALT, and we can add TYPICAL OVER NON-TYPICAL, since the metonymy would be strange if the speaker meant 'Shakespeare's will', and, by the same token, IMPORTANT OVER LESS IMPORTANT, etc. At the same time Kövecses and Radden are careful to point out that the principles are not equivalent in terms of their 'local' weight, for example in the metonymy *The buses are on strike*, meaning 'the bus drivers are on strike', the principles INTERACTIONAL OVER NON-INTERACTIONAL and IMPORTANT OVER LESS IMPORTANT override the principle HUMAN OVER NON-HUMAN (cf. Ruiz de Mendoza and Mairal Usón 2007 for an explanation). Among the factors which cause such violations Kövecses and Radden mention social-communicative effects, for example the impact of social taboos and rhetorical effects, as non-default cases are unusual and hence more linguistically and conceptually intriguing.

Summing up Kövecses and Radden's attempt at constraining metonymy, we may conclude that their proposal is by all means an important contribution to the study of metonymy. At least in some cases, however, it is difficult not to notice redundancies in the proposed principles. For instance, it is hard to imagine a good Gestalt that is not bounded, although there are entities, such as units of time, which are bounded but are not good Gestalts, so probably the GOOD GESTALT principle is a particular instance of the more general BOUNDED OVER UNBOUNDED principle. On other occasions, the proposed principles are so vague that they leave room for almost any interpretation or need considerable revision, such as the principle MORE OVER LESS, which is supposed to explain why we say *How old/big/tall is X?*, as well as many cases when we refer to small amounts using nouns denoting whole substances, for example *Have you got butter?* But the principle is obviously wrong given the huge number of

PART FOR WHOLE metonymies. The principle is there but it must be reformulated. Or, perhaps there are reversible and non-reversible principles? BOUNDED OVER UNBOUNDED would surely be a candidate for such a reversible principle, since on the one hand there are cases like Kövecses and Radden's example *We had chicken today* or *I smell skunk*, but on the other hand, and contrary to their claim that they are "much less productive and more likely to be felt to be metonymic" (1998: 67), there are probably just as many reversed UNBOUNDED OVER BOUNDED cases, such as *gold* for things (e.g. medals) made of gold, *glass* for things made of glass.

Finally, it is difficult to understand Kövecses and Radden's rationale for including in their list the communicative principles of clarity and relevance. First of all, as slight reformulations of two of Grice's maxims of conversations (cf. Grice 1975), they hold for any act of communication, and thus *ipso facto* they should also hold for metonymic communication. In fact, it would be more interesting to find a communicative property of metonymy which makes it different from other acts of communication. The principle that suggests itself is not qualitatively different from one of the aspects of Grice's Maxim of Manner, namely Be Brief, but in the case of metonymic communication the maxim takes on a rather special significance and form, which is why I shall call it the Principle of Verbal Economy:

> Be brief. Don't repeat what your addressee(s) already know from their experience and context. Make maximal use of their ability to form conceptual associations and construct relevant meaning on the basis of the words they hear, their perception of context and their knowledge of the world.

Another attempt to constrain metonymy has been made by Ruiz de Mendoza and Mairal Usón (2007), who suggest three kinds of principles constraining metaphoric and metonymic mappings: the Extended Invariance Principle, the Correlation Principle and the Mapping Enforcement Principle. The Extended Invariance Principle (an extension of Lakoff's Invariance Principle to non-topological structures, cf. Lakoff 1990, 1993) says that in the case of metaphor "the generic-level structure of the metaphoric target has to be preserved in a way that is consistent with the generic-level structure of the source" (Ruiz de Mendoza and Mairal Usón 2007: 37), while in the case of metonymy the principle preserves the generic-level structure configuration of domain-internal relationships, for example the sentence *The buses are on strike* preserves the controlled-controller relationship between the bus and the driver. The Correlation Principle says that the implicational structure of the source elements should match the implicational structure of the target elements. Ruiz de Mendoza and Mairal Usón (2007) argue that the Correlation Principle determines the most appropriate choice of the source concept for accessing the intended target, such as *the ham sandwich* in the example

The ham sandwich is waiting for his check. Finally, the Mapping Enforcement Principle says that "no item will be discarded from a mapping system if there is a way to find a corresponding item in the source" (*ibid.*: 38). According to this principle, the clash between the ditransitive structure of *He gave John a kick* and the monotransitive structure of kicking is resolved by metonymically conceptualising effects of kicking as possession.

In Chapter 6 I will attempt to show how these principles can be reformulated in terms of blending of Damasio's image and dispositional spaces. We also return to Kövecses and Radden's principles and consider them briefly from the point of view of their neural basis.

1.5   Metonymy and cognitive domains

Because of the crucial role of contiguity and conceptual unity of entities involved in metonymic relations, it had been believed for a long time that metonymy should be distinguished from metaphor on the grounds that it is restricted to a single cognitive domain. Accordingly, Lakoff and Turner argued that metonymy "involves only one conceptual domain. A metonymic mapping occurs within a single domain, not across domains" (1989: 103). That view was, however, challenged by Croft (1993), who showed that, given the encyclopedic view of semantics, whereby the meaning of lexical items is represented in terms of domain matrices, the metonymic mapping in fact usually does involve mapping from one domain onto another. The crucial constraint on the metonymic mapping is that the two domains must both belong to the same domain matrix, while in metaphoric mapping the source domain and the target domain belong to two independent matrices. Thus, in both the well-known examples (1) and (2) below (17 and 18 in Croft 1993: 348), the complex matrix of *Proust* is evoked.

(1)   Proust spent most of his time in bed.
(2)   Proust is tough to read.

The semantic intuition that (1) is more literal than (2) stems from the fact that in (1) the central domain in the characterisation of Proust is evoked (i.e. the domain of PEOPLE specifying Proust as a person). In contrast, example (2) is felt to be figurative (metonymic) because the meaning of *Proust* has been transferred to the domain of his LITERARY WORK. To describe this cognitive mechanism, Croft uses Cruse's (1986: 53) term 'domain highlighting' and comments briefly: "metonymy makes primary a domain that is secondary in the literal meaning" (Croft 1993: 348). The difference between metonymy and metaphor can thus be described in terms of domain highlighting and domain mapping.

I find the argument convincing. The only doubtful aspect of Croft's formulation (embraced by Barcelona 2000) is that in Langacker's original formulation words are not characterised in terms of domains alone, but rather, in terms of salient parts of domains, called 'profiles'. Therefore, I suggest that the above quote should be changed to *metonymy makes primary the profile in a domain that is secondary in the literal meaning*. In addition, this formulation excludes active zones from the scope of metonymy, which, by definition, are not profiled (cf. §1.9.1 for a detailed discussion). Finally, as we have seen in the discussion of Koch's example, the above formulation may be at times too restrictive and should be relaxed somewhat in order to accommodate the possibility of modifying the domain as well (e.g. in the case of *chasing*, the domain of CATCHING may disappear altogether).

Another claim Croft makes in his paper is that if it is accepted (following Langacker, 1987: 300) that most complex symbolic expressions consist of dependent and autonomous predications, then "the dependent predication can induce domain highlighting in the autonomous one, and the autonomous predication can induce domain mapping in the dependent one" (Croft 1993: 359). For instance, in *She likes to read the Marquis de Sade*, *Marquis de Sade* is an autonomous predication, while *read* is dependent, so the predication *read* induces the metonymic highlighting of the TEXT domain of the predication *Marquis de Sade*. In examples of metaphors, for example *He entered a state of euphoria*, the autonomous predication *a state of euphoria* induces domain mapping in the interpretation of the dependent predication *enter*, whose 'literal' domain of physical SPACE has been mapped onto the domain of PSYCHOLOGICAL STATES. The same is true of noun-noun compounds like *bra cup*, where the autonomous modifier *bra* induces the metaphoric interpretation of *cup*, which designates its dependent part, since it is a cup *of* a bra.

Although Croft's generalisation holds true for most cases, it is probably untenable in its strong version, which we have presented above. The reason why the principle must be weakened is that there are cases where the same dependent predication may be elaborated either by a metonymic or metaphoric expression. Consider these examples:

(3)   I have to give back some change to the pork chop.
(4)   I have to give back some change to the block of ice in the corner.
(5)   The pork chop is waiting for his check.
(6)   The block of ice is waiting for his check.

It would be odd indeed to claim that in (3) it is the dependent predication *give back some change to* that induces the metonymic reading of *the pork chop*, while in (4) it is the autonomous predication *the block of ice in the corner* that induces the metaphoric reading of *give back some change to*. Of course the relevant part of the verb phrase in (4), *give back some change to*, is no more metaphorical than the same phrase in (3). Rather, it is the semantics of the head verb and the direct object that induce the metaphoric construal of the indirect object. The same can be said about (5) and (6), where again the subject NPs are both autonomous predications, whose figurative meanings, metonymic and metaphoric respectively, are induced by the dependent verb. The obvious conclusion is, therefore, that the dependent predication may induce either metaphoric or metonymic construals of the autonomous expressions. Thus we can fully agree with Croft's weaker position that "there is an attempt to 'match' the domain of the dependent predication and of the autonomous predications that elaborate it" and that "either the autonomous or dependent predication in a grammatical unit can have its domain adjusted, via domain mapping [i.e. via metaphor – BB] or domain highlighting [i.e. via metonymy – BB]" (1993: 360).

An interesting extension and modification of Croft's analysis was presented by Ruiz de Mendoza (2000). First of all, Ruiz de Mendoza suggests that metaphors can be broadly divided into 'one-correspondence metaphors' and 'many-correspondence metaphors'. An example of the former is the metaphor *Achilles is a lion*. The reason why it is called 'one-correspondence metaphor' is that what is mapped onto the domain of PEOPLE is a single attribute profiled in the whole conceptual structure of the source. In contrast, such metaphors as ARGUMENT IS WAR involve a whole set of systematic correspondences, and thus are called 'many-correspondence metaphors'. Turning to metonymy, Ruiz de Mendoza claims that it is possible to reduce all types of metonymy to two general categories: PART TO WHOLE and WHOLE TO PART. Thus, he argues, there are no PART-TO-PART metonymies. His argument is based on his analysis of the metonymy in *The ham sandwich is waiting for his check*, where he claims *ham sandwich* is part ('a sub-domain') of the whole of the domain matrix of CUSTOMER, rather than both the customer and the sandwich being distinct parts of the RESTAURANT domain. I find this claim justified (cf. Bierwiaczonek, 2007b). It does not follow, however, that the expression in question is not an instance of PART-FOR-PART metonymy. I think the argument is mistaken because it stems from confusing the concept of CUSTOMER with that of a PERSON. Quite obviously, the concept of CUSTOMER has as its fairly central parts (subdomains) the domains of PEOPLE as well as DISHES they order (or, more generally, PURCHASES they make). In *the ham sandwich* metonymy it is the DISH as one part of the whole representation (domain matrix) that is used to access another part, that is the PERSON (as a single instance of the category PEOPLE), rather than the whole representation of the CUSTOMER (cf. Bierwiaczonek, 2007b and Chapter 6 for a more exhaustive discussion).[9] Furthermore, there are other cases of predicative metonymy which quite clearly involve PART-FOR-PART relations. Consider, for instance, the following exchange:

(7)   A: How did you spend the weekend?
       B: Tom presented us with theatre tickets.

Even ignoring the fact that a VISIT TO A THEATRE is itself a part of the whole WEEKEND domain (scenario), the precondition (possession of tickets) is used to access other parts of the scenario, such as going to and watching a performance at the theatre, to the exclusion of the part representing necessary preconditions, such as choosing the performance and buying the tickets (cf. Chapter 4 for details).[10] Interestingly, even the highly conventionalised metonymy *not to have a roof over one's head* usually does not refer to the whole house but, rather, to a small flat (i.e. one part of the house stands for another part of the house). Similarly, in ironic expressions based on antonymy (cf. Chapter 5), one profile in the region on a scale of a property, for example the profile of *bad* in the negative region on the scale of INSTRUMENTAL or SENSORY VALUES, may be used to access another profile in the opposite region of the same scale, that of *good*. Clearly, both profiles are just different parts in the same scalar domain. Finally, in Chapter 3.3 we shall discuss cases of exocentric compounds, for example *pickpocket*, which also involve part-for-part mappings. In these compounds, Verb+Object part of a sentential construction stands for its agentive-Subject part of the same construction.

1.6   Metonymy vs. synecdoche

As we have already seen in the quote from Aristotle's *Rhetoric*, the GENUS-SPECIES relation was at first considered as a kind of metaphor. This view was quickly abandoned, however, and replaced by other approaches. Accordingly, classical rhetoric distinguished three master tropes: metaphor (based on analogy), metonymy (based on contiguity) and synecdoche (based on GENUS-SPECIES and PART-WHOLE relations). With Jakobson's metaphor-metonymy dichotomy, the traditional synecdoche was included in metonymy. As a result, both GENUS-SPECIES and PART-WHOLE relations began to be regarded as metonymic, the tradition still very much alive in Lakoff and Johnson (1980), who explicitly referred to PART-FOR-WHOLE synecdoche as a kind of metonymy, in Kövecses and Radden (1998), who included *pill* used for *birth-control pill*, clearly a genus-species relation, in their list of metonymies, and in the work of Barcelona (2000). Halliday (1994 [1985]: ch. 10) separated synecdoche from metonymy but continued to define it in terms of PART-WHOLE relations. On the other hand, in the 1970s and 1980s a number of scholars associated with Group μ in France and Todorov resurrected the classical tradition and emphasised the role of synecdoche at the expense of metonymy (see the discussion in Nerlich and Clarke 1999). It seems that the terminological confusion was

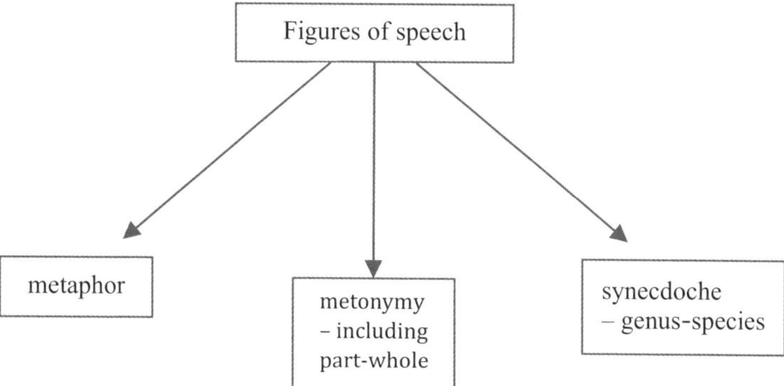

Figure 1.6 General typology of figures of speech according to Nerlich and Clarke (1999).

finally resolved with the realisation, voiced emphatically by Burkhardt (1996), Seto (1999, 2003) and Nerlich and Clarke (1999), but anticipated by Esnault (1925), that PART-WHOLE relations, as other relations based on contiguity, are essentially qualitative, whereas genus-species relations, based on set-inclusion, are quantitative. Since I return to this issue in Section 8 of this chapter, I will confine myself now to the reproduction of the typology of figures of speech as they were presented by Nerlich and Clarke (1999), enriched, however, by the notion of synecdochic metonymy, which will be discussed in Section 8 of this chapter. The term 'metonymy' (which may be interpreted as 'associative metonymy') denotes other, non-controversial kinds of metonymy, including those based on part-whole relations. In what follows I will be using the term 'metonymy' in this sense.

1.7   Beyond reference: typology of metonymy

If, as we have mentioned, Lakoff and Johnson (1980) saw metonymy as a basically referential device, operating on the level of individual words and more complex expressions used referentially, subsequent research has shown that it may be at work also on other levels of linguistic organisation. As we shall see in Chapter 2, it crucially determines some formal properties of language, while in Chapter 3 its importance in morphology will be discussed. However, even in its basic, semantic (or conceptual) sense metonymy cannot be restricted to simple reference. Numerous researchers (see Chapter 5 for references) have noted that metonymy often goes beyond the level of lexical semantics and motivates larger units, such as phrases and sentences, as well as pragmatic aspects of language, such as indirect speech acts and implicature.

Given this wealth of manifestations of metonymy, it comes as no surprise that there have been attempts to provide a more adequate taxonomy of metonymy.

1.7.1 Propositional metonymy

One of the most interesting proposals of this kind was made by Panther and Thornburg (1999, 2003a, 2005, 2007), who have drawn an important distinction between propositional and illocutionary types of metonymies. The propositional type consists of ordinary referential metonymies (of the DISH-FOR-CUSTOMER kind) and what Panther and Thornburg call 'predicational' metonymies (i.e. the metonymies whereby the predication *p* is intended to mean predication *q* implicated by *p*). An example of such predicational metonymy is the high-level metonymy POTENTIALITY-FOR-ACTUALITY, illustrated by the expression *was able to finish her dissertation* in sentence (8a) with its metonymically implicated predication *finished her dissertation* in (8b):

(8)   (a) She was able to finish her dissertation.
       (b) She finished her dissertation.

As an example of referential propositional metonymy, we may consider Panther and Thornburg's example (9a) (cf. Panther and Thornburg 2003a: 4) with its implicated extension in (9b):

(9)   (a) General Motors had to stop production.
       (b) The executive officers of General Motors had to and actually stopped production.

In metonymic terms, the proposition expressed by (9a) functions as the vehicle for the target proposition represented by (9b). Although the distinction drawn by Panther and Thornburg is extremely important, I find their proposal to refer to the mappings in (9) as propositional metonymy a little confusing. For the fact that the subject or any other referring expression is metonymic does not make the proposition metonymic or the metonymy propositional. Thus in (9) the expression *General Motors* represents a case of referential metonymy and the predicate *had to stop production* represents predicational metonymy. This does not mean, however, that there are no cases of true propositional metonymy. On the contrary, they are quite common and indeed involve propositions. Therefore, in the present work I propose that the term propositional metonymy should be reserved for the cases when it is the whole propositional content p of a sentence S that is used to access another propositional content q within the same ICM or the whole ICM, or integrated whole. The predicational metonymy in (8) above is one example of such propositional metonymy. Other examples are not hard to find. In fact, the exchange in (7), repeated below as (10), is another example:

(10)   A: How did you spend the weekend?
          B: Mary got some free tickets to the movies.

In the pragmatic account, B's answer is taken as conversationally implicating that B and Mary went to the movies. It should be observed, however, that the implicature is based on the PART-FOR-PART metonymy, whereby the precondition in the scenario of GOING TO THE CINEMA stands for the other parts of the scenario. The metonymy does not stop there, though, and in the next metonymic step, the whole script of GOING TO THE CINEMA is conceptualised as the central event of the whole WEEKEND scenario, which, through PART-FOR-WHOLE metonymy, gives rise to other implicatures, which are simply default values of the other subevents of the weekend scenario.

The main difference between referential and propositional metonymy is that, in the clear cases, referential metonymies can only be interpreted figuratively, because otherwise they simply do not make good, conceptually acceptable propositions. This property of referential metonymies manifests itself in the fact that when they are interpreted 'literally', they often violate selectional restrictions of the predicates with which they co-occur. Thus, in the well-known examples, repeated below as (11)–(15) with underlined referential metonymies, the propositions are conceptually acceptable and coherent only if they are interpreted metonymically.

(11)   <u>The buses</u> are on strike.
(12)   <u>The pork chop</u> is waiting for his check.
(13)   <u>The kettle</u> is boiling.
(14)   She introduced me to <u>the biggest brains</u> of their department.
(15)   He never played in <u>the football cup</u>.

In contrast, propositional metonymies make perfectly well-formed propositions, which, however, violate maxims of conversation and thus give rise to implicatures. Such is the case of B's answer in the short exchange above, and B's answer in the following exchange:

(16)   A: How are you and Sue getting on?
          B: Oh, she moved out only yesterday.

In the ICM of a good EROTIC RELATIONSHIP people usually live together. If one of them is moving out, it is usually because the relationship is coming to an end or at least is going through a serious crisis. Therefore B's answer, through EFFECT-FOR-CAUSE metonymy, implicates that B and Sue are not getting on very well at all.

Predictably, using the criterion of the conceptual well-formedness of the literal interpretation as a distinctive property of propositional metonymy, it is necessary to classify the cases of predicational metonymy discussed above as a special kind of propositional metonymy. Notice how B's answers in the two exchanges given above in (10) and (16) can be changed into predicational metonymies:

(17) A: How did you spend the weekend?
      B: I got a free ticket to the movies.
(18) A: How are you and Sue getting on?
      B: Well, we have just seen a psychotherapist.

It seems that the only difference between ordinary propositional and predicational metonymies lies in the fact that in ordinary propositional metonymy (as in (10) and (16)) it is the whole sentence that is used metonymically, while in the predicational metonymy it is only the predicate. For this reason, we shall modify the terminology and use the term 'predicative' instead of 'predicational'. Consequently, we shall distinguish two subcategories of propositional metonymy: propositional sentential metonymy and predicative metonymy.

1.7.2 Illocutionary metonymy

Panther and Thornburg suggest that illocutionary metonymies arise when "an attribute of a speech act can stand for the speech act itself" (2003a: 4). Since the attribute of a speech act is often expressed by a different kind of speech act, illocutionary metonymy often has the general form: ONE SPEECH ACT (SA1) FOR ANOTHER SPEECH ACT (SA2), where both speech acts are components of the same speech act scenario. Thus, illocutionary metonymies underlie what Searle (1975) called 'indirect speech acts' (i.e. cases where one 'explicit', direct speech act stands for another speech act), for example the uttering of sentence (19a) below, which has the direct illocutionary force of an assertion, may be used with the illocutionary force of an inquiry, represented by (19b):

(19) (a) I don't know where the bath soap is.
      (b) Where is the bath soap?

In Example (20), discussed by Panther and Thornburg, the speaker's expression of a wish in (20a) conventionally stands for a request, as in (20b):

(20) (a) I would like you to close that window.
      (b) Please close that window.

1.7.3 Formal metonymy

Before we close our discussion of the typology of metonymy, it is necessary to point out that in order to make this typology complete one more kind of metonymy should be distinguished, i.e. the metonymy based on purely formal relations between various units of language. This kind of metonymy, which is usually based on the mapping SALIENT PART OF FORM FOR WHOLE FORM, was dubbed 'form-level metonymy' by Barcelona (2005) and 'formal metonymy' by Bierwiaczonek (2007a). It is the latter term that I will continue using here. Barcelona (2005, 2007) and Bierwiaczonek (2007a) have shown that formal metonymy operates on various levels of linguistic organisation. For instance, on the level of morphology it makes it possible to use just one part of the form of a word, for example *fridge*, to access the whole form, i.e. *refrigerator*, while on the level of syntax, the same kind of PART-FOR-WHOLE formal metonymic process motivates ellipsis of the verb in gapped sentences, for example *John ordered meat and Bill fish*. This kind of metonymy, operating on the linguistic forms of different levels of complexity, is discussed in greater detail in the next chapter.

If we add formal metonymy to Panther and Thornburg's taxonomy, the picture seems complete. There are four kinds of linguistic metonymy:

A. Formal metonymy
B. Referential metonymy
C. Propositional metonymy (with its two subtypes: predicative and sentential)
D. Illocutionary metonymy

We shall discuss these in turn in subsequent chapters.

1.8 Peirsman and Geeraerts' prototype approach to metonymy vs. metonymy based on conceptual structure

The main point of Peirsman and Geeraerts' (henceforth P&G) proposal is that it is impossible to define metonymy in a single, unitary and uncontroversial fashion and, therefore "a non-unitary definition of metonymy is called for" (2006: 270).[11] Such a non-unitary characterisation of metonymy, P&G argue, can be best achieved if one resorts to "a prototype-theoretical model of categorization" (*ibid.*). According to this model, there should be one central and basic kind of metonymy, functioning as the prototype, while other kinds and types of metonymy should be derivable from this prototype. Since P&G find the attempts at defining metonymy in terms of domains unsatisfactory, and since many researchers agree that the definitional property of metonymy

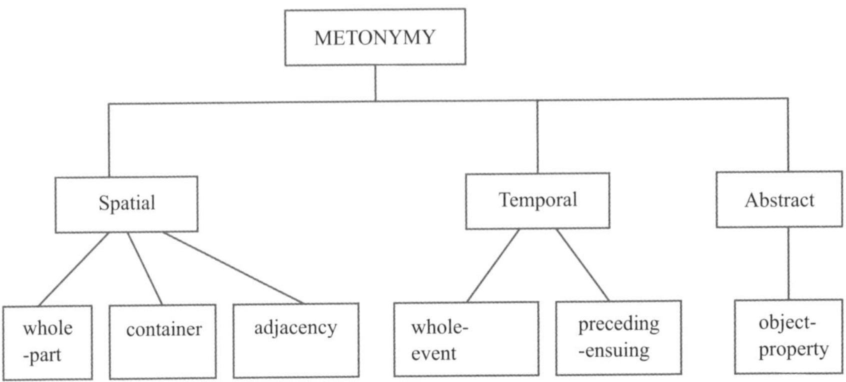

Figure 1.7 Typology of metonymic relations according to Seto (1999).

is contiguity, they try to construct an explanatory model of metonymy accounting for the prototype effects within the broad category of metonymic links in terms of different kinds of contiguity. The proposal that they find particularly useful as a starting point for their own attempts is Seto's classification of metonymy, as reproduced in Figure 1.7.

As can be seen, Seto's classification distinguishes three main domains and different metonymy-producing relations within those domains, with significant conceptual cross-domain parallelisms between the domains. The parallelisms concern the part-whole relations and various construals of proximity, from containment to adjacency. P&G modify and extend Seto's classification in the following ways:

1. They introduce a scale of spatial contiguity from part-whole, through containment, through contact to adjacency.
2. They add the dimension of various degrees of boundedness of the entities involved in metonymic relationships.
3. They add two other categories of domains to Seto's account: the domain(s) of actions, events and processes on the one hand, and the domain(s) of assemblies and collections on the other.

The result is a 3-dimensional model, reproduced here as Figure 1.8, with three coordinates: the first specifying the degree of association of the two concepts, the second specifying the degree of boundedness of the two concepts, and the third the domains extending from the basic spatial domain to more abstract domains of time, action/event/process to assemblies and collections.

The two questions that immediately arise are: is the model adequate and is the model exhaustive? It must be admitted that the authors themselves answered the second question in the negative, so all we should do is point to

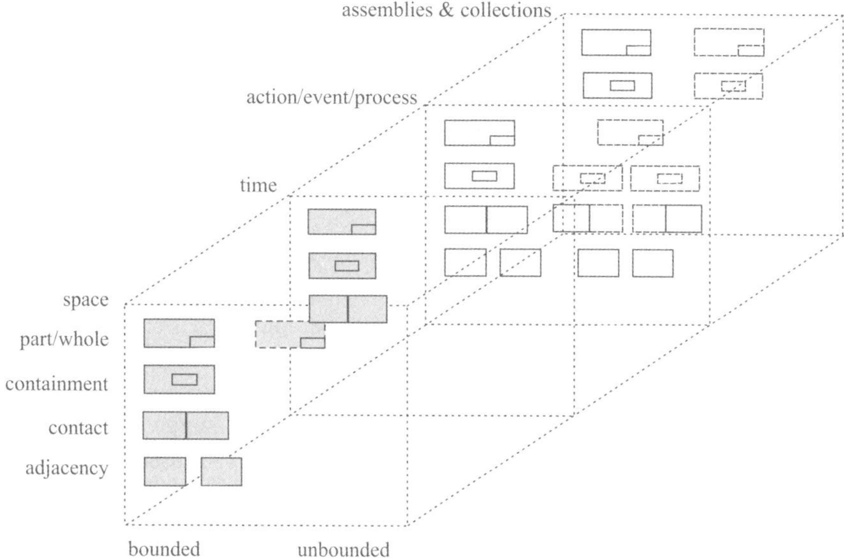

Figure 1.8 Peirsman and Geeraerts' prototypical model of metonymical patterns (scanned from Peirsman and Geeraerts 2006: 310, Figure 18).

the areas of metonymy unaccounted for by the model, which I will do later on. Now we shall focus on the adequacy. My answer is the model is interesting but it needs serious revisions both in its general structure and in its details. Below I set out my four objections to it.

Objection one

As for the general structure, it is rather difficult to understand the logic of the order of domains suggested by P&G. Granting that the physical SPACE domain is somehow intuitively basic, there is no reason why the next domain should be the domain of TIME, and why TIME should be followed by EVENTS/ACTIONS, and why EVENTS/ACTIONS should be followed by ASSEMBLIES and COLLECTIONS. The order does not seem to indicate increasing levels of abstractness as there is no reason why EVENTS should be considered more abstract than individual physical objects. Perhaps the order indicates that the domains are increasingly more complex? But then P&G never explain how they arrived at this particular scale of complexity.

Secondly and relatedly, it seems rather strange that ASSEMBLIES and COLLECTIONS form different categories of domains than SPACE. P&G may argue that ASSEMBLIES are so heterogeneous that it would be misleading to put them into a single ontological category. I can agree with that. Nevertheless, COLLECTIONS are prototypically just sets of similar physical entities; therefore, they should be classified within the domain of SPACE, perhaps as a special kind of contact or adjacency (see below). On the other hand, if the domain homogeneity is regarded as criterial, then it is extremely difficult to tease out TIME as a separate domain, independent of ACTIONS/EVENTS/PROCESSES, and ACTIONS/EVENTS/PROCESSES as independent of TIME, as the domain of TIME is crucial for their characterisation.

Objection two

The second argument against P&G's account is that they have not defined the notion of adjacency with sufficient precision. What is it that makes two or more concepts adjacent rather than separate, and therefore suitable for metonymic rather than metaphoric mapping? Is it just a matter of physical and/or conceptual distance or is it rather a matter of stronger or weaker association? This indicates that Croft is probably right suggesting that it's much better to see metonymy as a phenomenon based on association than on contiguity. His argument is that "contiguity unlike association implies a notion of spatial nearness" (2006: 319), which often simply does not occur because metonymy may and often does apply to non-spatial concepts, for example TIME FOR EVENT in *Sept. 11th*. In fact, spatial contiguity may be the prototypical kind of association and that is why, as a technical term, it is used metaphorically to denote various kinds of non-spatial associations as well. A likely reason why it has been so often used and misused is that conceptual domains, domain matrices and more generally semantic representations are usually construed as spatial objects, which means that what is conceptually associated is construed as spatially near. P&G provide an excellent example of this kind of metaphorisation by showing how the term 'contiguity' may be used with reference to the domain of TIME. In Bierwiaczonek (2007b) and in Chapter 6 below I argue that from the point of view of neural organisation, it is the association (synaptic links and circuits) of neural assemblies that matters, not their actual physical proximity or contiguity.

Objection three

The third, and perhaps the most serious, objection that can be raised against P&G's account is that they confuse what Seto calls 'E(ntity) relations' with 'C(ategory) relations' and discuss them all in terms of assemblies and collections. Surprisingly, they start off by presenting a threefold classification of part-whole relations, reproduced here as Figure 1.9.

The representations are, however, misleading in that they present taxonomies, assemblies and collections as the same kinds of relations, whereas taxonomy is quite different from the other two. This is what Burkhardt (1996) calls the equivocation of the word *part*, which may mean 'component' ('Bestandtail') or 'subset' ('Teilmenge'). In particular, assemblies and collections are rather uncontroversial E-relations, based on

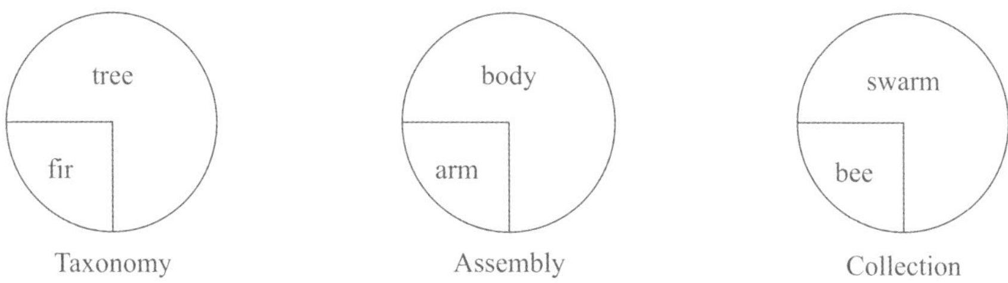

Figure 1.9 Peirsman and Geeraerts' classification of part-whole relations.

the conceptualisations of real-world part-whole relations, where the whole perceptually and conceptually consists of parts regarded as subsets or members. Accordingly, it is natural to say that an arm is part of a body and a bee is part of a swarm. In contrast, taxonomies are typical C-relations, whose extensional definition may treat them as collections, but then it is a definition of a collection of trees (e.g. *park* or *forest*, which are the same collective concepts as SWARM), rather than *tree*, and thus we cannot say *A tree consists of firs, oaks*, etc. or *A fir is a part of a tree* in the way we can say *A body consists of arms, legs,* etc, *A swarm consists of many bees* or *An arm is a part of a body* or *A bee is often part of a swarm*. In addition, Seto himself makes it clear that the diagram is just 'a spatial metaphor': "Since there is no natural form given to the fir class, when we speak of it as being a part of the tree category, we are thinking metaphorically" (Seto 1999: 94). The literal, 'real world' parts of a tree are branches, trunk and roots, not firs and oaks. Therefore we may agree with Seto that "to avoid theoretical confusion, the uses of 'whole' and 'part' should be restricted to partonomy, for example the whole-part relation in the world" (*ibid.*: 94). But there is one more reason why P&G's proposal should be rejected. As Panther and Thornburg (2000b) observed, metonymies are based on contingency (see also Brdar 2007 and Chapter 5 below). Although the concept of contingency is rather vague and subject to gradation, there is no doubt that the condition of contingency is satisfied in assemblies and collections (i.e. a body without an arm is still a body and a swarm without a bee is still a swarm), whereas it is systematically violated in taxonomies. In fact, the special 'necessary' link between C-relations is often definitional, as traditionally taxonomies underlying hyponymy are defined in terms of unilateral entailment: for example cutting a fir tree entails cutting a tree, but cutting a tree does not entail cutting a fir tree. The conclusion is that neither relation discussed by P&G, that is HYPERONYM FOR HYPONYM (e.g. *pill* for *contraceptive pill)* nor HYPONYM FOR HYPERONYM (e.g. *Kodak* for *camera)* are true cases of metonymy! Admittedly, P&G do see the problem and acknowledge that "we should be careful not to range the hyperonym and hyponym pattern too rapidly with metonymy. In any case, we seem to have reached the borderline of metonymy with hyperonym and hyponym pattern: to the extent that it is a metonymy at all, it is a highly specific and peripheral case" (Peirsman and Geeraerts 2006: 308). As we have seen in Section 1.5 above, a number of researchers (e.g. Burkhardt 1996; Seto 1999, 2003; Nerlich and Clarke 1999) have already decided that the transfer of meaning based on genus-species relations should be restricted to synecdoche, considered as an independent figure of speech. In the section *An Alternative*, below, I present a theory of metonymy based on conceptual relations which avoids at least some of the problems raised by P&G's excessively inclusive account.

Objection four

Finally, if the category of metonymy has indeed a prototypical structure, it is hard to interpret the model proposed by P&G as the prototypical category of metonymical structures. The point is that prototypical categories have proto-typical and less prototypical members and the models of such prototypical categories should show how the more peripheral subcategories are related to the prototype. In P&G's model there is no indication which 'metonymical pattern' is to be considered as prototypical, nor how the metonymical patterns in various domains are related. To be sure, P&G explicitly state that "spatial part-whole relations [are] the core of the category" (Peirsman and Geeraerts 2006: 309), but, as Croft pointed out, this has not been at all demonstrated by means of any well-known prototypicality tests, for example graded accept-ability judgments, order of mention, frequency of occurrence. However, even if it is accepted that the area in the left upper corner of each domain is to be interpreted as prototypical (i.e. the area of part-whole bounded relations), we are still left with the problem of how to interpret the linear ordering of domains. The diagram suggests that what happens in the domain of SPACE is somehow related to, or perhaps projected on, the domain of TIME, which in turn serves as the source domain for the domain of ACTIONS, EVENTS and PROCESS, which in turn provides the model for the domain of ASSEMBLIES and COLLECTIONS. However, P&G do not give any arguments that this indeed is the direction of extension, nor do they explain why and how the domain of ASSEMBLIES and COLLECTIONS should need the domain of TIME in order to develop its metonymic senses, rather than the domain of SPACE, with which it has much more in common.

An alternative

The alternative I offer is not radically different from P&G's proposal, although it does differ from it in a number of crucial respects. What the two approaches have in common is that indeed metonymy is not a unitary phenomenon as it uses different kinds of conceptual structures. We differ, however, in that what P&G regard as different forms of contiguity I regard as different forms of associa-tions between concepts, where association may be defined as a relationship between two or more concepts $C_{a1}, C_{a2}, \ldots C_{an}$, such that an activation of one of those concepts, for example C_{a1}, is likely to cause systematic activation of the other concepts C_a. Furthermore, associated concepts may or may not form coherent conceptualisations; it is only those associations that form integrated conceptualisations that are used in metonymy.[12] In other words, I agree with both P&G and Feyaerts that "The essence of metonymy resides in the nature of the relationship that connects two concepts with each other" (Feyaerts 1999: 329), but I consider association as a better, more neutral term than contiguity. In addition, there are three other important differences: First I propose two basic kinds of metonymy-producing relations between concepts (with P&G's distinctions exhibiting specific elaborations of the two); second I offer a substantially different treatment of concepts based on inclusion; and third I argue that any attempt to define metonymy in terms of particular kinds of domain (e.g. spatial, temporal) is wrong as it distorts the fundamentally conceptual nature of metonymy. The main advantage of the alternative discussed below is that it provides a single basis of analysis not only of metonymy and metaphor but also of all semantic relations. In addition, it offers new ways of distinguishing metonymy from metaphor and sheds new light on their mutual relationship.

The details of my proposal are as follows: First of all, my position is that the cases of taxonomic elaborations and generalisations (schematisations) should not be regarded as metonymic at all (see Koch 1999 for a similar view). As we saw in Section 1.5, any transfer along the axis of generality-specificity should be classified as synecdoche. Apart from the conceptual and logical differences between those relations and the relations based on contingent associations characteristic of metonymies, which could be explained away in a model with prototype structure, there is another reason why taxonomic relations should be excluded from the scope of metonymy. The reason is practical: the taxonomic relations should be excluded, because if they are not excluded, the scope of metonymy will be so large that it will become virtually void of content. What would make the scope of metonymy so dangerously large is the fact that each denotational language usage is schematic with respect to the conceptualisation it designates (which is known as 'indeterminacy' of language by philosophers (cf. Ingarden 1960). Take for example the statement I *bought a flower*. Here *flower* denotes some particular flower, for example a rose. If I say *I bought a rose*, *rose* denotes a particular kind of rose, for example a hybrid tea. Granting the indeterminacy of language, most linguistic expressions can be viewed as superordinate with respect to their target meanings, which in turn implies that if, in addition to the relations based on association, hyperonymic and hyponymic relations are also considered as metonymic, then each denotational expression is metonymic, which renders the concept of metonymy descriptively and theoretically useless.

As for borderline cases, it is surprising that in their discussion of taxonomies P&G have ignored (or overlooked) one particularly important relationship, namely that between the members of a category on the same level of schematicity/elaboration (e.g. when one refers to an Alsatian as *a Pekinese*, or an Opel Corsa as *a Mercedes)*. On the level of lexical semantics the transfer has been dubbed aptly 'co-hyponymous transfer' (cf. Blank 2003), which may result in new senses, as in the case of Late Latin *talpus* meaning 'mole', which in Italian (*topo*) and Sardinian (*topi*) developed the sense 'mouse', and French *rat* and dialectal Italian *rat* (from **ratt-* = 'rat'), which also developed a new sense of 'mouse'. The relationship is important because it seems to provide good ground for distinguishing metonymy from metaphor, or at least for drawing a sharp line in the fuzzy area separating the two phenomena. My proposal, which may be called the Principle of Minimal and Maximal Overlap (PMMO), is this:

> Principle of Minimal and Maximal Overlap – When one basic or higher level category is used as a source for another basic or higher level category, the transfer is metaphoric. When one lower-than-basic level category is used as a source for another lower-than-basic level category, the transfer is metonymic.

Let us illustrate this using two folk taxonomies (Figure 1.10) which represent, respectively, natural and artifact taxonomies, and in which the basic level of categorisation is marked by thick boxes. According to PMMO, if speaker S says *crocodile* referring to a dog, or *boat* referring to a motor car, s/he is speaking metaphorically, because s/he is transferring one basic level concept to another basic level concept. If, however, S uses *bulldog* referring to a dachshund, or *limousine* referring to a sedan, then S is speaking metonymically, as s/he substitutes one member of the sub-basic category for another member of that category.[13]

At this point we might be prompted to ask what makes the basic level so critical in distinguishing the two kinds of transfer. In fact the answer to this question has been known at least since the first publication of Rosch's studies of basic level categories and prototypes (Rosch 1978; cf. also Taylor 1995: ch. 3), where she pointed out that basic level categories a) maximise the number of attributes shared by members of the category and b) minimise the number of attributes shared with members of other categories. Thus the basic level is the level which determines the greatest conceptual distance between the categories of a single taxonomy. The categories on the basic level are maximally distinct, while the categories below it are considerably similar. In terms of domains or ICMs often referred to in the definitions of metaphor and metonymy, it may be suggested that a basic level category provides most of the central domains of the domain matrices of its lower-level subcategories,

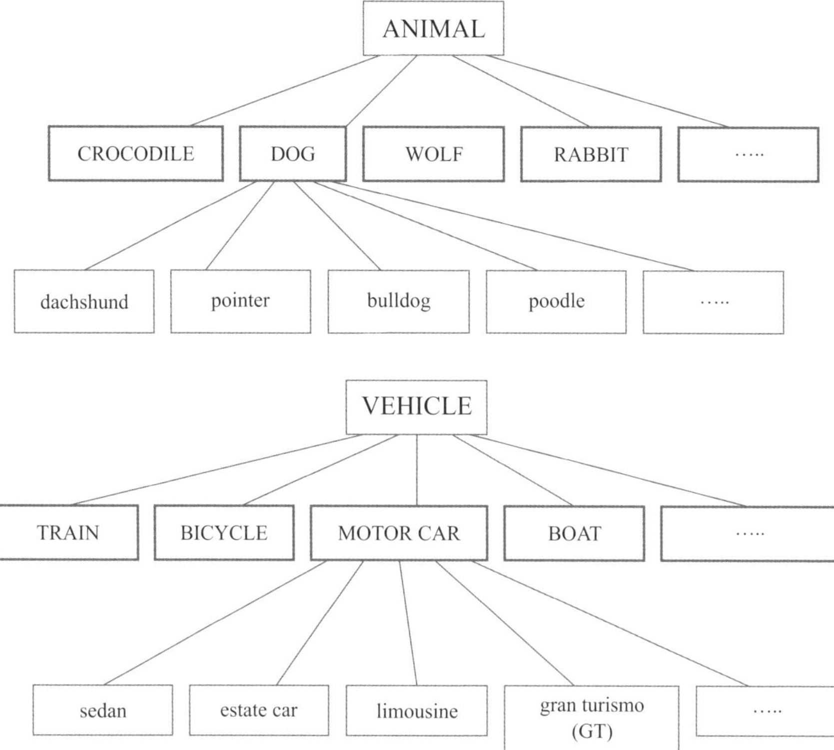

Figure 1.10 Superordinate, basic and subordinate levels of categorisation as basis for metaphoric and metonymic transfers of meaning.

while the basic-level categories differ in most of their domains, and hence may be considered to belong to different domain matrices.

The proposed analysis, outlined in Bierwiaczonek (2002), is based on different relations between concepts, which are defined as conceptual regions within conceptual space determined by profiles in conceptual domains and other concepts. In general, the more central domains and concepts the two concepts share, the more they overlap, and the more distinct the domains and concepts that determine their conceptual regions, the more separated they are.[14] The different relations can be represented diagrammatically as shown in Figure 1.11.

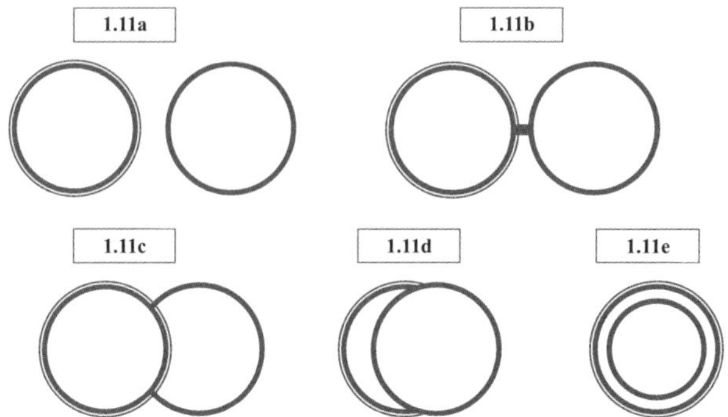

Figure 1.11 Five basic kinds of conceptual relations: (1.11a)–(1.11e).

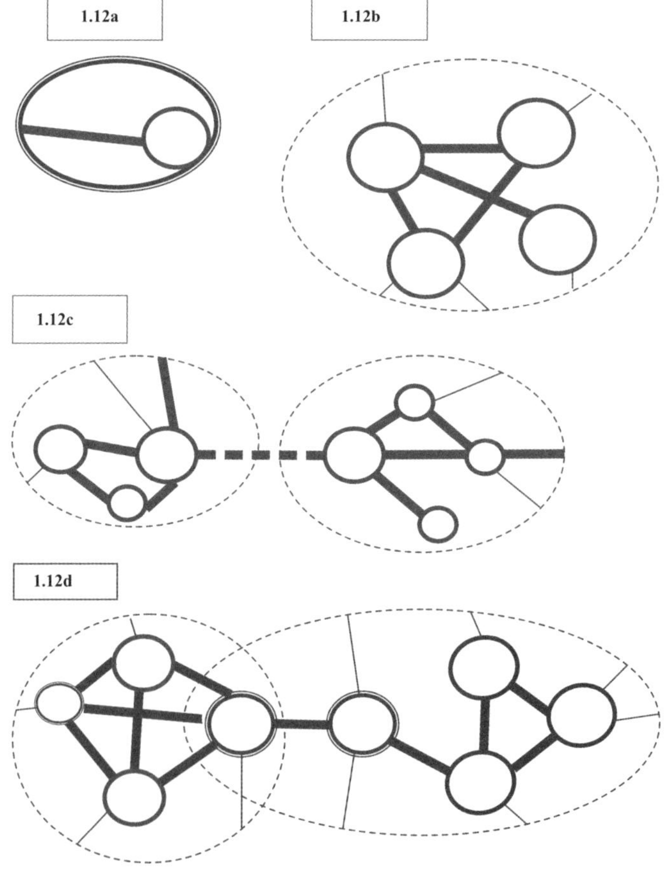

Figure 1.12 Specific realisations of conceptual relations as reflected in lexical relations (1.12a)–(1.12d).

As the diagrams show, there are five basic kinds of conceptual relations (Figure 1.11) which in various forms are reflected in lexical relations (Figure 1.12):[15]

    i.   unassociated separation (i.e. no overlap and no link at all), for example the concepts of FLOWER and DEMOCRACY or AIR and SENTENCE. At times unassociated separation manifests itself in 'distant' ontological metaphors, and double scope integration networks, for example the conceptual regions of the concepts of LOVE and FIRE are determined by different domains (LOVE: INTERPERSONAL RELATIONS, FEELINGS, VOLITIONS; FIRE: ELEMENTS, TEMPERATURE, DESTRUCTION), thus they may be linked only indirectly, for example through the domain of TEMPERATURE which is part of the folk cognitive model of FEELINGS. Since the link is so indirect, the two concepts are not part of the same larger integrated conceptualisation and can only be connected metaphorically. Thus, in Figure 1.11, the configuration represented in 1.11a may be linked, through metaphor and change into the configuration 1.12c, in Figure 1.12, which may lead some researchers (e.g. Lakoff and Johnson 1999: 71f) to believe that some concepts, like LOVE, are never independent of the metaphors for those concepts.

   ii.   associated separation, which manifests itself in meronymy, antonymy, reversiveness, metonymic synonymy and other non-semantic relations, as in the strong unidirectional associative link between KETTLE and WATER. If the two concepts are ontologically similar, their conceptual regions may overlap but they may be still associated as two independent concepts, shown in 1.12a, in Figure 1.12, as in the case of LOVE and CARE discussed in Chapter 5. On account of the overlap, this is a non-prototypical case on the borderline between true separation and overlap shown in 1.11d, in Figure 1.11.

As I already pointed out above, associated concepts may or may not form integrated conceptualisations, which, depending on their particular characteristics, may be referred to as conceptual domains, spaces, frames and Idealized Cognitive Models, as shown in Figure 1.12. All the conceptual regions form an integrated whole, as opposed to the association between the two concepts belonging to two different domains linked with a dotted line, shown in 1.12c, which may represent a well-established conceptual metaphor, such as the conceptual metaphor LOVE IS A JOURNEY.[16]

Disregarding the problem of constraints and optimality principles, we may say that metonymy is a process of co-activation of strongly associated concepts within single integrated conceptualisations as they are represented in 1.12a and 1.12b.

iii. small partial overlap, typical of relations between basic level categories, which manifests itself in 'proximal' ontological metaphors, metaphorical synonymy and single scope integration networks, for example in the metaphor MAN IS A WOLF the conceptual regions of MAN and WOLF share the conceptual region of the concept of MAMMAL. There is no link. The intuition that the two concepts are somehow related stems from the fact that their conceptual regions overlap and thus co-activate parts of their shared conceptual domains, which corresponds to Seto's c-relation. The configuration looks as shown in Figure 1.12d. In the one-correspondence metaphor MAN IS A WOLF one of the concepts associated with WOLF (say HOSTILITY) is associated with the concept of HOSTILITY in the representation of MAN. In the case of many-correspondence structural metaphors the two domains share their image schematic structure (generic space in the sense of Turner and Fauconnier 1995; Fauconnier and Turner 1998), which may co-activate correspondences between other concepts.

iv. large partial overlap, which manifests itself in co-hyponymy below the basic level, synonymy A (cf. Chapter 5) and mirror scope integration networks. Some examples were discussed above – what they share is a rich, well-defined conceptual region of the hyperonym, hence the intuition that they are related, which stems from the overlap and not from the link. This is another case of c-relation.

v. inclusion, which prototypically manifests itself in hyponymy and plesionymy and converseness, for example PEKINESE shares all the central domains of DOG but in addition is linked with some more specific domains. The conceptual region of DOG is smaller but probably cognitively and neurally more deeply entrenched on account of being activated each time any breed is mentioned. The relation is again based on c-relation.

In sum, although association is a gradient notion, the five relations shown in Figure 1.11 constitute five cardinal points on the scale of association-inclusion which provide the basis for metonymy, synecdoche and metaphor.[17] In terms of co-activation, 1.11a represents the case of unlikely co-activation (brought about by some contextual clues or perceived remote analogy), 1.11b – likely but contingent, 1.11c – necessary but small and hence conceptually negligible, unless further elaborated, 1.11d – necessary but partial, conceptually meaningful, 1.11e – necessary and total for one of the concepts in prototypical cases.

It follows from P&G's account that most metonymies identified by linguists represent either relations 1.11b or 1.11d or 1.11e, although they have not distinguished the basic level and sub-basic level associations represented in 1.11c and 1.11d. In contrast, what I propose is that metonymy should be limited to the relations represented by 1.11b (whole-part and part-part association) and, at least partly, 1.11d (sub-basic level overlap). Consider what this implies. First, it excludes from the scope of metonymy all the cases of greater or smaller schematicity of semantic scope, typical of taxonomic relations, shown in 1.11e. Second, apart from the sub-basic level cases discussed above, substantial overlap will also cover cases of facets and dimensions which are not conceptualised as autonomous parts of certain concepts. Consider, for example, the dimensions of TIME and PLACE in activities. While the place may be conventionally linked with certain activities (cf. 1.12b) and so it may be used in predicative PLACE-FOR-ACTIVITY metonymies, for example *Eve is in the bathroom* for 'Eve is having a pee', time is an inherent, and hence inseparable dimension of activities (1.12a) but it is also used in metonymies, for example *a night with Eve, Sept.11*. Another relation that may be regarded as metonymic in virtue of substantial overlap is the highly intrinsic relation between an object and the material it is made of: the domain of the material is quite central in the representation of some categories, but never exhausts it. Third, the conceptual relations and the resultant lexical relations are very different from the construal of those relations suggested by Cruse (2000), where he discusses hyponymy, meronymy and synonymy as relations of identity and inclusion, and incompatibility, co-meronymy, and various kinds of opposites (e.g. complementaries, antonyms, converses) as relations of opposition and exclusion. We have already seen why hyponymic and meronymic relations should be regarded as crucially different. Converses in my account activate exactly the same domains (frames), though in different ways, therefore they should be considered as inclusions, not available for metonymic mappings.[18] Antonyms and complementaries both have considerable overlaps, for example they share the primary domain and are thus more like co-hyponyms below the basic level which may be called 'sub-basic incompatibilities', for example *Alsatian* and *poodle*, which share their 'dogness'. As we have seen above, this kind of overlap is simply a kind of link motivating metonymic mappings.

Interestingly, the parallel and rather marginal nature of metonymies based on antonymous and complementary relations is further enhanced by the fact that these metonymies usually have a jocular, humorous, or ironic effect, for example *man* for 'woman' (complementaries), *smart* for 'stupid' (gradable antonymy) and *poodle* for 'Alsatian' (sub-basic incompatibility), though at times they may be truly extended to cover lexical gaps, as in the extension of the European Spanish *léon* ('lion') to American Spanish 'puma' (cf. Blank 1999a). Incompatibility and co-meronymy are also treated differently. The basic-level incompatibility (and above), as a c-relation, does not involve total exclusion, since the terms share the conceptual region of the hyperonym, while co-meronyms represent the conceptual relation of association (an e-relation). They are all related within the same integrated conceptualisation of their holonym.

In contrast to metonymy-generating relations depicted in Figure 1.11 (1.11b and 1.11d), the conceptual relations in 1.11a and 1.11c represent more and less 'distant' metaphors, for example *My husband is an ice cube* vs. *My husband is a lion*, respectively. The distance is due to the fact that the two corresponding concepts in the first sentence do not share the superordinate category, while the concepts of HUSBAND and LION do share the superordinate category (LIVING BEING). 1.11d shows the relation between two sub-basic level categories which have a great deal in common because they share the same basic level category. Finally, 1.11e illustrates the relation of total inclusion typical of hyperonym-hyponym patterns, where the inner circle (i.e. the hyperonym) has no cognitive autonomy and represents the schematisation of commonalities shared by the whole category. I suggest that the term 'metonymy' in taxonomic relations be applied only to the relations between concepts represented by 1.11d. What distinguishes this kind of 'taxonomic' metonymy from metaphor is that the two concepts share all the properties of the common basic level concept, which makes them conceptually contiguous (or at least 'close') and what distinguishes it from the hyponymic relations is that neither of them is totally included in the other and thus they fail to exhibit the resultant logical property of unilateral entailment. Still, however, the relations 1.11b and 1.11d are different and it seems justified to differentiate them terminologically. I suggest that the mappings based on these relations are always classified as metonymic; however, since relation 1.11d involves substantial overlap, which makes it similar to the conceptual structure underlying synecdoche, as described in Section 1.5, we may refer to this particular kind of metonymy as 'synecdochic'. Thus, I will say that calling an Alsatian *a poodle* or a dentist chair *an armchair* represents cases of synecdochic metonymy. With these observations and

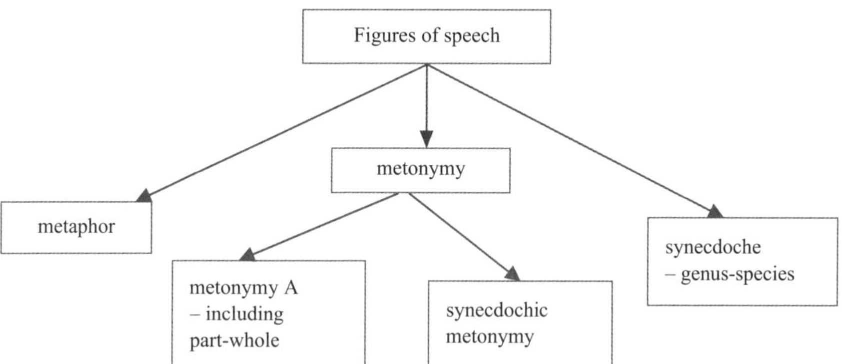

Figure 1.13 Extended general typology of figures of speech.

suggestions in mind, we can now extend slightly the typology of figures of speech presented in Section 1.5 to distinguish two basic types of metonymy: the basic metonymy A (short for 'associative') and synecdochic metonymy.

1.9 Residual problems: active zones, perspectivisation and what we do with proper names

1.9.1 Active zones

The present account also allows us to shed a new light on the problem of active zones. Let us recall that, as originally defined by Langacker, active zones are "those portions of a trajectory or landmark that participate directly in a given relation" (1990: 190).[19] Thus, to take one of Langacker's standard examples, in sentence (21) it is not the whole of the trajector *dog* and the whole of the landmark *cat* which participate in the relation designated by the verb *bite* but their 'focal areas', which in this case involve the dog's teeth and jaws.

(21)   Your dog bit my cat.

It is important to observe that the active zones in (21) are not salient, discrete parts or sharply bounded regions. Moreover, as Langacker insightfully observes "the participation of certain regions is obviously more direct and more central to the relational conception than that of others" (*ibid.*). Other examples are (Langacker 1990: 191):

(22)   (a) Roger ate an apple.
      (b) Roger heard a noise.
      (c) Roger walked faster.
      (d) Roger is digesting.

In the above examples the different 'selected facets' of the same trajector *Roger* are active as the primary participants in the relation designated by the verb (cf. Kalisz 1998 for a similar set of examples and discussion). In addition, however, Langacker argues that "active zones are not limited to subparts of the profiled entity. More generally, they need only be associated with that entity" (1999: 63). This is illustrated by sentences (23)–(25) below:

(23)   I'm in the phone book.
(24)   Kettle is boiling.
(25)   That car doesn't know where he's going.

The target concepts (i.e. the active zones) in the above sentences are, respectively, the speaker's name and phone number, the water in the kettle and the driver of the car. Here Langacker's suggestion becomes much more controversial, since most researchers would agree that the relevant expressions in sentences (23)–(25) are par excellence metonymic. In fact Langacker is aware of it, for he argues that active-zone phenomena "display a kind of metonymy, wherein a pivotal entity (here a part) is referenced only indirectly, via the term for another, associated entity (the whole)" (Langacker 2000: 62). Langacker's view, without any modifications, is endorsed by Taylor (2002: ch. 6.3) and Radden et al. (2007).

If active-zone phenomena are indeed 'a kind of metonymy', the question arises what kind of metonymy they are. One obvious property of most of Langacker's examples of active zones is that they are all transfers from wholes to parts or from parts to parts. Langacker (2000: 63) shows this in two diagrams reproduced below, in which *tr* and *lm* represent vehicles (sources) of metonymies and *az* (active zone) represents their targets.

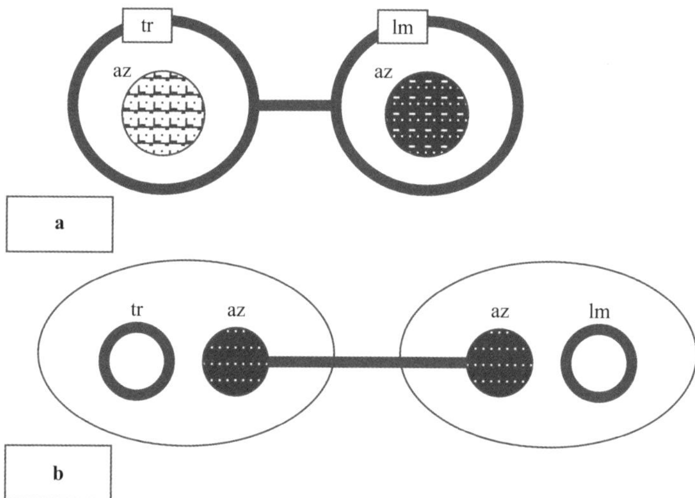

Figure 1.14 Active zones vis-à-vis trajectors and landmarks according to Langacker (2000).

As we can see, Langacker's examples have something in common. However, they also differ rather significantly. First of all, as already noted, in Examples (21) and (22) the active zones are largely indeterminate and vague. In other words, they indicate that the speakers resort to active-zone phenomena when they cannot precisely or adequately designate the target concept. A typical example would be the nominal expression *my finger* in sentence (26):

(26)   I cut my finger.

It is impossible to cut the whole finger (unless one talks about cutting it OFF), so the expression *my finger* designating the landmark of CUT does not as a whole participate in that relationship. However, it is impossible to designate the cut with absolute precision. To some important extent the same is true of examples like (21). Note that, even in such seemingly clear cases, it is not just the teeth that are the target of the nominal *your dog*. If they were, sentences like (27) would be perfectly normal, and (28) would sound strange:

(27)   ??Your dog's teeth bit my cat.
(28)   Your dog bit my cat with its sharp teeth.

Instead, what happens is that in (28) the active zone is construed as an instrument, i.e. a different participant in the action schema, which means that the Agent is still the major participant. Taylor (2002:110f) provides what might be taken as prototypical active-zone phenomena in the examples below:

(29)   John kicked the table.
(30)   My car got scratched in an accident.

In (29) the active zones are the vague region of John's foot involved in kicking and the equally vague region of the table directly affected by the kick. In (30) the nominal *my car* activates even more elusive portions of the vehicle, which may even be spatially discontinuous. All this is of course very different from what we see in examples (23)–(25), where the targets are not only independent, autonomous entities, but they are also easily conceptualised and lexicalised.

Those two general observations indicate two possible ways of solving the definitional problem of establishing the relationship between active-zone phenomena and metonymy. One solution is that in fact all WHOLE-FOR-PART and PART-FOR-PART transfers of meaning should be regarded as special cases of active-zone phenomena. This would leave us with two broad kinds of non-metaphoric mapping, namely PART-FOR-WHOLE metonymy and active-zone phenomena. The other solution is that cases like those illustrated by (23)–(25) are not regarded as active-zone phenomena at all and that PART-FOR-PART metonymy is retained as a separate subcategory of metonymy (based on association of concepts). Besides, WHOLE-FOR-PART metonymy is also retained as a separate subcategory, with the prototypical members having both the WHOLE and the PART clearly conceptualised and lexicalised. Finally, the term 'active-zone phenomenon' would be restricted to the WHOLE-FOR-PART designations where the part is indeed a conceptually vague 'zone' rather than a clearly identifiable, bounded and lexicalised region.[20]

There are three arguments in favour of the latter alternative, which are also the reasons why this latter solution will be adopted in this study. First of all, good metonymies allow for straightforward, grammatical paraphrases, which is much harder for typical active zones. Thus sentences (23)–(25) can be easily paraphrased, as in (23′)–(25′) below, while those in (22) cannot. Consider the sentences below:

(23′) My name and phone number are in the phone book.
(24′) The water in the kettle is boiling.
(25′) That car's driver doesn't know where he is going.
(22a′) ??Roger's mouth (and teeth) ate an apple.
(22b′) ??Roger's ears heard a noise.
(22c′) ?? Roger's legs walked faster.
(22d′) ?? Roger's digestive system is digesting.

As Langacker pointed out "a discrepancy between profile and active zone represents the NORMAL situation" (1990: 65), much in the way various degrees of categorical schematisation, which I have also excluded from the scope of metonymy, represent a normal situation. Both result from the grossly asymmetric relation between the finite resources of language and the infinity of conceptualisations which can only be designated with a considerable degree of underspecification. In that sense, both schematisation and active-zone phenomena are inevitable and necessary for human language to work as it does (cf. Radden et al. 2007).[21] This is the reason why Nerlich and Clarke rightly observe that synecdoche, defined as figure of speech exploiting various degrees on the schematicity-specification scale, is, compared to metaphor and metonymy, "the least figurative of the three master tropes" and that in fact it has "become a general semantic and stylistic mechanism" (1999: 206). In contrast, although metonymy may be said to be natural and extremely communicatively useful, it cannot be said to be inevitable or necessary.

The second argument, showing the difference between WHOLE-FOR-PART metonymies and active-zone phenomena, is that, unlike active zones, metonymies often violate ordinary selectional restrictions of the predicates with which they co-occur. Consider the standard metonymies below:

(31) The sax has flu.
(32) The pork chop is waiting for his check.

None of the instances of *Roger* in the examples in (22) above violated the selectional restrictions of the verbs with which they co-occur, whereas both (31) and (32) are only interpretable and acceptable as metonymies, in which *the sax* and *the pork chop* are construed as people and are thus compatible with the normal human subjects selected by *have flu* and *wait for a check*.

The third, somewhat related, argument for distinguishing active-zone phenomena from metonymy is that they do not exhibit identity transfer typical of true metonymies. As an illustration, consider sentences (33) and (34) below, borrowed from Nunberg (1995):

(33) Yeats is still widely read even though most of it is out of print.
(34) *I punched Bill and it started to bleed.

The pronoun *it* in (33) is acceptable through metonymic transfer from
YEATS (human) to YEATS' POETRY (inanimate). In (34), where *Bill* is the source
for the active zone, say, BILL'S NOSE, the anaphoric reference to the active zone
is impossible.

The final argument, already noted above and also adduced by Croft (1993),
is that there are important differences between typical metonymies and
active zones in terms of the place of the vehicle and the target on the scale of
extrinsic versus intrinsic relations. In particular, metonymies tend to rely on
extrinsic relations, while active zones are usually rather intrinsic. Of course
the terms extrinsic and intrinsic are probably as hard to define as association
and contiguity, but we may define them as prototypically structured notions,
with the highly contingent relation between the container and its content as a
prototypical extrinsic relation and the scratched area of the car and the body
of the car as the prototypical intrinsic relation.

Separating active-zone phenomena from metonymy does not preclude
cases of metonymy-active-zone chains. For instance, the nominal *car* in *I'm
having my car fixed* may metonymically stand for its part, say the engine,
while the specific parts in the engine (if the speaker has any idea what they
are) which are being fixed may only be accessed as active zones. In order to
realise how vague that target is, it is enough to point out that fixing an engine
often involves replacing some of its parts, so the active zone before and after
fixing may be referentially different.

Apparent counter-example
Langacker (1990: ch. 7) proposes an analysis of sentences reproduced here
as (35)–(37) in terms of active-zones, which suggests that active zones may
also involve transfer from parts to wholes. If it were so, Langacker's analysis
would constitute a serious challenge to the claim made above that active-zone
phenomena are restricted to the transfer from wholes to their conceptually
vague parts.

(35) (a) He began eating dinner.
      (b) He began dinner.
(36) (a) The orchestra started playing the next song.
      (b) The orchestra started the next song.
(37) (a) The author finished writing a new book.
      (b) The author finished the new book.

Langacker argues that while in the (a) sentences above the main clause verbs
profile relations with nominal trajectors and processual landmarks represented
by their gerundive complements, in the (b) sentences it is the landmark of the

'embedded' process that functions as the landmark of the main clause relation and the whole process is the active zone. For reasons that I find difficult to understand (cf. Croft 1993, who also finds this proposal difficult to explain), Langacker suggests that the contrast has to do with the systematic ambiguity of the main verbs in (35)–(37) and presents the contrast between the first pair of sentences as shown in Figure 1.15.

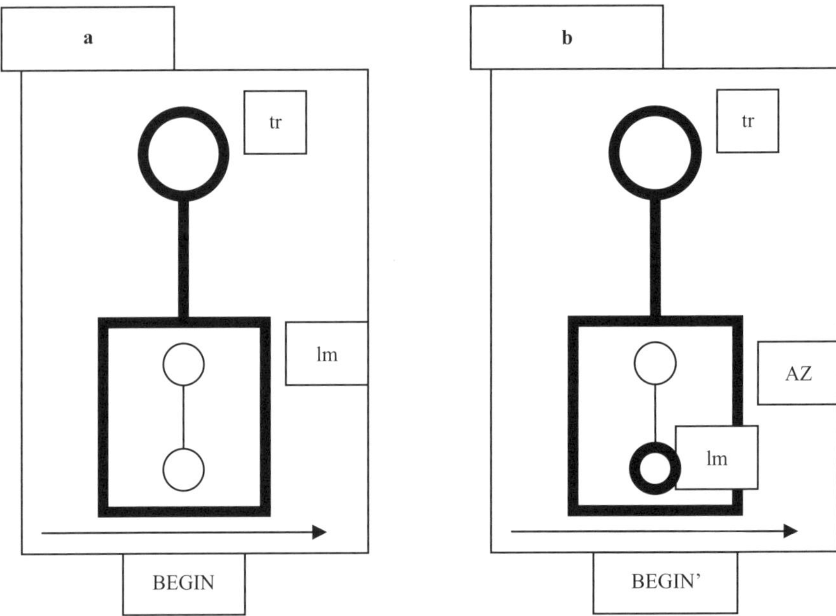

Figure 1.15 Representations of sentences (34a) and (34b) according to Langacker (1990).

It follows from Figure 1.15 (b) that the landmark of the complement of the relation BEGIN metonymically provides access to the whole of that relation construed as an active zone (AZ). In general, I find Langacker's analysis convincing; however, if we adopt the terminology proposed in the previous section, there is no reason why the whole relation should be considered as an active zone. On the contrary, the relational predication activated by the nominal landmark consists of three sharply bounded conceptual parts (trajector, relation, and landmark) and two equally sharply bounded formal parts (the gerund and the object nominal); thus the whole transfer has all the crucial distinctive characteristics of the PART-FOR-WHOLE metonymy, both on the conceptual and formal level. This argument is further reinforced by the fact that the same participant-relation (or alternatively, predicate-argument, or more generally, the event schema) structure is often employed as the basis (i.e. an integrated whole) for conversions (discussed in more detail in Chapter 3), where, for example, the landmark of the relation may be used to stand for the relation itself, as in converted verbs (the so-called 'object verbs', cf. Dirven 1999) like *to fish, to crew, to skin,* etc. or where the relation itself may stand for the trajector of the relation, as in converted nouns like *a cheat, a bore, a flirt, a tease,* etc.

Langacker's representations are misleading, if not downright contradictory, in that the active zone (or, according to my suggestion, the target of the PART-FOR-WHOLE metonymy) is profiled (cf. Figure 1.15 (a) and (b)), although as an active zone, by definition, it should be unprofiled.[22] We shall suggest a slightly modified representation of sentences (35) in Chapter 2. In addition, Langacker (1990) believes that *mutatis mutandis* active zones are also involved in various raising constructions illustrated by the (b) sentences below:

(38) (a) To fix Hondas is easy.
     (b) Hondas are easy to fix. (Object-to-Subject)
(39) (a) For the dog to escape is likely.
     (b) The dog is likely to escape. (Subject-to-Subject)
(40) (a) I would expect for the Clippers to lose again.
     (b) I would expect the Clippers to lose again. (Subject-to-Object)

Langacker claims that in the (a) sentences in (38)–(40) it is the whole process which functions as the trajector, while in the (b) sentences the role of the trajector is taken over by the profiled participant and the remaining infinitival part of the process becomes "the trajector's active zone with respect to the scale of difficulty (or pleasure, etc.)" (Langacker (1990: 200). Here Langacker's analysis is even more problematic because the putative active zones are actually explicitly specified and thus become indistinguishable from the regions or parts designated directly. Again, we return to the raising constructions in Chapter 2.

The above considerations suggest that what Langacker considers as active zones should be divided into three separate phenomena: a) regular WHOLE-FOR-PART metonymies, where the target PARTS are conceptualised and lexicalised, b) PART-FOR-WHOLE metonymies working on syntactic structures and c) non-metonymic active-zone phenomena where the potential target is not conceptualised and lexicalised, or if it is conceptualised it is not lexicalised. Thus, for example, if I say *I'm going to wash my car*, the target of expression *my car* is not conceptualised because it may involve not only the body of the car but also its windshield, windows, number plate, and presumably the wheels. Similarly, if I say *Tom hit me on the head*, *me* may stand for some unidentified spot on the speaker's head that the speaker can have great difficulty identifying conceptually and denoting lexically. If, however, on seeing a picture of Eve's face, the speaker says *This is Eve*, or refers to the

US as *America*, she is definitely speaking metonymically. And she is also speaking metonymically when she says that landscapes are easy.

Active zones in hyperbole
In general, the suggested dissociation of active zones from metonymy reduces the number of linguistic and conceptual phenomena that fall within the scope of active zones; there may be cases, however, that used to be considered metonymic and that now should be regarded as active zones. One of such cases seems to be the hyperbole. In Bierwiaczonek (2001, 2002a) I suggested that hyperbole should be analysed as a special case of metonymy whereby certain extreme points on the scale stand for the quantities relatively close to those points. Thus, in what I call positive hyperbole, the metonymy has the form ALL CATEGORY C FOR A LOT OF CATEGORY C, as in (41) and the second clause of (42) below, while in what I call negative hyperbole, the metonymy has the form NO AMOUNT (OR NUMBER) OF CATEGORY C FOR A SMALL AMOUNT (OR NUMBER) OF CATEGORY C, as in the first clause of (42):

(41)   Everybody knows that Sue is having an affair with the boss.
(42)   Nobody cares for French anymore; everybody's trying to learn English.

The exact referents of *everybody* and *nobody* in the above examples are theoretically possible to conceptualise and to lexicalise, but because the hyperboles are usually used when no such exact numbers or amounts are available, they should now be considered as active-zone phenomena, albeit very close to metonymy.

1.9.2 Perspectivisation vs. metonymy

In trying to delimit the scope of metonymy, another question to consider is whether perspectivisation can be seen as a form of metonymy. In other words, how should we deal with dot objects (cf. Pustejovsky 1995), that is cases of categories whose semantic representations consist of two (or more) domains which are mutually dependent, for example *book* – [PHYSICAL OBJECT] and [WRITTEN TEXT], *school* – [INSTITUTION] and [BUILDING] (likewise – *church, parliament*), *man* – [BODY] and [MIND] (SOUL). The question is: do the above capitalised elements represent two (or more) autonomous senses of the given lexemes or, rather, are they two different components of a single meaning? If the two senses can be separated, one of them should be regarded as a metonymic extension of the prototype; if not, no metonymy is involved and the components should be regarded as facets of a single sense, keeping in mind that facets are defined as "fully discrete but non-antagonistic readings of a word" which are somehow "fused into a single conceptual unit" (Cruse 2000: 114). In terms of association, facets represent the strongest form of association between two concepts, which manifests itself in the fact that the two concepts are co-activated each time the lexeme that denotes them is normally used. Consequently, different facets may be perspectivised on different occasions of usage. Nonetheless, each time a dot object lexeme is normally used all its facets are activated as well. For example, in sentence (43) below, the physical, BODY aspect of the lexeme *boy* is perspectivised but [MIND] is activated as well and the separation of the two results in a non-synonymous and distinctly odd sentence (44). In sentence (45) the perspective is changed but the co-activation remains and an attempt to disassociate the two again results in the oddity of (46):

(43)   I saw two very tall boys yesterday.
(44)   ?? I saw two very tall bodies of boys yesterday.
(45)   I talked to that boy yesterday.
(46)   ?? I talked to the mind of that boy yesterday.

Thus we may conclude that, in most cases, the use of dot object categories represents simple cases of perspectivisation. Although the perspective changes, usually the whole category is evoked and no WHOLE-FOR-PART metonymy is involved. This does not mean, however, that dot object lexemes cannot be used metonymically. In sentence (47) below the lexeme *boy* is used metonymically and its non-metonymic paraphrase (48) sounds perfectly felicitous:

(47)   Take the boy to the morgue.
(48)   Take the body of the boy to the morgue.

Consider now the lexeme *newspaper*, which consists of two facets [SET OF FOLDED SHEETS] and [TEXT] and other associated components of meaning such as [BUILDING], and [JOURNALISTS]. The sentences below highlight different aspects of this complex semantic structure:

(49)   It says in our newspaper that a new bridge will soon be built here.
(50)   Our local newspaper has only six pages.
(51)   That's our local newspaper (pointing at a building).
(52)   We are still waiting for our local newspaper (= journalists).

According to the criteria for perspectivisation and metonymy, examples (49) and (50) are both non-figurative and should be regarded as different perspectivisations of the two central facets of the lexeme *newspaper*, whereas (51) and (52) are metonymic, involving transfers from central to associated domains. The obvious difference is that perspectivisation does not create potential ambiguities and its explication is usually felt to be not only odd but also redundant, if not pleonastic. Like examples (44) and (46) above, the explications of (49) and (50) sound odd and redundant, while the explications of metonymic (51) and (52) seem perfectly natural:

(49′)   ? It says in the text of our newspaper that a new bridge will soon be built here.

(50′)   ?? The set of sheets (or the material form) of our local newspaper has only six pages.

(51′)   That's the building of our local newspaper (pointing at a building).

(52′)   We are still waiting for the journalists from our local newspaper.

Although sentences like (49) and (50) are rather clear examples of perspectivisation, the exact relation between different facets of the multifaceted nominal in them is usually indeterminate and, if one insisted on analysing them as metonymies, it would be impossible to distinguish the source and the target. Therefore, I am inclined to agree with Langacker (2010), who claims that they should be regarded as cases of profile/active-zone discrepancy. However, since facets are well conceptualised and easily lexicalised (though not so easily explicated in contexts) I propose that they are a special subcategory of active-zone phenomena on the borderline with WHOLE-FOR-PART metonymy.

In some cases, different perspectives may become fully semantic. A good case in point is the word *school*. Normally, the representation of *school* consists of such facets as [TEACHING INSTITUTION] and [BUILDING], with [TEACHERS], [STUDENTS], and [WAY OF THINKING] as associated components. In sentences (53) and (54) probably the whole representation is evoked, although the facets which are perspectivised are respectively [TEACHING INSTITUTION] and [BUILDING]:

(53)   My son said he didn't want to go to school any more.

(54)   The authorities recently closed down a lot of local primary schools.[23]

However, *school* can also be used metonymically, as in (55) and (56) below, where only one facet (in 55) or one associated concept (in 56) are activated: building in (55) and pupils representing the school in the game in (56) (note the plural concord!):

(55)   A bomb hit their school a week ago and now they have classes in private houses.

(56)   Our school have lost the game although they were leading after the first half.

Thus example (55) shows how a multifaceted item like *school* can be used metonymically. In addition, the comparison of (53) and (54) shows that changes of perspective may have grammatical consequences. In particular, when the INSTITUTION facet is perspectivised, as in (53), *school* is an uncountable noun, while when the BUILDING facet is perspectivised, *school* is countable. In sentence (57) below the word *church*, which is uncountable in its institutional sense, as in *separation of church and state*, is used in a fully autonomous metonymically extended sense of 'building' converted into a countable noun.

(57)   The Catholic Church was strong but there were too few churches in big towns.

All in all, we may conclude that:

(a)   The uses of lexical units denoting dot object categories, whereby the whole representation is activated but one facet is particularly salient, should be considered as cases of perspectivisation, as a special subcategory of active-zone phenomena, not metonymy, since there is no stand-for relation and there is no source distinct from the target.

(b)   A dot object category can be used in ad hoc referential WHOLE-FOR-PART metonymic expressions, whereby the whole is used to access only one of its facets and the other facets are suppressed.

(c)   Some facets of dot object categories may develop into full-fledged lexicalised and grammatically distinct separate senses of their source concepts.

Finally, it is worth noting that metonymic uses of lexemes denoting dot object categories are extremely difficult to account for in terms of Koch's theory of metonymy based on figure-ground effect (see §1.4.1 above) since in the case of dot objects there are two or more equally central – and hence figure-like – domains, and thus, when one of these domains is activated particularly strongly, there is no real figure-ground shift, but change in the perspective within the facets of a single figure.

A note on proper names

In our earlier discussion of an alternative to Peirsman and Geeraerts' prototype theory of metonymy, we suggested that according to the Principle of Minimal and Maximal Overlap (PMMO), when one lower-than-basic-level category is used as a source for another lower-than-basic-level category, the transfer is metonymic. We also argued that it is theoretically advantageous to exclude the cases of specification and generalisation from the scope of metonymy. This leaves us with the problem of proper names re-categorised as a class. There are two common versions of this kind of re-categorisation: paragons and common proper names used in the generic sense.[24]

Paragons

In the expressions *Bill is a Judas* or *Bill is a second Chomsky* the terms of the lowest possible level of categorisation, the level of unique designators (i.e. the proper names *Judas* and *Chomsky*) are used as common nouns to denote the most salient property of the individual they normally refer to. Kövecses and Radden (1998) tried to account for such cases in terms of a metonymy CATEGORY FOR DEFINING PROPERTY. The problem with their proposal is that it is not clear where the 'category' comes from as names refer to individuals and do not denote categories. Therefore, I suggest that the paragon name is first mapped onto the higher node of the whole class of similar entities, for example *Judas* onto treacherous members of a group and *Chomsky* onto brilliant linguists, thereby losing its proper name grammatical status. Since the re-categorised paragon name is strongly associated with the defining property of the category, it may then metonymically stand for this defining property. A solution along these lines was recently suggested by Barcelona (2004). Barcelona argues that in sentences like (58), *Shakespeare* denotes 'immense literary talent' through PART-FOR-WHOLE metonymy, whereby the stereotypical model of Shakespeare, which associates his name with 'immense literary talent,' is mapped onto the whole class of important talented writers.

(58)   Lope de Vega was not a Shakespeare.

The specific metonymy typical of paragons which makes this mapping possible is IDEAL MEMBER FOR CLASS.

I have two objections to Barcelona's account. Firstly, it is not at all obvious exactly what 'the stereotypical model of Shakespeare' is. Barcelona regards it as 'entrenched', but the fact that it is entrenched does not entail that it is fixed. In fact, in the construction of meaning of expressions with *Shakespeare,* different components of the model may be perspectivised and it is doubtful that any of those components can be considered as 'defining'. Barcelona's proposal in this respect sounds rather essentialist. However, essentialism does not work in language, as has been shown many times (see Taylor 1995 for a review of familiar arguments), and no wonder it does not work in this case, either. It is significant that even Quirk and his colleagues give two different interpretations of the sentence (59) below:

(59)   There were no Shakespeares in the nineteenth century.

Thus in Quirk and Greenbaum (59) is paraphrased as "writers who towered over contemporaries as William Shakespeare did over his" (1990: 76), while Quirk et al. interpret it as meaning "authors like Shakespeare" (1985: 289). Clearly, the first paraphrase perspectivises the greatness and importance of Shakespeare in relation to other contemporary writers. The latter interpretation is seriously underspecified and itself may be interpreted in a number of very different ways, which could also be taken as interpretations of the original sentence, depending on which aspect of Shakespeare's work is highlighted. Thus *Shakespeares* in the sentence could mean 'authors like Shakespeare in their ability to depict the intricacies and contradictions of human nature' or 'authors like Shakespeare in his ability to use creatively the linguistic resources of English' or 'authors like Shakespeare in his ability to combine the mundane with the sublime' or simply 'great playwrights'.[25] Secondly, what is strange in Barcelona's proposal is that he claims that the model of Shakespeare somehow conditions the emergence of the subcategory of great writers,[26] whereas exactly the opposite seems to be the case. Thus, for instance, most readers probably identify the subcategory of great playwrights in the category of writers, and it is this subcategory that Shakespeare belongs to and, as its particularly salient member, may be used to stand for the subcategory. Let us assume that the taxonomy has the form shown in Figure 1.16.

Given the taxonomy, *Shakespeare* can be used metonymically in two different ways. The first use is predicative, as in examples (58) and (59). In such cases the PART FOR WHOLE metonymic process operates, whereby the name of Shakespeare gets elevated to the status of the category name through the

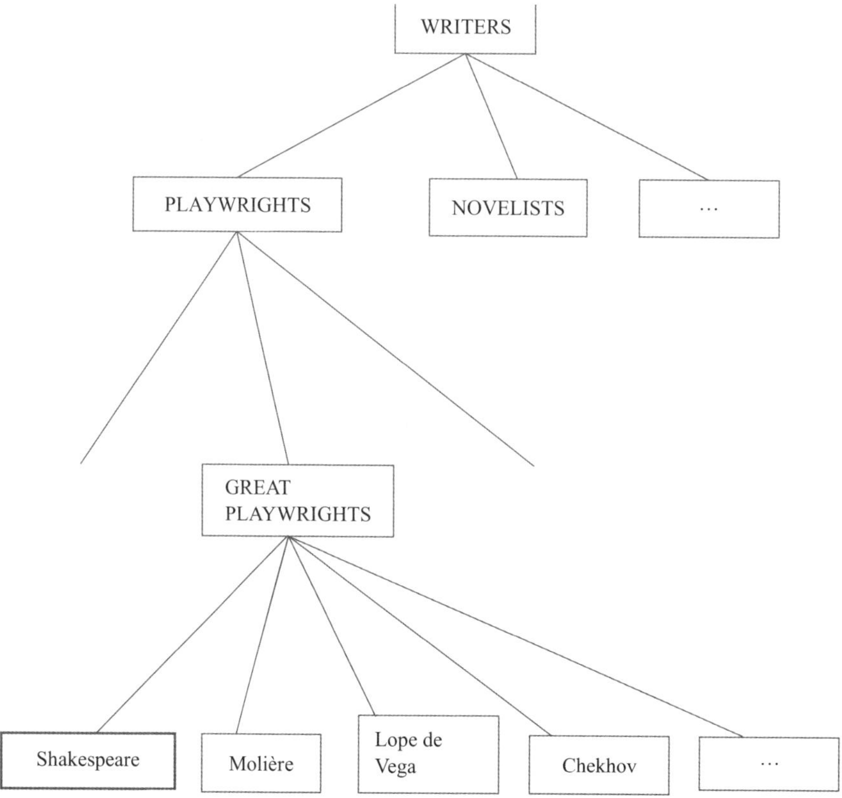

Figure 1.16 A likely taxonomy of GREAT WRITERS used in the re-categorisation of ***Shakespeare***.

IDEAL MEMBER FOR CLASS metonymy. Although the line between ordinary generalisation (schematisation) and this kind of transfer is thin, I call this particular kind of transfer metonymic because, as pointed out above, it relies on the concepts strongly associated with a given individual, but not immanent to them. Consequently, it would be hard to re-categorise *Shakespeare* to denote the whole category of WRITERS, that is to construe sentence (59) as meaning 'There were no writers in the nineteenth century'. The other context in which paragons are used is strictly referential, illustrated by (60) below:

(60)   How many plays did that Shakespeare of yours write?

Suppose that the referential target of the expression *that Shakespeare of yours* is Lope de Vega. I claim that in such examples the paragon's proper name is used to refer to another individual that shares some substantial part of the cognitive structure with the individual normally referred to by that name, and thus, according to the criteria laid out Section 1.6 above, it should be regarded as synecdochic metonymy, comparable to *Mercedes* or *Mini Fiat* standing for another car.

The examples above do not by any means exhaust the figurative potential of paragon proper names. As Brdar and Brdar-Shabó (2007) have demonstrated, strictly metonymic use of a proper name may shade into increasingly more metaphoric use. For instance, the English construction [Det – Noun$_{Paragon}$ – of – Y] may be used either strictly metonymically, with Noun and Y denoting entities in the same domain (as in 61 below), in the overlapping, albeit distinct domains (as in 62) and completely separate domains (as in 63) (examples are all Brdar and Brdar-Shabó's):

(61)   Steven has a bag of tricks, a good passer, can operate in confined areas and is the Zidane of Villa whose left foot is nearly as good as his right.

(62)   Described, to his slight embarrassment, as the '*Michael Jordan of the Rugby League*' Lauitiiti has arrived at Leeds with a reputation of being the most exciting ball-handling forward in the world.

(62)   Sarkozy is described by MEDEF, French CBI, as '*the Zidane of Finance*'.

In (61) the common domain for both *Zidane* and *Villa* (an English football club) is FOOTBALL, in (62) the domain of Michael Jordan is BASKETBALL, while the domain of rugby league is of course RUGBY – the two kinds of sport having a lot in common: both are physical, team games played with a ball, involving passing the ball and scoring by properly locating the ball in a designated location. Finally, in (63) *Zidane*, again, evokes the domain of FOOTBALL mapped onto a very distinct domain of FINANCES, hence a clear case of metaphor though metonymically motivated. An interesting point Brdar and Brdar-Shabó have made is that the more distinct the domains are the more specific intensionally and the more narrow is the metonymic target of the source. In the examples above, in (61) Zidane is still an outstanding footballer, in (62) Jordan is just an outstanding ballplayer, and in (63) *Zidane* is almost entirely reduced to axiology and stands simply for a genius in his field. The process could be called 'metonymic bleaching', comparable to the development of the adjective *fine* in English, discussed by Wells (1977) and a number of examples of semantic bleaching discussed by Hopper and Traugott (2003).

Common first names
Finally we should also mention the case whereby common first names, for example *Jack* or *John*, are used as common nouns. The study by Grygiel (2007) indicates that male proper names have been used as common nouns in essentially four cases:

(a) as synonyms of *man* (i.e. 'male human being')
(b) more specialised meanings, often denoting groups of particular occupations, such as servant, policeman, soldier, sailor
(c) euphemistic WHOLE-FOR-PART metonymies, in the sense of 'sexual organs'
(d) (rare) metaphoric extensions in instrumental senses, for example *jack* as 'a device for lifting heavy objects off the ground'.

Cases (a) and (b) are particularly relevant to our present considerations. Grygiel suggests that these extensions are best accounted for in terms of conceptual blending. For instance, the generic senses of proper names emerge from the blending of the domain of male proper names, where they have specific reference, and the domain of man/male human being, which is characterised by the relation of generic reference. A similar explanation may be proposed for the senses in point (b). In general, Grygiel's analysis is convincing; however, he offers no explanation why only a small group of names tends to be re-categorised as common nouns and why they are extended to rather special groups of occupations. In my opinion, what Grygiel has ignored in his account is the rather special status of the names in question, namely, the fact that, paradoxically, although they are proper names, they are in fact, extremely common proper names, such as *John, Jack, Richard (Dick), Joe, Tom* and *Harry*. In other words, they have a semi-proper name status in that they hardly ever refer to a specific man because a lot of men bear them: they are ordinary and common. This ordinary and common status makes them suitable for referring to a generic, ordinary man, or a man doing, like many others, an ordinary, common job. These are the reasons why *John* or *Jack* are extremely unlikely to be used with reference to the boss, a famous politician or a movie star, nor are they used in the sense of 'a member of a group of managers, politicians or celebrities'. If *Shakespeare* is a paragon of a literary genius, *John, Jack,* and *Tom* are paragons of ordinary common people doing ordinary, common jobs. Calling generic men or men doing common jobs *John* or *Jack* is metonymic due to the Principle of Minimal and Maximal Overlap (PMMO): the cognitive representations of individuals called *John* or *Jack* and the cognitive representations of those who are referred to by those names (although their actual names are different) exhibit substantial overlap.

1.10 Why metonymy?

As we have already seen and will see again and again in the remaining parts of this book, metonymy is ubiquitous in language and thought. It is therefore natural to ask why it is so ubiquitous. The most common answer to this question is that metonymy is an 'abbreviation device', which allows us to use the already existing or contextually given associative links between concepts in order to "say things quicker" (Nerlich et al. 1999: 362). In addition to economy, Cruse (2000: 212) points out that metonymy also serves to ease access to the intended referent and highlight the relevant associative relation. In addition, as Panther and Thornburg (particularly in 2003b, 2005) have repeatedly shown, metonymic patterns may provide the necessary basis for efficient processes of inference, and may therefore underlie all the most important aspects of communication and cognition. Thus, in terms of Levinson's (1995) heuristics, it is metonymy that makes the R-heuristic work. For, being a combination of Grice's Maxim of Quantity (submaxim 2) and Relevance, R-heuristic says: "Say/write no more than you must, and mean more thereby."

All this is no doubt true. We must not forget, however, that metonymy also serves a more practical and yet equally important function, namely it helps us to fill the lexical gaps in the cases of *inopiae causa,* that is lexical gaps in the vocabulary of a language (cf. Ziomek 1990: 169, see Chapter 5). This is particularly true of new categories in science or industry and new categories of artifacts, which are named metonymically on the basis of the conceptual link between the new category and its inventor/discoverer (eponymy) or the conceptual overlap between the representation of the new category and the representation of some other, already existing category. The former case may be illustrated by the name of Parkinson used to denote a new disease (and, also, referentially, patients suffering from the disease) or the founder's name *Opel* used for a subcategory of cars. The latter case is most common in the systematic way the meanings of personal professional nouns are extended to cover the new devices which do the same jobs, for example *printer, player, speaker* (see Chapter 5 for more examples and discussion). In this sense metonymy is one of the most powerful means of semantic change as it was discussed by Ullmann (1972 [1962]) and, more recently, by Blank (1999a). Of course in such cases metonymy is fully lexicalised and becomes part of the semantic system of a language and is no longer contingent.

Notes

1 Aristotle's example is particularly telling as it involves quantification where *thousands* is used to mean 'numerous', implying that THOUSANDS is included in the target NUMEROUS. In Bierwiaczonek (2000) I suggested that in fact all cases of hyperbole and litotes should be regarded as instances of metonymy. I believe now that that suggestion was mistaken for reasons that will be made clear later on.
2 The quote and the translation are Koch's (1999).
3 The status of the hypallage is not entirely clear, but it should probably be regarded as a kind of metonymy restricted to the relations of cause–result, attribute–bearer of attribute and temporal relations, for example *sleepy* in *a sleepy day* designates the property of the day by means of its effect (result) on people (cf. Ziomek 1990: 224f).
4 It is interesting to note that for a long time metaphor was also regarded as a trope based on syntagmatic relations. The tradition probably goes back Quintilian, who defined metaphor as *metaphora brevior est similitudo,* apart from Jakobson, the theory reducing metaphor to simile was later criticised by Max Black in his classic papers (e.g. 1993 [1979]), in which he put forward his interactional theory of metaphor.
5 I have modified some of the subcategories of metonymy in accordance with Norrick's original formulation.
6 Norrick (1981: 100) claims that this particular metonymic principle follows from the more general principle of reference which states that a person may be referred to by his/her role. In addition, this relationship is covered by Norrick's Metaphoric Principle 2, which describes the specific-generic relation. I have decided to include it as a separate type of metonymic relationship because there are clear cases where nouns denoting the office are used in the personal sense, for example *the cabinet* as office and individual ministers. In Polish the noun *Wysoki Sąd* (high court) is conventionally used as a form of addressing judges during trials (i.e. as an equivalent of the English *Your Honour*).
7 ICM stands for Idealized Cognitive Model, as it is described and used in Lakoff (1987). The formulation of the definition leaves little doubt that its authors were inspired by Langacker (1993), where metonymy is considered to be part of a more general cognitive operation of accessing different mental entities (targets) by means of more salient 'reference points' within one domain. For instance, SHAKESPEARE may be used as a reference point by means of which the conceptualiser may invoke LITERARY OUTPUT OF SHAKESPEARE.
8 I must admit that calling non-activated links 'metonymic' seems unacceptable to me. As a matter of definition, what makes metonymy what it is, is precisely the activation of certain links. The other links may be associative but as long as they are not activated they are not metonymic.

9   Ruiz de Mendoza (p.c.) argues that "In the restaurant context the concept 'person' is not relevant; the relevant concept is 'person that takes on the customer's role'". I cannot agree with that. It seems that all we can say for sure on the basis of linguistic data is that waitresses conceptualise customers as people who order dishes, sit at certain tables, wear certain clothes, behave in a certain way, etc. Thus they form complex gestalts consisting of a number of 'relevant parts', such as person (whether we call her *customer* or not), dish, table, chair, etc. which can all be used in PART-FOR-PART metonymic reference. For example the person may be accessed by the dish or the table (cf. *Number six is waiting for his check*). The dish may be referred to by the person or table as well, for example when a waitress points at a dish and asks *Is this the guy in the corner* or *Is this number four or six* (see Chapter 6 for more discussion). Such reference would not be possible if the person, dish and table were not conceptually distinct as parts of a single gestalt or image space.

10   Ruiz de Mendoza insists that the precondition stands for the whole event: "the possession of tickets allows one to go to the theatre and have leisure time there" (p.c.). I agree but this is just the second part of the whole scenario; its BEFORE part is not targeted (cf. Chapter 4). Ultimately the problem is resolved if we analyse it in terms of conceptual integration: the question evokes the WEEKEND space, the answer evokes the POSSESSION space and the whole GOING-TO-THE-THEATRE scenario (evoked by the expression theatre tickets). Thus the whole scenario is evoked but only the actual event part is targeted as relevant answer to the question *How did you spend the weekend*?

11   This non-unitary nature of metonymy is important to bear in mind in order to avoid the kind of considerations that recently led Barnden (2010) to question the usefulness of the terms 'metonymy' and 'metaphor' altogether on the grounds that it is impossible to find clear criteria for separating these notions. It is of course true that, depending on our purpose at hand, we might have to specify exactly what kind of metaphor or metonymy is at work on each particular occasion. Then such modifiers, representing different subcategories and levels of generality, are available, for example WHOLE-FOR-PART, MATERIAL FOR OBJECT. Ignoring some very problematic arguments adduced by Barnden in his paper, it is surprising that, as a linguist, Barnden considers fuzziness and internal complexity of metaphor and metonymy as a linguistic curiosity, while in fact their internal structure is similar to most other basic-level categories. The fact that they may be defined in terms of a bundle of non-necessary conditions does not make them any more useless than categories such as GAME, CHAIR or LOVE or WORD or NOUN or CLAUSE.

12   I am grateful to Ruiz de Mendoza (p.c.) for motivating me to try to define the term 'association' as precisely as possible. I believe that, as it stands, the definition enables empirical, language-independent studies of association, which of course have a long tradition in psychology, for example in the studies of stereotypes (cf. Kurcz 2000). For comparison, recall that Gestalt psychology defines association more narrowly, for example as "a bond between two experiences which enables us to recall the second experience when only the first is given again" (Köhler 1975[1947]: 152).

13   See 'A note on proper names' below for other, though related, cases.

14   Although the analysis in Bierwiaczonek (2002b) is based on purely linguistic observations and the *but*-test for identifying the domains and concepts determining the conceptual region of different subcategories of LOVE, I believe that, ultimately, they will be identified neurally along the lines of Hauk, Johnsrude and Pulvermüller's (2004) fMRI study which demonstrated that words denoting activities such as *smile, punch, kick* differentially activate face, arm/hand and leg regions in the somatomotor neural maps, showing that the conceptual regions of activities are defined, inter alia, by the relevant profiles in the domain of body.

15   This is an extension of the proposal made in Bierwiaczonek (2005), where it was suggested that there were only three basic kinds of relationships: separation, overlap and inclusion. It seems to me now that 'overlap' was too general as it comprised three relationships, i.e. part-whole, partial overlap and substantial overlap, which have quite different properties.

16   Of course LOVE IS A JOURNEY is a many-correspondences metaphor. The details of those correspondences have been ignored for expository purposes.

17   Warren suggests that there are four kinds of non-literal senses: metaphor, reversal, hyperbole and litotes, and metonymy, which are based, respectively, on the following 'connections': reminiscent property, polarized property, property "the intensity of which needs to be up- or downgraded", and "relation of concomitance" (contiguity) (1999: 225).

18   Indeed, there is nothing figurative about denoting the same event in terms of BUYING or SELLING, or describing a relation of POSSESSION in terms of OWNER or PROPERTY.

19   The main arguments of this section are presented in Bierwiaczonek (2010).

20   The observation that active zones are typically non-lexicalised suggests that they may be phylogenetically and ontogenetically earlier and more basic than metonymies. This means that the early humans and young speakers often use holophrases as vehicles for lexically unknown targets. This may suggest that we should distinguish two kinds of active zones: those that are both unconceptualised and unlexicalised and those that are simply lexical gaps, either in the lexical system or in the lexical competence of particular speakers.

21   For some reason, Radden et al. treat active zones as a kind of incompatibility, which "requires the interlocutors to construct meanings in order to reconcile the conflict between expressions" (2007: 7ff), and illustrate it with Langacker's example *The cigarette in her mouth was unlit*. This suggests that there is a conceptual conflict between the part of the cigarette that actually touched the mouth and the whole cigarette on the one hand and the part of the mouth that touched the cigarette and the whole mouth. I must admit I do not see any conflict here. On the contrary, the target is absolutely dependent on the whole. In my view, what applies to the active-zone kind of under-specification is what Radden et al. call 'indeterminacy': "the situations in which a linguistic unit is underspecified due to its vagueness in meaning" (2007: 6).

22   Langacker runs into the same kind of problem in his analysis of internally headed relative clauses in Japanese (cf. Langacker 2010), where he explicitly admits that "the landmark's active zone is explicitly mentioned at a lower level of organization" (p. 65).

23   The Polish translation of (54) *Władze pozamykały wiele lokalnych szkół podstawowych* is interesting as it exhibits the ambiguity between the perspectivised reading 'close down' and metonymic reading 'lock the school', which targets only the BUILDING facet. Given the context, however, the perspectivised reading is much more likely.

24   In classical rhetoric the semantic shift from the proper name to the name of a category is known as antonomasia. The term would be useful if it were not for the fact that it has also another meaning, namely the replacement of the proper name by a salient epithet of the name's referent, for example *the Thunderer* for Zeus. This is the reason why some researchers distinguish antonomasia-1 (for the latter) and antonomasia-2 (for the former, cf. Płuciennik 2007). Since the term comes from Greek *anti-* ('instead') and *onomazein* ('to name'), it seems preferable to restrict it to the latter case. Therefore I shall not use it in the discussion of the proper name re-categorisation, which I shall refer to as proper name hyperonymisation.

25   Notice that the same argument applies to the expression *a second Chomsky*, which may describe someone as intellectually brilliant but may easily be construed as denoting a linguist obsessed with the idea of autonomous syntax and/or innate linguistic faculty.

26   Here is the relevant quote: "It is important to insist upon the idea that a prerequisite for the application of this metonymy [IDEAL MEMBER FOR CLASS – BB] in this case is the creation of the mental class of immensely talented writers (…), and that a prerequisite for the creation of this class is the existence of the culturally entrenched metonymic model of Shakespeare (…) (Barcelona 2004: 369).

2 Formal metonymy

The main focus in this chapter is formal metonymy, which is the metonymy based on a formal relation between the vehicle and the target. This metonymy is typically a PART-FOR-WHOLE metonymy or, more specifically, SALIENT PART OF FORM FOR WHOLE FORM (cf. Barcelona (2005), whereby a part of the formal representation of a linguistic unit stands for the whole formal representation of this unit. The most obvious cases of formal metonymy are alphabetisms (initialisms), acronyms, clips and various kinds of ellipsis in syntax. Several examples of such formal metonyms are discussed. In addition, it is shown that formal metonymy may well underlie a number of spelling conventions as well as syntactic and pragmatic phenomena.

2.1 Form as an ontological realm

Following traditional semiotics (cf. Ogden and Richards 1985 [1923]), which distinguished three ontological realms relevant to the analysis of signification (i.e. the realm of forms, the realm of concepts and the realm of referents),[1] Radden and Kövecses (1999; henceforth R&K) distinguished three kinds of fundamental 'semiotic' Idealized Cognitive Models (ICMs), namely Sign ICMs, Reference ICMs, and Concept ICMs. Sign ICM is defined as "the pairing of a concept and a form" (R&K: 23). Reference ICM is defined as "the pairing of a thing or event and a sign, form or concept" (R&K: 23). Concept ICM involves links between concepts, which usually are, but do not have to be, associated with forms. What is important about Sign and Reference ICMs is that they link entities from different ontological domains, while Concept ICM relates entities within the same realm: the realm of concepts.[2]

As already mentioned in Chapter 1, according to R&K, the three kinds of ICMs give rise to three kinds of metonymies: Sign, Reference and Concept Metonymies. What R&K have overlooked in their account is the possibility of what we shall refer to here as 'formal metonymy'. This is the metonymy whereby a part or some salient aspect of the form of a linguistic unit is used to access the whole form of this unit. Formal metonymy is like concept metonymy in that it stays within the confines of a single ontological realm: that of form.[3] In a more recent paper, Radden and Panther (2004) have distinguished metonymies based on form-form relations and those based on form/

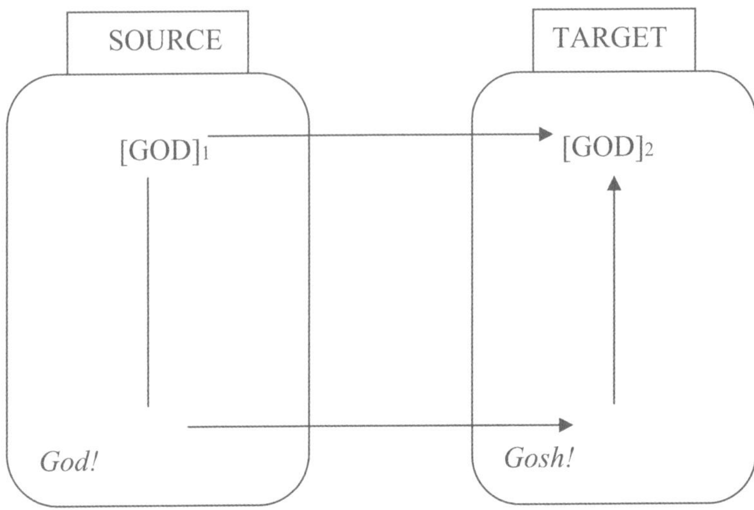

Figure 2.1 Motivational structure of ***Gosh!*** according to Radden and Panther (2004). The arrow from *God!* to *Gosh!* shows the motivated form-form relation; the arrow from *Gosh!* to [*GOD*]₂ shows the motivated semiotic relation; the arrow from [*GOD*]₁ to [*GOD*]₂ shows the motivated content-content relation.

content-form/content relations. The former involve purely phonetic and phonological structures in regular phonological processes such as assimilation, vowel harmony. The latter are connected with metonymies that are formally motivated, but, in Radden and Panther's view, they apply to the symbolic unit as a whole. It follows from Radden and Panther's account that the euphemistic use of *Gosh!* instead of *God!* is motivated formally and conceptually in the manner depicted in Figure 2.1.

In opposition to Radden and Panther's proposal, in Bierwiaczonek (2007a) I suggested that in the case of the formal metonymy represented by *Gosh!* the target does not involve any new content; on the contrary, the primary reason for introducing abbreviations and euphemisms is to access (at least part of) the same content by means of a shorter or modified form. Accordingly, the metonymic link between *God!* and *Gosh!* should be represented as shown in Figure 2.2.

Figure 2.2 indicates that, as a target, *Gosh!* is an expression that has the same expressive value as the expression *God!* without actually mentioning the sacred name. The mention of God is thus evaded, although the form of the unit *God!* motivates the form of the unit *Gosh!* As indicated by the dotted lines, *Gosh!* has probably developed its own conceptual structure, but this

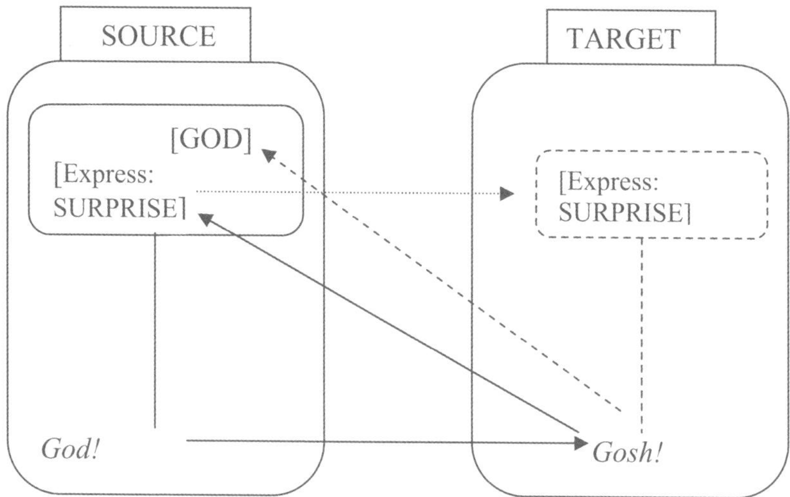

Figure 2.2 *Gosh!* as a unit whose form and conceptual structure are motivated by its link with ***God!***

conceptual structure is motivated by the link with the expressive component of the conceptual structure of *God!* In other words, I believe that the form of *Gosh!* does not motivate its content directly, but by way of its original link with the expressive part of the expression *God!* In general, it seems that the motivational dependence of one expression on another is a matter of degree. The most conceptually dependent expressions are abbreviations: at first they are always used in order to access the same conceptual structure as the full complex expression they stand for.

Coming back to the *Gosh!* example and using the terminology of the present work, it may be said that *Gosh!* is a formal vehicle which makes it possible to access the pragmatic part of the unit *God!* without strongly activating the conceptual structure associated with GOD since it has developed its own pragmatic meaning, say [Express: SURPRISE]. Thus it has become a more or less independent unit which may activate the conceptual structure [GOD] of *God!* only indirectly and hence weakly via its formal link with *God!*, as shown in Figure 2.3.[4]

Less-controversial examples of formal metonymies will be discussed below (cf. Figure 2.4 and Figure 2.5).

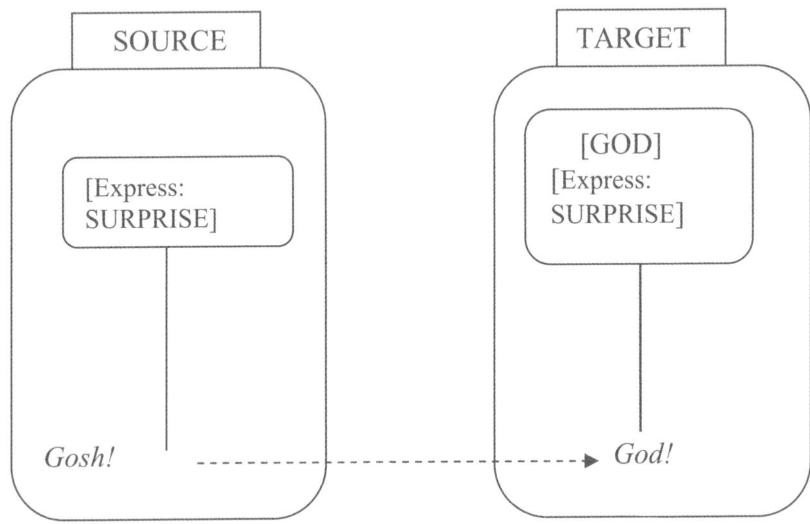

Figure 2.3 *Gosh!* used metonymically as a vehicle accessing the formal component of the unit *God!* and indirectly its conceptual structure.

2.2 Formal metonymies

At least two domains within the ontological realm of linguistic form should be distinguished: the domain of SOUND and the domain of GRAPHIC REPRESENTA-TIONS.[5] Accordingly, two Form ICMs can be proposed: the SPEECH-SOUND ICM, associating concepts with sounds, and the WRITING ICM, in which graphemic symbols represent speech sounds. It should be observed that the SPEECH-SOUND ICM is like SIGN and REFERENCE ICMs in that it involves cross-realm relations, while the WRITING ICM is like the CONCEPT ICM in that it involves relations within the same realm, namely the realm of form, although it links two different kinds of formal representations: the sound representation and its graphemic representation.

Although the SPEECH-SOUND ICM is quite similar to the SIGN ICM in that they both link the phonological representation with the concept, I suggested in Bierwiaczonek (2007a) that they should be regarded as qualitatively different. The difference is the contrast between the semasiological and onomasiological perspective on linguistic units. Accordingly, I suggested that the SIGN ICM takes the semasiological perspective and links each linguistic form with a semantic-conceptual representation. In contrast, the SPEECH-SOUND ICM represents the onomasiological perspective, whereby a single concept may have a number of phonological representations. It is on the level of those forms that some formal metonymies operate. In order to draw a distinction between the metonymies produced within the WRITING- and the SPEECH-SOUND-ICMs, the relevant metonymies will be referred to, respectively, as 'WRITING metonymies' and 'SPEECH-SOUND metonymies'.

2.2.1 Writing metonymies

WRITING metonymy is a cognitive process whereby one written representation of the phonological form of a linguistic expression is used as a vehicle to access another written representation of the same phonological form.

2.2.1.1 Letters for words

Perhaps the simplest form of WRITING metonymy is the convention that dirty words are typographically indicated by means of the first grapheme or graphemes only, as in *f..., sh....* In English, this metonymy is clearly an instance of the graphemic PARS PRO TOTO. Thus our first metonymy has the following form: INITIAL GRAPHEME(S) FOR THE WHOLE GRAPHEMIC REPRESENTATION.

2.2.1.2 Homophonic alphabetism

Another kind of WRITING metonymy, which I shall refer to as 'homophonic alphabetism', is represented by alternative shortened forms of spelling in which the sound representations of letters or numbers are usually used. Examples abound, especially in various forms of modern texting: *2* for *to* or *too, 4* for *for, U* for *you, C* for *see.* Historically speaking, this spelling convention may be regarded as a move toward a syllabic system, in which single graphemes stand for clusters of phonemic units. The SYLLABIC WRITING ICM is of course different from ALPHABETIC WRITING ICM, and thus gives rise to different kinds of WRITING metonymies.

In principle, any homophonic spelling of a word is a possible candidate for a WRITING metonymy. In most cases, the metonymy may be explained in terms of the Principle of Least (manual!) Effort, so the metonymy is acceptable as long as it is intelligible and shorter than the ordinary written form, such as *nite* for *night, thru* for *through, For chrissake!* standing for *For Christ's sake!* There are cases, however, when the modification of spelling is motivated by mercantile reasons, such as an attempt to attract attention, as in numerous trade names (e.g. *Kwick Kopy* may stand for *Quick Copy,* as a name of a photo-copying firm, while a dry cleaners shop may be called *Mr Kleen*).[6] Usually, however, the attention-getting and shortening tendencies go hand in hand, as in snack bar names like *Lite Bite* and *Snax,* a shoe-shop *Shusella,* or a hairdresser's studio *Lookrite.* All these strategies may be subsumed under a single kind of metonymy: HOMOPHONIC GRAPHEMIC REPRESENTATION OF X FOR ESTABLISHED GRAPHEMIC REPRESENTATION OF X.

2.2.1.3 Alphabetisms

The most common and the most pure form of WRITING metonymy is alphabetism (also called 'initialism'): a part, consisting of the first letters of all or most words, stands for the whole consisting of all the letters. Since the letters do not function as representations of the actual sounds occurring in the abbreviated expression, they are pronounced just as letters. Of course such 'alphabetic metonymies' typical of simple alphabetisms become meaningful only through the whole chain of metonymies, ultimately linking the form with the conceptual content: ALPHABETIC PHONETIC REPRESENTATION OF LETTERS FOR FIRST LETTERS OF WRITTEN REPRESENTATION OF WORDS OF COMPLEX EXPRESSION (CE) FOR FIRST SOUNDS OF WORDS OF CE FOR WHOLE PHONETIC REPRESENTATION OF CE FOR CONCEPTUAL REPRESENTATION OF CE. As an example, let us consider the alphabetism AO for *accountant officer*. The alphabetic phonetic representations of letters A and O, i.e. [ei] and [ou], stand for the first letters of the written representation of the words *accountant officer*, which stand for the first sounds of the words of CE *accountant officer*, which stand for the whole phonetic representation of the CE *accountant officer*, which stands for the conceptual representation of the CE ACCOUNTANT OFFICER.

At times the whole metonymic chain may be further complicated, as in the case of M.A., in which the alphabetic phonetic representations of M and A in MA, i.e. [em] and [ei], stand for the first letters of the lexical words in the CE *Master of Arts*, which stand for the first sounds of the words *master* and *arts*, [m] and [a:] respectively, which stand for the whole phonetic representation of the words *master* and *arts*, which in turn stand for the phonetic representation of the CE *master of arts*, which stands for the conceptual representation MASTER OF ARTS of CE *master of arts*.

2.2.1.4 Acronyms

The case of true acronyms is less compositional and hence more complex. Although their graphic representation is a clear PART-FOR-WHOLE metonymy, their pronunciation is a blend representing a relatively autonomous unit, 'borrowed' from its graphic constituents but not fully predictable from them in terms of sound representation, for example while the graphic representation of NATO is a simple metonymy, the diphthongs [eɪ] and [əʊ] in its sound representation are a product of the conceptual integration of the graphic representation and its default (prototypical) sound representation (or alternatively, alphabetisms), while the sound representation of the consonants [n] and [t] is based directly on their form in the full representation (or perhaps again their prototypical sound form). In any event, the degree to which the sound form of an acronym is determined by its graphemic aspects or the actual sound properties of the whole expression must be determined individually for most acronyms.

I suggest that the metonymy, call it 'acronymic metonymy', has the following form: LETTERS STAND FOR LETTERS OF THE FIRST SOUNDS OF THE WORDS OF CE, WHICH JOINTLY STAND FOR THE PHONOLOGICAL REPRESENTATION OF CE, WHICH STANDS FOR THE CONCEPTUAL REPRESENTATION OF CE. For instance, in the acronym *AIDS*, the letters A, I, D, S stand for the letters of the first sounds of the words *acquired, immune, deficiency*, and *syndrome*, which letters jointly stand for the phonetic representation of CE *acquired immune deficiency syndrome*, which jointly stands for the conceptual representation ACQUIRED IMMUNE DEFICIENCY SYNDROME of CE *acquired immune deficiency syndrome*.

The chain of acronymic metonymies suggested above accounts for the fact that acronyms exhibit a considerable degree of phonetic autonomy and non-compositionality, namely their constituent phones are often different from the phones in the full CE, for example [s] of *syndrome* is pronounced [z] in the acronym, and both diphthongs in *NATO* (North Atlantic Treaty Organization) are quite different from their counterparts in the actual name. Since letters motivate the phonetic representation of acronyms more than the actual sounds used in their full expressions, it seems quite reasonable to regard them as a special case of spelling pronunciation, based on global properties of written representations in conjunction with suprasegmental aspects of pronunciation, such as vowel reduction (e.g. the final vowel in *NASA*) or assimilation (e.g. the voicing of the final [s] in *AIDS*).

There is little doubt that the degree of autonomy of an acronym from its formal source is a matter of degree and, in general, depends on such factors as entrenchment (caused by high frequency) and the complexity (or simply length) of the source. It seems that the oft-quoted examples *laser* and *radar* may be considered as fairly independent. Because of high frequency and the length as well as the complexity of their sources (*light amplification by stimulated emission of radiation* and *radio detection finding and range*, respectively), the two acronyms have all but lost the formal link with their sources and probably few speakers are aware of what they originally stood for. At the other extreme of the scale one may find the acronyms and alphabetisms standing for less-complex and less-common expressions often limited to specialised domains or even particular texts, for example *NP* in linguistics, R&K for Radden and Kövecses in this text. Often, the formal link, especially between the source and an alphabetism, is likely to survive simply because it may be confused with other sources, for example *GP* may stand for 'Gallup Poll', 'gas-permeable' (of contact lenses), 'general paralysis', 'general pause' (in music), 'general practitioner', 'general purpose', 'Gloria Patri', 'graduated pension', 'Graduate in Pharmacy', 'grand(e) passion', 'Grand Prix' (*Oxford Dictionary of Abbreviations,* 1992).

In languages like Polish, with rich nominal and verbal inflections, the degree of autonomy of an acronym and alphabetism may be measured by the way it sets up its concord relations. Thus a well-entrenched alphabetism *PRL* [pe-er-el], for *Polska Rzeczpospolita Ludowa* ('Polish People's Republic') usually takes masculine concord on account of its consonantal *-l* ending occurring in a number of masculine nouns (*knebel* 'gag', *szczebel* 'rung', *badyl* 'dry stalk', *ul* 'beehive' etc.), even though the head of the vehicle *Polska* is feminine and, when unabbreviated, the expression takes feminine concord, as in (2) below:

(1)   PRL skończył się wraz z pojawieniem się Solidarności.
       [PRL ended (Pret.3sg.masc.) Refl. together with appearance Refl. Solidarity (Gen.sg.)
       PRL came to an end with the advent of Solidarity]

(2)   ?PRL skończyła się wraz z pojawieniem się Solidarności.[7]
       [PRL ended (Pret.3sg.fem.) Refl. together with appearance Refl. Solidarity (Gen.sg.)]

(3)   Polska Rzeczpospolita Ludowa skończyła się wraz z pojawieniem się Solidarności.
       [Polish People's Republic (Nom.sg.fem.) ended (Pret.3sg.fem.) Refl. together with appearance Refl. Solidarity (Gen.sg.)]

(4)   *Polska Rzeczpospolita Ludowa skończył się wraz z pojawieniem się Solidarności.
       [Polish People's Republic (Nom.sg.fem.) ended (Pret.3sg.masc.) Refl. together with appearance Refl. Solidarity (Gen.sg.)]

Figure 2.4 shows that *PRL* has acquired the status of an independent unit, which accesses the conceptual structure directly, without strongly activating its full formal representation.

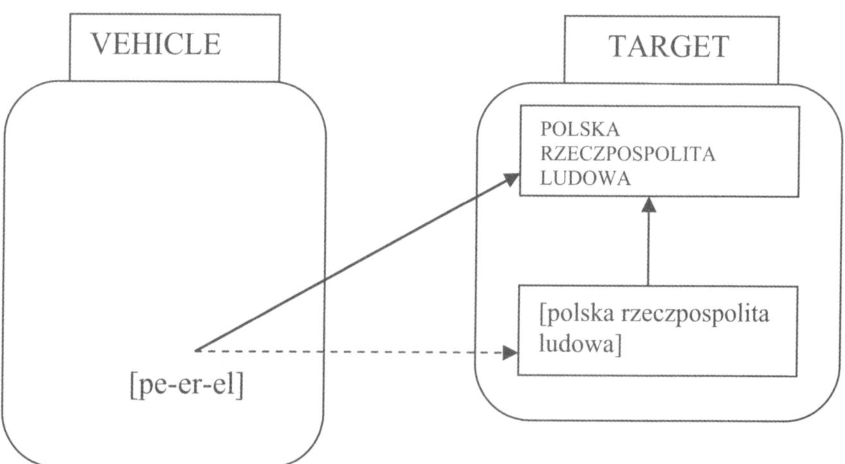

Figure 2.4 Direct activation of the conceptual content of [Polska Rzeczpospolita Ludowa] by the alphabetism *PRL.*

In the case of new political parties, the situation is less stable. For instance, the acronym for one of them, PiS [pis] for *Prawo i Sprawiedliwość* ('Law and Justice'), may be inflected as a masculine noun, by analogy with other nouns ending in *-is*, e.g. *lis* 'fox', *urwis* 'rascal, *cis* 'yew tree', pronominalises like masculine nouns and takes masculine concord (as in (5)), but may be used as a neuter noun as well, which is presumably based on the neuter first noun of its name *prawo* 'law', and, consequently, takes neuter concord, as in (6). It will be noticed that both quotes come from the same issue of a quality newspaper *Gazeta Wyborcza* (Oct. 28th, 2005), which shows how unstable the situation is.

(5) PiS wielokrotnie pokazał, że można z nim współpracować.
PiS many-times showed (Pret.3sg.masc.) that [one] may with it (3sg. masc) co-operate
PiS has shown on numerous occasions that it was possible to co-operate with it.

(6) PiS z trudem odrobiło straty.
PiS with difficulty made-up-for (Pret.3sg.neut.) losses.
With some difficulty PiS managed to make up for its losses.

Thus, in the case of the acronym *PiS*, there are two competing ways of accessing its conceptual structure: one direct, like [pe-er-el] in Figure 2.4, and the other indirect, via a metonymic link with its full formal representation, shown in Figure 2.5.[8]

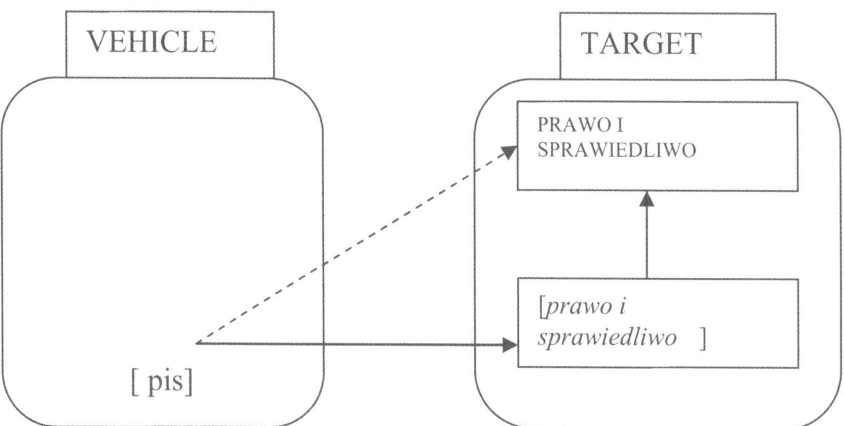

Figure 2.5 The form [pis] metonymically activates the form of the symbolic unit ***Prawo i Sprawiedliwość.***

2.3   Speech-sound metonymies

Speech-sound metonymy is a cognitive process whereby one sound, or a group of sounds, of a phonetic representation stands for the whole representation. This is the kind of metonymy which motivates what Barcelona (2005) call 'non-prototypical constructional forms'. Defined in such a broad way, the concept of speech-sound metonymy applies to a rather wide range of phenomena from vowel reduction in English to clips. In the case of vowel reduction, the schwa sound [ə] may stand for a number of other vowels in the unstressed position.[9] The justification for this analysis, which also motivated the underlying representations of these phonemes in generative phonology, is the fact that when stressed the same vowels are pronounced with their full value, for example the first vowel of the words *photography* and *photograph,* and many others.

Beside simple segments, some acronyms, especially those where it is impossible to determine whether the source is provided by the graphemes or the initial sounds of the full expression, as in the case of *PiS* discussed above, might also be called Speech-sound metonyms. However, prototypical instances of Speech-sound metonyms are clips (truncations), such as *doc* for *doctor, math* for *mathematics, fridge* for *refrigerator*. The formal metonymy involved in clips is: REDUCED PHONOLOGICAL FORM OF X FOR STANDARD PHONO- LOGICAL FORM X.

Nevertheless, it seems that clips may be considered to be just a subcategory of a more general, higher-level formal metonymy, whereby a modified phonological form of an expression stands for the standard phonological form of the expression, i.e. the metonymy MODIFIED PHONOLOGICAL FORM OF X FOR STANDARD PHONOLOGICAL FORM X. The modification of form is particularly common in what might be called 'formal euphemisms', where the euphemistic effect is achieved by a modification of the form of a taboo expression. We have already discussed the case of *Gosh!* as a euphemistic substitute for *God!* Other examples are not hard to find: *heck* for *hell, Stripe!* for *Strike!* (see below), *Tarnation* for *Damnation,* and *Darn, Dang, Drat* for *Damn. Brother* may stand for *Bother* (Allan and Burridge, 1991: 126), and, rather extreme, *Dagblag it* for *God damn it.*

Again it must be stressed that the actual activation of the target form may be a matter of degree, with some clips and euphemistic modifications probably preserving a strong link with the full expression, for example *math,* and others acquiring the status of increasingly independent units, for example *fan,* a truncated form of *fanatic.*

2.3.1 Morphological metonymy

Morphological formal metonymy is a process whereby a single morpheme stands for the whole word of which it constitutes a part. Below are examples of rather straightforward types of this general phenomenon.

2.3.1.1 The root for the whole derived form

The root (or base of derivation) may stand for the derived form, such as *Damn!*, which, as Allan and Burridge (1991: 125) argue, is derived from *condemn* (rather than from the cohort *Damnation!*), *damn* as an expressive modifier standing for the participial *damned*. Arguably, other 'reduced' participles should also be included here, e.g. American irregular past and participial forms of such verbs as *fit* (*fit, fit*), *quit* (*quit, quit*), *wet* (*wet, wet*), as well as a few participles derived from former strong verbs, such as *drunk* from *drunken*, *got* for *gotten*, *forgot* for *forgotten* although in most cases the formal difference has also led to conceptual and distributional differentiation.

2.3.1.2 A prefix for the whole derived form

A prefix may stand for the whole derived word, such as *sub >> submarine, subscription,* or *subeditor, mini >> miniskirt, ex >> ex-husband, ex-wife.*

2.3.1.3 A suffix for the whole word or words

A suffix may stand for the whole word or words, such as *various -isms*, where *-isms* stands for the whole category of abstract, often learned words (e.g. *materialism, consumerism, dualism, Marxism*).

2.3.1.4 One component of a compound for the whole compound

One component of a compound may stand for the whole compound:

(a) HEAD OF A COMPOUND FOR THE WHOLE COMPOUND (e.g. *paper >> wallpaper, chair >> electric-* or *wheelchair, or highchair*). It should be pointed out that the formal metonymy here accompanies a conceptual synecdochic shift from a hyponymic term to its hyperonym, so a more general term stands for a less general term (see Chapter 1). Blank (2003) calls this process 'absorption into the *determinatum*' and illustrates it with Spanish *coche* (coach, car) ellipsed from *coche automóvil* and German *Schirm* (shelter, umbrella) from *Regenschirm*.

(b) MODIFIER OF A COMPOUND FOR THE WHOLE COMPOUND, for example *submarine >> submarine boat, sedative >> sedative drug, defective >> (mentally) defective person, Fifth >> Fifth Avenue, gold >> gold medal, return >> return ticket, apple >> apple juice* or *apple-tree, mobile >> mobile phone, human >> human being*).[10] Blank (2003) calls this process 'absorption into the *determinans*' and illustrates it with

French *diligence* ('velocity', 'stage coach'), ellipsed from *carosse de diligence* and German *Weizen* ('wheat, 'beer made from wheat') from *Weizenbier*. The last example is particularly telling since *Weizen* meaning 'wheat' is masculine (*der Weizen*), while in the sense of 'beer' it is neuter (*das Weizen*), thus retaining the neuter gender of its original head (*das Bier*) and showing that the suggestion that the head has been 'absorbed into the *determinans*' must be rejected. In Polish this kind of metonymy is particularly common in culinary vocabulary, where the adjectival modifier stands for the whole NP with the ellipsed head noun denoting the most common categories of dishes and drinks. The target compound usually has N + Adj structure, for example *grochowa >> zupa grochowa* ('pea soup'), *pomidorowa >> zupa pomidorowa* ('tomato soup'), *schabowy >> kotlet schabowy* ('pork chop'), *czysta >> wódka czysta* ('clear vodka'), *żytnia >> wódka żytnia* ('rye vodka'). Another domain in which this metonymy is common is SPORT, for example *skrzydłowy* ('winger' in football), *środkowy* ('centre' in basketball), *rozgrywający* ('setter' in volleyball).

It is well known, however, that the boundary between compounds and so-called syntactic phrases is rather fuzzy (cf. Szymanek 1998: ch. 2); therefore, I shall postpone a more thorough discussion of the combinations of free morphemes till the next section. Summing up, the morphological metonymies discussed above seem to conform to the general metonymic mapping: MORPHEME M (FREE OR BOUND) OF A MORPHOLOGICALLY COMPLEX WORD X FOR THE WHOLE X.

A note on phonaesthemes
It has been known for a long time that, apart from traditional morphological formatives, phonaesthemes also form form-meaning pairs. For instance, in English the initial [*sw-*] cluster is systematically linked with lexemes denoting 'a curved, fast motion', as in *swerve, swoop, swish, swipe, swift, swathe, swirl* (see Dirven 1985 for discussion), the initial cluster *fl-* is also systematically linked with lexemes designating 'sudden or violent movement', as in *flap, flail, flee, flick, flutter, flurry*, and verbs ending in *-ash* tend to designate 'violent impact', as in *bash, clash, crash, dash, flash, gash, gnash, lash, smash, thrash* (cf. Allan and Burridge 1991). More recently, Bergen (2004) demonstrated that the well-known English phonaesthemes *gl-*, associated with VISION and LIGHT, as in *glimmer, glisten, glow*, and *sn-*, associated with MOUTH and NOSE, as in *snore, snack, snout*, display priming effects much like those exhibited by ordinary morphemes. However, as opposed to regular morphemes, phonaesthemes do not appear as formal metonymic parts that can stand for the whole word. Therefore, it may be suggested that they are based on the SIGN ICM. As part of the phonological representation of a word, the phonaestheme alone

stands for a part of the semantic structure of the word (one of its central domains).

A note on rhyming slang

It seems that ordinary rhyming slang expressions should be considered as sound metonyms formed according to the metonymic principle (COMPOUND) EXPRESSION (X)Y FOR AN EXPRESSION Z WHICH RHYMES WITH Y, for example *Aristotle >> bottle, pig's ear >> beer, orchestra stalls >> balls, stammer and stutter >> butter*. However, since most rhyming slang expressions are compounds or, in Nunberg et al.'s (1994) terminology, idiomatic phrases, and since they are usually used without the rhyming component of the expression, it seems reasonable to regard them as cases of morphological metonyms whereby the modifying (non-rhyming) constituent of the compound stands for the whole compound. The metonymy in question is: EXPRESSION X OF THE RHYMING SLANG COMPOUND XY FOR XY. In the examples above, this metonymy produces expressions such as *pig's, orchestra* and *stammer*, which, owing to the chaining of the two metonymies, stand respectively for *beer, balls* and *butter*. The chains of morphological and sound metonymies in those cases can be represented as follows:

> *pig's >> pig's ear >> beer*
> *orchestra >> orchestra stalls >> balls*
> *stammer >> stammer and stutter >> butter.*

2.4   Syntax – constructional metonymies

As already discussed in Chapter 1, there is a tradition in the studies of metonymy, going back to Jakobson's theory, which restricts it to *"a transfer along the syntagmatic axis"* (Karolak in Polański 1993: 364; transl. mine – BB). As we saw, this narrow, purely syntactic view cannot be maintained. This does not mean, however, that there are no syntactically based metonymies. On the contrary, there are plenty.

My presentation of syntactic metonymies is based on the constructionist view of syntax as first formulated by Langacker (1987) and Fillmore et al. (1988), and subsequently developed by Goldberg (1995) and more recently Croft and Cruse (2004). Without going into details, I shall follow and define the construction as "a syntactic configuration with one or more substantive items (e.g. the words *let alone, have a …*, and *away*) and sometimes not (as with focus constructions, exclamative constructions and resultative constructions). A construction also has its own semantic interpretation and sometimes its own pragmatic meaning (as with tautological constructions)" (Croft and Cruse 2004: 247).[11] Again following Croft and Cruse, all constructions are viewed as atomic or more or less complex and as more or less schematic, or more or less substantive, with complex, totally schematic syntactic structures at one extreme of the continuum and atomic, substantive words at the other. From the point of view of construction grammar, with its insistence on the lexicon-syntax symbolic continuum (cf. Fried and Ostman 2004; Croft and Cruse 2004), it makes little sense to distinguish phrases from sentences as they are all constructions. However, for expository purposes I have divided the two kinds of 'purely' syntactic metonymies into phrasal and sentential metonymies. Since both phrases and sentences are constructions, they may be regarded as two kinds of constructional metonymies.

2.4.1 Phrasal metonymy

Phrasal metonymy is a metonymy whereby part of a phrasal construction stands for the whole phrasal construction. This kind of metonymy was already alluded to by Ullmann as a transfer of meaning resulting from ellipsis based on the 'contiguity of names'. Ullmann describes it as follows: "in a set phrase made up of two words, one of these is omitted and its meaning is transferred to its partner" (1972 [1962]: 222). The examples Ullmann discusses include *the main* for *the main sea*, *a daily* for *a daily newspaper*, as well a number of French examples, such *diligence* for *carrosse de diligence* and as *un première* for *un billet de première class*. Ullmann's account is inadequate in two ways. First of all, as the last example shows, the 'set phrase' may well consist of more than two words. Secondly, he fails to explain why the phrase resulting from ellipsis preserves the grammatical properties of the full phrase, such as the determiner and the categorial properties of the remaining constituents (e.g. an adjective remains an adjective). Nor does Blank's (2003) contention that such examples are cases of lexical ellipsis or (as he prefers to call them) 'absorption' explain much if we cannot show what their conceptual basis is. Moreover, Blank's conclusion that "absorption as a diachronic process has no proper synchronic counterpart" (*ibid*: 269) is only tenable given an arbitrarily restricted concept of synchronic semantic relations, as otherwise the conclusion must be that 'absorption' has a synchronic counterpart either in idiomatic constructions (e.g. *the poor*), or some metonymically motivated conversions (e.g. the adjective *black* converted into the noun meaning 'a black person').

In what follows I will demonstrate that the ellipsed expressions discussed by Ullmann and Blank are parts of larger constructions, that is combinations of the form and meaning of the whole phrase, which they access metonymically. The same approach is also represented by Barcelona (2005) in his analysis of the example *Interstate 70* metonymically standing for *Interstate number 70*. As another illustration I shall analyse two adjectival head NP constructions consisting of the definite article and an adjective. I shall argue that the construction should be considered as a case of phrasal metonymy targeting the full NP.[12] It will be observed that the proposal made below is fully compatible with the claim that the Art-Adj construction is elliptical, discussed and defended by Balteiro (2007: ch. 3).

The Art-Adj construction comes in three varieties (cf. Quirk et al. 1972: 5.20). The first involves generic plural personal nouns in combinations with adjectives designating "a particular physical or social condition" (Swan 1995: 18), as in *the blind, the deaf, the rich, the poor, the needy, the jobless* which stand for the blind, the deaf, the rich, the poor, the needy, the jobless people. The second involves nationalities, designated by the adjectives ending in *-(i)sh, -ch* and *-ese* (plus *the Swiss*). Since other aspects of the construction remain the same, both these cases represent the same kind of formal metonymy, which has the form [*the* ADJ$_{ph/s\ condition;\ nationality}$] >> [*the* ADJ$_{ph/s\ condition;\ nationality}$ [PEOPLE]]. Accordingly, the inner construction, represented schematically in Figure 2.6 as a boldface box, is used as a vehicle to access a larger phrasal construction represented as the outer box of the diagram.[13]

Syn	*the*	Adjective
Sem	GENERIC	PROPERTY$_{COND/NATIONAL}$

>>

Syn	*the*	Adjective	Noun
Sem	GENERIC	PROPERTY$_{COND/NATIONAL}$	PEOPLE

Figure 2.6 Construction *the* ADJ$_{CONDITION/NATIONALITY}$ as a vehicle (part) to target construction *the* ADJ$_{CONDITION/NATIONALITY}$ N$_{PEOPLE}$ (whole).

The plural noun [PEOPLE] in the target construction, which should be interpreted conceptually not lexically, explains why the phrases in question take plural concord. The third case of the adjectival head NP involves the most general and abstract concept (and noun) of the THING or, more specifically, such items as *news* (probably determined pragmatically), modified respectively by some non-inherent descriptive/evaluative adjective or a superlative, for example *the sublime* and *the ridiculous* in *He went from the extremely sublime to the ridiculous*, and *the latest* in *The latest is that he is going to run for election* (Quirk et al. 1972: examples in 5.23). The relevant metonymy seems to be [*the* ADJ$_{d/e;superlative}$] >> [[*the* ADJ$_{d/e;superlative}$] [THING]], as shown in Figure 2.7. The singular [THING] in the target construction makes sure that the metonymy takes singular concord.[14]

Syn	*the*	Adjective
Sem	GENERIC	PROPERTY$_{\text{DESC/EVAL}}$

\>\>

Syn	*the*	Adjective	Noun
Sem	GENERIC	PROPERTY$_{\text{DESC/EVAL}}$	THING

Figure 2.7 Construction *the* ADJ$_{\text{DESCR/EVAL}}$ as a vehicle to target Construction *the* ADJ$_{\text{DESCR/EVAL}}$ N$_{\text{THING}}$.

If the metonymies in question were analysed in purely conceptual terms, for example as instances of the metonymy PROPERTY FOR BEARER OF PROPERTY, the grammatical characteristics of the elliptical expressions would have to be determined anyway, in order to rule out the wrong examples, involving concord and/or semantic selectional restrictions.

One of the interesting consequences of the proposed analysis is that it offers a cognitively realistic explanation of the fact that the ADJ>N conversion often appears in two varieties: so-called partial and total conversions (cf. Bauer 2005; Balteiro 2007). The expressions analysed above are usually considered partial on the grounds that they do not exhibit the full range of nominal inflections and distributional properties while retaining some of the adjectival properties; in particular:

(a) they do not take nominal inflections
(b) they do not co-occur with the indefinite article and other nominal modifiers, for example *a poor, *their poor
(c) they can be premodified by adverbs, for example *the comparatively poor*
(d) they can be graded, for example *the poorer, the poorest.* (Balteiro 2007: 80)

Thus the adjectives in the construction in question retain their ordinary adjectival status.

A similar metonymy-based analysis can be proposed for participial adjectives accessing the whole NPs, such as *twenty wounded, 200 killed,* or the singular ones like *the deceased* or *the accused,* etc. Needless to say, the fact that the *the*-ADJ construction is motivated metonymically does not prevent it from having the status of an autonomous construction in English, as argued by Fried and Östman (2004: 75), but it does explain where the semantics of the construction comes from.

The whole process need not stop at the level of an idiosyncratic construction, however. On the contrary, Balteiro (2007: 81) rightly points out that there is no shortage of adjectives which have undergone total conversion and exhibit the whole range of the inflectional and distributional characteristics of nouns, for example *an intellectual, a private (soldier), a musical (comedy), a capital (city)*. What I suggest is that in the case of Adj>N conversions metonymy is a necessary intermediate stage on the way to total conversion, defined as "unmarked change of word category" (Schönefeld 2005: 138), whereby a word changes its conceptual status, from being a dependent relational unit to being an independent THIING and, as a result, acquires nominal inflections and begins to function as an ordinary common noun. In Polish the phrasal metonymic motivation can be proposed for a number of nouns ending in -owy. The suffix is primarily adjectival and the nouns are morphologically identical to the adjectives, for example *szeregowy* ('private') vs. *żołnierz szeregowy* ('private soldier'), *dzielnicowy* ('local') vs. *policjant dzielnicowy* ('local constable'). Grzegorczykowa claims that the suffix has been "abstracted away from original substantivised adjectives" (1984: 41) [transl. mine – BB]. Interestingly, it has become productive and semantically quite fixed, denoting prototypically employees responsible for or operating or using some particular piece of equipment, named in the base, as in *aparaturowy* ('apparatus (operator)'), *kadłubowy* ('working in the hull'), *wagowy* ('scales (operator)').

Alongside adjectives ending in -*owy*, there are other converted adjectives, whose phrasal source is easy to trace. Here is a short list of examples which still can be used as adjectives but which are increasingly common as autonomous nouns: *zdrowy* (a healthy (person)), *chory* (a sick (person)), *biedny* (a poor (person)), *bogaty* (a rich (person)).

What argues in favour of the phrasal motivation of those nominals is the fact that they retain the semantic properties of the whole phrase. Thus, *pijany* ('drunk') retains the temporary construal of the NP *pijany mężczyzna* ('drunk man') as opposed to *pijak* ('drunkard'), which is a derived nominal having a habitual meaning. Moreover, all these adjectives can still be graded, as in the following sentences:

(7)   Na naszym oddziale, bardziej zdrowi pomagają bardziej chorym.
      [At our ward, the more healthy (patients) help the sicker (patients)]
(8)   Najbogatsi pomagają najbiedniejszym.
      [The richest help the poorest]

However, the most important category of Polish NPs based on formal metonymies is represented by participial postmodifiers. Sentences (9) and (10) below illustrate the metonymic PART-FOR-WHOLE relation between, respectively, the present and the past participial headless NP and full NP:

(9)   Siedzący przed bramą nie zauważyli jak książę wymyka się tylnymi drzwiami.
>> LUDZIE siedzący przed bramą nie zauważyli jak książę wymyka się tylnymi drzwiami.
[(People) sitting in front of the gate didn't notice the prince sneaking out through the back door.]

(10)   Nikt nie troszczy się o zwolnionych z pracy i opuszczonych przez najbliższą rodzinę.
>> Nikt nie troszczy się o LUDZI zwolnionych z pracy i opuszczonych przez najbliższą rodzinę.
[Nobody cares for the (people) made redundant and forsaken by their closest family.]

It is important to notice that the above sentences do not illustrate a simple purely syntactic deletion rule which would allow the head postmodified by participial phrases to be deleted, because the headless NPs are permitted only when the target head of the whole NP is personal.[15] Consider these unacceptable sentences:

(11)   *Leżace na ziemi zostały wyrzucone do kubła na śmieci.
> Rzeczy leżące na ziemi zostały wrzucone do kubła na śmieci.
[The (things) lying on the floor have been thrown into the dustbin]

(12)   *Nikt nie troszczy się o wrzucone do kubła na śmieci.
> Nikt nie troszczy się o rzeczy wrzucone do kubła na śmieci.
[Nobody cares for the (things) thrown into the dustbin]

The relevant metonymy based on participial modification can be represented as follows:

Syn	Participle$_{\text{Past/Present}}$ Phrase
Sem	PROPERTY

>>

Syn	Noun	Participle$_{\text{Past/Present}}$ Phrase
Sem	PEOPLE	PROPERTY

Figure 2.8 The headless participial postmodifier as the vehicle activating a full personal plural NP in Polish.

In addition, we may distinguish formulaic metonymies, whereby a part of a well-entrenched formula activates the whole formula. However, if a formula is defined as a substantive construction with a strong pragmatic component, it may be argued that some formulas are also constructional phrasal or sentential metonymies (see below). For instance, Allan and Burridge (1991: 125) speculate that 'Oh dear' comes from 'Oh dear God'; and *Strike* (often euphemised as *Stripe*) is all that is left from *God strike me dead if (I'm not telling the truth)*. They also suggest that *Blast it* and *Bother it* may in fact come from *May God blast/bother it*. *Oh my!* stands for *Oh my God*. Consider also *Many happy returns*, which stands for *Many happy returns of the day*. The metonymy in question is PART OF FORMULA FOR WHOLE FORMULA.

2.4.2 Sentential metonymy

Sentential metonymy is a metonymy in which a formal part of a sentential construction stands for the whole sentential construction. Five kinds of sentential metonymies will be discussed: question tags, sentences involving reduced comparatives, anaphoric ellipsis, gapping and reduced raising constructions.

2.4.2.1 Tag questions

My claim is that tag questions are syntactically determined metonymic constructions which access larger syntactic wholes made conceptually available by the sentences with which they co-occur.[16] It should be noted that I have avoided any reference to the actual lexical words used in the sentence preceding the tag because, as the data discussed by Langendoen (1970) show, speakers construct their tag questions on the basis of their conceptualisation of the content of the preceding sentence, rather than on the basis of its strictly syntactic or even semantic properties. Sentences (7) through (9) show what kinds of alternate construals speakers choose in tag questions. The data come from a questionnaire Langendoen gave his forty-six students as a homework exercise:

(13)   I may see you tomorrow (Langendoen's 19)
       Won't I?   17
       May I not?   11
       Mayn't I?   10
       Might I?   3
       Mightn't I?   2
       Can't I?   1
       Shall I?   1
       Will I?   1

(14) I believe that Dr. Spock is innocent (Langendoen's 42)
      Don't I?   36
      Isn't he?   10

(15) Either John or Sue will stay (Langendoen's 61)
      Won't they?   22
      Won't she?   19
      Won't he?   3
      Won't he or she?   1
      no reply   1

The tag questions to sentence (13) indicate that the choice of the auxiliary may be quite free, the questions to sentence (14) demonstrate that the verb phrase accessed by the tag question is motivated but not fully determined by the preceding sentence, and tag questions in (15) show that the selection of the 'subject' of the tag, serving as the point of reference for the pronoun, is also a matter of construal and cannot be totally determined syntactically. Thus the sequence Aux PRO, which functional linguists call the Mood (Halliday 1994 [1985]: 72) of the tag, is not totally determined by the preceding 'main' clause. However, the rest, or what functionalists call the Residue (Halliday 1994 [1985]: 74) and what I shall indicate simply by VP, is determined: grammatically – by the Mood of the tag, and lexically – by the preceding sentence. As Halliday observes "It is always possible to 'reconstitute' the ellipsed item so that it becomes fully explicit. Since ellipsis is a lexico-grammatical resource, what is taken over is the exact wording, subject only to the reversal of speaker-listener deixis (*I* for *you* and so on), and change of mood where appropriate" (1994 [1985]: 321). In terms of formal metonymy, the 'taking over' means accessing the whole clausal structure by means of its modal part consisting of AUX PRO. Although the details of the formulation may need refining, approximately, the formal metonymy involved in the interpretation of tags may be represented as follows: $[[\text{NP}_i \; (\text{-/+ Neg}) \; \text{VP}_j], \text{AUX}_j \; (\text{+/-Neg}) \; \text{PRO}_i] >> [[\text{NP}_i \; (\text{-/+ Neg}) \; \text{VP}_j], \text{AUX}_j \; (\text{+/-Neg}) \; \text{PRO}_{\text{NPi}} \; \text{VP}_j]$ where the subscripts indicate, broadly speaking, conceptual relatedness, including anaphoric relations and/or a lexical identity.

Taylor (2004: 64) argues that a construction is motivated "to the extent that it can be related to … various other facts about English, and thereby occupies an ecological niche within the language". In my view, the tag question construction is motivated by at least two other question constructions. One is negative questions with falling intonation. What the tag questions and negative questions of this kind have in common is their pragmatic component: given adjacency pairs, their preferred second part expresses agreement (cf. Levinson 1983: ch. 6; Halliday 1994 [1985]: ch. 4). Thus (16) and (17) below, with falling intonation, both invite agreement:

(16)   She's charming, isn't she?
         Yes, she is.
(17)   Isn't she charming?
         Yes, she is.

The second motivation is structural: it is the use of Aux SUBJECT sequences in utterances functioning as prompts for other-initiated self-repair (18) or for confirmation (19), although the latter may also be interpreted ironically, as other-initiated self-repair.

(18)   A: She was very kind.
         B: Was she?
(19)   A: She doesn't particularly fancy Bill.
         B: Doesn't she?

Neither in exchange (18) nor in exchange (19) are the answers genuine requests for information, which is typical of tag questions as well. Following Taylor's approach to the motivation of constructions (Taylor 2004), given the negative questions, as in (11), and short elliptical questions, as in (18B) and (19B), it may be concluded that tag questions occupy a niche ecologically motivated and in a sense prepared by these two related constructions.[17]

2.4.2.2 Reduced comparatives

A process formally similar to the reduced clauses in question tags can be observed in comparative constructions of equivalence, exemplified in the following sentences:

(20a) Bill is at least as tall as Jim.
(20b) Bill is at least as tall as Jim is.
(21a) Bill ran the distance as fast as Jim.
(21b) Bill ran the distance as fast as Jim did.

It will be observed that the meaning and structural properties of the reduced subordinate clause in (14) and (15) are completely determined by the meaning and structure of the main clause. Thus the sentences can be non-metonymically paraphrased as:

(20′) Bill is at least as tall as I am tall.
(21′) Bill ran the distance as fast as I ran the distance fast.

Admittedly, (20′) and (21′) sound rather awkward, probably due to the considerable grammaticalisation of the metonymic constructions represented by both versions of (20) and (21). However, the 'full' construction is still very much alive in sentences like (22) and (23):

(22) Bill is as strong as I am courageous.
(23) Bill sang as beautifully as Jim played his guitar awfully.

Clearly, the 'full' comparative construction is part of English grammar and thus there are good reasons to suggest that sentences (20) and (21) are sentential metonymies accessing the whole comparative construction of equivalence. The source and target constructions of (20a) are represented in Figure 2.9, whereas the source and target constructions of (20a) are represented in Figure 2.10.

Syn	NP$_1$	Verb	*as*	AdjP$_1$	*as*	NP$_2$
Sem	PATIENT	STATE	EQUI	ATTRIBUTE		PATIENT

>>

Syn	NP$_1$	Verb	*as*	AdjP$_1$	*as*	NP$_2$	Verb	AdjP$_1$
Sem	PATIENT	STATE	EQUI	ATTRIBUTE		PATIENT	STATE	ATTRIBUTE

Figure 2.9 Reduced comparative attributive construction activating the full comparative attributive construction.

Syn	NP$_1$	VP$_1$	*as*	AdvP$_1$	*as*	NP$_2$
Sem	AGENT	ACTIVITY	EQUI	ATTRIBUTE$_{MANNER}$		AGENT

>>

Syn	NP$_1$	VP$_1$	*as*	AdvP$_1$	*as*	NP$_2$	VP$_1$	AdvP$_1$
Sem	AGENT	ACTIVITY	EQUI	ATTRIBUTE$_{MANNER}$		AGENT	ACTIVITY	ATTRIBUTE$_{MANNER}$

Figure 2.10 Reduced comparative adverbial construction activating the full comparative adverbial construction.

By and large, the same analysis can be proposed for regular comparative structures involving contrast, as in these sentences:

(24a) James likes the theatre more than Susan.
(24b) James likes the theatre more than Susan does.
(24c) James likes the theatre more than Susan enjoys it.
(24d) James likes the theatre more than Susan enjoys the theatre.

Sentence (24d) represents a full comparative construction;[18] which has the form shown in Figure 2.11.

Syn	NP$_1$	VP$_1$	more	than	NP$_2$	VP$_1$
Sem	EXPERIENCER$_1$	PSYCH-STATE	GREATER DEGREE	COMPARED TO	EXPERIENCER$_2$	PSYCH-STATE

Figure 2.11 The comparative construction illustrated by sentence (24d).

While examples (24b) and (24c) may be said to involve different anaphoric pro-forms (*does* and *it*, respectively), example (24a) is clearly metonymic, although it may also represent two comparative constructions: one accessed through the subject of the comparative clause and the other accessed through its object. As is well known, the difference shows up when the subject of the comparative clause is pronominalised. Consequently, sentence (24a) can have two pronominal versions: (24a*) corresponding to (24b), and (24a**):

(24a*) James likes the theatre more than she (does).
(24a**) James enjoys the theatre more than her >> James likes the theatre more than he likes her.

2.4.2.3 Anaphoric ellipsis

The term 'anaphoric ellipsis' covers all the cases where an ellipsed element has an antecedent earlier in the sentence.[19]

Anaphoric phrasal head ellipsis

There are cases of ellipsis in English which are quite similar to the phrasal metonymies discussed above, whereby the head noun is not formally represented and the resultant NP has the actual form Def.Art.–Adj. Nevertheless, such cases must be classified as sentential metonymies since the ellipses must have an antecedent as the head of another phrase mentioned earlier in the sentence. As an example of this kind of metonymy we shall consider sentence (25) (discussed also by Balteiro, 2007: 81f):

(25)   It is a wet light rather than a dry ____.

Apart from the free choice of the determiner, the crucial difference between the phrasal metonymies like *the poor* and the ones illustrated by (25) is that in the former the head of the NP has no overt antecedent and is a fixed concept (i.e. PEOPLE) while in the latter the formally 'absent' head is determined by an antecedent which occurs earlier in the sentence. In example (25) the head of the elliptical NP *a dry* is the head of the NP *a wet light* (i.e. the noun *light*). Thus the conceptual head of the NP *a dry* stands in an anaphoric relation to the head of the earlier NP. Hence the term 'anaphoric ellipsis'. Nevertheless, for reasons I cannot explain, sentences like (25) – the ones involving anaphoric ellipsis – are much more unusual than the cases of cataphoric ellipsis, where the phonetic head follows the gap. Cataphoric ellipsis is illustrated by sentence (26):

(26)   It is a wet ____ rather than a dry light.

Anaphoric subject ellipsis

Consider the following sentence:

(27)   He applied and got the job.

This is another case of anaphoric ellipsis, called 'textual ellipsis' by Carter and McCarthy (2006: 181), where the co-referential subject of the second (and the following) co-ordinate clause is not expressed formally. Unlike the anaphoric head ellipsis, subject ellipsis has no cataphoric counterpart:

(28)   *Applied and he got the job.

Nor is it possible in English to ellipse objects:

(29)   *Bill kissed Mary and Paul kissed ___, too.
(30)   *I wanted to buy that book and I bought ___.

The reason for the unacceptability of (29) and (30) is that English already has a way of expressing their conceptual content by means of (anaphoric) auxiliary pro-forms. So a grammatical equivalent of (31) is (32):

(31)   Bill kissed Mary and Paul did too.
(32)   I wanted to buy that book and I did.

In languages which do not have grammaticalised anaphoric auxiliary constructions, like Polish, sentences structurally equivalent to (31) and (32) sound either much more acceptable or perfectly correct:

(33)   ?Bill pocałował Marysię i Paweł pocałował też.
(34)   Chciałem kupić tę książkę i kupiłem.

2.4.2.4 Gapping

Bach (1974) discusses the rule of gapping and in the age of total transformational generative absolutism declared that such structures seem to 'demand rule schemata rather than strict transformations'. The schema in question would have to relate the second sentence in each pair with the first one. On our metonymic account, sentences (35b) and (36b) (as pairings of form and meaning) are accessed through the vehicles of sentences (35a) and (36a), respectively:

(35a) John ordered meat; and Bill, fish >>
(35b) John ordered meat, and Bill ordered fish.
(36a) Mary went to New York; Harry, to Washington; and Sally, to Waukegan >>
(36b) Mary went to New York, Harry went to Washington, and Sally went to Waukegan.

In sentences (35) and (36), the following metonymy is at work: $[NP_1\ V_1\ X],[NP_2 \_\_ Y] >> [NP_1\ V_1\ X],[NP_2\ V_1\ Y]$. The relationship shows that gapping involves formal metonymy: the meaning of the whole sentential construction is accessed by means of a reduced form of the construction. The same explanation holds for a similar case, which may be called 'auxiliary gapping', discussed within the minimalist paradigm by Redford et al. (1999: ch. 20), illustrated by sentence (37):[20]

(37)   He was laughing and she _ crying.

2.4.2.5 Reduced raising constructions

The final example of formal sentential metonymy I shall discuss is based on ellipsed sentences based on structures involving so-called object-to-subject raising (cf. Langacker 1990: ch. 7, 1999: ch. 11; Lee 2004 [2001]: ch. 5). Recall that object-to-subject raising is a relationship between sentences, illustrated by (38) and (39):

(38)   To solve the crossword is difficult.
(39)   The crossword is difficult to solve.

Since the object-to-subject-raising predicates like *difficult, easy, tough, impossible* are normally used in descriptions of processes, such as solving the crossword, and not in descriptions of physical objects, such as a spoon, it has been suggested that sentences like (40) result from the same conceptual structure as (38) and (39), except that in (40) the process "remains unelaborated because its nature is evident by other means" (Langacker 2000: 340).

(40)   The crossword is difficult.

My claim is that the 'other means' involve also the whole raising construction represented by (39). In other words, the [Patient-Subject NP – be – Adj] syntactic pattern of (40) is metonymically used to access the [Patient-Subject NP – be – Adj – to V] pattern. The metonymy is pragmatic (see below) to the extent that the particular semantic properties of the verb are determined by the culturally determined nature of the typical human interaction with the entities denoted by the Patient-Subject NP, for example in the case of crosswords the typical interaction is solving, in the case of books it involves reading and so on.

However, the metonymic operations on raised constructions are not limited to the case of ellipsis illustrated by sentences like (40). As we have already seen in Chapter 1, Langacker suggests that the sentences in (41) below differ in that while in sentence (41a) the main clause verb profiles the relation between a nominal trajector and processual landmark, represented by its gerundive complement, in sentence (41b) it is the landmark of the 'embedded' process that functions as the landmark of the main clause relation and the whole process is an active zone.

(41a) He began eating dinner.
(41b) He began dinner.

Langacker presents the contrast between the pair of sentences in (41) in terms of the polysemy of the inceptive verb *begin* (see Figure 2.12).

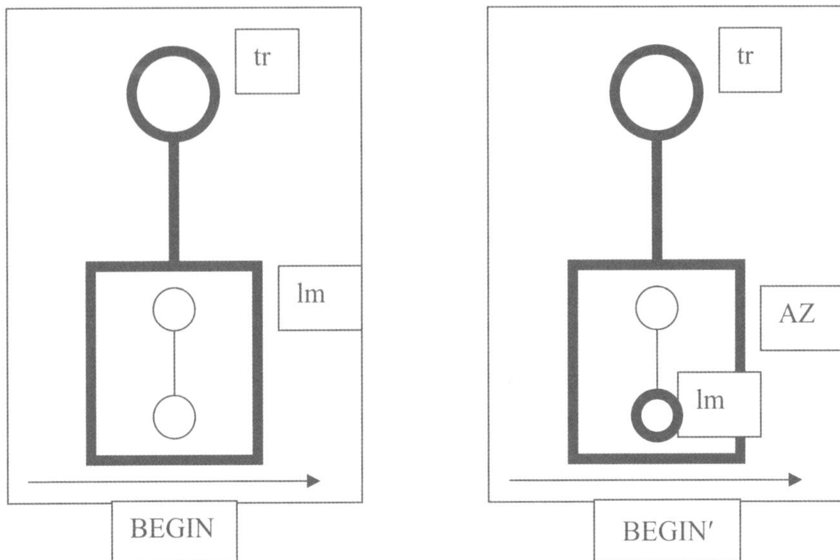

Figure 2.12 Representations of sentences (41a) and (41b) according to Langacker (1990: ch. 7).

As already noted in Chapter 1, Langacker's active-zone analysis of the sentences illustrated by (41) is at odds with the very concept of active zone, which normally accounts for the cases of under-specification, not alternate construals, which are clearly the domain of grammar. In fact, if the extension is accepted, the notion of active zone may be used to account for almost any kind of transfer of meaning and thus becomes descriptively useless. In Figure 2.13 I offer an alternative solution. The crucial difference between Langacker's and my accounts lies in the fact that in my analysis both sentences in (41) involve metonymy and neither of them involves active zones. As the diagrams show, in both cases the whole of the propositional structure of the complement clause is accessed. What is different are the vehicles of this formal PART-FOR-WHOLE metonymy: in (41a) it is the substructure consisting of the verb and direct object NP (functioning jointly as the landmark of the main relation), while in (41b) it is the direct object NP, which alone functions as the landmark of the main relation.

In terms of constructional representations, the whole semantic content of the construction may be represented as [AGENT-ASPECTUAL VERB-EVENT], where the Event itself consists of [Agent-Activity-Patient] with the Agent of the Event being co-referential with the Agent of the main clause. The difference between (41a) and (41b) lies in the complexity of the syntactic vehicle

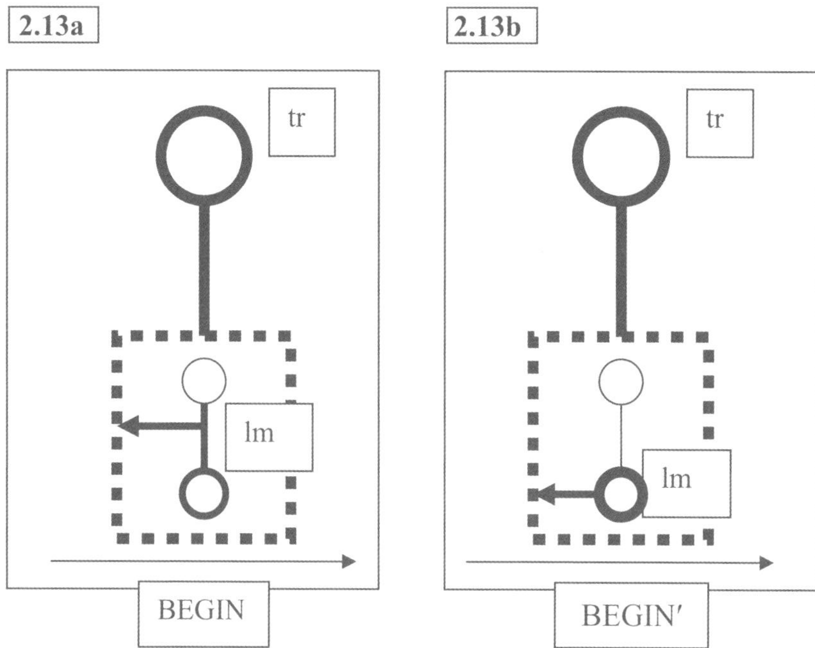

Figure 2.13 Modified representations of sentences (41a) and (41b).

selected to access the semantic structure of the 'embedded' Event; in (41a) it is the gerundive form of the verb designating the activity of the Event along with the NP designating the Patient, while in (41b) it is only the object NP designating the Patient. Accordingly, the two structures can be represented as in Figure 2.14. The boldfaced constituents of the Event represent the vehicle of the metonymy.[21]

2.14a

Syn	NP$_1$	Verb		**V-ing**	NP$_2$
Sem	**AGENT$_i$**	**ACTIVITY**$_{ASPECTUAL}$	E V E N T		
			Agent$_i$	**Activity**	**Patient**

2.14b

Syn	NP$_1$	Verb			NP$_2$
Sem	**AGENT$_i$**	**ACTIVITY**$_{ASPECTUAL}$	E V E N T		
			Agent$_i$	Activity	**Patient**

Figure 2.14 The grammatical constructions sanctioning (a) aspectual sentences like (41a) *He began eating dinner*, and (b) aspectual sentences like (41b) *He began dinner*.

In addition, I have demonstrated that it is perfectly possible to explain the meaning of (41b) in terms of standard PART-FOR-WHOLE formal metonymy without postulating a rather ad hoc polysemy of *begin*.

A detailed discussion of aspectual verbs is important because Langacker uses the same extended notion of active zone in his analysis of raising constructions arguing that it has 'independent motivation'. If the alternative non-active-zone analysis of aspectual verbs is accepted, Langacker's analysis of raising constructions loses its independent motivation and turns out to be unmotivated and, at best, ad hoc. If this is the case, a better motivated proposal is called for. I offer such a proposal below, but first we must consider the details of Langacker's account.

Langacker (1990: ch. 7) argues that in addition to the aspectual sentences, active zones are also involved in various raising constructions, known as Object-to-Subject Raising (OSR), Subject-to-Subject Raising (SSR) and Subject-to-Object Raising (SOR), illustrated by the (b) sentences below:

(42a) To fix Hondas is easy.
(42b) Hondas are easy to fix.
(43a) To paint landscapes is tough.
(43b) Landscapes are tough to paint. (Object-to-Subject Raising)
(44a) For the dog to escape is likely.
(44b) The dog is likely to escape. (Subject-to-Subject Raising)
(45a) I would expect for the Clippers to lose again.
(45b) I would expect the Clippers to lose again. (Subject-to-Object Raising)

Langacker claims that in sentences (a) of (42), (43) and (44) it is the whole process which functions as the trajector, while in sentences (b) the role of the trajector is taken over by the profiled participant and the remaining infinitival part of the process becomes the trajector's active zone with respect to the scale of difficulty (or pleasure [or likelihood – BB], etc.). In other words, despite their differences all the three kinds of raising are "alike in that the [raised] NP in question is analysed as the true subject or object of the main clause, both syntactically and semantically. In each case, moreover, the nominal referent stands metonymically for its processual active zone vis-à-vis the main clause relation" (Langacker 2000: 356). Langacker accounts for these differences between (a) and (b) sentences in terms of polysemy of the main clause adjective. Thus for the two sentences in (43), he suggests the representations shown in Figure 2.15.

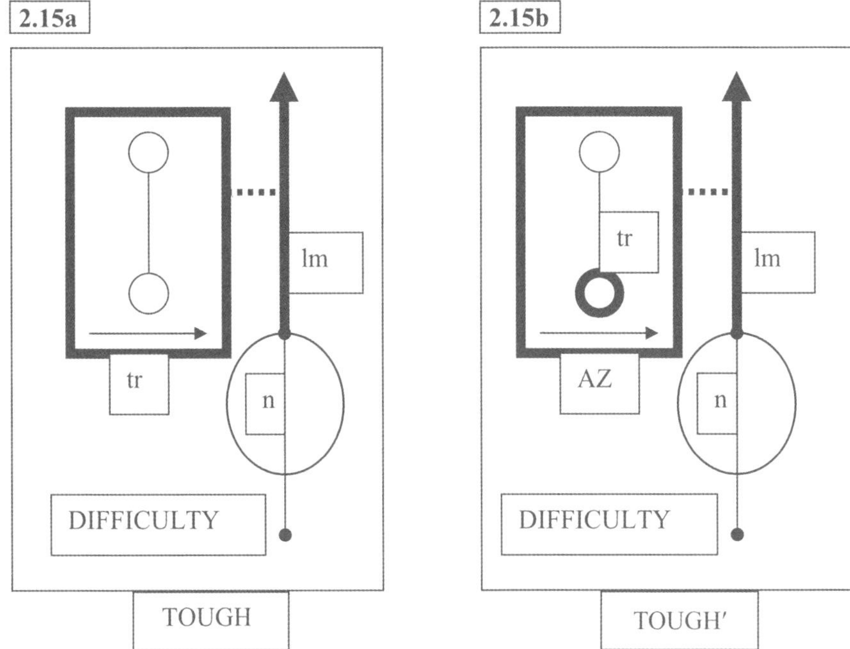

Figure 2.15 Representations of sentences (43a) and (43b) according to Langacker (2000).

Here Langacker's analysis is even more problematic than in the *begin* sentences because the putative active zones are actually explicitly specified (i.e. profiled), and thus become indistinguishable from the regions or parts designated directly. Since the process is specified, it is odd to claim that "the nominal referent stands metonymically for its processual active zone" (*ibid.*). It is also odd to call 'zones' two fully specified constituents of a relation, namely the relation itself (the verb) and its landmark (the object NP). What we have already said about the suggestion that there are two different senses of the verb *begin* in (41a) and (41b) applies also to the proposal that there are two different senses of *tough* in (43a) and (43b). Langacker is right that basically *tough* designates an e-site on the scale of DIFFICULTY which is usually elaborated by another relation. However, the fact that this elaborating relation may be construed in different ways does not affect the meaning of *tough*. As Langacker himself convincingly shows (cf. Langacker 2000: ch. 11), the possibility of multiple construals is constrained by the structural and semantic properties of the subordinate clauses (e.g. their analysability), as in the case of idiom chunks, and not the polysemy of the main clause predicate.

The representation of raised and non-raised constructions I propose below does not make use of the notion of active zone and the semantic polysemy of raising predicates. Instead, a number of constructions are suggested which differ in some respects and have certain characteristics in common. The formal metonymy is evoked in two cases: when the trajector of the subordinate relation is unspecified and when the infinitival complement is ellipsed, as in *The crossword is difficult*. For the sake of simplicity, I have ignored the exact specification of the semantic roles in the Sem(antic) part of the representations, reducing them to the two basic conceptual roles of the TRAJECTOR and LANDMARK. Likewise, the semantics of verbs was reduced to the elementary distinction between STATE and PROCESS. The same subscripts indicate co-reference (i.e. a single entity in Langacker's diagrams).

An attempt to combine Langacker-style representations of conceptual structures with syntactic representations in the Fillmore-style Construction Grammar was made by Leino (2005). Whether we combine them or not, some sort of interface mechanism relating conceptual structures to their syntactic representations is necessary anyway (see Jackendoff 2002 for general discussion). I believe what I propose below is a step, albeit a very tentative one, in this direction. In the constructions below the semantic role of ATTRIB with the subscript AA stands for 'Attribute of Activity for Agent', represented by the raising adjectives *easy, hard, difficult*, etc.

A. *Object-to-subject raising*

The non-raised construction with a clausal subject, e.g. *For a good mechanic to fix Hondas is easy, For my wife to sleep here is difficult* may be represented as shown in Figure 2.16.

Syn	Clause$_{inf}$	*be*	AdjP
Sem	EVENT	STATE	ATTRIB$_{AA}$

Figure 2.16

In sentences like *To fix Hondas is easy*, the whole of the subject clause is accessed by means of its Verb + object NP part. There is no active zone; the TRAJECTOR (Agent), easily conceptualised and potentially lexicalised (e.g. by *for anybody*), is construed as generic (the subscript G) (see Figure 2.17).[22]

Syn	⊙		Verb$_{inf}$	NP	*be*	AdjP
Sem		**EVENT**			STATE	ATTRIB$_{AA}$
		TRAJECTOR$_G$	**PROCESS**	LANDMARK		

Figure 2.17

In contrast, OSR construction involves co-instantiation in the sense of Fried and Östman (2004) (see Endnote 21), therefore the subject and the object of the complement clause must be co-indexed. Consequently, *Hondas are easy to fix, Landscapes are tough to paint* are examples of a construction which has approximately the form shown in Figure 2.18.

Syn	Np$_s$	*be*	AdjP	$\odot$	*to* Verb$_{inf}$	
Sem	TRAJECTOR$_i$	STATE	ATTRIB$_{AA}$	E V E N T		
				TRAJECTOR$_G$	PROCESS	LANDMARK$_i$

Figure 2.18

Given above formulation, sentences like *Hondas are easy* and *Landscapes are tough* can be interpreted as instances of an NP-*be*-ATTRIB$_{AA}$AdjP construction, which metonymically accesses the whole OSR construction and thus its main properties are determined by that construction (see Figure 2.16).

B. *Subject-to-subject raising*

The set of SSR predicates mentioned by Langacker is internally diversified and includes some of the verbs that most linguists would not consider raising predicates any more, for example modal verbs. Since a complete analysis of the whole set is irrelevant to my purposes, I only discuss non-raised construction and then go on to what I refer to as Adjectival SSR Construction (i.e. a construction with main clause SSR adjectives like *(un)likely, sure, certain, liable, apt*). In the construction, the role of ATTRIBUTE is subscripted as *Epist.* indicating its epistemic modal meaning.

Non-raised construction (e.g. *For the dog to escape is likely* or *That the dog will escape is likely* or *That he will win is certain*)

Syn	Clause	*be*	AdjP
Sem	EVENT	STATE	ATTRIB$_{Epist.}$

Figure 2.19

Adjectival SSR construction (e.g. *The dog is likely to escape* or *He is certain to win*)

Syn	NP$_s$	*be*	AdjP		VP$_{inf}$
Sem	TRAJECTOR$_i$	STATE	ATTRIB$_{Epist.}$	EVENT	
				TRAJECTOR$_i$	PROCESS

Figure 2.20

C. *Subject-to-object raising*

Again, the set of SOR predicates is internally diversified, ranging from verbs of emotional attitude, desire and intention, such as *like, want, mean*, through mental state verbs, such as *believe, expect, think, imagine*, to the verbs of communication, such as *state, declare, acknowledge*. As Langacker points out, however, the difference between the fully transparent SOR predicates and the so-called PRO (or Equi) verbs, such as *persuade* or *tell*, is by no means clear cut and often allows for double construals or at least a considerable degree of indeterminacy, as in the case of verbs of perception. Therefore, it is necessary to postulate representations that would allow for variable degrees of the object participant's involvement in the profiled main-clause relationship. Determining precisely how different degrees of this involvement should be represented would require a separate study. For our purposes, I will propose three cardinal options:

(a) prototypical, fully transparent SOR construction
(b) prototypical PRO construction
(c) blended SOR-PRO construction

In the representations below I will assume the following conventions:

– A syntactically and semantically complete subordinate clause is enclosed in a boldfaced box.
– A wall of the subordinate clause box may be open (is no longer boldfaced), which indicates that the elements on either side of the open 'wall' may syntactically or semantically affect the syntactic or semantic structure on the other side of the wall.
– A grey filling of the cell of a box indicates a blend (e.g. an element has a syntactic and/or semantic function in both clauses).
– In the semantic representations of construction only the general terms TRAJECTOR and LANDMARK and PROCESS are used, although in detailed analyses, most of them have much more specific semantic roles, such as AGENT, PATIENT, EXPERIENCER, and the verbs belong to different semantic classes as well.
– The subscripts S and DO stand respectively for 'subject' and 'direct object'.

To begin with, let us assume that the non-raised version of the SOR construction, represented by sentences such as *The judge declared that he was mentally incompetent* or *I believe that he is a fink* or *I would expect for the Clippers to lose again,* has the following form:

Syn	NP$_S$	Verb	Comp$_{for-}$ to/that	Clause
Sem	TRAJECTOR	PROCESS	EVENT	

Figure 2.21

The raised versions have the following forms:

A. SOR construction (e.g. *The judge declared him to be mentally incompetent* or *I believe him to be a fink* or *I would expect the Clippers to lose again*)

Syn	NP$_S$	Verb	NP$_{DO}$	VP$_{inf}$
Sem	TRAJECTOR$_0$	PROCESS	EVENT	
			TRAJECTOR$_i$	PROCESS

Figure 2.22

As the figure suggests, in the SOR construction TRAJECTOR$_i$ is semantically independent of the main clause, but on the syntactic level it has the function of the DO of the main verb. In Langacker's terminology, it is fully transparent.

B. PRO construction (e.g. *I persuaded my mom to see a doctor* or *I told Bill to stay*)

Syn	NP$_S$	Verb	NP$_{DO}$		VP$_{inf}$
Sem	TRAJECTOR$_0$	PROCESS	LANDMARK$_i$	EVENT	
				TRAJECTOR$_i$	PROCESS

Figure 2.23

As Figure 2.23 shows, the EVENT structure of the subordinate clause is open to the effect that the LANDMARK of the main clause determines the identity of the TRAJECTOR of the complement clause, indicated by the same subscripts. On the level of form, the TRAJECTOR$_i$ has no syntactic exponent.

C. Blended SOR/PRO construction (e.g. *Everyone heard Melvin entering the building*)

Syn	NP_S	Verb	NP_{DO}	VP_{ing}
Sem	$TRAJECTOR_0$	PROCESS	$LANDMARK_i$	
			$TRAJECTOR_i.$	PROCESS
				EVENT

Figure 2.24

In the blended SOR/PRO construction, the DO of the main clause has a double semantic function: it serves as the LANDMARK of the main clause as well as the TRAJECTOR of the EVENT designated by the complement clause.

With these rough representations of the three constructions, we may now consider the cases of metonymies, whereby parts of the constructions are used to activate the whole construction. Here are the relevant examples discussed by Langacker (sentence 40 is repeated):

(46)   The crossword is difficult.
(47)   Another war is likely.
(48)   Q: Who is coming to your party?
       A: I expect Tom and Sally.

Langacker argues that "As a general point, the complement clause in raising constructions functions as the periphrastic device allowing the raised NP's active zone to be spelled out explicitly when required" (2000: 341). Langacker's claim amounts to extending the definition of active-zone phenomena beyond their ordinary and explanatorily useful scope, namely, the active zone would involve PART-FOR-WHOLE transfers from well-conceptualised and lexicalised parts to the equally well-conceptualised and lexicalised wholes. According to my proposal, no such extension is necessary, since the way sentences (46)–(48) become meaningful can be accounted for in terms of a formal metonymy whereby a part of a construction is used to access the whole construction, with the details of the resulting meaning being determined either anaphorically (if the EVENT is specified in the preceding linguistic context, as in (48)), or pragmatically by the canonical activity associated with the particular TRAJECTOR or LANDMARK (see §2.6 below). Accordingly, the example *The crossword is difficult* involves a formal metonymy, which may be represented as in Figure 2.25.

Syn	NP$_s$	*be*	AdjP
Sem	TRAJECTOR$_i$	**STATE**	**ATTRIB$_{AA}$**

>>

Syn	NP$_s$	*be*	AdjP	⊙	*to* Verb$_{inf}$	
Sem	TRAJECTOR$_i$	STATE	ATTRIB$_{AA}$	E V E N T		
				TRAJECTOR$_G$	PROCESS	LANDMARK$_i$

Figure 2.25 Interpretation of the NP-*be*-ATTRIB$_{AA}$AdjP construction is motivated by its metonymic link with the full OSR construction.

Before we conclude this section, it is worthwhile observing that a fairly similar account can be proposed for two other phenomena of English syntax and semantics, both of which may involve formal metonymy. The first case has to do with the constructions illustrated by sentences (49)–(50) which, as Quirk et al. (1972: 828) argue, have adverbial transforms, seen here:

(49)   He was quick to react.
       = He reacted quickly.
(50)   He was slow to react.
       = He reacted slowly.

If the paraphrases are indeed adequate, then, on the conceptual level, the metonymy is ATTRIBUTE FOR MANNER. However, examples like (49) and (50) above also occur in sentences without the infinitive, as in (51) and (52) below:

(51)   He was quick.
(52)   He was slow.

I suggest that in such cases, the infinitival complement, with its behavioural meaning determined pragmatically, is accessed metonymically through the part of the construction which as a whole consists of the subject noun, the copula, an adjective and the infinitive. Thus, it is either given contextually or it is up to the hearer to infer what the Agents of (51) and (52) were involved in doing. The other example has to do with MANNER FOR LINGUISTIC ACTION metonymy analysed in English, Croatian and Hungarian by Brdar and Brdar-Shabó (2003), illustrated by (54) and (56):

(53)   Our boss was vague about when the pay-rise was due.
(54)   Our boss was vague.
(55)   Arthur was brief about the other teachers in his recollections.
(56)   Arthur was brief.

I believe that sentences (54) and (56) are possible only because the speaker and his interlocutor have mental access to larger portions of the content in the form of the target construction exemplified by (53) and (55). Or, rather, should we say 'used to have mental access' because, as Brdar and Brdar-Shabó have demonstrated, a number of such manner-of-speaking adverbs have extended their meanings and incorporated this new 'linguistic action' sense in their semantic structure, which has obviated the need for pragmatic inferencing altogether. English adjectives which have developed this extended polysemous structure are *articulate, blunt* and *open.*

2.4.2.6 From subordinate to main clause constructions

There are a number of independent subordinate clause constructions in Polish which are motivated by larger complex sentence constructions. They preserve the grammatical properties of the embedded clause and have the same illocutionary force as the complex sentence. The larger complex sentence constructions and the independent subordinate clause constructions are illustrated in the following sentences:

(57)   Chcę, żeby Tom przyjechał. [I want Tom to come]
(58)   Żeby (tylko) Tom przyjechał! [That Tom may come!]
     Illocutionary force: EXPRESSION OF A WISH
(59)   Złości mnie, że ty się zawsze musisz spóźniać.
     [It annoys me that you must always be late]
(60)   Że (też) ty się zawsze musisz spóźniać!
     [That you must always be late!]
     Illocutionary force: EXPRESSION OF ANGER

The fact that the constructions in question are motivated by formal metonymy and inherit the illocutionary force of the whole complex sentence does not mean that they do not have idiosyncratic formal and semantic/ pragmatic properties. For instance, the pragmatic particles in brackets (*tylko, też,* and the modal *musieć*) should probably be included in the formal description of those constructions. On the semantic/pragmatic side, we should indicate their axiological value (GOOD and DESIRABLE in the *żeby-tylko* construction, and BAD and UNDESIRABLE in the *że-też* construction) as well as their higher expressiveness.

Independent *if*-clause constructions in English have been recognised and described by Panther and Thornburg (2003b) and by Brdar-Szabó (2007), who calls them 'stand-alone conditionals', in terms of complex speech act scenarios (see Chapter 4). The approach is convincing but it fails to account for two aspects of the construction: its grammatical properties and the axiological value of the proposition expressed in the construction. As we have seen, the grammatical properties can be explained in terms of the formal metonymy motivating the emergence of the constructions in question, where the subordinate clause is simply a part of a complex sentence standing for the whole. As for the axiological value, it is probably an idiosyncratic property of the construction, but it is likely that it may be motivated by the frequency factors regarding the target complex sentences. We may find that the relevant sentences usually are used with those axiological values found in the constructions, thus it is only one, the more frequent axiological value that has been strengthened and conventionalised. Alternatively, as argued in Chapter 4, the positive evaluation of activity A belongs to the motivation part of the Request Scenario and it is only those activities (As) which are desirable that enter the Request Scenario and can have the illocutionary force of directives.

As an example of formal metonymy involved in independent *if*-clause constructions we may consider *if-only* construction in English. According to the formal metonymy account, the construction is motivated by the full conditional construction. As is well known, conditional sentences come in several varieties, but we shall consider only the past counterfactual kind. In general, following the mental space account of counterfactuals (Dancygier and Sweetser 2005), the past counterfactual *if*-construction sets up two spaces: *i)* the hypothetical space with the counterfactual premise p (the protasis expressing the negative epistemic stance) and the conclusion q (the apodosis) and *ii)* the reality space, which represents the opposite value of p. According to Panther and Thornburg (2003b), in the independent past *if*-clauses illustrated by sentence (61) (Panther and Thornburg's (21)), the *if*-clause evokes the general Reasoning Scenario reproduced here as Figure 2.26.

(61)   Judging from the spot where it lay it had been planted between the underside of the mattress and one of the cross-supports. **If I hadn't re-made the bed ... if Sonia and I hadn't made love ...** Sonia. Nothing else accounted for the presence of that hellish box ...

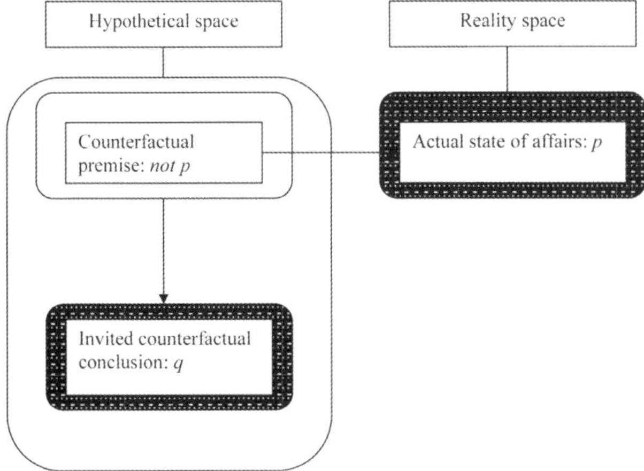

Figure 2.26 Reasoning Scenario based on Panther and Thornburg (2003b).

Now consider the propositions made in (61) expressed by means of the *if-only* construction:

(62)   If only I hadn't made the bed. If only Sonia and I hadn't made love.

I think Panther and Thornburg are right when they claim that the bold expressions in (61) "have a low degree of pragmatic independence; rather, they give the impression of being highly elliptical *if*-clauses" (2003b: 143). In comparison, *if-only* sentences are certainly more independent and less compositional, since the *if-only* construction is much more firmly established in English grammar (cf. Dancygier and Sweetser 2005: ch.8). There is one more difference, however. Notice that ordinary past counterfactual *if*-constructions are indeterminate regarding their axiological load. In particular, *p* may be evaluated as good or bad. In (61) both *I had made the bed* and *Sonia and I had made love* are viewed as bad, undesirable, and hence the hypothetical consequence of the hypothetical *not-p* clause is viewed as good. An opposite axiological configuration, however, is also perfectly possible, as sentence (63) shows:

(63)   If the ambulance hadn't arrived in time, I would have died.

Clearly, in (63) *p* (the ambulance had arrived in time) is viewed as good and desirable, while the hypothetical *q* (I died) as bad and undesirable. Interestingly, such axiology is not available for the *if-only* construction and sentence (64) implies that the speaker, who now may be extremely unhappy and would rather not be alive, views the fact that the ambulance had arrived in time as bad and undesirable.

(64)   If only the ambulance hadn't arrived in time.

The above considerations strongly indicate that the past counterfactual *if-only* construction is prototypically used in order to express not only a wish or desire, as argued by Dancygier and Sweetser (2005), but rather regret that some particular circumstance did or did not occur, in other words the actual state of affairs is viewed as bad and undesirable. Accordingly, the difference between the ordinary independent past conditional, as well as its elliptical versions illustrated in (61), and the *if-only* construction lies in the more specific axiological pattern of the latter, which may be represented as in Figure 2.27.

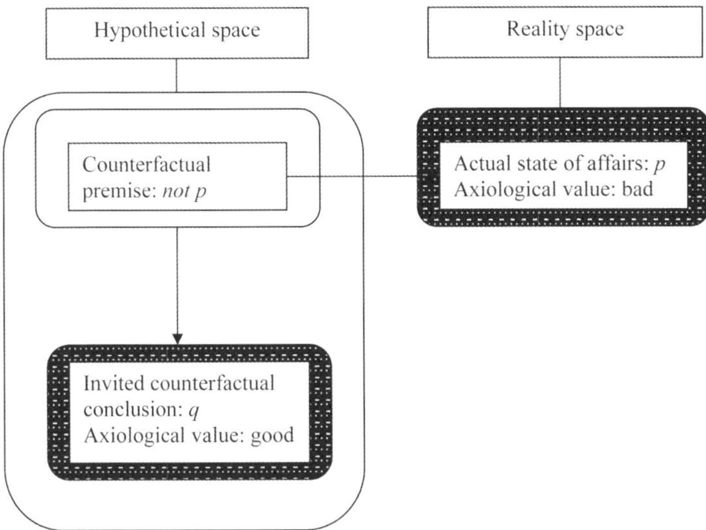

Figure 2.27 *If-only* Reasoning Scenario.

Semantically, past *if-only* sentences can be paraphrased using the formula 'It would have been good if *p*'; however, from the pragmatic point of view they are used to express regret that ~*p*. Moreover, the invited counterfactual *q* is not part of the past *if-only* construction at all, and, therefore, I suggest that the construction should be represented as follows:

Syn	*If only* NP *had* V_{PP} P
Sem	$PAST_{hypothetical}$ $EVENT_i$: Good
Pragm	Speaker regrets ~$EVENT_{i\ factual}$

Figure 2.28

I believe, however, that the construction is still, at least weakly, associated with its full motivating conditional construction (i.e. the one which does specify the 'good' consequence *q* in the Reasoning Scenario, and thus metonymically evokes it). The full construction is represented by sentence (65) with the negated negative consequence (i.e. in the hypothetical past nobody found out, which was good) or by sentence (66) with an affirmative positive consequence (i.e. in the hypothetical past they carried on living happily, which was good):

(65)   If only we hadn't re-made the bed, nobody would have found out what had happened.

(66)   If only we hadn't re-made the bed, they would have carried on living happily.

Schematically, the full construction can be represented as follows:

Syn	Clause$_1$: *If only* NP *had* V$_{PP}$P	Clause$_2$: NP *would have* V$_{PP}$P
Sem	Condition: PAST$_{hypothetical}$EVENT$_i$: Good	Consequence: PAST$_{hypothetical}$ EVENT$_q$:Good Or: PAST$_{hypothetical}$~EVENT$_q$:Good
Pragm	Speaker regrets ~EVENT$_{j\ factual}$	

Figure 2.29

I believe that the pragmatic component of the construction developed and was entrenched gradually. Since the event which constitutes the object of regret is mentioned in the protasis, the second clause (the apodosis) was felt to be so hypothetical that it became communicatively superfluous and was gradually dropped to become a monoclausal performative (cf. Dancygier and Sweetser 2005: 219).

2.5   Discourse metonymy

Generally speaking, discourse metonymy is a metonymy whereby a part of a construction used by speaker B accesses the whole construction which is grammatically and lexically determined by the construction used by speaker A. The standard examples of discourse metonymy are what Halliday (1994[1985]: 318) refers to as 'clause ellipsis', subdivided into *a)* yes/no ellipsis and *b)* WH- ellipsis. For the purposes of presentation, I shall ignore WH- ellipsis and discuss only yes/no ellipsis. Halliday illustrates clause ellipsis with the following examples:

(67)   A: Can you row?
        B: Yes.   [I can row]
(68)   A: Is that all?
        B: No.   [That is not all]
(69)   A: You're growing too.
        B: Yes [I'm growing too], but I'm growing at a reasonable pace.
(70)   A: I shouldn't be hungry for it, you know.
        B: Not at first [you wouldn't be hungry for it at first], but …
(71)   A: Would you like to see a little of it?
        B: Very much indeed. [I should very much indeed like to see a little of it]

The structures in brackets are the 'ellipsed' items suggested by Halliday. In terms of metonymic analysis put forward here, they should be interpreted as the whole structures accessed by means of their parts in B's rejoinders.

Example (69) shows that the metonymy is not confined to questions and answers, and examples (70) and (71) show that the vehicle need not stand first in the linear ordering of the sentence. Thus it may be proposed that the discourse metonymy illustrated in (67) through (71) has the form: {A: S_i} B: [LE] >> [$_{Si}$...LE....], where the expression in curly brackets represents speaker A's sentence, and LE stands for the 'lexical exponent' of the construction. The subscript indicates that A's sentence and the target S are related. In examples (67) through (71) the lexical exponents are, respectively, *Yes, No, Not at first,* and *Very much indeed.*

The above examples do not exhaust all the possible discourse metonymies. Other examples are easy to find. Consider, for example, the following exchanges with *Let's* and *You'd better* as fixed lexical exponents of the constructions whose instantiations are given in brackets:

(72)   A: Shall we go swimming?
       B: Let's.   >> [Let's go swimming]
(73)   A: Don't you think I should return the money straight away?
       B: You'd better.   >> [You'd better return the money straight away]

2.6 Pragmatic metonymy

Typically, pragmatic formal metonymies are based on partly substantive constructions where the substantive part of the construction stands for the whole construction in which the unuttered part is schematic and often conceptually filled in from the context or the general knowledge of the world. Thus pragmatic metonymies seem to be the least formal and most conceptual of all the metonymies we have discussed so far. It is true; nevertheless, as we shall see, because they do have a schematic formal component, therefore they may be counted among formal metonymies as well.

2.6.1 Ellipsed objects

As is well known, a number of English transitive verbs have developed formally intransitive constructions. Levin refers to the whole group of such constructions as "unexpressed object alternations" (1993: 33). The group includes unspecified object alternation, such as *bake, cook, draw, drink, eat, play,* illustrated by (74); understood body-part object alternation, such as *blink, nod, point, wave,* illustrated by (75); understood reflexive object alternation, such as *bathe, change, dress, shave, wash,* illustrated by (76); and PRO-arb(itrary) object alternation, such as *advise, warn, amuse, anger, please, shock,* illustrated by (77):

(74) (a) John has been drinking a lot of milk these days.
     (b) Bill has been drinking again.
(75) (a) The man waved his hand at the children waiting on the platform.
     (b) The man waved at the children waiting on the platform.
(76) (a) Sue dressed herself hurriedly.
     (b) Sue dressed hurriedly.
(77) (a) His views always shock people.
     (b) His views always shock.

Since the objects are 'understood' I suggest that in all of the above elliptical examples the Patient is metonymically accessed through corresponding transitive constructions with what I shall call 'default Patients' in their semantic structure. Thus the new construction is intransitive only on the syntactic level; on the semantic level the Patient is there as a biologically or culturally defined default. For instance, the verb *drink* in English has developed an intransitive construction, illustrated by (74b) above, with the culturally default Patient ALCOHOLIC BEVERAGE. Thus the intransitive construction is motivated metonymically. The phenomenon seems universal, although in different languages different verbs can appear in such constructions. For instance, in Polish, alongside the equivalents of the English verbs illustrated above such as *pić* ('drink'), *jeść* ('eat'), *palić* ('smoke'), *prać* ('wash'), *prowadzić* ('drive') etc., there are a number of verbs whose equivalents in English are often much less felicitous. Consider the following:

(78) Ona już nie bierze – *She does not take [drugs] any more.
(79) Przepraszam, czy tu biją – ?? Sorry, are they beating [ordinary people, customers] here?
(80) Opowiadasz – You're telling [a tall tale].

On the other hand, unlike in English, there is no reflexive object alternation, so most Polish equivalents of the English verbs belonging to that group take an obligatory reflexive object *się*, as in (81a), which is a translation of (76a):

(81) (a) Ona przebrała się pośpiesznie – She changed herself quickly.
     (b) *Ona przebrała pośpiesznie – She changed quickly.

This kind of ellipsis is not limited to objects of mono-transitive verbs but represents a more general principle. Goldberg (2005) has suggested that the omission of objects is linked with their prominence in discourse. Consider the following examples:

(82) The chef in training chopped and diced all afternoon.
(83) Tigers only kill at night.
(84) The singer always aimed to dazzle.

(85) Pat gave and gave, but Chris just took and took.
(86) The sewing instructor always cut in straight lines.

Since all the examples involve either mono- or di-transitive verbs with ellipsed objects, Goldberg accounts for the omissions in terms of the Principle of Omission under Low Discourse Prominence which states:

> Omission of the patient argument is possible when the patient argument is construed to be deemphasized in the discourse vis à vis the action. That omission is possible when the patient argument is not topical (or focal) in the discourse, and the action is particularly emphasized (via repetition, strong affective stance, contrastive focus, etc.). (Goldberg 2005: 29)

There is no doubt that the discourse functions are relevant to the omissions. However, the omission would be impossible without the metonymic link with the full construction in the first place. In short, all the sentences above activate the whole, semantically 'complete' constructions in which all the arguments are specified. Thus, what Goldberg calls Deprofiled Object Construction (Goldberg 2005: 31) results from its metonymic link with the central transitive constructions.

2.6.2 Ellipsed clausal complements

Beside omitted objects, pragmatic formal metonymies also involve more or less direct speech acts with lexically unspecified but pragmatically determined clausal complements. Consider the following examples along with the partial representations of the metonymies they represent:

(87) Condolences and apologies – *I'm sorry, I apologise.*
      Metonymy: [*I'm sorry*] >> [*I'm sorry that* ($_S$ E BAD FOR AD)]
      where E stands for 'event' and AD for 'addressee'.
(88) Thanking – *Thank you …*
      Metonymy: [Thank you] >> [I thank you for (VP-ing AD's ACT GOOD for S)]
      where S stands for 'speaker' and VP-ing for the gerundive form of the verb phrase denoting an act performed by the addressee.
(89) Threats – *You'd better stop hitting my little brother, or else!* (Swan, 1995: 181)
      Metonymy: [*p, or else*] >> [*p, or else* (S's ACT BAD FOR AD)]

The difference between [*p, or else*] construction and the constructions in (87) and (88) is that the former usually makes no reference to anything in the context and, as a result, its interpretation must rely on the class of S's undesirable acts defined culturally.

2.7   Conclusions

2.7.1   Properties of formal metonymies

One of the main cognitive principles governing the choice of conceptual metonymies discussed by Radden and Kövecses (1999) is the principle MORE OVER LESS. The main cognitive principle governing the choice of formal metonymies seems to be the reverse of that, namely the principle is: LESS OVER MORE. The specific instantiations of this principle are: LESS WRITING OVER MORE WRITING, LESS SOUND OVER MORE SOUND, SHORT MORPHOLOGICAL FORMS OVER LONG MORPHOLOGICAL FORMS, SHORT SYNTACTIC FORMS OVER LONG SYNTACTIC FORMS etc. Clearly the reduction comes at a cost – in terms of processing energy consumption, metonymy is probably quite costly; still, what is saved in purely physical energy that would have to be otherwise spent in the articulatory or manual effort seems to be worth it. This does not seem too surprising. After all, is it not part of human nature that we are better at and prefer sitting and thinking to actually speaking and writing?

2.7.2   Metonymic syntax

The analysis of phrasal and sentential metonymies proposed above has interesting consequences for the theory of syntax. For it follows from this analysis that in general there are three kinds of constructions: 'full' constructions, in which the syntactic representation is more-or-less isomorphic with the semantic representation, such as *I know that Bill is ill*, 'gapped' constructions, in which an incomplete 'gapped' syntactic structure activates a complete semantic representation, such as *I want to go home*, and 'ellipsed' constructions, which have arisen through entrenchment of formal metonymies whereby formal parts of the full constructions are used to access the full constructions, such as *the poor, Bill began a book, Hondas are easy.*[23]

In addition, the analysis strongly supports the claim often made by cognitive linguists, particularly Langacker (at least since 1986) and Tuggy (at least since 1987), that language depends much more on low level constructions and schemas than gross generalisations. The theory of formal metonymy presented in this chapter, in conjunction with the view that language is a structured inventory of grammatical constructions, explains some of the crucial commonalities between constructions as well as the principles of inheritance.

2.7.3 Single metonymic mechanism and processing help

The findings presented here show that, basically, the same cognitive metonymic mechanism is involved in accessing formal representations of linguistic units on the word level and on the level of constructions, again confirming one of the main and the most far-reaching claims of CG, namely that the same cognitive operations are at work in different aspects of language. I hope to have demonstrated that metonymy, which so far has been regarded as primarily conceptual, has its purely formal analogue as well. Langacker argues that "Grammar (…) is basically metonymic, in the sense that the information explicitly provided by conventional means does not itself establish the precise connections apprehended by the speaker and hearer in using an expression. (…) Explicit linguistic coding gets us into the right neighborhood, in other words, but from there we have to find the right address by some other means" (2009: 46). In general, Langacker's observation is true. However, as we have seen, formal metonymies may often help us establish quite 'precise connections' between what is said and what is intended and, before we resort to 'some other means', we are led quite a distance to 'the right address' by formal grammatical means.

Notes

1 We should bear in mind that different researchers put different labels on these notions; e.g. in Ogden and Richards's (1985 [1923]) original formulation the three realms were dubbed respectively symbol, thought and referent, while in Pierce's semiotic theory they corresponded to the representamen, the interpretant and the object (cf. Al-Sharafi, 2004: ch. 3 for discussion).

2 It should perhaps be pointed out that onomatopoeia represents a rather special case of the Sign ICM in which the auditory form of the sign is based on the auditory profile of the concept. In this case (as in the case of other iconic signs), there seems to be a natural association between the form (i.e. the vehicle) and the concept (i.e. the target) based on similarity, which brings onomatopoeia close to so-called Representational metonymy or REPRESENTEE FOR REPRESENTATION (e.g. when we use nouns denoting objects for visual representations of those objects). In his recent paper Barnden (2010) argues that Representational metonymy is in fact indistinguishable from image metaphor, as they are both based on similarity. It is definitely true that similarity (of whatever perceptual modality) is involved in both cases. What Barnden fails to notice, however, is that it is only in the case of metonymy that the target and source are strongly associated: in fact the existence and perceptual properties of representation causally depend on the existence and perceptual properties of the representee! This kind of link is totally absent from metaphor.

3 After my presentation of the first draft of that paper at the conference *Perspectives on Metonymy* in Łódź (May 6–7, 2005), Günter Radden pointed out to me that

they discussed such metonymies in their paper. I cannot but agree, but it should be stressed that they did not treat them as a qualitatively different kind of metonymy. In particular, they discussed abbreviations such as *UN* for *United Nations* as cases of FORM$_A$-CONCEPT$_A$ FOR FORM$_B$-CONCEPT$_A$ metonymy (i.e. a sign metonymy), which I think fails to represent the crucial formal link between FORM$_A$ and FORM$_B$. Secondly, while it is true that they distinguished PART OF A FORM FOR THE WHOLE FORM metonymy (Kövecses and Radden 1998: 36, for example *crude* for *crude oil*, or *tgif* for *Thank God, it's Friday*), as well as two other formal metonymies, namely MODIFIED FORM FOR ORIGINAL FORM (*ibid.*: 43), for example *effing* for *fucking*, and SUBSTITUTE FORM FOR ORIGINAL FORM (*ibid.*), for example *Do you still love me? – Yes, I do*), they discussed it in the section on "metonymy producing relationships" (§3) and did not set it off as an ontologically distinct category. Therefore, in section 2 on ontological realms in which metonymy occurs they distinguish only Sign, Reference and Concept metonymies. Thus, although Kövecses and Radden clearly recognised the phenomenon of formal metonymy, they did not categorise it as such.

4   I believe that this is a more satisfactory account than the one I first presented in Bierwiaczonek (2007a).

5   Another domain that should definitely be proposed as well, but which I shall not discuss here as it would take us too far afield, is the domain of gestures and signs in sign language (i.e. physical representations of concepts).

6   Of course the expression *Mr Kleen* and some other examples mentioned in this section involve a whole chain of other, conceptual mappings as well. A detailed analysis of all those mappings would take us outside the scope of this work so I will not attempt it here. It is important to note, however, that the formal metonymy in *Klean Kopy* is not a simple PART-FOR-WHOLE, but rather One member of a set (of possible graphemic representations) for another member of this set, *k* and *c* being two members of the set of possible graphemic representations of the phoneme [k]. Therefore, the metonymy in such cases should be considered as synecdochic.

7   The feminine concord is more likely in older texts, when *PRL* had not yet acquired its unit status.

8   This is not to say that *PiS* cannot develop its own autonomous links with other units in the conceptual systems of individual speakers. For instance, a Polish speaker of English, like myself, will inevitably associate it, again due to the formal link, with a rather unpleasant English unit *piss*.

9   I owe this observation to Ela Górska (p.c.).

10   The difference between this morphological kind of metonymy and the syntactic metonymy consists in their (gradual) grammatical determinacy. Consequently, the morphological metonyms acquire the status of independent units representing the category of the whole, hence *sub* exhibits the full range of nominal inflections and the freedom of co-occurrence characteristic of ordinary common nouns (e.g. *a sub, the sub, two subs, these subs*), while the syntactic metonyms are constructionally, and hence much more lexically, inflectionally and grammatically, fixed, e.g. *the rich, *a rich, ?these rich, *these riches*. There the sign >> is to be interpreted as 'stands for' or 'metonymically activates'.

11 The constructions mentioned in the quote can be illustrated by the following sentences:

He didn't make colonel, let alone general (let alone)
He had a walk (have a …)
Bill slept the afternoon away (V… away)
It is against pardoning these that many protest (focusing)
It's AMAZING *the amount I* SPENT (exclamative)
I had brushed my hair very smooth (resultative)
Boys will be boys (tautological)

Note too that according to Taylor's latest definition – "A construction is a linguistic structure that is internally complex, that is, a structure that can be analyzed into component parts" (Taylor 2004: 51) – all metonymies discussed in this paper are constructional.

12 Although Plag discusses the Art-Adj group in the context of conversion, he recognised its special syntactic status: "the non-idiosyncratic behaviour of adjectives used to refer to collective entities (e.g. *the poor, the blind*) can be taken as evidence for the syntactic nature of this special type of conversion" (2003: 116). The intuition behind Plag's comment is right but the formulation is clearly contradictory: if the adjectives are indeed converted into nouns why can't they, unlike ordinary collective nouns, take other determiners and why do they, again unlike ordinary collective nouns, require only plural verb inflections (i.e. plural concord). If that is not idiosyncrasy, what is?

13 Although here, and in other sections of the book, I will not follow any of the standard formalisations of construction grammars, I hope the format I am using is straightforward to anyone familiar with the basic idea of cognitive syntax, which is viewed as inherently symbolic, and thus always combines form and meaning. In fact, the tables I am using are a compromise between the formalism of construction grammar (cf. e.g. Östman and Fried 2005) and the idea of constructional schema used by Langacker, in the sense that the tables (or schemas) and their instantiations are represented in the same format, and differ only in the level of specificity. I assume that the syntactic notions (e.g. N, V, NP, VP) and semantic roles (e.g. Agent, Patient, Instrument) represent higher levels of syntactic and semantic schematicity than their instantiations but are always immanent in them (see Dąbrowska 2004: ch. 10 for a succinct discussion of Langacker's grammar).

14 It will be noticed that I have by no means exhausted the subject. To make my account at least slightly more complete, one should also consider metonymies involved in the 'bare' adjectives like *English*, meaning the English language and singular/plural personal reference of such expressions as *the accused, the deceased, the undersigned.*

15 The construction in question usually has the plural personal head and it is this variety of the headless construction that I represented schematically below. However, singular personal heads are also permitted, for example *Piszący te słowa wie, że nic nie wie* [[THE PERSON] writing these words knows that he knows nothing].

16 It follows from the present account that tag questions are dependent units, elaborated by the sentences which precede them.

17 At the conference *Semantics Without Borders*, Bielsko-Biala, September 11–13, 2008, Klaus-Uwe Panther and Linda Thornburg suggested an analysis of question tags in terms of metonymies based on prototypical scenarios of speech acts performed in the main clause. In the discussion that followed I proposed that the whole tagged sentence should be accounted for in terms of conceptual integration in which the main clause and the question part are phonologically and conceptually blended. Neither Panther and Thornburg's nor my proposal preclude the kind of formal metonymy discussed above. On the contrary, it seems that they both require it.

18 The suggested construction is only one of the whole family of comparative constructions, but an exhaustive analysis of the comparative constructions would go beyond the scope of the present study. I hope it is clear, however, that the same metonymic mechanism is involved when the whole of the comparative clause is activated by an object NP or an adverbial PP, as in *Bill is better at fixing cars than washing machines* and *Property in Moscow is more expensive than in New York*. I assume that the semantic category PSYCH-ACTIVITY is denoted by so-called mental state verbs or psych-verb (cf. Berk 1999: ch. 1)

19 It should be remembered that for a number of researchers, metonymy and ellipsis are two distinct phenomena (cf. Blank 1999b).

20 There are other possibilities as well. 'Subject + Copula ellipsis' may be also proposed to account for verbless clauses like *Whether right or wrong, Ed always loses his arguments* or *When ripe, these peaches will be delicious.*

21 In construction grammar, the identity of the subjects of the matrix verb and its complement is discussed in terms of co-instantiation and is also indicated by co-indexation of the appropriate participants of the valence relation of the matrix verb and the complement, which share the same syntactic properties but not necessarily the same relational properties (i.e. θ-roles or grammatical functions). There is no indication, however, that the absent constituents are accessed metonymically (cf. Fried and Östman 2004: 63f)

22 In construction grammar, the subject of the main clause would exhibit the syntactic properties of the object of the complement but would bear a null participant relation (θ null) to the matrix predicate (cf. Fried and Östman 2004). It is difficult to say how construction grammarians could handle such cases as *Landscapes are tough* without postulating constructional metonymy. Without a metonymic link with the full raising construction, the syntactic properties and the selection of the subject are totally inexplicable.

23 At least some elliptical constructions could be accounted for in terms of constructional metonymy. One obvious case is sluicing, illustrated by the sentences below (taken from Culicover and Jackendoff 2005: 266), where a bare interrogative phrase stands for a whole indirect question.

   i.   Harriet is drinking something, but I don't know what.

   ii. Harriet is drinking scotch again, but I don't know what kind.

3 Metonymy in morphology

As we saw in Chapter 1, the most important and the least controversial function of metonymy is reference: the vehicle is used to identify, or activate, the target for the sake of reference. Thus in the classic *The pork chop is waiting for his check*, the expression *the pork chop* is used to refer to a particular individual. Likewise, in the title of a recent film *The Devil Wears Prada*, *Prada* is used to refer to the clothes designed and sold by the famous brand. However, as I shall try to show below, metonymy should not be restricted to referential use of free lexical forms; it may affect every meaningful unit of language. Therefore, it should come as no surprise that we should find it on the level of morphemes as well. This is where we start.

3.1 Derivations

The question any student of morphology has to ask is to what extent the meanings of lexical items derived through various word-formation processes are determined by the semantics of the components of those items. In other words, the question is to what extent the meanings of derived morphologically complex lexical items are compositional and hence predictable. The answer cognitive grammar gives to this question is this: the meaning of morphologically complex lexical items is only partly compositional and, although it is motivated, it is never fully predictable. To see how unpredictable the senses of morphologically derived items can be, I shall briefly discuss the semantic potential of the nominal suffix *-er,* as analysed by Panther and Thornburg (2003c, henceforth P&T). For a discussion of the polysemous structure of a number of other English affixes, see Lehrer (2003). What P&T have found is that the suffix *-er* in English exhibits a range of senses which are all related to the central Agentive sense, which they characterise as PROFESSIONAL HUMAN AGENT (e.g. *teacher*). These senses can be broadly divided into two groups: object-level metaphoric and metonymic extensions from the central sense and event-level metonymic extensions from the central sense. Modifying slightly P&T's description, the object-level extensions are as follows:

1. **Personal senses motivated by the location a person lives in or is related to**
    For example *Londoner, New Yorker, Wall Streeter* (person professionally employed on Wall Street)

2. **Animate and inanimate Agents**
    (A) Animals: *retriever, pointer, setter, biter, nightcrawler, grasshopper*
    (B) Inanimate: *gas-guzzler, skyscraper*

3. **Instrumental**
    (A) Instrument (V+er): *dishwasher, can opener, muffler*
    (B) Instrument-means, often having a prepositional base or a numeral modifier: *upper* (anti-depressant pill): *downer, three-incher* (nail), *three-wheeler*
    (C) Quasi-instruments (articles of clothing): *clamdiggers, pedal-pushers, sneakers, waders*

4. **Purpose-locations (i.e. locations defined by their purpose)**
    Sleeper, diner, bed-sitter, larder, shitter

5. **Purpose-patients**
    scratcher (lottery ticket you scratch), *reader; broiler, fryer, roaster* (types of chicken), *sipper, slurper, gulper* (types of drinks), *stocking stuffer* (small Christmas gift)

6. **True patients**
    beater (beaten-up old car)

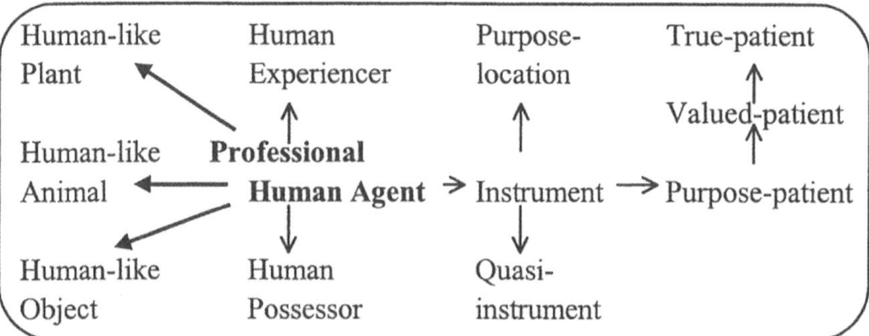

Figure 3.1 Object-level metaphoric and metonymic extensions from the central sense of *-er*. (scanned from P&T: 297).

The event-level extensions can be further subdivided into the central case of causative events, such as *thriller, groaner, stunner, bummer;* (weather events:) *drencher, scorcher*, and more peripheral categories:

A. **Instrumental**: *mixer* (party), *fundraiser, season-opener*
B. **Patientive**: *keeper, forgetter*
C. **Semantically unspecified**: *beaner* (hit on the head), *rear-ender* (kind of car accident), *backhander* (kind of stroke in tennis), *bender* (drinking binge)

Interestingly, the different construals of the relation between the base and the suffix do not exclude each other, hence a single derived lexical item may exhibit a number of quite distinct senses. One such item in English is *sleeper*, whose polysemous semantic structure P&T represent as in Figure 3.2.

OBJECT LEVEL

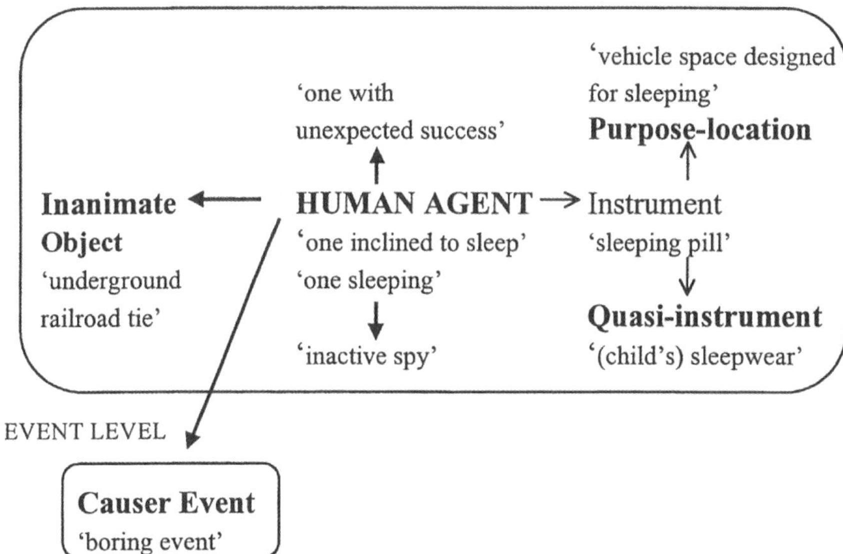

Figure 3.2 The polysemy (or multi-functionality) of *-er* as manifest in *sleeper* (scanned from P&T: 310).

Barring the clear cases of metaphor, such as *sleeper* meaning 'underground railroad tie', the picture that emerges is one of a dependent symbolic unit *-er*, which can be elaborated by almost any concept somehow associated with a given event schema, whether as a participant, a part of the setting (i.e. an adverbial), or as an emotional or cognitive consequence of that event on a putative perceiver. The multiplicity of the possible emergent meanings of *-er* derivatives shows quite clearly that they cannot be analysed in terms of Langacker's (1991) Energetic Chain and the coding hierarchy, as suggested by Kardela (2000: ch. 1), because the Energy Chain comprises only the Agent, Instrument and Patient. Thus, the only explanation seems to be that most of the derived meanings of *-er* derivatives are motivated metonymically: the same *-er* designates very different, yet associated entities: from the prototypical Agents, through the Instruments they use and the Locations where an activity is performed to the whole events. What all these multifarious concepts have inherited from the prototypical agentive meaning is its 'nouniness': they all denote regions bounded in the conceptual space, hence grammatically they are all nouns.

Quite another set of metonymies are at work in the selection of the base of *-er* nouns. P&T show that although they also exhibit considerable diversity, they are motivated by a number of high-level metonymies, differing in the degree of prototypicality and productivity.[1] Thus the meaning of the whole derived nominal is the result of combining the target concept of the base and one of the senses of the suffix *-er*. Of course the most prototypical base of *-er* formations is a verb, denoting, again most prototypically, a transitive activity such as *to teach, to bake, to write*, although intransitive activities are by no means rare, as in *to run, to swim, to sleep* for *runner, swimmer* and *sleeper*, which we have discussed above. At the same time, there are also a number of non-verbal bases, as in *tinner, hatter, whaler, driftnetter, Wall Streeter, submariner, philosopher*, and it is these bases that require explanation. The explanation P&T offer is this: non-verbal bases are allowed in *-er* nominals because they are conceptually related to activities. To give just one example, *Wall Streeter* is an acceptable derivation because WALL STREET is metonymically related to a famous financial INSTITUTION, which in turn is related to the ACTIVITY of the people working for that institution. Consequently, the locative base is motivated by the metonymic chain: PLACE for INSTITUTION for ACTIVITY. As a result, the meaning of the whole nominal is 'person professionally employed on Wall Street'.

In conclusion, P&T's analysis demonstrates that, using Langacker's ontology, *-er* nominals in English denote THINGS characterised in terms of their TEMPORAL RELATIONS. Prototypically, the THINGS are PROFESSIONAL HUMAN AGENTS but they may be metonymically extended to other participants of the ACTION ICM, or even external EVENTS. In contrast, the RELATIONS are prototypically ACTIVITIES (i.e. PERFECTIVE PROCESSES) which may be metonymically accessed through a variety of other participants of the ACTION ICM, such as LOCATION, PATIENT (e.g. *hatter, rear-ender*), MANNER (e.g. *backhander*) or PROPERTY (e.g. *three-incher*).[2]

Thus it is incorrect to claim, as Kosecki does, that "Since only a single property of a person can be focused on at a time, such an instance of facetisation can be formulated as PROPERTY FOR PERSON" (Kosecki 2005: 69). While it is perfectly possible that an ACTIVITY (or LOCATION, etc) is construed as a PROPERTY (cf. Grzegorczykowa 1984: 40; and §3.3.1 below) contributed by the root (base), it must be borne in mind that in the complex nominals in question, the profile of the derivative (i.e. the person or other entities) is determined by the suffix (cf. Langacker 1987, 1991; Waszakowa 1998; Kardela 2000: ch. 1). Incidentally, the same is true of other kinds of derived nominalisations whose emergent profiles are also determined by various nominalising suffixes (i.e. 'nominalisers' in Langacker 1991). Consequently, I cannot agree with Szawerna (2007), nor with Radden and Kövecses (1999), that such nominalisations as *murderer* or *killer* represent metonymies PROCESS FOR PARTICIPANT of this process or, as Radden and Kövecses put it, ACTION FOR AGENT. Notice that in those examples the process components (i.e. *murder* and *kill*) do not stand for any participants; it is the whole integrated expression that has the participant meaning. Metonymy should not be confused with integration, although, as P&T's analysis clearly shows, it may affect the target meaning of the particular components of the integration process and motivate non-prototypical formations.[3] In cognitive linguistic terms, derivation is more similar to compounding than to conversion (both these processes are discussed in subsequent sections), in that compounding also involves integration of two semantic units, although the affixes' meanings are more abstract than those of more independent lexemes. Thus the emergent meaning of derivations is always a blend of the two components induced by the dependent status of the affix, while conversions depend on metonymic mappings alone. The distinction is necessary in order to distinguish the metonymic processes involved in the two components of the derived nominals from the true PROPERTY FOR PERSON metonymies involved in Adjective > Noun conversions (e.g. *a black* in English or *chory* 'a sick person' in Polish; see Chapter 2).

Another important reason why we should bear in mind the composite nature of such derivations is that it is only through the semantic properties of both components that we can account for the differences between various 'rival' personal suffixes, such as *-ist, -nt*, in English and numerous personal suffixes in Polish, for example *-nik, -ista, -owiec, -ek, -as, -iel, -ator, -acz, -arz* etc. (cf. Szober 1966).

Comparing *-er* with *-ist* and *-nt* in English, P&T show that *-ist* exhibits metonymic processes on the base (e.g. *cyclist* vs. *novelist*) but not on the suffix itself, while precisely the opposite is true of *-nt*, which tends to be almost entirely restricted to verbal bases, but represents considerable polysemy as a suffix, ranging from Agentive senses, such as *servant, defendant*, through numerous instrumental senses, such as *stimulant, coolant*, to Purpose-Patient senses, as in *ingestant, inhalant*.

A similar observation may be made about two Polish suffixes *-arz* and *-acz*. For instance, the Polish suffix *-arz* is used to form personal nouns and is only peripherally used to form (metaphoric) animal and (metonymic) instrumental nouns. In this respect, its conceptual polysemy cannot be compared to the

English *-er.* However, the grammatical and conceptual complexity of its bases is comparable: Verbs (Activity): *malarz* ('painter'), *piekarz* ('baker'), Nouns (affected Patient): *grzybiarz* ('mushroom picker'), *łapówkarz* ('bribe taker'), *tapeciarz* ('wallpaperer') (Kosecki 2005: 87); Nouns (effected Patient): *czapkarz* ('hatter'), *plotkarz* ('a gossip'), Nouns (Means, Material): *włókniarz* ('textile worker'), *wikliniarz* ('wicker worker'), Nouns (affected and enjoyed Patient): *karciarz* ('card player'), *kawiarz* ('coffee connoisseur'), *herbaciarz* ('tea connoisseur'), and syntactically less obvious Locations: *kioskarz* ('kiosk assistant'), *poczciarz* ('post office worker'), *wyspiarz* ('islander'), *bramkarz* ('goalkeeper'), Manners: *motylkarz* ('butterfly swimmer'), *żabkarz* ('breast-stroke swimmer') (cf. Grzegorczykowa 1984: 41); Instruments: *piłkarz* ('footballer'), *lotniarz* ('hang-glider'), *kajakarz* ('canoeist'), Experiencers: *szczęściarz* ('lucky man'), *nędzarz* ('pauper') (Kosecki 2005: 79). In contrast, the Polish suffix *-acz* allows predominantly for verbal bases (but see nomina attributiva *siłacz* ('strongman'), *bogacz* ('rich man'), *brodacz* ('bearded man')); instead, however, it itself exhibits a large polysemous network of metonymi-cally related senses, almost comparable with the English *-er*. Here is a sample: Human Agents: *biegacz* ('runner'), *podpalacz* ('arsonist'), *oblatywacz* ('test pilot'), Non-human Agents and Instruments: *powielacz* ('copier'), *rozpylacz* ('sprayer'), *wybielacz* ('bleach'), Locations: *sracz* ('shitter').[4]

Conclusions

A small sample of examples of morphological derivatives drawn from English and Polish shows that metonymy, as a process of meaning extension motivated by conceptual association, applies both to the affix of a complex word and to its root. In the case of affixes, the prototypical meaning (profile) may be extended to other participants of the relation designated by the base, elements of its ground (e.g. location) as well as a closely associated external event. In the case of derivational base, the prototypical base (i.e. a verb denoting a perfective process) may be also extended and allow for other related concepts related to activity, such as nouns denoting location, instrument or manner. It must be remembered, however, that the relation between each affix and its elaborations is unique and must be determined in terms of its characteristic autonomy-dependency parameters.

3.2   Conversions

The simplest and least theoretically biased definition of conversion is "the use of a word of a particular word category as a word of another category, without this being indicated by any formal marker or change" (Schönefeld 2005: 131).

In comparison to other languages, in English conversion is exceptionally common. Bauer (1983: 226) made a comment which aptly characterises the status of conversion in English:

> Conversion is an extremely productive way of producing new words in English. There do not appear to be morphological restrictions on the forms that can undergo conversion, so that compounds, derivatives, acronyms, blends, clipped forms and simplex words are all acceptable inputs to the conversion process. Similarly, all form classes seem to be able to undergo conversion, and conversion seems to be able to produce words of almost any form class, particularly the open form classes (noun, verb, adjective, adverb). This seems to suggest that rather than English having specific rules of conversion (rules allowing the conversion of common nouns into verbs or adjectives into nouns, for example) conversion is a totally free process and any lexeme can undergo conversion into any of the open form classes as the need arises.

As we already mentioned in Chapter 2, two kinds of conversion are often distinguished: so-called partial and total conversions (cf. Bauer 2005; Balteiro 2007), depending on the number of inflectional and distributional properties of the new category a converted word exhibits. This is why so-called transpositions (e.g. a *stone wall*), where *stone* occupies an attributive position typical of adjectives, are sometimes regarded as partial conversions. The reason why *stone* is regarded as a partial conversion is that, although it occupies a typically adjectival position and has a typically adjectival modifying function, it fails to exhibit other properties of adjectives, for example comparative and superlative inflections, predicative positions and certain adverbial modifications. In Section 3.3, below, we shall classify expressions like *stone wall* as compounds and explain their adjective-like properties in terms of the modifier-head construction.

Nor shall we consider as conversions the cases of ellipsis which we discussed in Chapter 2 as instances of formal metonymy (e.g. *the poor, the sick*) although, as we already pointed out, some of these adjectives may have acquired a full (or almost full) nominal status (e.g. *black*), and thus should be counted as conversions. In general, the problem has to do with the graded and fuzzy nature of grammatical categories (cf. Hopper and Thompson 1985; Taylor 1995; Bauer 2005). It seems that a reasonable proposal regarding Adj>N conversions is that converted adjectives start as ordinary adjectives in ellipsed NP-s and are gradually transferred from the modifying position to the nominal head position in the structure of NP.

Rather informally, the process can be presented as in Figure 3.3, where each table represents an NP and the lowercase strings of letters in the lower boxes stand for actual phonetic realisations of the words of a given category.

Stage A

Det	Adj	N
ddd	*aaa*	*nnn*

Stage B (formal metonymy: DET-ADJ FOR THE WHOLE NP)

Det	Adj	N
ddd	*aaa*	⊙

Stage C (conversion via conceptual metonymy: PROPERTY FOR THING HAVING THIS PROPERTY)

Det	Adj	N
ddd	⊙	*aaa*

Figure 3.3 Adj>Noun conversion through formal metonymy.

It seems quite plausible that it is the process shown in Figure 3.3 that has led to the emergence of such de-adjectival nouns as *a daily, a weekly, a regular, a dyslexic, a crazy*. Another problem with conversions is that, given Schönefeld's rather broad definition of the process, it is not clear what is meant by 'word category'. As we already mentioned, the term 'grammatical category' itself is far from clear. In addition, each major category also has its subcategories, for example nouns can be countable or uncountable, verbs can be stative or dynamic, adjectives can be gradable or ungradable. I believe that both kinds of category changes should be considered as conversions. Furthermore, in what follows I will try to show that both the major category conversions and the minor category conversions are essentially metonymic;[5] however, the metonymies they employ are quite different.

3.2.1 Minor conversions

Minor conversions are ordinary conceptual metonymies based on a shift in construal. Although in general I agree with Kardela (1996) that at least some of the distinctions illustrated below have prototype representations and are a matter of degree, the examples provided here are rather uncontroversial (cf. Radden and Dirven 2007: ch 4 and 8 for more detailed discussion).

(a) ***Countable nouns >> uncountable nouns***, for example *chicken, duck* [construed as food]; *brick, stone* [construed as material] (cf. Bauer 1983; see Brdar 2007 for cross-linguistic corpus-based studies of 'animal grinding' and tree-wood names)

(b) ***Uncountable nouns >> countable nouns*** MATERIAL FOR OBJECT MADE OF THIS MATERIAL (e.g. *glass >> a glass*); MATERIAL FOR COLLECTION OF OBJECTS (e.g. *silver >> the silver* ['silverware']) (cf. Dancygier 1980).

(c) ***Proper nouns >> common nouns (eponyms)*** PRODUCER FOR PRODUCT (e.g. *[Henry] Ford >> a Ford [car made by the Ford company]*); PLACE FOR PRODUCT (e.g. *[Channel Island] Jersey >> knitted woollen fabric made there* [hence *a jersey*]; names of beverages (e.g. *cognac, burgundy, champagne*) (cf. §5.2.1.5 below)

(d) ***Common nouns >> proper nouns*** (e.g. *Bath, Oxford, Newcastle*, or Polish *Piasek* [sand], *Łódź* [boat], *Zielona Góra* [green mountain]. Cf. 'A note on proper names' in Chapter 1 on the role of this kind of metonymy in onomastics.

(e) ***Abstract nouns >> concrete nouns*** PROPERTY FOR BEARER OF PROPERTY (e.g. *beauty* for 'a beautiful person', *talent* for 'a talented person' as well as, for some obscure reason, 'sexually attractive people'). In Polish *inteligencja* has both meanings of English *intelligence* and *intelligentsia*.

(f) ***Non-gradable adjectives >> gradable adjectives***, for example *He's more French than his father. I was more dead than alive*).[6]

(g) ***Stative verbs >> dynamic verbs;*** in English any instance of a proto-typically stative verb used in progressive aspect, underscoring its boundedness (cf. Langacker 1987) such as *The defence are wanting to change the course of the interrogation now,* or (in a New Model Army lyric) *I'm wondering, I'm asking, I'm reaching, I'm finding, I'm wanting.*

(h) ***Dynamic verbs >> stative verbs***; arguably, in English any dynamic activity construed as an unchangeable routine (e.g. *Bill plays tennis every Tuesday*).

(i) ***Transitive verbs >> intransitive verbs*** (e.g. *eat, smoke, wash, paint, write*) As noted in Chapter 2, most cases can be regarded as cases of formal metonymy, whereby the omitted object is accessed metonymically.

(j) ***Intransitive verbs >> transitive verbs*** (e.g. *He's walking > He's walking his dog*).

A problem arises how these conversions differ from ordinary lexical polysemies. Probably, at least in some cases, the main difference is that minor conversions correspond to the change in the schematic profile of the designated entity, for example a normally bounded region such as CAT may be construed as unbounded; an imperfective process such as LOVE, which is unbounded within the immediate temporal scope, may be conceptualised as bounded, as in *I'm loving it* vis-à-vis *I love it*; an ungradable adjective like *French* may be conceptualised as gradable in *He's more French than his father*, which means that a region in a quality space is temporarily put on a scale. Apart from the shift in profile, the conceptual meaning of these expressions remains the same as in their primary sense.

In contrast, in prototypical polysemy, the change of the conceptual subcategory involves more than just a new profile: those senses usually require new domains and new profiles in the semantic representation because they have usually developed new, idiosyncratic meanings, for example *a paper* is much more than just a piece of paper, non-gradable *alive* does not entail gradable *alive*, the stative and dynamic senses of *hold* are quite different. Still, it seems that the difference between minor conversions and polysemy is a matter of degree. It is also likely that minor conversions simply mark the first step in some of the semantic extension processes leading to true polysemies. For instance, in the case of *paper* in English, the minor metonymically motivated conversion from unbounded THING to bounded THING has led gradually to the proliferation of countable senses of this new converted schematic sense (cf. Chapter 5).

3.2.2 Major conversions

In this section we shall focus on total conversions (i.e. cases when a word originally belonging to one category exhibits the full range of conceptual, inflectional and distributional properties of another category). First of all, I shall argue that conversion should not be regarded as a derivational process involving zero-derivation. Secondly, I will try to show that conversion is crucially based on metonymy. The reason conversion should not be regarded as a kind of derivational process has been laid out convincingly by Štekauer (1996), who has pointed out that the hypothetical zero-morpheme would have to cover the range of functions unprecedented anywhere else in grammar. Thus the same zero-morpheme would have to convert verbs to nouns, nouns to verbs, nouns to adjectives, adjectives to verbs, etc., or else "scores of homonymous zero morphemes" (*ibid.*: 40) would have to be postulated. Furthermore, as Cetnarowska (1993) has shown in her study of bare nominalisations in English, bare nominalisations (i.e. V>N conversions) differ from suffixal action nouns in that they exhibit different kinds of semantic properties. In particular, the derived "action nouns in English tend to occur more often in actional readings whereas bare nominalisations which compete with them tend to exhibit concrete readings" (Cetnarowska 1993: 139). In addition, they are much more independent of the predicate-argument structure of their 'source' verbs and develop their concrete readings "in a non-rule governed fashion, as non-derived nouns do" (*ibid.*:139).

This seems to be true of other kinds of conversion as well (cf. Dirven 1999), which means that we should agree with Štekauer that "The process of conversion should be regarded as a unique, specific, word-formation process, based upon principles different from those that characterise the process of derivation" (1996: 43). Dirven (1999) suggests that this 'unique, specific' process is metonymy based on event schemas. Since the purpose of this process is not reference but change of profile on the predicate-argument level (or, as Dirven calls it, 'nucleus' level), it should be distinguished from referential metonymy. Although both processes are metonymic, event-schema metonymy singles out a salient participant to become "the main designation for the event itself" (Dirven 1999: 279). This means that, in Dirven's view, event-schema metonymy is, generally speaking, restricted to PARTICIPANT FOR PROCESS metonymy and this is what Dirven presents in his study: object, instrument, manner, locative and essive verbs converted from various participants of event schemas. There is no reason, however, to limit the notion of event metonymy to this unidirectional mapping. A much broader understanding of event-schema metonymy is suggested by Schönefeld, who argues that "in event-schema metonymies, the re-categorised word stands for a different type of conceptual category and hence is a representative of a different word category" (2005: 153). Following Schönefeld's suggestion, I also define event-schema metonymies as metonymies in which various concepts belonging to some particular event schema are used to access other concepts belonging to the same event schema. An extensive list of such metonymies was proposed by Kövecses and Radden (1998: 54), which, slightly modified, is reproduced in Table 3.1.

We shall not go into the details of the differences between Dirven's and R&K's approaches. Suffice it to say that all R&K's metonymies are event-schema metonymies in the broader sense suggested above and hence they can represent a much wider range of conversions than the mappings proposed by Dirven. Notice, for instance, that the high-level metonymies formulated by R&K account not only for N – V conversions, but may be extended to other categories (e.g. RESULT FOR ACTION (f) accounts also for Adj>V conversions,

Table 3.1 List of event-schema metonymies.

(a)	INSTRUMENT FOR ACTION:	*to ski, to shampoo (one's hair)*
(b)	AGENT FOR ACTION:	*to butcher (the cow), to author (a book)*
(c)	ACTION FOR AGENT:	*snitch (slang: to inform and informer)*
(d)	OBJECT INVOLVED IN AN ACTION FOR THE ACTION:	*to blanket (the bed)*
(e)	ACTION FOR OBJECT INVOLVED IN THE ACTION:	*(give me one) bite*
(f)	RESULT FOR ACTION:	*to powder (the aspirin)*
(g)	ACTION FOR RESULT:	*(a deep) cut*
(h)	MEANS FOR ACTION:	*to sneeze (the tissue off the table)*
(i)	MANNER OF ACTION FOR THE ACTION	*to tiptoe (to bed)*
(j)	TIME PERIOD OF ACTION FOR THE ACTION:	*to summer (in Paris)*
(k)	DESTINATION FOR MOTION	*to porch (the newspaper)*
(l)	TIME OF MOTION FOR AN ENTITY INVOLVED IN THE MOTION	*(The) 8.40 (has just arrived)*

such as *empty, clean, dry, blind*, which Dirven's proposal leaves out). At the same time, some of R&K's suggestions may raise doubts. For instance, the example in (e) should probably be better, or at least partly, analysed in terms of the [give-sb-*a*-v] construction than event schema metonymy (cf. Croft and Cruse 2004) and the metonymy in (l) looks like a referential metonymy (TEMPORAL) PROPERTY OF AN ENTITY X FOR ENTITY X.

In whatever ways the list could be modified, what is striking about it is that most of the metonymies (9 out of 12) convert Participants into Actions. If this is juxtaposed with Hopper and Thompson's observation that "languages often possess rather elaborate morphology whose sole function is to convert verbal roots into N's, but no morphology whose sole function is to convert nominal roots into V's" (1984: 745), we may suggest that verbal N>V conversion is the counterpart of nominal derivation. If this is a plausible answer, the next question that immediately arises is: Whence this asymmetry? Why should derivation be better for nouns and conversion better for verbs? It seems that the answer in this respect lies in the conceptual content of the target categories. As Langacker (1991) has observed, and as we have seen in English *-ing* nominalisations and Polish transpositional nouns, the change from verb to noun does not change the conceptual content of the verb. We may even add that it often simplifies it by demoting the participants and focusing on the relation itself. For instance, in the sentence *Giving can be easier than taking* the verbs' e-sites have virtually disappeared and *giving* and *taking* function as autonomous units. In contrast, Langacker observes that the change from noun to verb "is generally accompanied by the addition of conceptual content" (1991: 25). The reason for this is rather straightforward: each verb implies an event schema, characterised in terms of its participants and setting, for example the noun *butter* designates an unbounded region defined in terms of colour, smell, taste, density, and function (and perhaps a few more qualia), whereas the verb *butter* evokes a whole scene, involving not only butter, with its qualia, but also the Agent (+ his/her active zone), Instrument (+ its active zone), Patient conflated with Location, and the change in the original shape of the butter resulting from the activity of spreading it on the Patient. And this is just the beginning (see Jackendoff 2002 for a complex but still considerably underspecified semantic representation of the verb *butter*). The same is true of the contrast between relatively simple adjectives and de-adjectival verbs. Given this conceptual complexity of verbs, it is quite likely that conversion, with its indeterminacy and unpredictability (see Szymanek 1998: ch. 3 for discussion), is the best way to activate the complex event structures through one profiled participant (e.g. in N>V conversions) which metonymically stands for the whole process. Moreover, the function of the derived noun must be clear because there is competition. The Agent (e.g. *employer*) should be kept apart from the Patient (e.g. *employee*) because those two have very different functions in that particular event, hence a more definite and specific semantics of nominalising affixes. In contrast, there is usually one kind of prototypical activity associated with a given participant, so it is enough to profile this single participant to access the process and other participants as well.

Finally, Szymanek (1998: ch. 3.3) argues that, in general, also in the case of Adj>Noun derivations, the predominant direction goes from adjectives to nouns, resulting in a large number of *nomina essendi*. Both Polish and English have developed such general and extremely productive de-adjectival suffixes; Polish *-ość*, such as *szary > szarość, młody > młodość;* English *-ness* (alongside much less productive *-ity* and *-ency/ancy*), whose function is the nominalisation of the adjective serving as its base (i.e. changing the profile from an atemporal RELATION to THING, but otherwise exhibiting no new semantic elements). Since it seems that there is no equally semantically schematic suffix changing nouns into verbs, the question arises what makes nominal derivation so special. Part of the answer probably lies in one of the most basic aspects of human cognition and thought, namely the need for reification which turns abstract entities like RELATIONS and PROCESSES into THINGS (cf. Langacker 1987), which can be thought about and talked about much more easily. The same tendency manifests itself in ontological metaphors, whereby abstract concepts acquire properties of things (cf. Szwedek 2002).

In summary, our observations suggest the following generalisation: derivational morphology is better suited for regular and conceptually simpler changes of construal such as reification, whereas more subtle, contextually flexible and less predictable and often more complex sense modifications are carried out on the conceptual level, by means of event-schema metonymy. The predominance of both de-verbal and de-adjectival nominalisations reflects the need for nominal concepts in human cognition.

A note on eponymy

Kosecki (2005: ch. 6) discusses a number of cases whereby the surnames of well-known people have been converted into verbs, according to the metonymic pattern: PERSON FOR BEHAVIOUR ASSOCIATED WITH THAT PERSON. Here are the relevant examples:

(1) They Khadaffi'd the USA Embassy.
(2) They Bin Laden'd Madrid.
(3) He's going to OJ his way out of the marriage. (discussed also by Gibbs 1999)
(4) He Raul'd the ball into the net.

Kosecki argues that the above examples involve the metonymies PERSON FOR ACTION "followed by the metonymies PROTOTYPICAL MEMBER OF CATEGORY FOR WHOLE CATEGORY" (2005: 120). However, it is not clear what kind of prototypicality he has in mind. It seems that the reason why proper names are used as the basis for those conversions is that these people performed certain activities in a unique way. So, it is true, as Kosecki argues, that the verbs illustrated in the examples above "are linked to the semantic role of manner" (2005: 120); however, it is not true that either the person or the manner in which they perform their activity is 'prototypical'. On the contrary, what makes that person and the activity they perform salient is the uniqueness of the person (comparable to that of paragons) as well as the uniqueness (albeit stereotyped) of the manner in which they perform this activity. Consequently, a more precise, if cumbersome, formulation of the metonymy in question should be: SALIENT PERSON FOR ACTIVITY ASSOCIATED WITH THAT PERSON PERFORMED IN A UNIQUE MANNER TYPICAL OF THAT PERSON.

3.2.3 A minor-major conversion borderline case

REIFIED ACTIVITY FOR OBJECTS INVOLVED IN THE ACTIVITY

The borderline case we shall discuss now owes its borderline status to the borderline status of the category of gerunds, or more generally *-ing* forms in English. Quirk et al. (1972: 133f) give fifteen examples in which the same *-ing* form of the verb *paint* is used, beginning with a purely nominal sense

(9), classified as 'de-verbal noun', through verbal nouns (8), gerunds (7), participles (6), to totally verbal (5). Since the basic meaning of *paint* is verbal, I have rearranged the examples showing the gradual progression from this purely verbal sense to the purely nominal. The examples I have chosen should be understood as cardinal points on a scale exhibiting various modifications in between:

(5) He is painting his daughter.
(6) Painting his daughter, Brown noticed that his hand was shaking. (i.e. while he was painting) [present participle]
(7) Brown's deftly painting his daughter is a delight to watch. [gerund]
(8) Brown's deft painting of his daughter is a delight to watch. (i.e. it is a delight to watch while Brown deftly paints his daughter) [verbal noun]
(9) Brown's paintings of his daughter (i.e. paintings owned by Brown, depicting his daughter but painted by someone else) [de-verbal noun]

Looking at the data in (5)–(9), two related questions immediately arise:

i.   What is the status of *-ing*? Should it be regarded as an inflectional ending or a suffix?
ii.   Where do *V-ing* forms cease to be verbs and begin to be nouns?

An answer to (i) might be as follows: in English the affix *-ing* is multifunctional, with one prototypically inflectional function (i.e. marking the participial form of verbs), and the other derivational function as a nominaliser (i.e. a suffix changing verbs into nouns). An answer to (ii) may be as follows: gerunds are still verbs, although they already exhibit a number of nominal properties (possessive determiner and nominal participant functions in the sentence structure); whereas verbal nouns are nouns although they still exhibit a number of verbal properties (e.g. some aspects of the verb's argument structure; cf. Langacker 2000: ch. 3 for an analysis of a phrase *the breaking of the glass by Floyd*). Assuming the tentative plausibility of the above answers, they have the following consequences for our analysis:

(a) Conceptual reification is not a sudden shift in profile, but may be a gradual process involving different degrees. In other words, nominalisations are not classical categories but, rather, should be viewed as categories with a prototype structure.
(b) If *-ing* nominalisations in English are not derived from verb roots, but are converted from the verbal gerundive *-ing* forms, sometimes the major category change may in fact be conceptually small, as in the case of conversion gerundive *V-ing* verb >> verbal *V-ing* noun. In cognitive terms, the metonymy is based on substantial conceptual overlap: PARTLY REIFIED PROCESS FOR PROCESSUAL THING (i.e. a more extensively reified PROCESS).

(c) Minor conversions based on verbal nouns, which preserve aspects of their base-verb's argument structure, will involve event-schema metonymies.

Point (c) is particularly important because it predicts that *-ing* nominals will develop some meanings based on the event structure associated with the base-verb. Although a definitive answer would require more extensive discussion, some of the initial data I have examined bear the prediction out. Here are some common examples:

> PROCESSUAL THING FOR INSTRUMENT: *bindings, wrapping, dressing* [in both its culinary and medical senses]
>
> PROCESSUAL THING FOR (AFFECTED OR EFFECTED) PATIENT: *washing, painting, writing*
>
> PROCESSUAL THING FOR RESULT: *swelling*
>
> PROCESSUAL THING FOR AN EPISODE: *thrashing, telling-off*
>
> PROCESSUAL THING FOR TIME: *beginning, ending.*

In Polish there is no gradation from purely verbal to nominal meanings. The three basic allomorphic nominalising suffixes *-anie, -enie, -cie* [7] have no inflectional functions and are unmistakably nominal, although they differ from other nominalising suffixes in that they are almost completely productive, they preserve reflexivity (e.g. *bić się>bicie się*, 'fight, fighting'), they preserve their base-verb's aspectual profile[8] and they preserve most of their base-verb argument structure (Grzegorczykowa and Puzynina 1984). Therefore they represent the clearest case of what is known in Polish linguistics as 'transposition': the change of syntactic category without any change in meaning. In cognitive terms, we might say that the three suffixes change the processual profile into a nominal profile comprising the whole relation. In Quirk et al.'s terminology (1972), they would be called 'verbal nouns'. Consider the translation into Polish of sentence (8) from the set we have discussed above:

(8ˇ)   Zręczne malowanie córki przez Browna jest radością dla oczu.
         ['deft painting of his daughter by Brown is a delight for eyes']

Consequently, unlike English V-*ing* forms, Polish transpositional action nouns do not represent any cases of major conversion. However, there is evidence that, like English converted *-ing* nouns, they might undergo minor conversions, also based on event-schema metonymy. The most important property of Polish *nomina actionis* is that they are abstract nouns denoting reified processes. Now with this general characterisation, what often happens is that they develop new senses and metonymically stand for different participants of the process designated by their base-verb. Thus, like the major conversions in English we have discussed above, they may be considered as event-schema metonymies. Consider the following mappings:

-   PROCESSUAL THING FOR AGENT (or EFFECTOR) (a more specific variant of: RESULT FOR CAUSE), for example *zmartwienie* (worrying >> worry), *utrapienie* (worrying >> nuisance, pain in the neck), *rozczarowanie* (disappointing >> disappointment)
-   PROCESSUAL THING FOR INSTRUMENT, for example *wiązanie* ((ski-)binding), *oparcie* (leaning >> back (of a chair)), *wsparcie* (supporting >> support), *zaproszenie* (inviting >> invitation), *wezwanie* (summoning >> summons)
-   PROCESSUAL THING FOR (AFFECTED OR EFFECTED) PATIENT, for example *pranie* (washing >> laundry), *ubranie* (clothing, dressing >> clothes), *jedzenie* (eating >> food), *picie* (drinking >> drink (*Gdzie jest nasze picie?* [Where is our drinking?]), *nagranie* (recording), *nacięcie* (cutting >> cut), *spuchnięcie* (swelling), *złamanie* (breaking >> fracture), *zranienie* (wounding >> wound), *zadrapanie* (scratching >> scratch), *zabrudzenie* (soiling >> smudge of dirt), *draśnięcie* (grazing >> graze), *wyobrażenie* (imagining >> idea, notion), *marzenie* (dreaming >> dream), *odzienie* (clothing >> clothes)
-   PROCESSUAL THING FOR LOCATION, for example *spanie* (sleeping >> place for sleeping), *więzienie* (keeping (sb) prisoner >> prison), *wgłębienie* (deepening >> hollow)
-   PROCESSUAL THING FOR TIME, for example *rozpoczęcie* (beginning), *zakończenie* (ending).

3.3 Compounds

Probably nowhere is the metonymic flexibility of language more conspicuous than in English compounds. Lyons (1977: 538) discusses the expression *London train* in sentences (10) and (11) and observes that in (10) it denotes 'a train going to London' while in (11) it denotes 'a train coming from London':

(10)   Has the London train left yet?
(11)   Has the London train arrived yet?

In contrast, Lyons pointed out that while *the London taxi* usually refers to taxis operating in London, *the London bus* can have both the meanings 'a bus going to London' and 'a bus coming from London', but, in addition, it may also denote 'a bus which operates in London'. In conclusion, Lyons observes that "It is inconceivable that the syntactic and semantic sub-classification of either *London* or *train*, *bus* and *taxi* in the language system could be such that these differences could be accounted for by rule" (1977: 538). Lyons is absolutely right: the emergent meanings of English compounds are non-compositional and unpredictable, but they are motivated metonymically by the conceptual structures denoted by their components and the blending operations connecting these structures. Of course context usually has a priming effect on the potential ambiguities; it restricts them but never really eliminates them. Using the basic classification and terminology proposed by Bloomfield (1933), Bauer (1983) and those who follow him (e.g. Szymanek 1998), I argue that, according to semantic criteria, compound nouns can be divided into four groups:

(a) **endocentric** compounds, for example *beehive, armchair*, which are hyponyms of the grammatical head – a beehive is a kind of hive, an armchair is a kind of chair;[9]

(b) **exocentric** compounds (also called 'bahuvrihi compounds'), for example *redskin* and *highbrow*, where the compound is not a hyponym of the grammatical head (i.e. a *redskin* is not a kind of skin, a *highbrow* is not a kind of brow). Bauer comments that "this type of compound is a hyponym of some unexpressed semantic head ('person' in the examples given here). Since the semantic head is unexpressed in such compounds, the compound is frequently seen as metaphorical or synecdochic" (1983: 30). Relatively new examples are *skinhead* and *hatchback*. Importantly, Bauer mentions such nouns as *pickpocket, scarecrow, spoilsport, wagtail,* and *telltale* and also refers to them as exocentric compounds (*ibid.*: 31).

(c) **appositional** compounds, for example *maidservant*, which are hyponymic for both their components (i.e. *maidservant* is a kind of maid and a kind of servant).

(d) **dvandva (copulative)** compounds, such as *Alsace-Lorraine* or *Bosnia-Hercegovina*, where "it is not clear which element is the grammatical head and the compound is not a hyponym of either element, but the elements name separate entities which combine to form the entity denoted by the compound" (Bauer 1983: 31).[10]

Categories c) and d) are briefly discussed by Kosecki (2007b). In what follows we shall focus on the first two categories, a) and b), firstly, because they are by far more common and secondly because they are more relevant to the subject matter of this study (i.e. they would be inconceivable without metonymy).

3.3.1 Endocentric compounds

For reasons which will become clear shortly, we shall start our discussion of endocentric compounds by considering nonce formations. Bauer defines a nonce formation as "a new complex word coined by a speaker/writer on the spur of the moment to cover some immediate need" and notes that "[it] is not sufficiently appreciated ... how large a proportion of complex forms that are heard every day are nonce formations" (1983: 45). As an example he quotes a sentence uttered by a commentator on the lying-in-state of George VI: *the twilight of his death has dimmed the whole world-sky*, where the compound *world-sky* is a nonce formation – one of many senses of *world* is blended with one of few senses of *sky*. The nonce compound formations are important for three reasons. First, they are 'adult' versions of the same basic mechanism that children use at the two-word stage in their first language acquisition (discussed in Chapter 6). Second, and more importantly for our present purposes, nonce compound formations use the same cognitive strategy as lexical compounds, which are nothing but nonce compound formations that have become conventionalised and cognitively entrenched. The strategy is basically the strategy of blending, but what is blended both in nonce and conventionalised units is usually particular senses of the component lexemes. There are three processes that may govern the emergence of the meaning of compounds: active zones, perspectivisation and metonymy. In compounds the formal part of each component word (i.e. the phonological representation) stands for some more or less easily identifiable part or domain of its conceptual representation. Thus in the nonce formation cited above, the form [wɜːld] appears to perspectivise the sense 'human affairs', while the form [skai], although it is used metaphorically, perspectivises the sense 'where we see the sun, the stars and the moon', much in the same way as in a compound *teacup*, the form [tiː] activates the 'liquid made from tea leaves' sense of *tea*, while the form [kʌp] activates the 'porcelain container' sense of *cup*. Third, nonce formations in English are almost invariably right-headed (cf. Bauer 2009 for cross-linguistic tendencies in the head-modifier linear ordering). Since the same regularity is evident in compounds as well, these formations are indicative of a single extremely powerful conceptual process enabling a staggering diversity of conceptual structures to acquire a simple two (or more)-word form. I take the view that the process which makes this possible is metonymy coerced by the semantics of the English [XY] constructional schema with X functioning as a modifier denoting PROPERTY and Y functioning as a categorially unspecified head, determining the profile of the combination. Thus the proposed theory, while based on blending operations, overcomes the major objection to the theory of compounds based on purely conceptual blending, as it was propounded by Fauconnier, Turner and Sweetser, and used extensively by Benczes (2006), namely that "The language user (…) does not always construe compounds as blends or mappings of two different conceptual frames: in a large majority of English compounds, XY are instead asymmetric constructions in which one element (Y) evokes the schematic frame and the other element (X) serves to specify it in greater detail: that is, the 'mental spaces' which blending theory posits for compounding do not have the same weight and do not assume the same function" (Heyvaert 2009: 251f).

It is worth recalling at this juncture that several linguists distinguish a third category of endocentric two-word combinations, namely 'syntactic phrases', which consist of fully compositional phrases like *high chair* ('a chair which is high') as opposed to a much less compositional and more tightly integrated compound *'highchair* ('a chair with long legs for a child to sit in while he/she is eating'). Whether the distinction is warranted and whether the criteria (e.g. stress shift) adduced by the proponents of the strict division are indeed reliable is not our concern here (cf. Bauer 1983: ch. 5.2; Plag 2003: ch. 6, and particularly Balteiro 2007: ch. 3 for discussion).[11] What is important for us is that nonce formations, syntactic phrases and compounds use the same constructional schema, namely [XY] with position Y taken by the head of the construction and X functioning as a modifier.

Before we look at how the theory of coerced metonymy works, consider these examples (based on Quirk et al. 1972):

A. Noun compounds
    (a) subject and verb compounds: *bee sting, earthquake, landslide, playboy, crybaby*
    (b) verb and object compounds: *book review, haircut, birth control, handshake*
    (c) verb and adverbial compounds: *diving board, frying pan, rope-dancer, handwriting*
    (d) verbless compounds (most of them N+N): *windmill, oak tree, sandwich man*

B. Adjective compounds
    (a) verb and object compounds: *breathtaking, heartbreaking, life-giving*
    (b) verb and adverbial compounds: *heartfelt, thunder-struck, good-looking, far-fetched, widespread*

C. Verb compounds
    brainwash, fire-watch, lip-read, chain-smoke, sleepwalk, babysit.

The first most obvious observation we can make is that most compounds are noun and adjective compounds. Moreover, even the verb compounds are in fact 'nominal-based' since, as it is claimed in Quirk et al. (1972), they are usually derived from *-ing* nominalisation (e.g. *babysit* is back-formed from *babysitting*). This observation is crucial for my argument that both NP-s and AdjP-s in English are prototypically right-headed, which means that there is a well-established constructional schema determining the semantic interpretation of XY sequences in such a way that the first component denotes a property of the second component, which denotes an entity. Since noun compounds far outnumber other categories, it may be safely assumed that the entity is prototypically a THING, but it may also be an ATEMPORAL or TEMPORAL RELATION (i.e. an adjective or a verb, respectively, so I will use the term ENTITY for THINGS and RELATIONS). Thus the construction schema, which I shall refer to as Compound Schema, can be represented diagrammatically as in Figure 3.4.

Syn	X $_{\text{Modifier}}$	Y$_{\text{Head}}$
Sem	PROPERTY	ENTITY

Figure 3.4 The Compound Schema in English.

The essence of my theory of endocentric compounds in English is that compounds in English involve blending the Compound Schema with the blended mental space resulting from the conceptual integration of the mental spaces evoked by the head and the modifier of the compound. As a result, the conceptual properties of the head (i.e. the fact that it is the most salient element of the two spaces) determine the grammatical category of the compound, while the identifying element of the mental space evoked by the modifier is metonymically conceptualised as a PROPERTY and connected with the modifier box of the Schema. For instance, for a compound like *bee sting,* the integration will look as shown in Figure 3.5.

In Figure 3.5 the double-line box indicates the blend whose structural and semantic properties are inherited from the Compound Schema but

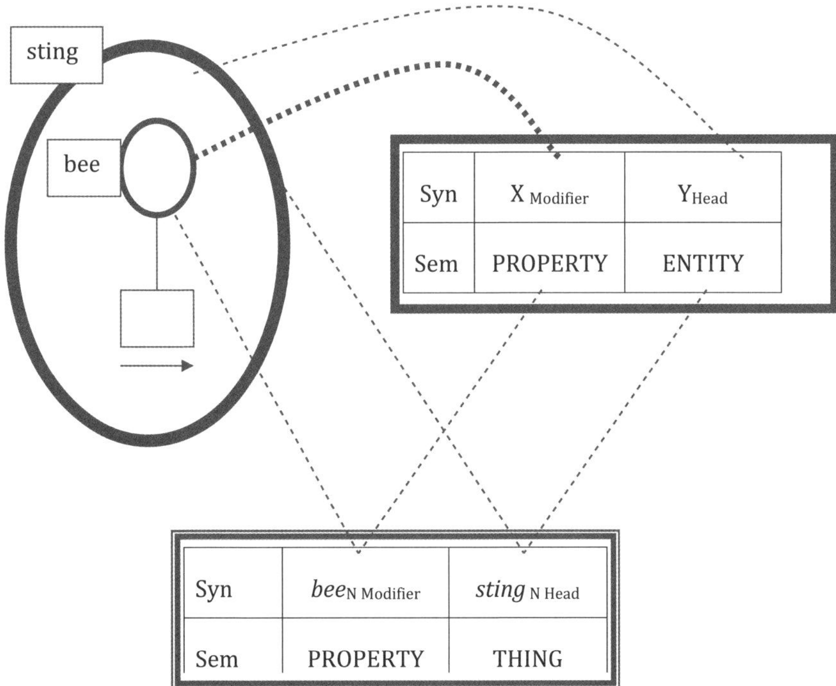

Figure 3.5 The blending of the Compound Schema and the mental space evoked by the processual head noun *sting* in the compound *bee sting.*

are elaborated by the STING Input Space. It follows from the diagram that the high-level metonymy THING FOR PROPERTY, indicated by the bold dotted connector, has been coerced by the semantic part of the Compound Schema. The metonymy is coerced insomuch as the entities belonging to different conceptual categories (THING in the *bee sting* example) are conceptually 'made' to stand for the identifying PROPERTY of the head ENTITY. Notice also that the emergent blend is specified with respect to the grammatical categories of its components, which follow naturally from their conceptual characteristics. Since in the analysed example both components denote bounded regions, they are both categorised as nouns. The blend represents a double scope network in the sense used by Fauconnier and Turner (2002): it is through the THING-FOR-PROPERTY metonymy that the conflict between the two categories is resolved. It must be remembered, however, that the STING space (on the left) itself represents a blend of two autonomous spaces, namely STING space and BEE space. A more complete representation of the whole integration process is shown for the compounds *jar lid* and *lid jar* (Figure 3.8 and 3.9), although the expressions *jar lid* and *lid jar* may sanction other conceptualisations as well.

The theory of coerced metonymy explains why sometimes researchers have doubts about the grammatical status of the modifier constituents (cf. Jackendoff 2009). In particular, since different grammatical classes all occupy the attributive position in the NP, prototypically occupied by adjectives, and since they all have a modifying function, also prototypically realised by adjectives, some linguists considered the first components in compounds as conversions into adjectives. The conversions were regarded as partial because those would-be adjectives did not exhibit other adjectival properties (see above), but they were felt to be conversions nonetheless (cf. Schönefeld 2005 for discussion). On our account, no conversion needs to be postulated since the categories retain their grammatical status and acquire the modifying function from the constructional schema. Moreover, they differ from the metonymies involved in conversions in that their target is always PROPERTY, regardless of their grammatical category. Thus, looking again at the examples given above, the following metonymic mappings can be distinguished:

A.   ***Noun compounds*** – the ENTITY in the Compound Schema is a THING[12]
   (a)   subject and verb compounds:
        bee sting, earthquake, landslide: AGENT/PATIENT FOR PROPERTY
        playboy, crybaby: ACTIVITY FOR PROPERTY
   (b)   verb and object compounds:
        book review, haircut, birth control, handshake: PATIENT FOR PROPERTY
   (c)   verb and adverbial compounds:
        diving board, frying pan: REIFIED ACTIVITY FOR PROPERTY
        rope-dancer: MANNER FOR PROPERTY
        handwriting: INSTRUMENT FOR PROPERTY

    (d) verbless compounds (most of them N+N):
        windmill: EFFECTOR FOR PROPERTY
        oak tree: SUBCATEGORY FOR PROPERTY
        sandwich man: POSSESSION FOR PROPERTY

B.   ***Adjective compounds*** – the ENTITY of the Compound Schema is an ATEMPORAL RELATION, that is the compounds designate a PROPERTY modified by another PROPERTY
    (a) verb and object compounds:
        breathtaking, heartbreaking, life-giving: PATIENT (LANDMARK) FOR PROPERTY
    (b) verb and adverbial compounds:
        heartfelt: LOCATION FOR PROPERTY
        thunder-struck: AGENT (FORCE) FOR PROPERTY
        far-fetched, widespread: MEASURE FOR PROPERTY

C.   ***Verb compounds***: the ENTITY of the Compound Schema is a TEMPORAL RELATION:
    brainwash, fire-watch, lip-read, babysit: PATIENT FOR PROPERTY
    chain-smoke: MANNER FOR PROPERTY
    sleepwalk: STATE FOR PROPERTY

Note that the present proposal differs considerably from an account of compounds suggested by Langacker (2000: ch. 1). In particular, Langacker claims that Figure 3.6 "characterizes an open-ended set of … noun-noun compounds" (*ibid.:* 19). In the case of the N-N compound *jar lid* the schema has the concrete realisation shown in Figure 3.7.

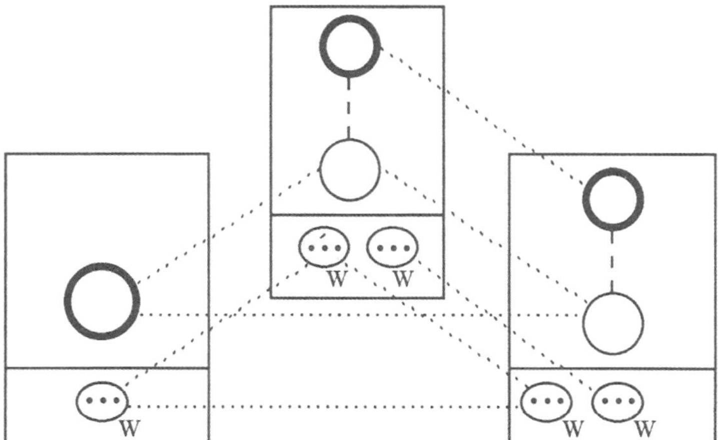

Figure 3.6 Compounding constructional schema according to Langacker (scanned from Langacker 2000: 19).

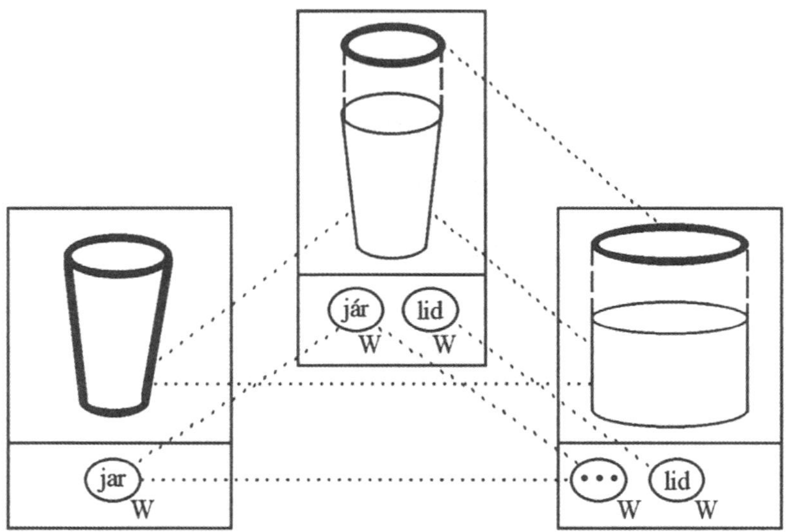

Figure 3.7 Integration of *jar lid* according to Langacker (2000:17).

Clearly, Langacker suggests that the constructional properties of N-N compounds (lower boxes) constitute integral parts of the representation of the components of the compound.[13] This implies, however, that there is a grammatical difference between nouns like *jar* and *lid* in terms of their constructional possibilities. In Langacker's terms, the word *lid* has an elaboration site (e-site), which in the compound in question is elaborated by *jar*, while *jar* does not exhibit this property. This is intuitively correct, but it does not explain why the compound in which the order of precisely the same components is reversed (i.e. *lid jar*) is a well-built and meaningful expression, although of course its meaning is quite different because of the reversed modifier-head relation. In our account, the Compound Schema is independent of actual expressions and makes no presuppositions about the combinatorial properties of its components. On the contrary, the order of components of a compound is determined solely by the background/foreground alignment of the composite structure, with the profile determinant taking the head position and specifying the category of the whole expression.

Accordingly, a more-or-less full analysis of *jar lid* in terms of the present theory based on the Compound Schema and coerced metonymy can be represented as in Figure 3.8.

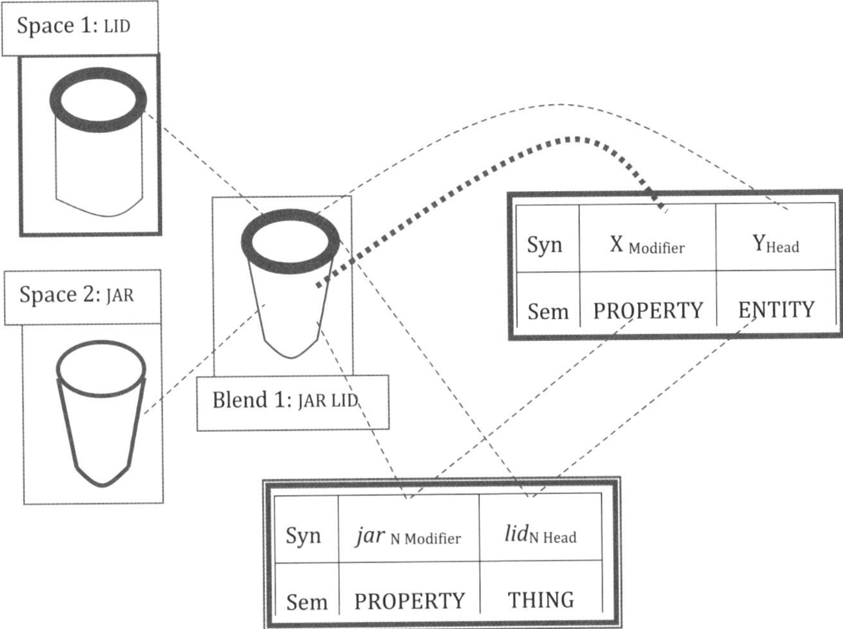

Figure 3.8 Integration of the compound *jar lid.*

As in the previous example, the bold dotted connector indicates a coerced high-level metonymy whereby a THING (JAR) stands for a PROPERTY of the ENTITY (LID) which determines the profile of the whole composite structure, which in this case is elaborated as a THING, and hence the whole compound is categorised as a noun. As seen in Figure 3.9 the compound *lid jar* has the same input spaces but they differ in relative salience: this time the profile determinant is JAR, which, therefore, elaborates the Head position of the Compound Schema, while LID – via coerced metonymy THING FOR PROPERTY – functions as a Modifier and PROPERTY of JAR.

As we have already mentioned, another advantage of the proposal made here is that its structure is linked, as a part, with other Modifier-Head sequences in English, which adds to its explanatory power. It also explains why the Modifier position of the compound may be filled by words belonging to almost any grammatical category or even multiple-word expressions as in phrasal compounds like *floor of a birdcage taste* or *pipe and slipper husband* (cf. Scalise and Bisetto 2009). At the same time, there is nothing in the present proposal that would rule out the possibility of the modifier being based on metaphor, as in *heartland*, discussed by Benczes (2006: 91f). It is important, however, that such cases must be viewed as instances of metaphor in metonymy. Thus, in the case of *heartland*, meaning 'the central part of a

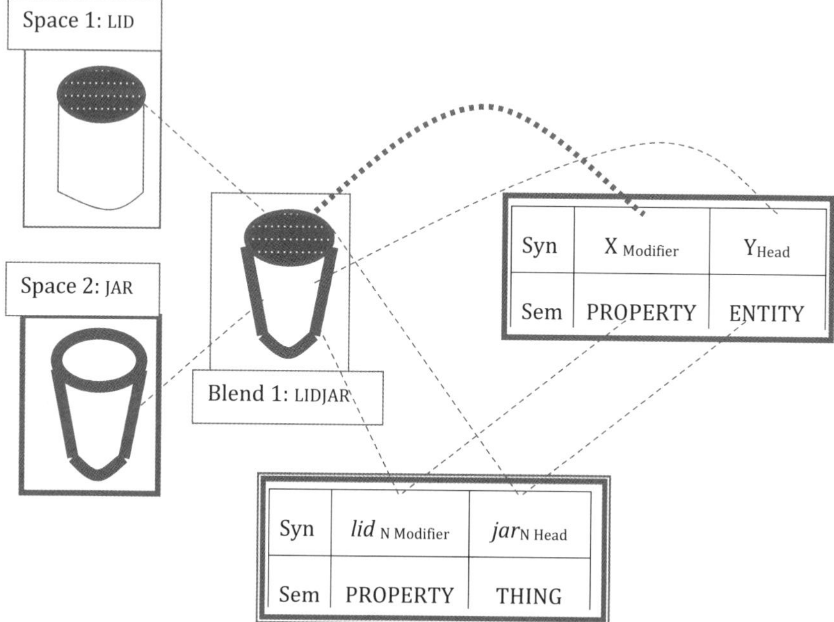

Figure 3.9 Integration of the compound *lid jar.*

country or area of land,' the modifier CENTRAL LOCATION is designated metaphorically as *heart* through conceptual metaphor LOCATION IS BODY, and then conceptualised as PROPERTY through metonymy CENTRAL LOCATION FOR PROPERTY. It
also follows from the proposed theory that all modifiers in N-N compounds
(and in fact all non-Adjective-N compounds) are designated metonymically;
therefore, there are no N-N compounds which have only 'metonymy-based
profile determinant' in the sense intended by Benczes (2006: 153ff). Benczes
argues that in compounds like *handwriting* and *gaslight* it is only the head
of the compound that is metonymic. However, it seems that she confuses
the entrenched contribution of the modifier to the meaning of the compound
with clearly metonymic motivation for this contribution. For instance, since
writing presupposes not only active body part and instrument but also material
on which it is performed, in appropriate contexts, *handwriting* could easily
mean 'writing with one's hand only used as an instrument, such as in sand or
snow' (on analogy with attested *pen-writing*) or 'writing on hand' (on analogy
with, again, attested *wall painting*). In fact those very different conceptualising possibilities sometimes surface as systematic ambiguities, as in *eardrop*,
which means either 'liquid medicine you put in your ear' or 'an earring with
a pendant', not to mention 'a daily uncensored morsel of comedy for our

Earwolves to enjoy for five minutes or so a day' which you can find on www. earwolf.com.

Words as property
We finish our discussion of endocentric compounds in English by considering a rather extreme form of compounding known as 'hyphen construction' (cf. Królak 2005). We shall see that given the general account of endocentric compounds in English proposed in the previous section, the analysis of hyphen constructions poses no special problems, despite the rather idiosyncratic formal characteristics of the construction. Królak illustrates the hyphen construction with the following expressions:

(12)   Hi-honey-I'm-home happiness.
(13)   What 'peace movement', or do you mean the don't-get-drafted movement?
(14)   You'll-be-sorry-for-this quality of resentment.

As the term suggests, the construction consists of a group of hyphenated words functioning as a pre-modifier – *hi-honey-I'm home, don't-get-drafted* and *you'll-be-sorry-for-this*. Interestingly, Królak points out that "hyphenated strings of words precede a noun and thereby occupy the position normally held in a sentence by an adjective" (2005: 197), and adds that "a hyphenated modifier fulfils the same function as an adjective, namely that of elaborating a noun" (*ibid.*: 197). Królak's observations clearly suggest that in terms of the theory of compounds presented above, the hyphenated group in the hyphen construction should, via coerced metonymy, stand for the PROPERTY of the head THING. This seems intuitively correct. What is less clear is the precise nature of the vehicle of that metonymy. I believe the solution lies in Królak's analysis, although she never explicitly expresses it. For the essence of Królak's analysis is that "the elaboration of the noun by a complex 'hyphenated modifier' serves to evoke, and metonymically stands for, an appropriate scenario" (*ibid.*: 197). Crucially, she argues that "the phrases joined with hyphens resemble citations incorporated in a text. Although they lack quotation marks, these expressions are used to convey some statement expressed by an imaginary speaker" *(ibid.*: 198). Of course the metonymy Królak refers to is quite different from the metonymy that enables the quotes to appear in the ordinary modifying position in compounds, but it does indicate what the vehicle of that metonymy is. For the hyphenated groups evoke scenarios involving turns of speech characterised by more-or-less conventional, often hackneyed expressions symptomatic of the speaker's emotion, attitude or personality. If these expressions are indeed symptomatic, it comes as no surprise that they may in fact be used for emotional, attitudinal and personality traits. In short, the metonymy coerced by the Compound Schema in hyphen-constructions is

WORDS PEOPLE SAY FOR PROPERTY. All in all, in the integration of the hyphenated compounds the hyphenated groups serve a double purpose: first, as speech acts, they metonymically evoke a particular speech act space (i.e. scenario) they are part of, and then they serve as vehicles for WORDS PEOPLE SAY FOR PROPERTY metonymy, which enables them to function as modifiers in ordinary right-headed compounds.

The final comment that needs to be made about the theory of English compounds proposed here is that despite the productivity and great grammatical freedom with which English compounds are formed, there is one crucial conceptual constraint on the components that function as modifiers (i.e. the parts of the compounds metonymically conceptualised as PROPERTY of the head ENTITY): they must designate a conceptual content that can felicitously restrict the reference of the head. As we have seen, the PROPERTY may be accessed by almost any entity – a THING, an ATEMPORAL, or TEMPORAL PROCESS, or even a string of hyphenated words; they are all acceptable as long as they are not conceptually redundant. Therefore, unless the world changes in such a way that new distinctions have to be made, compounds like *thing-table, animal rabbit, dead corpse, breathing dog, foot shoes* or *I'm-hungry sort of person* will probably not emerge.

3.3.2 Exocentric compounds reconsidered

In what follows I will focus on the category of exocentric compounds, since in the light of what we know about metonymy, it seems that this subcategory of compounds should be reconsidered and seriously revised. Let us recall that, as opposed to endocentric compounds, exocentric compounds are in fact defined negatively: the exocentric compound is not a hyponym of the grammatical head (i.e. a *redskin* is not a kind of skin, a *highbrow* is not a kind of brow). Bauer comments that "this type of compound is a hyponym of some unexpressed semantic head ('person' in the examples given here). Since the semantic head is unexpressed in such compounds, the compound is frequently seen as metaphorical or synecdochic" (1983: 30). However, as already mentioned, later in the same work (1983: 60) Bauer refers to nouns such as *pickpocket, scarecrow, spoilsport, wagtail,* and *telltale* as 'exocentric compounds' as well. The question is: if metaphor and metonymy are indeed at work in compounds like *redskin*, do they operate in the same way in compounds like *pickpocket*?

First of all, it should be emphasised that Bauer's view (that exocentric compounds are radically different from endocentric compounds) is not the only view. For instance, Hockett considers compounds such as *redcap* ('porter') as 'boundary-line cases' and concludes that "it seems preferable to class the construction of *redcap* as endocentric" (1958: 185). However, Hockett arrives at this conclusion on the grounds of a rather limited set of distributional data (e.g. the fact that *cap* and *redcap* can both occur in the same contexts in sentences such as *I saw the cap – I saw the redcap, The cap sat on the table – The redcap sat on the table*. These data suggest, according to Hockett, that after all, at least grammatically, a redcap is a kind of cap (although he admits that it isn't!). The argument is mistaken for, if Hockett added a few more examples, the clearly referential differences would soon turn up and exhibit distributional contrasts. The examples below show it quite clearly:

(15)   This cap needs ironing.
(16)   ?? This redcap needs ironing.
(17)   Suddenly the redcap screamed, got into my car and drove away.
(18)   ?? Suddenly the cap screamed, got into my car and drove away.

Plag (2003) comes to the same conclusion as Hockett but on categorial grounds. The logic of the argument is this: since it is the right-hand member of a compound which determines the grammatical category of endocentric compounds, and since in bahuvrihi compounds it is the right-hand member which determines the category (e.g. *redcap* is a noun and so is *cap*, *pickpocket* is a noun and so is *pocket*, ergo bahuvrihi compounds are endocentric). What Plag apparently overlooked is that the denotation of the compound is very different from its head (e.g. *cap* denotes a category of articles of clothing, while *redcap* denotes a group of people and, similarly, *pocket* denotes a part of an article of clothing, while *pickpocket* denotes a group of people.

Thus the reason why *redcap* should be classified as endocentric is not that it shares the distribution or grammatical category of its head. The reason why I also believe that *redcap* should be classified as an endocentric compound is that the head of the compound is not really absent but it is accessed as the target through PART-FOR-WHOLE metonymy, i.e. the porter is accessed through its perceptual part: a red cap.[14] In addition, the compound has the same ADJ-N structure as many other endocentric compounds. A number of other compounds, e.g. *loudmouth, paleface, skinhead*, can be analysed along the same lines (cf. Kosecki 2007b, who, however, treats them as exocentric compounds). In other words, I propose that these expressions should be classified as ordinary endocentric compounds whose conceptual head is accessed through the lexical head of the compound via metonymy. This is the reason why Geeraerts (2003) calls them 'metonymical compounds'. In true exocentric compounds, the head is indeed absent and is also accessed metonymically but not through one of its parts, but through its predicate part, designated by the verb and its object, where the object NP does not denote a part or property of the target but another entity with which the targeted Agent interacts, e.g. in *pickpocket* the pocket of course does not belong to the petty thief but to some other individual, so it is not a part of the individual denoted by the compound. Similarly, a killjoy spoils other people's fun, not his own, and so on. Thus the strategies employed in the formation of the two kinds of compounds are very different. The difference can be represented as follows:

(19) For *redskin, redcap, highbrow,* etc:
      If a distinctive (salient) part of X is [Property+Part], use an expression Y designating [Property+Part] to denote X
(20) For *pickpocket, killjoy, scarecrow,* etc:
      If X characteristically does [Activity+Patient], use the expression V(-NP) designating [Activity+Patient] to denote X

Notice that the procedure characterised in (20) indicates that the same metonymic mechanism is involved in conversions of verbs into personal nouns (e.g. *cheat, creep, cook, tear-away, layabout*), the only difference being that the latter are construed intransitively.

Let us now consider a few more examples, most of which are also traditionally considered as exocentric compounds, which do not represent either metonymic or V+N exocentric compounds. The examples are: *rolling stone, big gun, lone wolf, road-hog, windbag, battleaxe, cold fish, rare bird, couch potato, dead meat, dead/lame duck, dark horse, rotten apple, old flame.* Since the target categories of those expressions are all human and the sources, functioning as heads, are drawn from distinctly other domains, such as animals, or inanimate (natural or man-made) physical objects, the conclusion is that they can also be considered as endocentric compounds, but, unlike metonymic compounds, they access their head through metaphor. Thus the proper term for this kind of compound is metaphoric endocentric compounds.

Finally, it should be mentioned that, in fact, most figurative compounds involve chains of extensions and those chains often involve both metaphor and metonymy. For instance, Geeraerts (2003: 456f) discusses the case of the compound *hanglip* and argues that it involves two metonymic extensions: the first from *hanglip* (i.e. 'hanging lip') to 'a person with a hanging or protruding (lower) lip', and second, extends it to mean 'an unhappy, sulking, pouting person' via (BEHAVIOURAL) EFFECT FOR CAUSE metonymy. The consecutive sequence involving first metaphor and then metonymy can be illustrated by the Dutch compound *shapenkop*, meaning literally 'sheep's head' and figuratively 'a stupid person'. The two steps are: a metaphor mapping a (stupid) sheep's head onto a human head and a PART-FOR-WHOLE metonymy whereby a stupid human head stands for 'a stupid person'.

Summing up, the above considerations show that the category of compounds that Bauer dubbed 'exocentric' in fact consists of two very different groups.

1. The first group is essentially endocentric but the grammatical head of the compound is related to its conceptual head through metaphor or metonymy. For instance, in *redskin* (as in *paleface*), *skinhead* (and in

egghead), *hunchback, loudmouth,* skin, face, head, back, and mouth are used as salient parts metonymically standing for the whole person. In other words, the concept of PERSON is accessed through a part (see Figure 3.10).

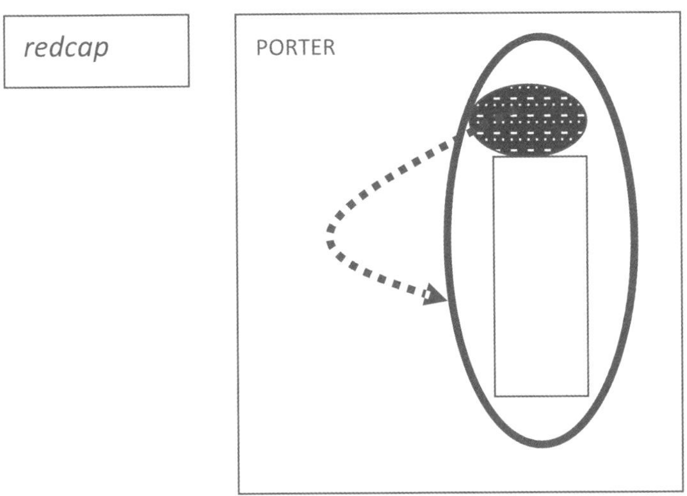

Figure 3.10 Representation of the activation of the conceptual head of the metonymic endocentric compound ***redcap***.

In metaphoric endocentric compounds the conceptually complex target is accessed through a lexically and conceptually complex expression belonging to a different cognitive domain, such as *road hog, rolling stone, big gun, lone wolf, windbag, battleaxe, cold fish, rare bird, couch potato, dead meat, dead/ lame duck, dark horse, rotten apple, old flame* (see Figure 3.11).

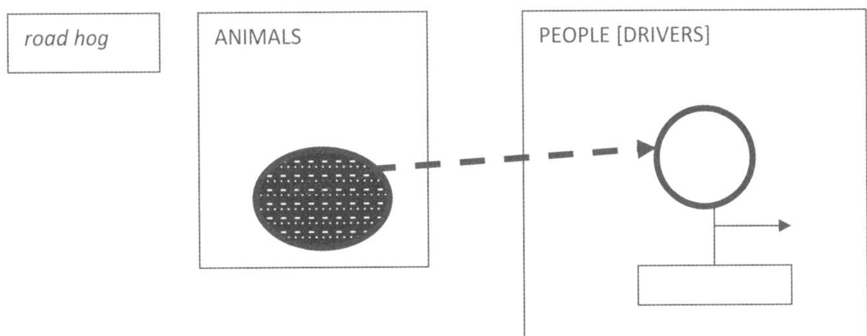

Figure 3.11 Representation of the activation of the conceptual head of the metaphoric endocentric compound ***road hog***.

All these examples can be straightforwardly accounted for in terms of Geeraerts' prismatic model, which represents not only the relationship between the literal compositional meaning of compounds and their conventional meaning but also shows the contribution of the components of compounds to the meaning of the compound as a whole.

2. The second group consists of truly exocentric compounds, such as *pickpocket, killjoy, scarecrow*, based on various syntactic and semantic relations between the compound and its conceptual target. To the extent that the access is determined by the syntactic structure of which the compound is a part, the relationship may be viewed as motivated by a formal PART-FOR-PART metonymy, whereby the predicate V-NP part of a sentential construction stands for the subject NP part of this construction, shown schematically in Figure 3.12.

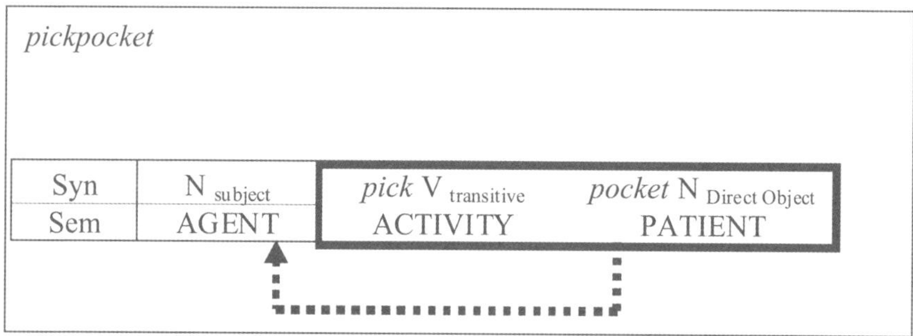

Figure 3.12 Representation of the activation of the target of the exocentric compound **pickpocket** based on formal metonymy.

The formal metonymy suggested above does not preclude conceptual metonymy, which may provide additional motivation for the exocentric compounds. The conceptual metonymy at work here is ACTIVITY FOR AGENT OF THIS ACTIVITY, which, as we have seen, motivates V>N conversions such as *flirt, cheat, success*. However, if we tried to account for exocentric compounds in terms of conversion alone, the resultant nominal compound would either have to be interpreted wrongly as other regular right-headed N-N endocentric compounds, or else we would expect some formal indication of the relation between the converted verb and its putative modifier (e.g. ungrammatical formations like **pick of pockets* or **pocket pick*). Therefore, the metonymy ACTIVITY FOR AGENT can only be seen as a conceptual reinforcement of the formal metonymy based on the clausal structure.

The uniqueness of the truly exocentric compounds in English illustrated above was recognised by Tuggy (1987), who called them '*scarecrow* nouns'.

Apart from *scarecrow*, the category consists of nouns such as *breakfast, skinflint, breakwater, catch-fly, cure-all, dreadnought, killjoy, pickpocket, spitfire, spendthrift*. Tuggy concludes that the compounds belonging to the *scarecrow* category, which, as usual, has more and less prototypical members, can be characterised in terms of the following properties:

1. They are exocentric (bahuvrihi): neither component stem is the head of the construction in the typical sense. Rather a verb and its object combine to designate the subject.
2. Besides the general V+O=S pattern, there are a few productive subpatterns, e.g. V +all=S (e.g. *cure-all, saws-all, carry-all, clean-all, copy-all, dust-all, farm-all, hide-all, lift-all, store-all,* etc.).
3. The construction is irregular; *saw-bones* (plural O), *saws-all* (3sg. verb).
4. Lexical dependence:
    (a) *Stretch*: *stretch-gut* (glutton), *stretch-halter/hemp* (gallows bird, one that deserves to be hanged), *stretch-leg* (death), *stretch-neck* (pillory), *stretch-rope* (bell-ringer)
    (b) *Lack*: *lack-land* (younger son), *lack-beard* (immature youth), *lack-all* (deficient person), *lack-brain/Latin/learning/mind/ sense/thought/wit*
5. V+O=N (e.g. *cease-fire, shut-eye, breakfast* [time, occasion?], *pastime, pick-lock, wardrobe* [instrument?])
6. O+V=S (e.g. *cow-poke, door-stop, paper-punch, nail-set, spoke-shave, water-shed, wind-break*)

Clearly, Tuggy's observations are not at odds with the analysis of true exocentric compounds proposed above. On the contrary, they underscore the semantic and compositional differences of those compounds from what I have called above metonymic and metaphoric endocentric compounds. They show, however, that the schema in Figure 3.12 does not account for all the scarecrow nouns. In particular, V-*all* compounds will be based on a partial elaboration of this schema, whereby the object of the verb is *all*. Similarly, in the cases of lexical dependence on verbs, the schema will be elaborated in two different ways with respect to verbs *stretch* and *lack*. The examples in point (5) are different in that they follow the general syntactic pattern of the vehicle ($V - N_{Direct\ Object}$), but select other targets, e.g., arguably, MEANS (or INSTRUMENT) in the case of *breakfast*, TIME in *cease-fire*, etc. Finally, the O+V=S pattern can be accounted for by blending the general transitive syntactic pattern of the schema in Figure 3.12 with another O-V compound schema.

3.4   Notes on metonymy in onomastics

3.4.1 Anthroponymy

Anthroponymy is the study of the origins and meanings of personal names. The obvious reason why I include a few remarks on anthroponymy in this book is that metonymy was crucial in the emergence of both first names and surnames. The reason why I include these remarks in the chapter on morphology is that most anthroponyms, as well as troponyms, involve conversions or compounding.

3.4.1.1 First names

A detailed anthroponymic account of the metonymic sources of first names would call for another long study; therefore I shall confine myself to just a few representative examples based on the data from the Oxford *Concise Dictionary of First Names*. Despite their great variety, first names can be broadly divided into those which are motivated by analogy and thus may be called 'metaphoric', as in *Peter* derived from Greek *petros* 'rock', and those which are motivated by an identifying salient property of the referent and thus may be called 'metonymic'. In what follows we shall focus on the latter group.

Abraham (Hebrew: *Avrtaham*) – the origin is uncertain but the Bible explains it as meaning 'father of multitude' (from Hebrew *av hamon*). Although in the original expression the word *father* might have been intended both literally and figuratively, we may suggest that in the end the name is motivated by the metonymy BIOLOGICAL (AND SOCIAL) FUNCTION FOR PERSON. *Paul* (from Latin: *Paulus*) – the original Latin name meant 'small'; thus the motivating metonymy was clearly: SALIENT PROPERTY FOR PERSON. Other names motivated by this metonymy are *Caesar* ('hairy'), *Justin* ('just') and *Felix* ('happy'). *Judith* is a biblical name meaning 'a woman from Judea', the motivating metonymy being NATIONALITY FOR PERSON. The metonymic principles behind first names are not limited to Hebrew and Latin traditions and in fact reflect an old process the traces of which can probably be found in all Indo-European languages, (e.g. Skr. *Su-śravas, Pari-śruta,* both meaning 'very famous', *Su-carus* 'very nice'). A number of Germanic first names are also metonymically motivated, such as SALIENT PROPERTY FOR PERSON, which motivates Richard (from OHG *ric-hart* 'mighty-strong'), while PLACE FOR PROPERTY motivates the compound Norman (from 'north man'; cf. Grygiel 2007).

Milewski (1993) argued that compounding as the main strategy of name-formation goes back to Proto Indo-European and was amply represented in the early stages of most Indo-European languages. Interestingly, there was a large number of verbal compounds, consisting of the verbal root and its object or some adverbial element, thus reminiscent of *scarecrow* nouns in English, in both O-V and V-O word orders, for example Skr. *Śatru han* '(the one) killing enemies' from the verb *hán ti* ('to beat'), Celt. *Virido-vix* '(the one) fighting courageously' from the verb *vincō* ('I win').[15] Thus they seem to represent the forms based on two kinds of metonymy: the formal metonymy PREDICATE FOR SUBJECT and a conceptual metonymy ACTIVITY FOR PERSON. The compounding tendency can be further observed in the nesting of compounds in larger units which also had the structure of compounds, such as Skr. *Vira-bhū-pati* 'the lord of the land of husbands', where *Vira-bhū* is 'the land of husbands', Aw. *Gaya-δā-stay* 'existing due to the giver of life', where *Gayō-δā* is 'the giver of life'.

Slavic first names are transparently meaningful. Milewski (1959; the same observation was made by Malec 1996) argued that there were three main ways of forming first names in medieval Slavic languages, which were all at least partly based on earlier forms present in Proto Indo-European or other Indo-European languages:

- Compound names, consisting of two or more words
- Clipped and diminutive forms of the compound names
- Appellatives, that is common nouns functioning as names.

Numerous Slavic compounds probably activated larger predicative structures denoting a desirable property or a wish for the new-born baby, with the formal vehicle consisting of Object and adjectival Predicate, for example *Bogumił* '(may he be) likeable to God' (< *Bóg* 'god', *miły* 'likeable').[16] There were, however, a large number of Slavic verbal compounds having V-O word order, for example Czech *Chotě-bor, Chotě-slav, Chotě-mir, Chotě-mysl, Chotě-voj* from the old Slavic verbal root *χotě-ti* 'to want', Serb and Czech *Brani-mir, Brani-slav*, Pol. *Broni-sław* from *brani-ti* 'to fight', *Budziwoj* (*budzi* + *woj*) – '(the one) waking warriors', *Zbysław* (Z-by + *sław*) – '(the one) enhancing fame/glory', *Zbygniew* (Z-by + *gniew*) – '(the one) enhancing anger'. Milewski (1993: 236) claims that V-O compounding was the most original feature of Slavic anthroponymy. Therefore, it is interesting that the same formal and conceptual mechanism was employed later in the formation of English exocentric compounds (discussed above in §3.3.2.), which indicates rather strongly that it had a conceptual and not only language-internal basis.

General tendencies notwithstanding, the meaning of numerous compound names was not fixed by a single interpretive formula but could be blended in a variety of ways. For instance, the root *-sław* could be construed in different names as a THING 'glory', PROPERTY 'famous', as in *Przesław* ('very famous'), or an CAUSATIVE ACTIVITY 'glorify', as probably in *Rodosław*, either '(May you) glorify (your) family' or '(the one) glorifying (his) family'.

Apart from anthroponymic derivations, a great many first names developed either through various forms of what we referred to in Chapter 2 as speech-sound formal metonymies, in particular clipping, or through morphological metonymies. The simple cases of clipping were relatively rare and can be observed in *Bogus* (< *Bogusław*), *Zdzis* (<*Zdzisław*), *Boża* (< *Bożana*). However, most clips were further modified either by means of phonemic changes, especially in the final syllable, for example *Bogusz* (< *Bogusław*), *Przemyk* (*Przemysław*). Morphological metonymies consisted of a single component of the compound standing for the whole, as in *Mir* (< *Mirosław*), *Slaw* (< *Sławomir*). Both the clipped forms and the morphological metonyms were often further modified by hypocoristic or diminutive suffixation, as in *Kazik* (< *Kazimierz*), *Sławko* (< *Sławomir*), *Staszko* (<*Stanisław*).[17] Slavic appellative first names were based on the metonymy SALIENT PROPERTY FOR PERSON, although the property was not always denoted by an adjective; nominals and prepositional phrases were equally productive, for example Czech names *Smil, Smir, Smysl,* which come from *sъmilъ* 'very nice', *sъmirъ* 'good peace', *sъmyslъ* 'good mind', and Polish *Zabor* (*za bor* 'behind forest'). In conclusion, the formation and development of most first names in Indo-European languages followed the familiar conceptual paths of metonymic integration and extensions typical of ordinary compounds and conversions, often followed by formal metonymies observed also in modern clips.

3.4.1.2 Surnames

Jäkel (1999) suggested a taxonomy of surnames in German based on the notions of motivation and metonymy. Ignoring the names whose origin and original motivation cannot be established, the taxonomy is shown in Figure 3.13.

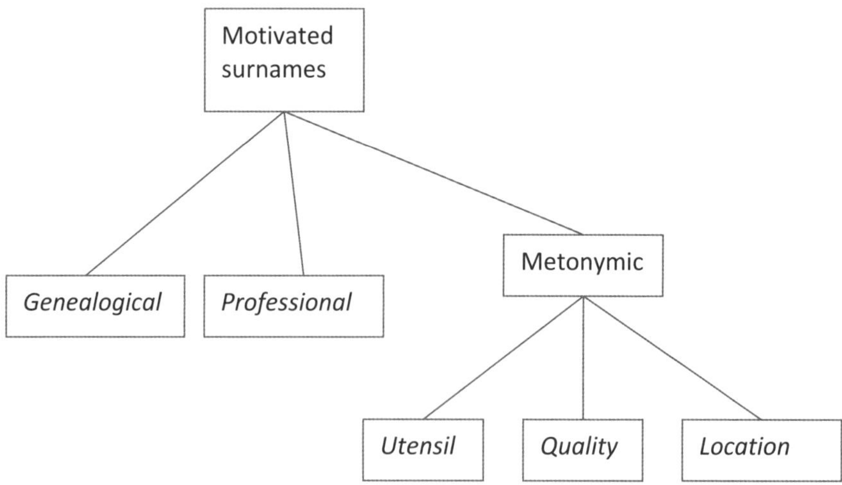

Figure 3.13 Taxonomy of surnames in German, based on Jäkel (1999).

Typical examples are:
(a) genealogical – *Thomas, Paul* (father's name) or *Jansen, Johnson, Andersson* (father's name + patronymic suffix grammaticalised from the lexeme for SON)
(b) professional – *Miller, Shepherd, Weaver*
(c) utensil metonymy[18] – *Hering* ('herring'), *Nagel* ('nail'), *Stein* ('stone')
(d) quality metonymy – *Hartmann* ('hard man'), *Kahlkopf* ('baldhead'), *Riese* ('giant')
(e) location metonymy – *Amende* ('at the end'), *Imhof* ('in the yard'), *Vormwald* ('in front of the wood')

It comes as no surprise that surnames are motivated since their function is and always has been to identify a singular personal referent, especially in situations where a number of referents bear the same first name. In order to restrict the reference to single individuals by-names were added, based on what was known about the intended referent, which gradually developed into fixed surnames. As Bach (quoted by Jäkel) pointed out: "Our surnames are by-names inherited from ancestors" (1952: 231). So, from the linguistic point of view, by-names and, subsequently, surnames may be regarded as modifiers restricting the reference of the head represented by the proper name (cf. Malec 1996 for a similar view). If this is accepted, we may regard first name-surname combinations as left-headed nominal grammatical constructions with the first name functioning as the head and the surname functioning as the restrictive modifier.

The above analysis raises the issue of the origin of this particular structural property of by-names. One possibility is that they originated from predicative descriptions at first added as non-restrictive appositions to the first names which subsequently became periphrastic antonomasias (cf. Endnote 8 of Chapter 1), for example *Zeus – the Thunderer, God – the Almighty, Mary – the Virgin, John – the Baptist, Bill – the Miller.* Through formal metonymy, the descriptive phrase could be used as a substitute for the whole phrase (e.g. *the Almighty* for *God the Almighty*), additionally motivated by the conceptual metonymy SALIENT PROPERTY FOR PERSON (cf. Płuciennik 2007). In time, the descriptive phrase might have become established as designating the identifying property of the referent and used restrictively as a by-name in conjunction with the proper name.[19] The general structure of the first name–surname construction is shown in Figure 3.14.

Syn	First name N $_{\text{HEAD}}$	X $_{\text{MODIFIER}}$
Sem	PERSON	IDENTIFYING PROPERTY

Figure 3.14 First name-surname construction in English.

The range of constructions represented schematically above had and to some extent still have rather idiosyncratic grammatical properties, but they were constructions nonetheless, and thus in all of them the modifier had the same identifying function implemented by specifying the identifying property of the individual denoted by the head. For instance, the modifier could have the structure of an entire NP, as in *John the Baptist* (mentioned by Jäkel), an entire NP without its determiner, as in *James son of Zebedee,* or a 'headless' NP reduced to its determiner and adjective, as in *Erik the Red* or *Ivan the Terrible,* or a PP, as in German *Amberg* ('at the hill') or *Bienwald* ('by the wood'). Gradually, however, most surnames were reduced to single units. This was done either by deleting the grammatical morpheme, as in *Cliff Richard, John Brown,* or by blending the two constituent lexemes into a single word, as in *Johnson* (John + son).

The history of surnames in Polish is similar to English, but there are also interesting differences. What follows is, by and large, based on an extremely detailed study of Polish surnames in the twelfth through the fifteenth century by Kowalik-Kaleta (2007: ch. 2). As far as the motivation of surnames is concerned, Kowalik-Kaleta distinguishes three main groups:

(a)   surnames motivated by location (*nazwiska odmiejscowe* – 'delocational surnames'), for example *Bykowski* (< *Byki*), *Lubomirz* (<*Lubomirski*), *Solecki* (< *Solec*).

(b)   surnames motivated by the name of the father (*nazwiska patronimiczne* – 'patronymic surnames'), for example *Sieciechowic* (< *Sieciech*), *Boguszewic* (<*Bogusz*).

(c)   surnames motivated by the properties of their bearers (*nazwiska odapelatywne* – 'deappellative surnames')

The last group confirms our analysis of English endocentric compounds since the same mechanism can be found also in Polish, where almost any predicative expression can be used as a distinguishing PROPERTY of the referent. Consequently, alongside predictable adjectives, such as *Bogaty* ('rich'), *Łakomy* ('gluttonous'), *Cichy* ('silent'), there are nouns *Kopyto* ('hoof'), *Staw* ('pond'), as well as prepositional phrases and whole verb phrases, as in

Z Bogiem ('with God'), *Z Krzywą Żoną* ('with a bent wife'), *Źle Wlazł* ('[he] got in badly'), *Tu Mi Grała* ('she played here for me').

Morphologically, surnames were formed in four ways:

(a) by using an ordinary common word converted to a by-name, such as *Bogaty* ('rich'), *Kopyto* ('hoof')

(b) by derivation (i.e. by means of affixing a specialised suffix to a chosen root), such as *Sieciech > Sieciechowic, Bartosz > Bartoszowicz*

(c) by compounding two free morphemes (often joined with the interfix -o-); as in *Mokronos* (< *mokry nos* 'wet nose'), *Miodowarzec* (< *miód warzy* 'brew honey')

(d) by whole clause-like phrases, for example *Tu Mi Grała* ('she played here for me'), *Źle Wlazł* ('[he] got in badly').

According to our criteria, although all the above names are motivated metonymically, only the names formed in the ways specified in (a) and (d) are clear examples of metonymy. The names in (b) are determined morphologically, while the examples in (c) must be considered individually, depending on whether or not the name has also the status of a common noun.

The same distributional, functional and general semantic properties of surnames accompanied by morphological differences suggest that Jäkel's taxonomy should be somewhat modified. It seems that, as in the case of modifiers in compounds (discussed in Section 3.3) all the surnames can be regarded from the diachronic point of view as modifiers specifying the identifying property of the head proper name. Since the PROPERTY part of the construction is accessed by various components of the idealised cognitive model of a given individual, such as [THE NAME OF THE FATHER], [THE PROFESSION], [THE CHARACTERISTIC TOOL OR ACCESSORY], it follows that, apart from metaphors, other surnames are motivated metonymically. The fact that they are motivated metonymically does not entail, however, that they are all metonymic, for example derived names like *Johnson* or *Sieciechowic* have their name-like status determined by the suffix, *-son* and *-wic*, respectively, and cannot, therefore, be regarded as metonymic, unlike *Paul, Amberg, Kopyto*, or *Tu Mi Grała*, which can.

3.4.2 Toponymy

In addition to anthroponyms, metonymy must also be taken into consideration in the study of proper names of geographical locations (i.e. toponyms).[20] What is of particular relevance to toponymy are the processes of conversion and compounding. In terms of their morphological and general conceptual structure, toponyms can be divided into four classes:

(a)   morphologically simplex names motivated metonymically or meta-phorically. In metonymic names, such as *Staines* 'stones', *Poplar*, *Bow*, a salient geological, botanical or architectural part of the place (i.e. stones, poplar trees or a bow-shaped bridge) may stand for the whole place.

(b)   morphologically compound names in which the modifying component is metonymic or metaphoric. If it is accepted that OE words *tun* and *burh*, which usually appear in the place names as *-ton* and *-bury*, had the primary senses 'village' or 'town', they may be considered as non-metonymic designations of places and it comes as no surprise that they should be found in toponyms. However, in order to designate places uniquely, they were often modified by characteristic properties designated metonymically, as in *Drayton* 'dragging town' (probably < OE *drag* 'something heavy that is used by being dragged along the ground or over a surface'), *Heston* 'town of bushes, bush town' (< OE *hese* 'bush, woodland country'), *Shepperton* 'shepherds' town', *Acton* 'oak town' (< OE *ac* 'oak'), *Kingsbury* 'king's fort, town'. The distin-guishing property was often designated also by the name of the owner or an important individual associated with a place, as in *Harlington*, *Kensington* (< OE personal name *Cynesige*), *Islington* (< OE personal name *Gisl*), Sunbury (probably < OE personal name *Sunna*).

(c)   morphologically compound names in which the head component is metonymic or metaphoric. This kind of toponym is similar to the ones discussed in (a) except that the metonymic head, usually based on the metonymy SALIENT GEOLOGICAL OR GEOGRAPHICAL PART FOR PLACE, is literally modified, as in *Hendon* 'high hill' (< OE *heah* 'high', *dun* 'hill'), Shadwell 'shallow stream' (< OE *sceald* 'shallow', *wylle* 'stream, spring'), *Ratcliff* 'red cliff' (< OE *read* 'red'), etc.

(d)   morphologically compound names in which both the head and the modifier are metonymic or metaphoric. The most typical examples of this kind of toponym are based on the head designating a salient building, business or estate and the modifier designating its distin-guishing property, for example *Chelsea* 'limestone port' (< OE *calc* 'lime', *hythe* 'a small port or haven'), *Chiswick* 'cheese residence' (< OE *cese* 'cheese', *wic* 'residence'), *Hanworth* 'cock enclosure' (< OE *hana* 'cock', *worth* 'enclosure'). However, other combina-tions were possible as well, particularly with the head designating some kind of geographical landmark, such as *Hanwell* 'cock spring or stream' (< OE *hana* 'cock', *wylle* 'spring, stream of water'), *Northolt* 'northern place' (< OE *hal* 'place, corner'), *Willesden* 'hill of the spring or stream' (< OE *wylle* 'stream, spring', *dun* 'hill').

We may note in passing that once the name of a place has been established it often serves as the vehicle for other referential metonymies, especially with respect to the inhabitants of the place. On the abstract level, where locations are conceptualised as containers (people live *in* places), the relevant metonymy seems to be CONTAINER FOR CONTENT. However, what is characteristic of those toponymic metonymies is that unlike in ordinary CONTAINER FOR CONTENT metonymy, the target is usually a subset of all the inhabitants, for example the name of a country may target its government or the national football team, as in (21) and (22) below, the name of the capital may also target the government, as in (23), but it may also, like other town names, target most of its inhabitants, as in (24). Finally, more specific locations, such as streets and even individual buildings may serve as vehicles for their salient inhabitants, as in (25) and (26).

(21) Poland will probably oppose Germany in their attempt to sign a bilateral gas deal with Russia.
(22) Henry's hand has led France to the Football World Cup finals.
(23) London has finally approved of the new energy-saving strategy.
(24) London celebrated all night as it was granted the hosting of the Olympic games in 2012.
(25) Downing Street has finally approved of the new energy-saving strategy.
(26) The White House may well reject the new energy-saving strategy.

3.5   Conclusions

We have seen that metonymy is a ubiquitous process in English morphology. In derivation it motivates the extension of derivational patterns both in the roots and in the affixes, for example it makes it possible to derive *-er* nominals not only from verbal roots but also from nouns and adverbials denoting various components of the event schema primarily evoked by a particular verb. Similarly, metonymy is instrumental in extending the prototypical Agentive meaning of the *-er* suffix to denote also Instruments, Locations and Causes. Conversions – both minor and major ones – are metonymic par excellence, while in endocentric compounding the conceptual metonymy X FOR PROPERTY constitutes the basis of a modification mechanism which, alongside the right-headed constructional schema, underlies the emergent meanings of compounds. I have also tried to show that exocentric *scarecrow* compounds are motivated not only by the conceptual metonymy ACTIVITY FOR PERSON but also by a formal PART FOR PART metonymy, where the verb phrase of a sentence stands for its subject. In addition, we have seen that the same general metonymic principles have motivated the formation of first names, surnames and troponyms.

Notes

1 For the sake of simplicity I ignore the role of metaphor in those integrations, which in any case is much less regular and productive.

2 A rear-ender is a car accident in which the back of one of the cars is crushed, a back-hander is a tennis stroke (in itself an extremely complex expression), cf. also *header* – 'a manner of hitting the ball with one's head in football' and *three-incher* – 'a three-inch long nail'.

3 Szawerna (2007) argues that there is a cline from perfect metonymies in conversions to less and less good examples of metonymy in stress shifts and derivations. I do not see any cline here: once the formal marker of the change of category (or subcategory) appears, metonymy disappears since the new target meaning is designated by a new form. As we shall see below, the conceptual metonymy PROCESS FOR PARTICIPANT of this process, which Szawerna mentions in his account, may crucially affect the way derived nominalisations extend their meaning, for example a derived nominalisation *washing* may change its designation from a reified process (i.e. an act of washing) to the landmark of the process (i.e. the clothes being washed). Note that this extension of meaning is not marked by any formal change (see also Schönefelt 2005).

4 A considerable overlap both in the semantics of various prototypically agentive suffixes and the availability of conceptual and grammatical categories of their stems often results in speakers' confusion about which form to choose, as Waszakowa (1998) amply demonstrated.

5 Their metonymic nature was already pointed out by Leech (1974: ch. 10).

6 Probably the reason why there are no gradable adjective >> non-gradable adjective conversions is that it would be tantamount to blocking a very basic mental ability of comparing.

7 I call them 'allomorphic' because they depend on the phonological properties of the verb stem (cf. Wróbel 2001: Part III) and as a result are in complementary distribution. Therefore in traditional terms they would be considered as allomorphs of a single nominalising morpheme.

8 Polish aspectual distinctions are usually conveyed morphologically through prefixation (cf. Wróbel 1984), for example imperf. *pisać* ('write') vs. perf. *napisać*, imperf. *pić* ('drink') vs. perf. *wypić*. All these verb forms may undergo the same kind of transpositional nominalisation: *pisanie, napisanie, picie, wypicie*.

9 Endocentric compounds, such as *beehive,* are typical 'two-component names' (nazwy dwuczłonowe) in Rozwadowski's (1921) theory of compound names. He argued that compound nouns consist of the head component (człon główny) denoting a general category, as in *hive,* and the modifying component denoting a more specific property, in this case the distinguishing 'inhabitant', as in *bee.* The theory of compounds proposed below owes a lot to Rozwadowski's insights.

10 A more systematic presentation of various views on classification of compounds as well the development of Bauer's views and recent alternative classifications can be found in Scalise and Bisetto (2009). Bauer's most recent position on the typology of compounds is presented in Bauer (2009).

11 Plag (2003: 159f) argues that one of the crucial differences between syntactic phrases and real compounds is the impossibility of separating the latter by other modifiers (e.g. *the two-year period – the two-year probationary period* vs. *waterbird – *water wild bird*). Given the usage-based theory of language adopted here (cf. Langacker 1990; Croft and Cruse 2004), the increasingly strong 'binding' of the two components in compounds can be accounted for in terms of conceptual and formal entrenchment of the blended structure: the more often it is used in its idiosyncratic meaning the less compositional and the more lexicalised it becomes. Ultimately, the shift of stress may be a reflex of this process as well, which is why it also occurs in conversions, as in *to put 'down – a 'put-down*. This suggests that compounds are the final result of the development I have already mentioned: nonce formation > syntactic phrase > compound.

12 Notice that the entities in the compounds discussed below are themselves a result of metonymic Verb>Noun conversions (e.g. *bee sting, earthquake, landslide*) whose nominal heads are based on metonymy ACTIVITY/PROCESS-FOR-INSTANCE OF ACTIVITY/PROCESS.

13 As we have already pointed out, the initial stress is not a constant property of the construction, therefore I will ignore it in the foregoing discussion.

14 It will be noticed that, prototypically, the metonymic endocentric compounds will involve what Cruse (2000) calls 'integral parts' (e.g. head, skin, mouth, back). If facultative parts are selected, as in *redcap*, they must have an unambiguously identifying function for a given subcategory (PORTER).

15 At first, the verbal concepts were denoted by the verbal element ('pierwiastek'). It was later, in the Slavic developments that full-blown verbal stems appeared in those compounds and became extremely productive (cf. Milewski 1993: 230f).

16 It should be remembered that the original meaning of *Bóg* was 'wealth, happiness' (Malec 1996: 10).

17 Needless to say all the above tendencies are still common in the various ways first names are modified in modern languages, for example in Polish clips *Aga > Agata, Tomek > Tomasz, Ala > Alicja, Staś, Stach, Stachu > Stanisław,* or in English *Tom > Thomas, Chris > Christopher, Bob, Bobby > Robert, Sue > Susan, Betty > Elisabeth,* etc.

18 I have been unable to find motivation for this rather strange label, because obviously Jäkel has not only utensils in mind, but any characteristic physical objects somehow associated with a given individual. It seems that the terms like 'tool' or 'accessory' metonymy would be more felicitous.

19 Another, though less likely hypothesis would be that the antonomasias were first by names which, through formal metonymy, began to function on their own. Thus the antonomasic *the Virgin* would result from deletion of the proper name in *Mary the Virgin*. The suggestion seems unlikely because antonomasia has always been thought of as a stylistic device making it possible to avoid the repetition of the

first name. So it would be strange to use *Mary* first and then 'pronominalise' it as *Mary the Virgin*, only to later reduce it to *the Virgin*.

20 The linguistic material discussed below is borrowed from the study of metonymy in onomastics by Niemczak (2008). A general account of toponymy in relation to reference within the cognitive framework can be found in Radden and Dirven (2007: ch. 5)

4 Metonymy in pragmatics

As Wells (1977) and Koch (1999) pointed out, most lexical metonymies appear first as ad hoc metonymies, interpretable only in specific contexts. This view is very much in keeping with the usage-based theory of language, as originally formulated by Langacker (1987, 1990, cf. also Croft and Cruse 2004), and it is this view that motivates our decision to begin the discussion of the impact of metonymy on the meaning of linguistic expressions beyond the level of morphemes with the way in which they are used metonymically in particular contexts, i.e. with pragmatics.

4.1 Referential metonymies

Nunberg (1978) and Lakoff and Johnson (1980) regarded metonymy primarily as a pragmatic linguistic device designed to facilitate reference. As Lakoff and Johnson expressed it, "Metonymy (…) has a primarily referential function, that is, it allows us to use one entity to *stand for* another" (1980: 36). Thus, in example (1) below, uttered by one waitress addressing another, the expression *the ham sandwich* stands for the customer who ordered the sandwich.

(1) The ham sandwich is waiting for his check.

Although, as we shall see in Chapter 5, the metonymic link between an expression and its meaning may be strongly conventionalised and thus become its permanent new sense, in the case of pragmatic metonymy, the relation between an expression and its target referent has to be inferred, or accessed, on the basis of the available contextual information, that is the representation of the context in the image space, i.e. the representation of the ongoing situation (see Chapter 6). For instance, given a different context of (1), e.g. a customer in a gallery who has just decided to buy a still-life with a ham sandwich in it, the same expression would refer to a completely different individual. However, the often purely contextual, incidental nature of pragmatic metonymy does not preclude systematic regularities. On the contrary, the pragmatic phenomena seem to exhibit and follow a set of well-defined high-level metonymic mappings, which form the basis for drawing valid implicatures and explicatures.[1] Many of these patterns, such as PART FOR WHOLE, CONTAINER FOR CONTENT, PRODUCER FOR PRODUCT, OBJECT USED FOR USER, CONTROLLER FOR CONTROLLED, INSTITUTION FOR PEOPLE RESPONSIBLE, PLACE

FOR INSTITUTION, PLACE FOR EVENT, are discussed briefly in Chapter 1. What needs to be added to that account is that referential metonymies often come in chains. Ruiz de Mendoza and Hernández (2003) argue that a metonymic chain is involved in the meaning of *Picasso* in sentence (3), whose intermediate metonymic shift is illustrated by (2):

(2) I love Picasso.
(3) I have a Picasso in the living room.

Sentence (2) is of course ambiguous because *Picasso* may be understood literally as 'a person' or metonymically as 'Picasso's work'. It is the latter sense that leads to the second step in the chain; namely, from 'Picasso's work' to 'a specific painting by Picasso' activated in sentence (3). Ruiz de Mendoza and Hernández represent this metonymic chain as shown in Figure 4.1.

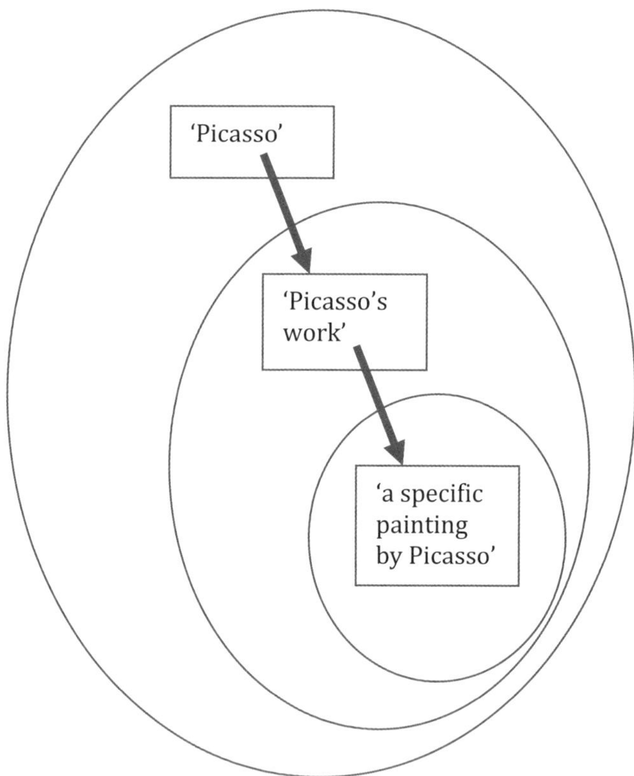

Figure 4.1 Double metonymy: AUTHOR FOR WORK FOR UNIQUE SAMPLE (based on Ruiz de Mendoza and Hernández 2003: 38).[2]

Other examples of metonymic chains are not hard to find. Ruiz de Mendoza and Hernández also discuss the possible double metonymies involved in the interpretation of *Shakespeare* in (4) below, where it stands first for 'Shakespeare's work', which in turn stands for 'a book (or books) containing Shakespeare's work':

(4) Shakespeare is on the top shelf.

Another example may be the development of meaning of the word *paper* in English (discussed in greater detail in Chapter 5), which may be used with reference to the content of 'a formal piece of writing about an academic subject', as in (5):

(5) His paper was so difficult that nobody had a clue what he was trying to say.

Hilpert (2006, 2007) suggests that the metonymic chain involved in the lexical development of *paper* is: MATERIAL >> WRITING (or PRINTED DOCUMENT) >> IDEAS, which means that it represents a case of double metonymy: MATERIAL FOR OBJECT MADE OF THIS MATERIAL WITH TEXT WRITTEN ON THIS MATERIAL FOR IDEAS EXPRESSED IN THIS TEXT. A metonymic chain seems also to have been involved in the semantic development of the word *glass* in the form of *glasses*, meaning 'spectacles'. The relevant metonymies are MATERIAL FOR PIECES OF THIS MATERIAL FOR AN OBJECT MADE FROM PIECES OF THIS MATERIAL. The latter development may be shown as follows:

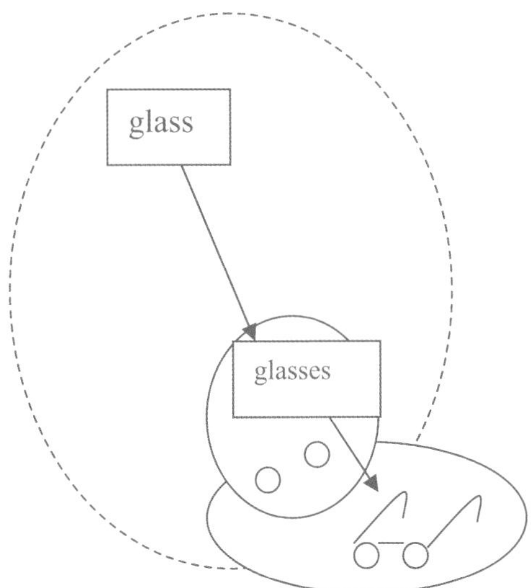

Figure 4.2 Double metonymy MATERIAL FOR SPECIALLY CUT PIECES OF THIS MATERIAL FOR AN OBJECT MADE FROM THESE SPECIALLY CUT PIECES OF THIS MATERIAL in the semantic development of the lexeme *glass* in English.

Since such referential metonymic chains are often lexicalised and grammat-icalised (cf. Hilpert 2007 for a review), we shall return to them in Chapter 5. Now we turn our attention to a less familiar and conceptually more complex case of propositional metonymy.

4.2 Propositional script-based metonymies

As defined in Chapter 1, propositional metonymy is a metonymy in which the whole propositional content p of a sentence S is used to access either the whole ICM or another propositional content q within the same ICM. If the proposition serving as the target is accessed by a sentence whose propositional meaning is completely different from the target (i.e. its subject and predicate are different), then the metonymy may be called 'sentential'. If the proposi-tional metonymy is limited to the predicate, the metonymy is referred to as 'predicative'. Following Panther and Thornburg (1999), I assume that most propositional metonymies are based on a conceptual Gestalt (scenario, a form of idealised cognitive model) they call State-of-Affairs Scenario (SAS). The states of affairs in the scenario include states, events, processes and actions. The scenario has the following general structure (cf. Panther and Thornburg 1999: 337):

i.   the BEFORE: *necessary precondition*: motivations, potentialities, capabilities, abilities, dispositions, etc., which can bring about the State of Affairs (SoA)
ii. the CORE: *the existing/true SoA*
iii. the EFFECTS: *necessary consequences* immediately following from the SoA
iv. the AFTER: *non-necessary consequences* of the SoA

The scenarios we discuss below are all particular elaborations of this general model, i.e. they are what Ruiz de Mendoza (2007) dubbed 'situational propositional models'. The psycholinguistic aspects and consequences of Panther and Thornburg's theory are discussed in Gibbs (2007).

Before we consider particular groups of examples one more comment needs to be made. A number of expressions we will discuss are already well-entrenched idiomatic expressions of English or other languages; however, they are included in this chapter because they represent cases of pragmatic strength-ening and thus illustrate the general principles of metonymy in language use. Traugott (1988), who was probably the first to describe the mechanism of pragmatic strengthening, identified three tendencies in the development of meaning:

- ***Tendency I***: Meanings situated in the external described situation > meanings situated in the internal (evaluative/perceptual/cognitive) situation
- ***Tendency II***: Meaning situated in the described external or internal situation > meanings situated in the textual situation
- ***Tendency III***: Meanings tend to be increasingly situated in the speaker's subjective belief-state/attitude toward the situation.

Tendencies I and II both involve change of domains, hence they are best described as metaphoric. In contrast, Traugott suggests, Tendency III should be viewed as "the shift from a conversational implicature to a conventional one" (Traugott 1988: 411), whereby a usually covert, more loosely associated implicature is strengthened and thus becomes a permanent aspect of meaning or what Traugott and Dasher (2002) call 'generalized invited inference' (GIIN) in their Invited Inferencing Theory of Semantic Change. The pragmatic strengthening which leads to permanent changes in meaning has a metonymic basis because, given the conceptual reality of SAS, the invited conversational implicature is just the target part of SAS accessed through an explicitly expressed other part of the same SAS, which constitutes the vehicle of this metonymic transfer (cf. Ruiz de Mendoza 2007 for a similar view). Thus what Traugott and Dasher regard as a salient conversational implicature (invited inference) arising from proposition p conveyed by expression e, as a part of the total truth- and non-truth-conditional meaning of e, which, through strengthening, becomes the conventional semantic (almost truth-conditional) meaning of e, may be viewed as a case of lexicalisation of metonymy. The metonymically accessed target part of SAS becomes the most deeply entrenched meaning of an expression. The metonymy is clearly of the PART-FOR-PART kind: the propositional, truth-conditional part stands for a non-truth-conditional implicature (invited inference). As we have seen, the wholes within which the mapping of those parts occurs are conceptual structures which we refer to as situational cognitive models or scenarios. A metonymic account of implicature was also suggested in Bierwiaczonek (2001, 2002a).

4.2.1 Travelling metonymies

The first well-known example of a propositional metonymy based on SAS was discussed by Lakoff (1987: 78f), who pointed out that the way Ojibwa speakers speak about getting to some destination is based on the cognitive model of going somewhere in a vehicle. The model consists of five stages:

i.   Pre-condition: You have (or have access to) a vehicle.
ii. Embarcation: You get into the vehicle and start it up.

   iii. Centre: You drive (row, fly, etc.) to your destination.
   iv. Finish: You park and get out.
   v. End point: You are at your destination.

It seems that Ojibwa speakers tend to access the whole scenario by means of the stage of Embarcation. Accordingly, when asked, for example, how they got to a party, they usually give answers which are translated as *I started to come, I stepped into a canoe, I got into a car*, and the like. As Lakoff himself points out, there is nothing unusual about the way Ojibwa speakers construct their utterances about travelling. In English people can also use the Embarcation stage for the whole scenario by saying, for example *I hopped on a bus* or *I just stuck out my thumb*. However, they also make use of other parts of the scenario, for example by saying *I have a car* or *I borrowed my brother's car*, they activate it through the stage of Precondition, while by saying *I drove* they activate it through the Centre. Notice that the scenario in question can also be activated by conceptually more distant propositional (sentential) metonymies, for example *My brother gave me a lift* or *My sister had lent me her car.*

4.2.2 Places for activities

A great deal of the activities we perform are confined to special culturally defined locations, which gives rise to strong associative links between those activities and locations. For example, we drink in pubs, read and study in libraries, work out in gyms. Consequently, utterances about locations often felicitously implicate activities. Thus, B's answer to A's question in the exchange below will in most contexts implicate that Tim is studying:

   (6)   A: What's Tim doing?
           B: He's in the library.

At times the strengthening of such implicatures may be reinforced by grammatical factors, which create increasingly conventionalised semantically determinate constructions. For instance, in English, expressions such as *go to school, go to jail, go to hospital* have acquired the status of constructions (marked by the absence of an article) based on the metonymy JOURNEY TO A DESTINATION FOR PERFORMING CANONICAL ACTIVITIES IN THAT DESTINATION, which in turn is based on a link between locations and typical activities (or events). Thus the target meanings of the above expressions are, respectively, 'to receive education', 'to serve time' and 'to undergo medical treatment'. They all designate the inceptive stage of those events, probably because, in the general scenarios of events, arriving in a particular place is strongly associated with the typical activity performed at that place, but they do not imply that the activity has been carried out to the point of completion. Thus, these expressions have the conventional meanings specified here:

(7)   a/ Bill went to school when he was ten >> Bill started to receive primary education.
b/ Bill went to gaol two years ago >> Bill started to serve a sentence.
c/ Bill went to hospital >> Bill started receiving treatment in hospital.

The high degree of conventionalisation of these implicatures does not, however, prevent them from being cancellable, as the following examples show:

(7)   a˘/ Bill went to school when he was ten, but nobody taught him anything.
b˘/ Bill went to gaol two years ago, but he escaped even before he moved to his cell.
c˘/ Bill went to hospital, but actually the hospital was full and they sent him home.

As opposed to those inceptive expressions, sentences denoting staying in a particular location imply that the activity or event is in progress, for example:

(8)   a/ Bill is at school >> Bill is receiving education.
b/ Bill is in gaol >> Bill is doing time.
c/ Bill is in hospital >> Bill is undergoing treatment in hospital.

Compared to such 'institutional locations' as school, gaol, or hospital, other locations are less entrenched. For instance, predications such as *go to the beach* or *go to the park* may well give rise to behavioural implicatures, but the implicatures are not conventionalised. There are, however, a handful of other locations which are so tightly culturally related to certain activities that their meaning is almost as fixed as that of the institutional locations discussed above. These are particularly common as metonymies for taboo activities related to excreting and sex. For instance, excreting can be accessed through such expressions as *go to the bathroom/be in the bathroom, go on the coal, go over the heap, go round the corner, go upstairs*, while having sex is euphemistically conveyed through such common metonymic expressions as *go to bed with someone*.

4.2.3 Metonymies of emotions

Emotions are notoriously difficult to conceptualise and to denote 'literally'; therefore they are usually accessed metaphorically or metonymically (cf. Lakoff 1987; Kövecses 1986, 1989; Nowakowska-Kempna 2000; Bierwiaczonek 2000, 2002b). We shall discuss three cases of metonymy of emotions.

4.2.3.1 Propositional metonymies of anger

In general, predications of emotions are based on scripts of emotional events, which have the following general structure:

i.   the BEFORE: Event 1 – Stimulus (Cause)
ii. the CORE: Experiencer's emotion
iii. the EFFECTS: various physiological effects
iv. the AFTER: Experiencer's behavioral responses.

As demonstrated by Kövecses (1986), Lakoff and Kövecses (1987), Lakoff (1987) and Bierwiaczonek (2000, 2000b), there are a number of systematic metonymic patterns in the language of emotions. Perhaps the most common, and the most productive, pattern is PHYSIOLOGICAL EFFECTS OF EMOTION STAND FOR EMOTION. For instance, in the predications of anger, physiological effects include body heat (example 9), internal pressure (10), redness in the face and neck area (11), agitation (12–13) and interference with accurate perception (14) (cf. Lakoff and Kövecses 1987: 197):

(9)   Don't get hot under the collar.
(10) When I found out I almost burst a blood vessel.
(11) She was scarlet with rage.
(12) She was shaking with anger.
(13) I was hopping mad.
(14) She was blind with rage.

Another high-level metonymy that follows from Lakoff and Kövecses' data is BEHAVIOURAL RESPONSES FOR EMOTION. The particular forms this metonymy takes in the predications of anger are INSANE BEHAVIOUR FOR ANGER (15–17), VIOLENT FRUSTRATED BEHAVIOUR FOR ANGER (18–20), AGGRESSIVE VERBAL BEHAVIOUR FOR ANGER (21–22) and AGGRESSIVE VISUAL BEHAVIOUR FOR ANGER (23–24) (Lakoff and Kövecses (1987: 204, 208):

(15) When my mother finds out, she'll have a fit.
(16) When the ump threw him out of the game, Billy started foaming at the mouth.
(17) He's about to throw a tantrum.
(18) He's tearing his hair out.
(19) If one more thing goes wrong, I'll start banging my head against the wall.
(20) The loud music next door has got him climbing the walls.

(21)   She gave him a tongue-lashing.
(22)   I really chewed him out good.
(23)   She was looking daggers at me.
(24)   He gave me a dirty look.

4.2.3.2 Propositional metonymies of love

The general patterns discussed above show up in the language of other emotions as well. As Kövecses (1986: 86ff) showed, there are a number of physiological effects that are conventionally associated with the concept of ROMANTIC LOVE, which give rise to a large number of metonymies. The most typical physiological bodily manifestations of love are:

— BODY HEAT: *I felt hot all over when I saw her; You really have the hots for her, don't you; 'I love you', she whispered in the heat of passion; It was a torrid love story;*

— INCREASE IN HEART RATE: *She had palpitations; He's a heartthrob; His heart was throbbing with love; Her heart began to pound when she saw him;*

— BLUSHING: *There was a glow of love in her face; She blushed when she saw him;*

— INTERFERENCE WITH ACCURATE PERCEPTION: *He saw nothing but her; I only had eyes for her.*

The concept of ROMANTIC, or as I prefer to call it EROTIC, LOVE can also be accessed through the lovers' characteristic behaviours and activities. As I have shown in Bierwiaczonek (2002b), as opposed to anger and similar short-lived emotions, the script of LOVE is much longer, so there are also numerous metonymic expressions based either on more controlled, even deliberate activities of the lovers or their culturally defined interactions, for example *I think the world of you, Bill goes out with Jane, Who are you dating now? Eve makes eyes at Frank, Tom sleeps with Sue,[3] They are always together.* Significantly, *Roget's Thesaurus* also cites other behavioural expressions, such as *necking, billing and cooing, courting, walking out, sighing, suing, pressing one's suit,* as synonyms of *love.* In addition, lovers are often referred to, again metonymically, as POSSLQs (i.e. 'Persons of Opposite Sex Sharing Living Quarters'). In the case of EROTIC LOVE but also in other subcategories of LOVE, particularly in CHILD'S LOVE OF PARENT, such forms of behaviour as simple physical closeness and communication are often synonymous with LOVE, for example *She was always by my side, My dad and I could talk for hours, He was the only one who really understood me.* Apart from different behavioural manifestations of LOVE as compared to other emotions and feelings, LOVE is different in its internal structure in that it cannot be described as a single emotion, but rather as a complex emotion, consisting not only of other, more basic emotions, but also rather long-standing volitions and attitudes. Consequently, it is also those parts of the whole conceptual representation of *love* that can be used as metonymic predications of LOVE. Here are some representative examples:

ONE EMOTIONAL CONCEPT FOR THE WHOLE CATEGORY
Most metonymies do not involve the whole category of LOVE but subcategories such as EROTIC LOVE, MOTHERLY LOVE, BROTHERLY LOVE.[4]

In sentence (25) the concept of INTEREST stands for the category of EROTIC LOVE:

(25)   I'm interested only in Eve, I'm not interested in any other girl.

Other elements of the same domain that are particularly common as metonymies of LOVE are AFFECTION and ATTACHMENT, as in (26):

(26)   I've never felt so much affection for anybody, I'm so attached to her. I couldn't live without her.

SALIENT VOLITION FOR THE WHOLE CATEGORY
The most general element of the volitional structure of LOVE is LOVER WANTS OBJECT OF LOVE TO BE HAPPY. Consequently, utterances (27) and (28) may be interpreted as declarations of love:

(27)   I want you to be happy.
(28)   I would do anything to make you happy.

SALIENT ATTITUDE FOR THE WHOLE CATEGORY
Probably the most common ways of accessing the whole representation of LOVE are the evaluative propositions: LOVER BELIEVES THAT OBJECT OF LOVE IS THE MOST BEAUTIFUL PERSON IN THE WORLD and LOVER BELIEVES THAT OBJECT OF LOVE IS SPECIAL. As conceptual elements, those attitudes may be accessed through a variety of lexical means, which can metonymically stand for the whole category, for example:

(29)   There is no one like you.
(30)   I think she's the one.
(31)   I've never met anyone like you.

Apart from the PART-FOR-WHOLE metonymies illustrated above, where the parts were elements of the domains constituting the domain matrix of the representation of LOVE, the language of LOVE offers two more possibilities. First of all, the predication of LOVE may be accessed through its participants, for example *She's my baby* or *She's my girl* may be tantamount to saying *I love her*, and *Jesus is my Lord* in the mouth of a devout Christian implicates 'I love Jesus'. It will be noticed that in such cases the metonymy is sentential rather than merely predicative, since it affects the structure of the whole sentence.

The second option resulting from the complex conceptual structure of LOVE is the metonymy WHOLE FOR PART, that is the predicate *love* can be used for specific conceptual components of the whole representation. Thus, *I love you* may mean radically different things depending on the speakers and their targets. For instance, a passionate lover may communicate in this way his SEXUAL DESIRE without declaring his DEVOTION, RESPONSIBILITY and other parts of the full representation of LOVE, while an aunt may say it to her baby nephew meaning that she enjoys the INTIMATE CLOSENESS of the baby, without implying that she is ready to CARE for the child (e.g. change his nappies). Within the same high-level WHOLE-FOR-PART mapping we can also distinguish a special case of referential metonymy whereby the whole is used for one of its participants, as the expression *love* in (32):

(32)   My love says she will never leave me.

4.2.4 POTENTIALITY FOR ACTUALITY

Panther and Thornburg (1999) argue that English speakers make extensive use of the metonymy POTENTIALITY FOR ACTUALITY. They claim also that this metonymy determines the meaning of a number of constructions in other languages as well. In particular, they show that the metonymy is operative in Hungarian, although its currency is more limited. Below, we briefly present Panther and Thornburg's findings about English and compare them with the data from Polish. It will be noticed that in terms of the State-of-Affairs Scenario, the metonymy activates the CORE component of the scenario through one of its NECESSARY PRECONDITIONS.

4.2.4.1 ABILITY TO PERCEIVE FOR ACTUAL PERCEPTION

Regardless of perceptual modality, the ability to perceive is a necessary condition for the actual perception. This link is systematically exploited in English, in which the modal verb *can* is conventionally used in utterances about actual perceptions. Consider the following:

(33)   Can you see him?
(34)   Can you see well?
(35)   I can't see the screen while you have that hat on.
(36)   The whole town can be seen from the window.
(37)   I could hear his sneering laughter as her arms carried me off through the fire of oblivion.
(38)   I'm on a lucky streak tonight, I can feel it.
(39)   I can taste the vanilla.
(40)   I can smell the garlic.

The above examples show that the metonymy ABILITY TO PERCEIVE FOR ACTUAL PERCEPTION is fully grammaticalised in English, in the form of the [*can – VERB OF PERCEPTION*] construction. However, this metonymy seems to be rare in other languages, e.g. as Panther and Thornburg (1999) demonstrated, it is not used in Hungarian. Polish sentences (41)–(48) below, which are the closest literal equivalents of (33)–(37), show that in Polish the metonymy is blocked as well. There are two basic ability verbs in Polish – *umieć* and *potrafić* – and a verb of permission *móc*, but none of them collocates with verbs of perception in the sense of actual perception. The only conventionalised way of denoting the actual perception is the regular tense, as in examples (49) and (50), which could be extended to other examples as well:

(41)   *Umiesz/potrafisz/możesz go widzieć?

(42)   *Umiesz/potrafisz/możesz widzieć dobrze?

(43)   *Ja nie umiem/potrafię/mogę widzieć ekranu, kiedy Pani ma na głowie ten kapelusz.

(44)   Całe miasto można widzieć z tego okna.

(45)   *Umiałem/potrafiłem/mogłem słyszeć jego szydzący śmiech, kiedy jej ramiona wynosiły mnie przez ogień zapomnienia.

(46)   Mam dziś wieczorem szczęście. *Umiem /potrafię/mogę to czuć?

(47)   *Umiem/potrafię/mogę czuć smak wanilii.

(48)   *Umiem/potrafię/mogę czuć zapach czosnku.

(49)   Widzisz go?

(50)   Widzisz dobrze?

As in Hungarian, sentence (44) is acceptable but it is not metonymic as it does not have the target meaning of actual seeing. It can only be construed as an expression of possibility or ability. The acceptability of sentences (47) and (48) could be enhanced if the prefix *wy-* was attached to the verb *czuć* ('feel'), i.e. if the verb was *wyczuć*. Nevertheless, then they too could only be construed 'literally' as denoting ability.

4.2.4.2 ABILITY TO PROCESS FOR ACTUAL MENTAL PROCESS

The POTENTIALITY FOR ACTUALITY metonymy is fully exploited in English in the domain of mental processes and states. Panther and Thornburg (1999) support this claim with the following examples:

(51)   I can't let her down just like that, yet one day it will have to come. I can see that now.

(52)   I can remember when we got our first TV.

(53)   Mary can't believe that Steve is guilty, but I can.

(54)   I can imagine how it happened.

In Hungarian, the metonymy is occasionally used, as in the translation of (54) and the negative (53). Likewise, in Polish, the sentences equivalent to (53) and (54) are on the whole acceptable. The Polish equivalent of sentence (51) is (55) below, and it is felicitous on condition that the verb *see* is translated as *rozumieć*, which is the closest equivalent of the English verb *understand* and is thus conceptually synonymous with *see* in this context. Nevertheless, an ordinary tensed version of the sentence sounds much more natural (cf. 56). The only sentence that cannot be translated as a Polish sentence with the verb of ability is (52); consequently, sentence (57) is distinctly odd.

> (55) Nie mogę jej tak zostawić, lecz kiedyś to będzie musiało nastąpić. Teraz umiem/potrafię/mogę to zrozumieć.
>
> (56) Nie mogę jej tak zostawić, lecz kiedyś to będzie musiało nastąpić. Teraz to rozumiem.
>
> (57) *Umiem/potrafię/mogę pamiętać, kiedy dostaliśmy nasz pierwszy telewizor.
>
> (58) Marysia nie umie/potrafi/może uwierzyć, że Steve jest winny, ale ja umiem/potrafię/mogę.
>
> (59) Umiem/potrafię/mogę sobie wyobrazić, jak to się zdarzyło.

These observations suggest that in general the metonymy ABILITY TO PROCESS FOR ACTUAL MENTAL PROCESS is used both in English and in Polish, but the constructions in the two languages differ in the degree of entrenchment as well as in the selection (or subcategory) of verbs which can fill in the main verb slot of the construction.

4.2.4.3 POTENTIALITY FOR ACTUALITY *in speech-act metonymies*

As Panther and Thornburg (1999) observe, POTENTIALITY FOR ACTUALITY metonymy is also common in direct speech acts, whereby the explicit performative verb is hedged with *can*. This observation is true of those speech acts which are positive or at least non-face-threatening, such as testifying, recommendation or promise, in these sentences:

> (60) I can testify that, seen from the surrounding heights, it is a fairyland of lights.
>
> (61) I can recommend this type of cage, as it is impossible for the birds to throw out seed husks.
>
> (62) I can give you my word that he is not at home.
>
> (63) I can promise you I'll be at home.

With more face-threatening acts, such as requests or impositions of obligations, other modal verbs are used, e.g. the verb *must*, based on a more general metonymic principle OBLIGATION FOR ACTUALITY, as in sentence (64):

(64)   I must ask you to leave.

Notice that the request is infelicitous with the modality of ability:

(65)   ?? I can ask you to leave.

The data adduced by Panther and Thornburg show that this metonymy is also freely exploited in Hungarian, although they do not give any Hungarian data that would be equivalent to (64).

The Polish translations of Panther and Thornburg's sentences (60)–(63), discussed above, indicate that the metonymy may be quite universal:

(66)   Mogę zaświadczyć, że, kiedy widzi się go z otaczających wzgórz, jest to bajeczna kraina świateł.
(67)   Mogę polecić ten typ klatki, bo uniemożliwia on ptakom wyrzucanie na zewnątrz łusek ziaren.
(68)   Mogę ci dać słowo, że nie ma go w domu.
(69)   Mogę ci obiecać, że będę w domu.

In general, Polish also follows the tendency to adjust the modality to the degree to which the act may be conceived as face-threatening. Thus, the Polish equivalents of (64) and (65) seem to exhibit a similar degree of acceptability:

(70)   Muszę cię poprosić, żebyś wyszedł.
(71)   ?? Mogę cię poprosić, żebyś wyszedł.[5]

In addition to direct speech acts conveyed metonymically, Panther and Thornburg (1999) propose also a metonymic account of three kinds of indirect speech acts: commissives, directives and imprecations. The sentences (72)–(77) serve as illustrations:

Commissives
(72)   John, I can make breakfast while you get dressed.
(73)   When you come to Budapest, I can be your translator.

Directives
(74)   Can you pass the salt?
(75)   Mary, you can peel the potatoes; John, you can set the table.

Imprecations
(76)   You can go to hell!
(77)   You can take this job and shove it!

The particular examples of POTENTIALITY FOR ACTUALITY metonymy in the domain of linguistic actions are also confirmed by the data from Hungarian and they seem to operate in Polish as well. Consequently, all the sentences from (72) to (77) sound quite natural when translated into Polish. The verb denoting potentiality is again the modal verb *móc*:

Commissives
  (78)   Janek, ja mogę zrobić śniadanie, a ty w tym czasie się ubierz.
  (79)   Kiedy przyjedziesz do Budapesztu, ja mogę być twoim tłumaczem.

Directives
  (80)   Możesz mi podać sól?
  (81)   Marysiu, ty możesz obrać ziemniaki, Janek, ty możesz nakryć do stołu.

Imprecations
  (82)   Możesz iść do diabła!
  (83)   Możesz sobie tę pracę wziąć i wsadzić!

4.2.4.4 ABILITY TO ACT FOR ACTUAL ACTION

As an essential condition for any action and thus an important constituent of the State-of-Affairs Scenario, the ability to perform an act is often used to access the corresponding activity itself. This metonymy in English is illustrated by sentences (84) and (85):

  (84)   John was able to finish his paper before the deadline.
  (85)   I can come to your party on Friday.

Panther and Thornburg (1999) are quite right to point out that the factual implication of (84) is stronger than that of (85). Perhaps the reason is that the modal expression *be able* in (84) is more 'rigid' in its designation of ability, while *can* in (85) is vague and can be interpreted as either ability or permission or even possibility. Since permission does not imply ability, nor does ability imply permission, although they both imply possibility, the factual implication is more diffuse.

In Polish, the ability verbs *umieć* and *potrafić* can only be used in the translation of (84), as in (86) below. Sentence (85) can only be translated by means of the verb *móc*, which exhibits a comparable semantic vagueness to English *can*, hence the factual implication of (87=85) is rather weak:

  (86)   Janek umiał/potrafił skończyć artykuł przed ostatecznym terminem.
  (87)   Mogę przyjść na twoją imprezę w piątek.

Hungarian translations of (84) and (85) display similar properties to their English equivalents.

4.2.4.5 DISPOSITION FOR ACTUALITY

Although dispositions are not necessary components of the State-of-Affairs Scenario, when they do occur, they strongly imply that the actual states of affairs do occur as well. No wonder we find them in English, Hungarian and in Polish. What is intriguing about the choice of the modal verb in Polish is that often the most natural verb in such utterances is the verb of ability *potrafić* ('to be able to').[6] This suggests a metonymic chain ABILITY FOR DISPOSITION FOR ACTUALITY in Polish. It will be noticed that I have changed Panther and Thornburg (1999)'s original formulation of the metonymy from DISPOSITION FOR OCCASIONAL BEHAVIOUR to DISPOSITION FOR OCCASIONAL ACTUALITY, because the metonymy applies not only to behaviours but also to processes and states, as in (90). Examples (88) and (89) are Panther and Thornburg's:

> (88)   Dogs can be very dangerous.
> (89)   He can be very unfriendly.
> (90)   It can be quite warm in England.

The Polish translations are not always equally felicitous. Consider the following:

> (91)   Psy mogą/potrafią/??umieją być bardzo niebezpieczne.
> (92)   On ?może/potrafi/??umie być bardzo nieprzyjemny.
> (93)   W Anglii ?może/potrafi/ *umie być bardzo ciepło.

The question marks before the verb *móc* in (92) and (93) apply to the sense of 'occasional actuality'. The preferred reading of 'future possibility' is perfectly natural and acceptable.

4.2.5 Propositional metonymy in cross-linguistic perspective

The studies and the Polish data discussed in this chapter show that, although there are a few cross-linguistic differences in the ways various kinds of metonymy are used in different languages, in general similarities prevail. One interesting difference is that stand-alone conditionals with directive force are systematically exploited in English and German, as well as in Polish, but not in Hungarian and Croation. There are some interesting hints at the plausible explanations suggested by Brdar-Szabó (2007), but on the whole it seems that it is still too early for any convincing generalisation. As for the POTENTIALITY FOR ACTUALITY metonymy the problem seems to be easier. It seems that what calls for explanation is not why Hungarian and Polish have not developed the ABILITY TO PERCEIVE FOR ACTUAL PERCEPTION metonymy, but rather: how come English has developed it? A possible solution is that English exhibits a systematic progressive/non-progressive contrast for the dynamic verbs, and since the verbs of perception are not prototypical dynamic verbs and yet there was a need for denoting perception in progress, the actual perception *can*-construction based on the ABILITY TO PERCEIVE FOR ACTUAL PERCEPTION metonymy has gradually developed to fill in this niche in English grammar. In the grammars of other languages, which do not exhibit the systematic progressive/non-progressive contrast, there was no such niche and hence the metonymy was not grammaticalised. Needless to say, the above hypothesis needs to be tested against other languages with an aspectual system comparable to English, but I believe that it has some initial plausibility (see Taylor 2004 for a similar view of the motivation for such constructions).

As for the other metonymies discussed in this chapter, a number of mappings can well be quite universal, owing to universally strong associations between certain components of the State-of-Affairs Scenario, for example travelling metonymies, places for activities and metonymies of emotions. It would be interesting to see if there are languages that do not make use of these high-level mappings. As we have seen, they are probably equally operative and common in typologically very different languages, such as English and Polish.

4.3 Illocutionary metonymies

As we already pointed out in Chapter 1, illocutionary metonymies are typical of 'indirect speech acts' (i.e. the cases where one 'explicit' direct speech act stands for another speech act), for example the uttering of a sentence which has the direct illocutionary force of an assertion may be used with the illocutionary force of an inquiry or warning. The most often studied kind of indirect speech act in English is probably the act of requesting and this is where we start.

4.3.1 QUESTIONS AND CONDITIONS FOR REQUESTING

According to Panther and Thornburg (2003b: 130), the indirect metonymic ways of expressing requests in English are all based on the REQUEST SCENARIO shown in Figure 4.3.[7]

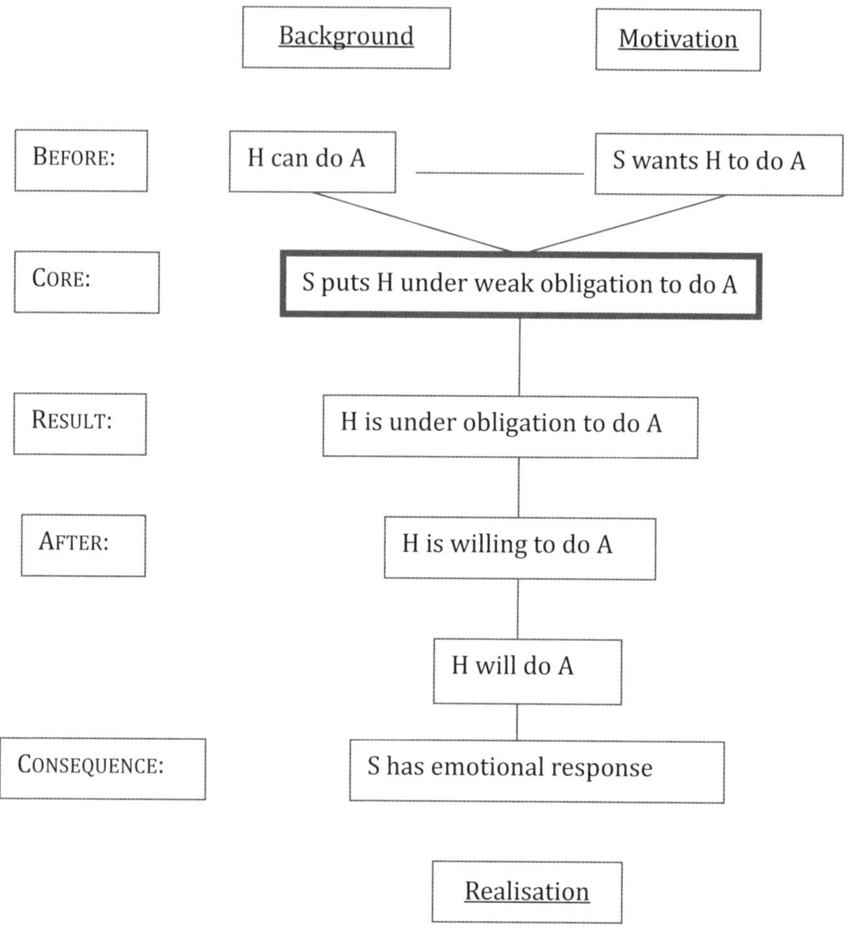

Figure 4.3 REQUEST SCENARIO according to Panther and Thornburg (2003b: 130).

Since the above scenario serves Panther and Thornburg as the basis of their analysis of a number of ways of making requests in English, it is important to consider it in detail. First of all, clearly the scenario is divided into three stages: the stage BEFORE the act, consisting jointly of the conditions for the performance of a request, the CORE, that is the central act of requesting, and the consequences of the act, again divided into the RESULT, AFTER and CONSEQUENCE. As it stands, the model is appealing and it successfully accounts for a number of indirect requests discussed by Panther and Thornburg in their paper. There are, however, a few modifications of the scenario that I wish to suggest.

The first modification concerns the background assumption *H can do A*. In my view, the assumption is too objectivistic and fails to explain why even a friendly H sometimes refuses to carry out the request. The reason is that it is S who makes this assumption and she may be wrong. Therefore I suggest the Background assumption should be formulated as *S thinks that H can do A*, which, incidentally, explains why requests often take the indirect form of questions about H's ability: S does not presuppose the ability but tries to make sure that her assumption is justified, hence the very common *Can you ...* requests. The second modification concerns the desirability of A, which I believe should be included in the motivation part of the scenario. Barring the situations when S conveys other people's orders, the common-sense argument in favour of this proposal is that we tell people to perform those activities which we consider good, worthwhile and desirable. Hence a rather contradictory:

> (94)   ?Take out the trash, please, but I don't think it's good to take out the trash.

A less common-sense and more empirical argument in favour of including the axiological component in the scenario is that explicating this component alone may have the illocutionary force of a directive. Consider a wife saying (95) to her husband:

> (95)   Isn't it good to take out the trash every now and then?[8]

Obviously, most husbands who still bother to infer the intended implicatures of their wives would take (95) as a request to take out the trash, which indicates strongly that the axiological part is an essential part of the Request Scenario which may also activate its other, more central parts or the whole. We may note in passing that Sokołowska (2001) in her analysis of the conditions that must be fulfilled for the act of invitation to be felicitous also included the condition that the Inviter should consider an activity A as desirable for the Hearer. She pointed out that the whole invitation scenario can be accessed by mentioning this condition. For instance, utterance (96) may be taken as an act of invitation, although, admittedly, it might be necessary to distinguish more precisely between the acts of invitation and that of suggestion and advice.[9]

> (96)   A cup of hot tea will do you good.

In addition, it is perhaps worth mentioning that advertising, which in its verbal part may be taken as a directive, also often achieves its success (i.e. makes viewers buy the advertised merchandise) by simply presenting its virtues and merits.

The third and last modification of Panther and Thornburg's proposal I wish to suggest has to do with the general structure of the scenarios of speech acts, which, I believe, can and should be reconciled with the traditional structure of speech acts. Bearing in mind that speech acts, in addition to various preconditions and motivations, have illocutionary and perlocutionary forces or effects as well, it seems advisable to distinguish these two parts in the scenarios, because after all it is the illocutionary part that constitutes the CORE of the scenario and the target meaning of various indirect speech acts. Accordingly, it may be suggested that in the Request Scenario the components BEFORE specify the preconditions of Request, the CORE specifies the central illocutionary force of the act, while all the components below it are elements of the perlocutionary effects of requests. This of course enables us to distinguish

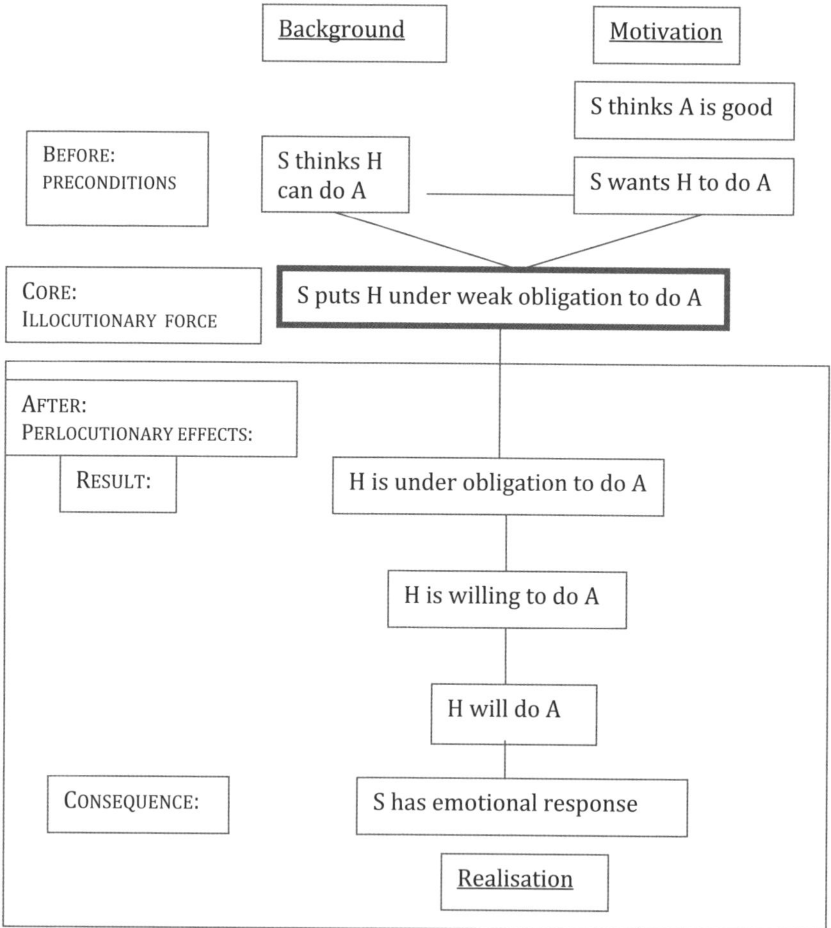

Figure 4.4 A revised REQUEST SCENARIO in terms of preconditions, illocutionary and perlocutionary components.

two high-level categories of illocutionary metonymies, such as PRECONDITION FOR ILLOCUTIONARY FORCE and PERLOCUTIONARY EFFECT FOR ILLOCUTIONARY FORCE.

In their analysis Panther and Thornburg assume that independent *if*-clauses are based on a conceptual space which consists of two components: 1) what is explicitly expressed – typically a hypothetical or possible situation or state *p* and 2) another statement *q*, which is implicated or metonymically activated and which denotes the consequence of *p*, the assessment of truth of *p*, an evaluation of the desirability of *p* or an emotional attitude to *p*. Thus in their view, there are in fact two components of the scenario that are metonymically accessed: what they call 'implicit part' and what is somehow implicated by the explicit + implicit combination. The problem with this proposal is that we have no way of knowing where the implicit part comes from. Now in the theory of independent subordinate clauses advanced here the solution lies in the integration of formal and conceptual metonymies. Thus, if the account I proposed in Chapter 2 is accepted, the implicit part is accessed through formal metonymy activating the whole of the conditional construction in the conditional space, while the core of the request is activated by blending the conditional space with the space of the Request Scenario. To take Panther and Thornburg's example (1), in the request reproduced here as (97), the suggested continuation *then I will begin the lecture* (2003b: 131) is clearly based on the second conditional construction, although it is only one specific consequent which realises the schematic representation of the consequent in the construction suggested in (98), which in request conditionals is also evaluated as good.

(97)   If you will come to order …
(98)   If you will come to order then [good event *q* happens]

In the blend the protasis of the conditional is connected with act A of the Request Scenario (i.e. both its components 'conspire' to activate the CORE part of the Request Scenario, whereby *S puts H under a weak obligation to do A*). The difference between ordinary *will*-requests (see below) and the *if*-conditional requests is that while the former focus on the act itself, the latter reinforce the motivation for A by activating the desirable consequence of A through formal metonymy, which also activates the schematic apodosis of the conditional construction.

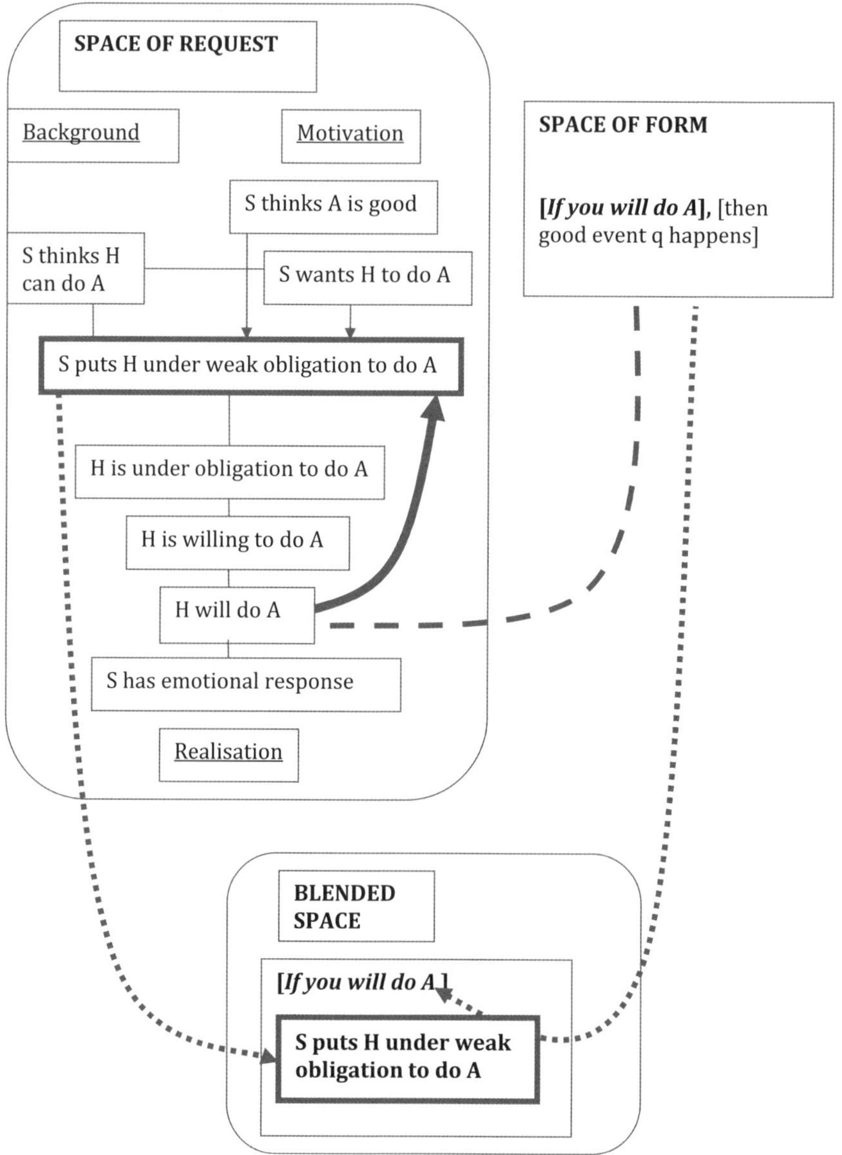

Figure 4.5 English *If you will do A* requests as blends integrating conceptual metonymy within Request Scenario and formal metonymy based on the future conditional construction.

4.3.2 Conditions for expressions of regret

Given the analysis of the formal metonymy involved in the past *if-only* construction suggested in Chapter 2, the illocutionary force of the construction can also be accounted for in terms of the conceptual integration of the EXPRESSION OF REGRET scenario, *if-only* Reasoning Scenario and the metonymically accessed full counterfactual past conditional construction. The approximate Conceptual Integrated Network representing the past *if-only* construction and its conventional illocutionary force is shown in Figure 4.6. The symbols *p(E)*, *q(E)* and *w(E)* stand for propositions designating events.

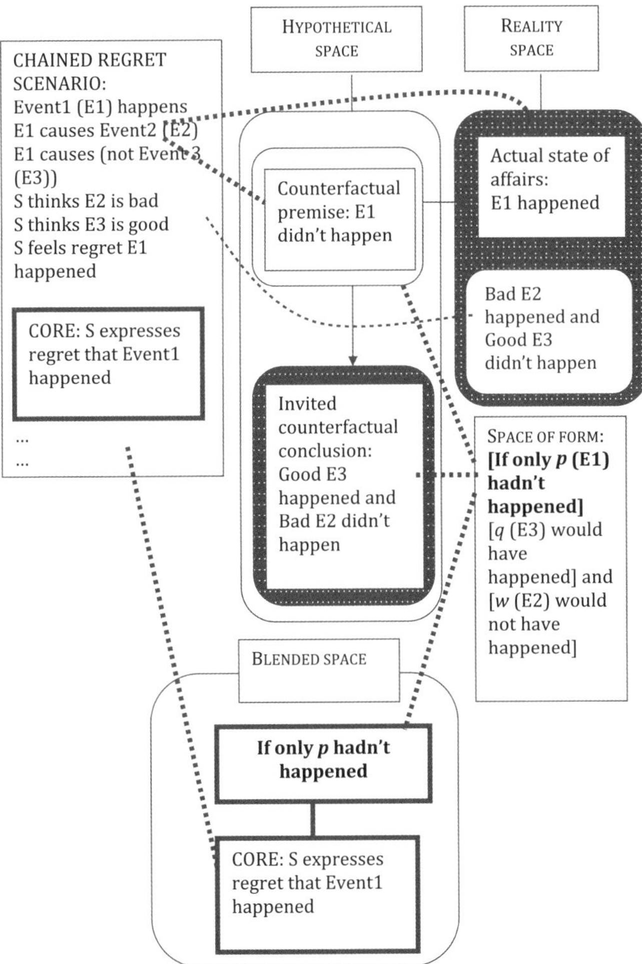

Figure 4.6 Conceptual Integration Network representing the stand-alone past *if-only* construction with the conventional illocutionary force of expression of regret.

The Chained Regret Scenario in Figure 4.6 should be considered as an extended form of the ordinary Regret Scenario, whereby there is only a single event causing the feeling of regret in S, who subsequently expresses this emotion. There are a number of constructions employing the Chained Regret Scenario, for example the constructions represented by these two sentences:

(99)   Isn't it a shame Pete didn't bring his sister to the party?
(100) I wish Pete had brought his sister to the party.

In the Chained Regret Scenario, the actual event causing regret is often not mentioned at all. Rather, S focuses on the first event (E1) which in the end led to some unfortunate result (E2), or, at least prevented some good result (E3). Thus both (99) and (100) could be continued, as in (101) and (102) below, by explicating the actual cause of regret. Consequently the first event is judged as regrettable on account of its causative role in a series of events which have led to some undesirable end:

(101) Isn't it a shame Pete didn't bring his sister to the party? There was
       nobody I could dance with.
(102) I wish Pete had brought his sister to the party. I spent the whole night
       alone.

A similar chaining of causes may be conveyed by means of the [X *should (not) have* PAST PARTICIPLE] construction, as illustrated by sentence (103):

(103) We shouldn't have bought that house. The mortgage is so high we
       cannot even afford to go on holiday.

The same considerations apply to other parts of Panther and Thornburg's analysis, such as example (104), (P & T's (13)), which has the illocutionary force of suggestion. According to Panther and Thornburg, the implicit consequent *q* may be 'then I will reveal to you my interesting discovery'. Again, it seems that this kind of *q* is not inferable but should be regarded as a formally ellipsed part of the conditional construction in which the consequent designates a situation which is beneficial to both S and H (rather than H alone as suggested by Panther and Thornburg, although in (104) indeed it is H that is the main beneficiary of A).[10]

(104) I have made a discovery, sir. It may be of no account, but I think you
       will find it interesting. If we could go up to your room, sir …

4.3.3 OBLIGATION FOR FUTURITY

As demonstrated by Hernández (2007), a number of European languages have developed future senses of deontic modal verbs. This semantic shift is based on the high-level metonymy OBLIGATION FOR FUTURITY. In English the modal verb most often used in this sense is *should*, as in (105) and (106) – (Hernández' (2a) and (3a) respectively):

(105) Don't worry, I should think about it.
(106) Should he accept the deal, everything will turn out fine.

Hernández argues that the choice of *should*, rather than *must*, is not random "since the future is not fully known and it is always no more than a reasonable assumption that a future event will take place" (2007: 138).

It seems necessary to make two comments about the above analysis. First, the strong obligation designated by *must* in English is not entirely excluded from future meanings, although, in accordance with Hernández' explanation, it can only be used in this basically epistemic future sense when the future is a matter of careful and fixed calculations, as in (107):

(107) If he sets off at 10am, driving at an average speed of 90kph, he must arrive in Warsaw by 4pm.

On the other hand, as is well known, the epistemic *may* is also sometimes used with future reference, when the future event is likely though rather uncertain, as in (108):

(108) If he sets off at 10am, he may even arrive in Warsaw by 4pm.

Secondly, the analysis of sentence (106) may be challenged on the grounds that *should* is a fixed substantive component of this particular conditional construction, since grammatically the condition is normally expressed by the present tense. However, this putative counterargument completely loses its force if we observe that in such conditionals, *should* can also be used in the apodosis, as in (109), which is a modally modulated version of (106):

(109) If he accepts the deal, everything should turn out fine.

In Polish the deontic modal verb most often used in the future sense is, predictably, the closest equivalent of English *should* (i.e. *powinien*), although the equivalents of *may* – *móc*, and *must* - *musieć* are also possible:

(110) Ewa powinna tu być o piątej.
       [Eve should be here at five.]
(111) Jeśli wyruszy o 10.00 rano, to jadąc ze średnią prędkością 90 km/godz, musi dojechać do Warszawy przed czwartą. [= 107]
(112) Jeśli wyruszy o 10.00 rano, to może nawet dojechać do Warszawy przed czwartą. [= 108]

Hernández points out that in languages which do not have two verbs exhibiting varying forces of obligation, represented by *should* – *must* in

English and *powinien – musieć* in Polish, but only one, it is this verb that is used in the future sense. This is the situation in Italian, with *dovere* as the only verb of obligation, and French with *devoir*, which some researchers consider to be a marker of scheduled future (cf. Fleischman 1982, quoted by Hernández 2007: 140), not unlike English *must* and Polish *musieć*. The latter observations have prompted Hernández to call this kind of metonymy OBLIGATION FOR FACTUAL FUTURITY. It seems, however, that futurity is non-factual by definition (as Hernández herself admits); therefore, I suggest that this kind of mapping should rather be labelled OBLIGATION FOR SCHEDULED FUTURITY.

Apart from the synchronic data, the productivity of the OBLIGATION FOR FUTURITY metonymy is further corroborated by the semantic development of *shall* in English. As is well known, the Modern English *shall* comes from the Old English verb *sheall*, whose basic meaning was that of obligation (still preserved in its past-tense form *should*) (cf. Lass 1994). It is this meaning that still prevailed in the semantics of *shall* in the seventeenth century, when in the King James translation of the Bible the Ten Commandments were rendered as: *Thou shalt have no other gods before Me, Thou shalt not take the name of the Lord thy God in vain,* etc. In time, however, the deontic meaning almost completely gave way to the futurity sense it still has in a number of English dialects today. Thus, the case of *shall* demonstrates that the metonymy OBLIGATION FOR FUTURITY works on the lexical semantic level as well.

4.3.4 FUTURITY FOR OBLIGATION

As we have seen, the association of futurity and obligation makes it possible to access futurity through obligation. However, this associative link also makes it possible for the activation to go from futurity to obligation. Hernández (2007) shows that the metonymy FUTURITY FOR OBLIGATION operates in Italian and English. The relevant examples are respectively the following:

> (113) D'ora innanzi, i transgressori pagheranno il doppio della penale fissata in precendenza.
> [From now on, transgressors will pay twice the previous fine.]
> (114) I will take out the garbage.

As for the English examples, Hernández makes an interesting claim that the deontic meaning of sentences with future reference depends on whether or not the denoted act is beneficial to the speaker; in particular, the more 'costly' the future event is to the speaker, the more likely it is that the sentence will convey the sense of obligation. This is the case in (114), since the act of taking out the garbage is unpleasant and no one performs it unless one has to.

The analysis proposed by Hernández is fully corroborated by the data from Polish. For instance, sentence (113) is best translated into Polish by means of a futurity construction [future BE + infinitive], which has a strong deontic meaning, as in (115), which is virtually synonymous with (116), in which the obligation is expressed explicitly by the verb of obligation *musieć*:

(115) Od teraz, łamiący przepisy będą płacili dwukrotnie wyższe grzywny.
       [= 113]
(116) Od teraz, łamiący prawo będą musieli płacić dwukrotnie wyższe grzywny.
       [From now on, transgressors will have to pay twice the previous fine.]

There is one aspect of the FUTURITY FOR OBLIGATION that Hernández has not mentioned in her study, namely that questions and statements about the future are in many languages used as directives (i.e. speech acts where the speaker imposes an obligation on the addressee). Typically, the questioning intonation is used for tentative requests, while the flat statement has the illocutionary force close to an order. Consider the following pair of sentences:

(117) Wyniesiesz śmieci?
       [Will you take out the garbage?]
(118) Jutro wyniesiesz śmieci i odkurzysz klatkę schodową. Potem możesz iść na imprezę.
       [Tomorrow you will take out the garbage and vacuum the staircase. Then you can go to the party.]

The intuition that (117) is not a genuine question is confirmed by the fact that these interrogative sentences used as directives are usually impossible with the Yes-No question morpheme *czy* (as in 117a), although it is possible with a related expressive construction illustrated by (119):

(117a) ?? Czy wyniesiesz śmieci?
       [(Whether) will you take out the garbage]
(119) Czy ty mi dasz wreszcie spokój!
       [(Whether) will you leave me alone!]

4.3.5 Assertions for other speech acts

Prototypically, assertions should be used as representatives denoting states of affairs committing the speaker to the truth of the expressed proposition. As we have seen, however, assertions can serve other functions as well; for example in (115) and (118), a simple assertion of futurity may have the force of a directive. Thus it seems that it is the meaning of the assertion and its relation to the context, including the speaker's intention, that actually determines the illocutionary force of the assertion. Again, the resultant force depends on the metonymic mapping within various parts of the scenario typical of the given speech act. What follows is by no means an exhaustive list of all the possibilities; rather, it should be taken as an illustration of the general tendency.

4.3.5.1 ASSERTION OF NORM FOR OBLIGATION OR PROHIBITION

In Polish, impersonal *się*-sentences (cf. Kubiński 1982), which often denote generic statements, as in (120)–(121), are often used to express the directive force of obligation or prohibition. Thus, sentences (122)–(124), could easily be used as directives.

> (120) W Polsce pracę zaczyna się najczęściej o 8 rano.
> [In Poland (one) begins work usually at 8 am] >> You should begin work at 8 am.
> (121) W zimie jeździ się na nartach, a w lecie na rowerze.
> [In winter (one) rides on skis, in summer on a bike] >> You should ride on skis in winter and on a bike in summer.
> (122) Je się nożem i widelcem.
> [(One) eats with a knife and fork] >> You should eat with a knife and fork.
> (123) Starszym ustępuje się miejsca.
> [(One) gives up one's seat to the elderly] >> Give up your seat to the elderly.
> (124) Tak się nie je.
> [(One) does not eat thus] >> You should not eat in this way.
> (125) Tak się nie robi >> Tak nie powinnaś robić.
> [(One) does not do (it) thus] >> You shouldn't act in this way.

The deontic implicature of sentences (122) and (123) in Polish probably stems from the axiological model whereby social norms are good and compliance with social norms is viewed as a virtue. Therefore, as I already pointed out, the statement of the norm corresponds to the BEFORE-condition S THINKS A IS GOOD of the Request Scenario in Figure 4.4. The crucial difference between the Request Scenario and Obligation Scenario evoked by sentences (122) and (123) is that in the latter the CORE is S PUTS H UNDER STRONG OBLIGATION TO DO A. By the same token, the negative assertions, as in (124)–(125), denoting the breach of social norm, have the directive force of prohibition.

4.3.5.2 ASSERTION OF SKILL/PERMISSION/POSSIBILITY FOR EXPRESSION OF ADMIRATION, CONTEMPT ETC.

Apart from the high-level POTENTIALITY FOR ACTUALITY metonymy used in propositional script-based metonymies, assertion of potentiality may also serve additional illocutionary purposes.

(a) ***Directives*** (as an alternative to QUESTIONING FOR REQUESTING)
You could pick that up.
(b) ***Commissives***
I can give you a lift.
(c) ***Expressives***

In general, any assertion of an object or person having properties above or below the norm has a strong evaluative and hence expressive meaning. Thus in a country where a normal car needs about 10 seconds to accelerate to 100 kph, (126) may be taken as an expression of admiration. If, on the other hand, a car is slower than the norm, the statement of its poor acceleration (127) may have the force of an expression of contempt:

(126) The car can accelerate to 100 kph in just 6 seconds.
(127) The car accelerates to 100 kph in 14 seconds.

As we have already seen (in §4.2.4.3), the expressive potential of statements of potentialities is also used in fixed, often rude imprecations, e.g. *You can shove it*. The same transfer is common in Polish, e.g. in expressions *Możesz mnie pocałować w tyłek/dupę* ['you can kiss my ass'], *Możesz to sobie wziąć i wsadzić* ['you can take (it) and shove it']. At the same time, however, the transfer is also common in conventionalised expressions of compliments and admiration, e.g. *z nią można konie kraść* ['one can steal horses with her' = she is good for anything], or the English *Nobody can hold a candle to her*.

4.3.6 Shopping through metonymy

A rather interesting case of various illocutionary metonymies employed with different frequencies by speakers of different languages has been noticed in commercial interactions. In their study of shopping requests Radden and Seto (2003) have pointed out that various languages make use of different metonymic patterns, depending on their more general typological characteristics, such as the fact that they are classified as *have-* or *be-* languages.

The main difference between those two groups of languages lies in the way they conceptualise POSSESSION. *Have*-languages typically express POSSESSION by means of a verb of possession followed by a direct object denoting the object possessed, as the English verbs *have, own*, and *possess*, illustrated by (130) below. Other *have*-languages mentioned by Radden and Seto are German, Lithuanian and Croatian. To this list could be added most Italic languages. In contrast, *be*-languages express possession by means of the verb of existence followed by a prepositional phrase denoting location, as illustrated in the example (131) below. The best-known *be*-languages are Japanese, Chinese, Korean, Finnish, Hungarian and Russian.

> (130) John has two children.
> (131) John ni wa kodomo ga futari iru.
>   [Lit.: John at/to topic child subj two be]

Radden and Seto also count Polish among *be*-languages, which is clearly inaccurate, since the Polish possessive sentences follow the *have*-pattern, as shown here:

> (132) Janek ma dwoje dzieci.
>   [Lit.: John has two children]

In addition, absence in location is also expressed in Polish by the verb of possession *mieć*.

> (133) Janka nie ma w domu.
>   [Lit.: John not has at home = John is not at home]

With two different conceptualisations of possession, different languages convey their shopping requests differently, although they all use the same shopping script presented below, which Radden and Seto have dubbed 'Basic Shopping Scenario' (BSS). The difference lies in the way the whole scenario is evoked metonymically by its different parts.

Basic shopping scenario

   i.   **pre-condition** – the article is available.
   ii. **transaction** –
      (a) <u>Transfer</u>: the salesperson transfers the article to the customer.
      (b) <u>Reception</u>: the customer receives the article.
      (c) <u>Result</u>: the article passes into the customer's possession.

Without going into detail, let us consider how various stages of BSS may give rise to metonymic coding. In the English sentence (134) below the availability expressed by the verb of possession activates the whole event. In contrast, in the Polish sentence (135) this stage is expressed by means of an existential construction:

> (134) Do you have 40-watt light bulbs?
> (135) Czy są żarówki czterdziestowatowe?
>   [Are there 40-watt light bulbs?]

Radden and Seto's analysis is certainly illuminating, but it seems that their account falls short of presenting the whole range of metonymic possibilities on account of a rather restricted version of the shopping scenario they based their analysis on. In particular, what they overlooked is the customer's intentions and activities, which may also produce metonymic expressions standing for shopping requests. The three elements of BSS ignored in Radden and Seto's account are the CUSTOMER'S VOLITION/NEED, her SEARCH FOR THE DESIRED PRODUCT and THE REQUEST TO SEE AND INSPECT THE PRODUCT before the decision to purchase it. The first two elements belong to the PRECONDITION stage, while the REQUEST TO SEE THE PRODUCT and the inspection belong to the TRANSACTION proper. It seems that it is the first two of these elements of the scenario that are particularly common in Polish shopping requests but they are no doubt perfectly felicitous in English too, as in these sentences:

(136) Potrzebuję dobre buty do chodzenia po górach.
[I need a pair of good climbing boots.]
(137) Szukam pary dobrych butów do chodzenia po górach.
[I'm looking for a pair of good climbing boots.]

Although Radden and Seto argue that various elements of the scenario, such as availability of the product, stand for the whole scenario, it seems equally likely that they may activate only some chosen parts of the scenario. Thus, sentences (134)–(135) may activate the REQUEST TO SEE AND INSPECT part of the scenario, while sentences (136)–(137) could easily implicate the question of availability of the boots and, through the chaining of metonymies, the REQUEST TO SEE AND INSPECT them.

It is enough to consider the possible responses to the above utterances to see that this is how they are actually construed. For instance, upon hearing (134) the shop assistant may felicitously respond saying (138), while an equally natural response to (136) and (137) may be (139) or (140):

(138) Tylko te drogie Philipsa, ale teraz wszystkie są w magazynie, więc nie mogę ich Panu pokazać.
[Only the expensive Philips ones, but they are all in the storeroom now so I can't show them to you.]
(139) W tej chwili nic nie mamy, bo czekamy na nową dostawę.
[We've got none at the moment but we're waiting for a new shipment.]
(140) (*presenting a pair of boots*) Czy o coś takiego Panu chodzi?
[Is this what you had in mind?]

Since the shopping scenario consists of activities as well as speech acts performed by its participants, which have different direct illocutionary forces, it comes as no surprise that at least some of the metonymies used in the shopping interactions will involve illocutionary transfers, whereby one kind of speech act related to some part of the scenario stands for another speech act representing another part of the scenario. The illocutionary metonymies of this kind illustrated by the speech exchanges discussed above are:

QUESTION ABOUT AVAILABILITY OF X FOR STATEMENT OF THE READINESS TO PURCHASE X

DECLARATION OF NEED TO POSSESS X FOR REQUEST TO SEE AND INSPECT X

STATEMENT OF SEARCH FOR X FOR REQUEST TO SEE AND INSPECT X.

It remains to be seen if culturally more distant languages make use of the same metonymic coding strategy, but the strategy is certainly common in Polish and in a number of other European languages.

4.4 Concluding remarks

In this chapter I have demonstrated that a wide range of linguistic facts traditionally associated with linguistic pragmatics and language in use can be successfully elucidated and explained in terms of metonymic mappings, acting on conceptual structures known as cognitive models (including frames and mental spaces) and scenarios. In particular, I have shown that it is possible to account for a number of propositional as well as illocutionary transfers of meaning in particular contexts in terms of the same basic cognitive metonymic mechanism. It follows from the analysis presented above that in the end it may well turn out that what is known as pragmatic inferencing is just a conceptual counterpart of a more basic process of co-activation of different parts of neural circuits which support integrated knowledge structures and it is these integrated knowledge structures that are used in various forms of metonymic meaning construction. This suggests that a great deal of seemingly complicated cases of inferencing may be in the end reduced to simple co-activation of associated elements, which is typical of other kinds of metonymy as well.

Notes

1 The question of the conceptual and metonymic basis of pragmatic inferences, both implicatures and explicatures, was discussed in detail by Ruiz de Mendoza and Pérez Hernández (2003) and Panther and Thornburg (2003b, 2007).

2 A different diagram showing this chain as well as other examples are discussed in Ruiz de Mendoza and Mairal Usón (2007) and Ruiz de Mendoza (2007), where it is suggested that there are four types of double metonymy types: a) double domain reduction, b) double domain expansion, c) domain reduction and domain expansion and d) domain expansion and domain reduction. I do not follow this

classification because I do not find it convincing. For instance, I do not see why *head* in *His sister heads the policy unit* should involve double domain expansion from HEAD to LEADER and then from LEADER to LEADING. I agree that the second step (i.e. from LEADER to LEADING) indeed involves expansion, but, in my view, the transfer from HEAD to LEADER is clearly metaphoric, based on the metaphor ORGANISATION/INSTITUTION IS BODY and thus involves a cross-domain mapping from the domain of HUMAN BODY to the domain of ORGANIZATION/INSTITUTION, and thus, by definition, has nothing to do with domain expansion (see Bierwiaczonek 2007d). In Goossens' (1990) terms, it could be considered a case of metonymy from metaphor.

3　It will be remembered that one of the synonyms of *lover* is *concubine*, which comes from Latin 'lie with' and thus is derived from a similar behavioural metonymy.

4　See Bierwiaczonek (2002b).

5　Sentence (71) would be perfectly acceptable with the rising questioning intonation but, in that case, *mogę* ('can') would be just a politeness marker.

6　A short Google search confirms my intuitions. Here are a few examples: *Publiczność potrafi być bezwzględna* (Audiences can be ruthless), *Zielonogórski urzędnik potrafi być grzeczny* (The civil servant from Zielona Góra can be polite), *Szczerość dziecka potrafi zabić* (A child's honesty can kill), *Barack Obama potrafi być bardzo brutalny* (BO can be very brutal).

7　All the models proposed could be probably expressed in terms of Ruiz de Mendoza's (2007) expanded version of the Cost-Benefit ICM. I will not pursue this possibility here but I hope to do so in a future work. Notice, however, that some of the suggestions made here are consonant with Ruiz de Mendoza's model (e.g. the importance of the states of affairs as being 'beneficial' or not is clearly reminiscent of my insistence that the models should contain an axiological component).

8　As moralists have repeatedly claimed, values have a compelling force: they compel responsible agents to fulfil them, for example a value judgment *It's good to feed the hungry* may be interpreted as implicating an obligation: *Feed the hungry* (see Bierwiaczonek 1990 for discussion). Thus, the implicature may be based on another high-level metonymy VALUE JUDGMENT FOR OBLIGATION.

9　Cf. Kalisz and Kubiński (1993) and Fabiszak (2001) for interesting demonstrations of the prototypical nature of speech acts.

10　Panther and Thornburg's analysis of the Suggestion Scenario raises other doubts as well. I do not see any reason why *H wants to do A* is the Motivation for suggestion. It seems more likely that the motivation for suggestion is axiological: under the circumstances, *S thinks it best for himself and H to do A*. Also, proto-typically, the suggestion affects both S and H, clearly signalled by the plural subject of suggestions, as in (104).

5 Metonymy in semantics

As already noted in Chapter 3, some examples of minor conversions may be regarded as side-effects of metonymic extensions of meaning, e.g. the lexeme *painting*, which grammatically belongs to the category of de-verbal nouns and which basically means 'an act of painting', has acquired a new metonymic sense, namely 'a painted picture', and thus has been converted from an uncountable to a countable nominal.

However, regardless of such category shifts, metonymy has long been recognised as one of the most powerful processes of lexical meaning extension.[1] Without going too deep into the past,[2] we may mention Waag (1901), discussed briefly in Peirsman and Gearerts 2006: 288), who recognised PART FOR WHOLE in the development of German:

(a) *Morgen*: 'morning'>> 'the whole next day'
(b) *Sonnabend* 'the evening before Sunday' >> 'the whole Saturday'

Similarly, the PART-FOR-WHOLE relationship motivates the polysemy of *day* and *night*, which, depending on the perspective, may both denote the 24-hour period. Thus, holidaymakers may talk about spending ten days in Paris, but the hoteliers will charge them for ten nights (cf. Taylor 1999: 30).

In English lexical semantics, Ullmann (1972: 1963f) discussed metonymy in the context of such words as *board*, which in one of its senses means 'table' but can also mean 'persons sitting around the council-table', *surgery*, which may denote 'the art of a surgeon' as well as 'the room where patients are seen and medicine is dispensed', and *youth*, whose original meaning in Old English was 'youngness, the fact, state or time of being young', extended metonymically to 'young persons collectively', but which later, in Middle English, developed the sense 'young man between boyhood and maturity'.

These observations could be multiplied but they do not answer the fundamental question: why metonymic extensions have become part of semantics at all. As we saw in Chapter 4, given the ease with which our mind processes metonymically encoded information, metonymy could just as well be confined to the domain of pragmatics without getting strengthened and becoming part of the semantics of words. Still, it is a simple semantic fact that a lot of lexical units do have well-established metonymic senses. In fact the question is more general and concerns metaphor as well: why do words develop their extra metonymic and metaphoric senses? As we shall see below, there are two reasons for that. However, it is important to note that whatever the reasons for lexical metonymies are, their development is by no means unconstrained. Some of the cognitive principles of those metonymic extensions were discussed in Chapter 1. In addition, as Barcelona (2003) showed, they usually follow the general patterns of metonymic mappings and must be socially and culturally sanctioned.

5.1 Catachresis and metonymic synonymy

The metonymic and metaphoric extensions of the prototypical senses of lexemes arise in two cases:

(a) *inopiae causa* – this is because of a lexical gap in the vocabulary of a language (cf. Ziomek 1990: 169), such as *V-neck, heel* ('a part of a shoe contiguous with the heel'), or extremely common cases of various inventions named according to the metonymy PERSON FOR INSTRUMENT, for example *printer, mixer, dishwasher*. Since traditionally the trope used when the speaker encountered a lexical gap was called 'catachresis', this kind of metonymy may be called 'catachretic'.

(b) as colloquial or poetic synonyms of already existing lexemes, for example *the crown* as a synonym of *the king* or *the royalty, cup* as a synonym of *competition* or *tournament*. Since such metonymic synonyms have, broadly speaking, rhetorical function, we may call them 'rhetorical' (see Bierwiaczonek 2007b).

Thus, considering the origin of a metonymic expression and its place in the lexical structure of a language, we may divide all metonyms into catachretic and rhetorical metonyms (i.e. metonymic synonyms of other expressions).

5.2 Metonymy in cognitive semantics

In one of the first studies of lexical polysemy in cognitive semantics, Dirven (1985) showed that alongside metaphor, metonymy is a major way of extending the number of senses of lexical items. This is what Koch (1999) calls 'metonymic polysemy', as opposed to ad hoc pragmatic metonymies created 'on the fly', like the famous *pork chop* in the waitresses' conversation. In other words, metonymic polysemies are well-established and conventionalised, and as such constitute comparatively stable non-prototypical senses of words whose prototypical senses function as their vehicles. In the light of the conception of metonymy suggested in Chapter 1, it is important to consider the conceptual relationship between particular senses of a given lexeme. As we shall see, the conceptual relations within a particular lexical item are strikingly similar to some of the basic conceptual relations between particular lexical items.

The relations are: inclusion, small overlap, substantial overlap, association, and separation. As I tried to show in Chapter 1, metonymy should be defined in terms of concepts and conceptual structures which are relatively strongly associated or exhibit substantial overlap within a single integrated conceptualisation. I suggested also that the latter variety, owing to its similarity to synecdoche, should be called 'synecdochic'.

5.2.1 Referential metonymy conventionalised: polysemy of nouns

5.2.1.1 *The problem of polysemy*

Discussing the problem of lexical polysemy, it is necessary to give criteria for distinguishing separate senses of lexemes. Without going into great detail, I will follow the account of Cruse (2000: ch. 6), who proposed that two (or more) discrete senses of a lexical item can be distinguished if the following criteria are satisfied:

A. the identity constraint, that is if a polysemous lexeme appears or is somehow activated twice in a sentence, only one of its senses is chosen for its interpretation (i.e. the senses must be identical). Thus in (1) below, *light* means either 'light in colour' or 'light in weight' for both coats; it cannot mean 'light in colour' with reference to Mary's coat and 'light in weight' with reference to Jane's coat:

   (1)   Mary is wearing a light coat; and so is Jane.

B. independent truth conditions, that is a sentence with lexeme X can be true in one sense of X but false if another sense is chosen, for example (1) may be true in the 'colour' sense of *light*, but false in the 'weight' sense.

C. independent sense relations, that is the 'colour' sense of *light* has different synonyms, antonyms and homonyms from the 'weight' sense.

D. autonomy, that is it is possible to deny a sentence containing lexeme X in one sense, and assert it in another without contradiction, for example sentence (2) sounds quite acceptable, because the two senses of *light* are autonomous:

   (2)   Mary's coat was light, I mean not heavy, but it was not light at all, in fact it was rather dark.

It seems that autonomy follows from the fact that the two senses have independent truth conditions. Having established two or more senses associated with a single linguistic form, we must decide whether the form is indeed polysemous or, rather, homonymous. If the lexeme is polysemous, the discrete senses must be somehow related to each other, or in other words – motivated. Cruse suggests that there are two kinds of relations that may link the discrete senses of polysemes: linear and non-linear relations. The linear relations are based on the different degrees of specialisation or generalisation. Cruse proposes four kinds of specific linear relations:

(a) autohyponymy – "when a word has a default general sense, and a contextually restricted sense which is more specific in that it denotes a subvariety of the general sense" (Cruse 2000: 108), for example dog_1 as 'member of canine race' and dog_2 as 'male member of canine race'.

(b) autosuperordination – the opposite of autohyponymy, whereby the default more restricted sense becomes generalised to the position of hyperonym, for example the shift of *man* from 'male member of human species' to 'human member of human species'.

(c) automeronymy – when a word has a default sense denoting the whole X and a more specific meaning denoting a subpart of X, for example the word *door* meaning the whole door set-up or only its leaf (*ibid.:* 109)

(d) autoholonymy – the opposite of automeronymy, whereby the name of the part denotes also the whole, for example *arm* denoting in its basic sense 'the upper limb without the hand' coming to denote both arm and hand.

5.2.1.2 Synecdochic extensions

It will be noticed that in the theory of metonymy outlined in Chapter 1 only the cases described in (c) and (d) above are relevant to metonymy; the first two types of relations may be considered to involve specialisation and gener-alisation and hence would be referred to as instances of synecdoche. Although metonymy seems more common, such cases of synecdoche are also quite frequent. Consider, for instance, the basic meaning of *ball* as 'round object', which, through autohyponymy, acquired a more specific sense of 'testicle', but also, in conjunction with formal metonymy, such senses as 'cannonball', 'eyeball', but also 'ball of foot' or 'ball of thumb'. Other examples are not hard to find. For instance, there is a productive synecdochic pattern whereby names of geometric shapes acquire additional senses of objects having those shapes, for example in Polish *koło* 'circle' developed a more specific sense of 'wheel',[3] in English *square,* alongside its basic geometrical sense, denotes also 'a large open area in the centre of a town or city, usually in the shape of a square' and *triangle* has developed the autohyponymous senses 'musical instrument bent into the shape of a triangle' and (in American English) 'a flat plastic object with three sides that has one angle of 90° and is used for drawing angles' (cf. Bierwiaczonek 2004a). An extreme form of autohyponymy is represented by common nouns restricted to definite descriptions, marked orthographically by the capital initial letter, as in the case of *the City, the House, the Tower* (cf. Ullmann, 1972: 162).

Autosuperordination is typical of schematisation, which may be illustrated by the well-known example of English *mill*, which used to be restricted to 'place where flour is produced' and now may denote almost any 'factory'. Another example is the word *ball* in the sense of 'a formal occasion for social dancing', which has become more general and now may also mean 'an instance of having a good time'. An interesting case of autosuperordination is discussed by Norlander (2007) in the semantic development of an English-based creole language Krio, in which English *beef* has acquired a much more general meaning 'meat, animal flesh of any kind'.

5.2.1.3 Metonymic extensions

Since automeronymy and autoholonymy are based on PART-WHOLE relations, in the present approach, they are obvious cases of metonymic extensions.[4]

Automeronymy

Automeronymy is typical of conventionalised WHOLE-FOR-PART metonymies or TARGET-IN-SOURCE metonymies, in Ruiz de Mendoza's terminology. A good example of a fully lexicalised case of automeronymy is the noun *earth* and its Polish equivalent *ziemia* as 'the planet on which we live' and its two chained extensions 'the land surface on which we live' and 'the substance on the land surface of the earth'; and *kuchnia* in Polish, which may mean the whole 'kitchen', 'furniture in the kitchen' and a 'stove in the kitchen', in addition to its non-automeronymic sense of 'cuisine'. Automeronymy is also involved in the ambiguity of some body parts, e.g. *eye* and *ear*. Thus alongside its holonymic sense 'the part of your body with which you see', *eye* also has the meronymic senses 'iris', as in *Eve has brown eyes* and 'eyeball', as in *Eve has big eyes*. Similarly, *ear*, alongside its holistic sense 'the part of your body with which you hear sounds', has at least two meronymic senses: 'inner ear', as in *I have an earache*, and 'auricle', as in *Bill has big ears.*[5] Less prototypical cases of automeronymy are represented by the lexemes denoting dot objects which systematically denote their particular facets, such as *book, man, church*, etc., discussed in Chapter 1.

Autoholonymy

One of the most common kinds of autoholonymy, probably stemming from the general anthropocentrism of language, is based on the metonymy PART OF PERSON FOR THE WHOLE PERSON, which, as we have seen, is often used in ad hoc referential metonymies. The parts chosen for this particular kind of extension are *head*, as in *headhunter, Two heads are better than one, We gave them two rolls per head, talking heads, skinheads, redhead, hothead*, etc., *hand*, as in *a farm hand* ('a man who does hard work on the farm'), *mouth*, as in *mouths to feed*, etc. In addition, the words for our private parts are used as offensive expressions for particular kinds of people, for example *arsehole* (*asshole*), *prick, tit*.[6]

In other languages the parts of the body also have metonymic extensions, but both the parts of the body and their meanings may be language specific. For instance, in Polish the equivalent of English *head* (*głowa*) has also often neutral meanings, as in *Co dwie głowy to nie jedna* (Two heads are better than one) or *Daliśmy im dwie bułki na głowę* (We gave them two rolls per head), and *hands* (*ręce*), as in English, are strongly associated with manual work, for example *ręce do pracy* (hands for work, 'labour'), *złota rączka* (golden hand, 'handyman'). On the other hand, *dupa* (arse) is ambiguous between the senses 'a clumsy, inefficient man' and 'an attractive female'.

Other fully lexicalised cases of autoholonymy are not difficult to find. For instance, names of fruit are often extended to the trees they grow on (see below), for example *cherry* in English and its Polish equivalent *czereśnia* may designate either the fruit or the species of tree on which the fruit grows. Likewise, both in English and in Polish salient parts of footwear and clothes often stand for the whole; for example English *spikes,* Polish *kolce*, both have developed a secondary autoholonymous sense 'shoes with metal points on the bottom (i.e. spikes – BB), worn by people who run races', Polish *korki* (studs) may also mean 'footballer shoes'. Similarly, *(high) heels/stiletto heels/stilettos* in English and *wysokie obcasy* in Polish may mean not only a part of a shoe but the whole shoe as well. In all those examples the low-level metonymy extending the original meaning of the lexemes is PART OF SHOE FOR WHOLE SHOE. Here are several other articles of clothing exhibiting similar polysemies: *V-neck, turtle neck*, and Polish *golf* (turtle neck) designate both the salient part (in English denoted metonymically by the name of the contiguous part of the body) and the whole sweater. In the case of *blue/white collars*, two metonymies are chained: autoholonymous PART OF OBJECT FOR WHOLE OBJECT (collars for shirts) and in the next step, CLOTHES WORN BY A PERSON FOR THAT PERSON. In another domain, the English *bar*, as discussed by Koch (1999), extended its more basic sense of a 'counter where alcoholic drinks are served' to the sense of the whole 'place to drink in'. Parts of events often develop secondary senses which designate the whole event as well, according to the metonymy SALIENT ENTITY OF EVENT FOR WHOLE EVENT, e.g. both in Polish and in English the word for CUP, which is the main prize in some sport events, stands also for the whole event, as in *football cup* or *puchar świata* (the World Cup). Similarly, in English *tea* has developed a secondary sense of a 'light meal eaten with a cup of tea'.

Autoholonyms are also common in the domain of music, for example *the strings* developed a chain from 'stringed instruments' to 'the people in an orchestra who play musical instruments that have strings' to 'the section of an orchestra which consists of stringed instruments played with a bow'; and *keyboard*, which extended its original partial sense 'a row of keys on some musical instruments' to the whole, that is 'an electronic musical instrument similar to a piano'. In Polish the word synonymous with electronic or acoustic piano is also autoholonymous; it is *klawisze* – plural of *klawisz* (piano key).

Apart from the linear relations motivating polysemy, Cruse (2000) has discussed also non-linear polysemy, in which various senses of the same linguistic form may be related by metaphor, metonymy and other 'miscellaneous' ways. Interestingly, Cruse argues that various kinds of non-linear polysemies differ in the degree of their systematicity. In particular, he claims that "probably the least systematic is metaphor", while "metonymy can be highly systematic" (Cruse 2000: 111). Although a detailed discussion of these intuitions would require a separate corpus study, it should be pointed out that the difference does not seem to lie in the systematicity as such, but rather in various degrees of generality of the conceptual mappings. In general, the more schematic the conceptual domains are, the more systematic the relations between them appear to be. As Lakoff repeatedly demonstrated (particularly in Lakoff 1987, 1990, 1993; Lakoff and Turner 1989; and Lakoff and Johnson 1980, 1999), conceptual metaphors are highly systematic and motivate a large number of linguistic expressions. Moreover, they form inheritance hierarchies whereby more specific metaphors are constrained by the image schematic structure of the more general ones. For instance, the metaphor ACTION IS SELF-PROPELLED MOTION provides structure for its more specific instances such as LOVE IS A JOURNEY, LIFE IS A JOURNEY, CAREER IS A CLIMB UPWARD, etc. (cf. Lakoff 1990, 1993; Bierwiaczonek 2002b). Consider also ontological metaphors such as ABSTRACT CONCEPTS ARE SUBSTANCES. On the other hand, there are highly specific metaphors, such as one-shot metaphors, for example Breton's famous line *My wife's waist is an hour glass*, discussed in Lakoff and Turner (1989).

Metonymies or, rather, metonymic patterns may be more or less general and productive as well, as Feyaerts (1999) has demonstrated. Cruse (2000: 111) cites such patterns as the following:

(a) TREE SPECIES – TYPE OF WOOD, for example *beech, walnut, oak*
(b) FRUIT – TREE SPECIES, for example *apple, pear, cherry*
(c) FLOWER – PLANT, for example *rose, daffodil, azalea*
(d) ANIMAL – MEAT, for example *rabbit, chicken, armadillo*
(e) COMPOSER – MUSIC BY SAME, for example *Do you like Beethoven?*
(f) FOOD – PERSON ORDERING SAME, for example *The omelette complained.*

What is confusing about Cruse's list is that while the mappings (a) through (d) are uncontroversial and well-established senses, probably stored individually in the mental lexicon and usually included in the dictionary entries of those words as separate senses, it is extremely unlikely for the metonymic senses in (e) and (f) to be listed in ordinary speakers' mental lexicons or dictionaries. Pattern (e) is a specific instance of a more general pattern PRODUCER FOR PRODUCT, and the relation FOOD – PERSON ORDERING SAME in (f) is almost completely context-dependent. In Blank's terminology, the patterns in (e) and (f) belong to "[discourse] rule-based non-lexicalized polysemy" (2003: 285), which should be distinguished from various rule-based and idiosyncratic lexicalised polysemies. Moreover, Cruse's list is extremely selective. There are certainly other more general and productive high-level metonymic schemas (or 'rules' in Blank's terms) not mentioned by Cruse. Here are some:

(g) MATERIAL FOR OBJECT MADE OF THIS MATERIAL, for example *paper – a paper, glass – a glass, oil – an oil* ('oil painting'), *plastic – a plastic* ('credit card'), *rubber – a rubber* ('eraser' or 'condom'), *iron – an iron*.

The relation between material and the objects made of it is not a prototypical PART-WHOLE relation typical of association (or continuity), since extensionally it involves a spatially unbounded entity and its instantiation (cf. Peirsman and Geeraerts 2006). This could, therefore, be regarded as another special kind of relation occupying the fuzzy borderland between synecdoche, which is based on GENUS-SPECIES C(ategory)-relations and prototypical metonymy, based on conceptual E(ntity) associations. What makes MATERIAL-OBJECT relations similar to synecdoche is the fact that, as in prototypical synecdoche, an object unilaterally entails its material. For example, *a glass* entails GLASS, *a rubber* entails RUBBER, or rather a proposition in which the word denoting an object is used entails the proposition in which the word denoting the material is used, as in (3):

(3)   I bought a glass > I bought (some) glass.

Of course, this logical parallelism between the GENUS-SPECIES relation and MATERIAL-OBJECT relation ends the moment we notice that in the latter relation the two entities involved may acquire autonomy, which suspends the logic of entailment; for example, when we come across papers which are not made of paper or irons which are not made of iron, or glasses which are not made of glass – in other words post-metonymies in the sense used by Riemer (2003). This shows that MATERIAL and OBJECT are, after all, two separate entities and thus the relationship is metonymic. In other words, extensionally, the material may be divorced from the object: a gold (medal) may be made of another metal or alloy. However, from the intensional point of view, the material is a rather central aspect (domain) of the semantic representation of the category of objects made of it, which means that there is conceptual overlap as well. As a result, classifying the relationship as metonymic is justified.

Finally, it should be pointed out that the crucial difference between GENUS-SPECIES and MATERIAL-OBJECT relations is also reflected in the fact that, in terms of *qualia* roles, the GENUS-SPECIES relationship belongs to the formal *quale*, while MATERIAL is part of the constitutive *quale* of the object, thus the place of the two relationships in the semantic structure of lexemes is quite different, which is another argument why the MATERIAL-OBJECT relationship should be regarded as metonymic.

(h) PROPERTY FOR OBJECT BEARING THAT PROPERTY. Since properties are usually denoted by adjectives, and the objects are denoted by nouns, this kind of metonymy often involves conversion of adjectives into nouns (discussed in Chapter 3). Polish examples include *zielony* (green – 'dollar' or 'member or supporter of an ecological party or organisation), *czerwony* (red – 'communist'), *rudy* (red-haired – 'redhead'), *łysy* (bald – 'bald person').

(i) CONTAINER FOR CONTENT. This kind of metonymy is common in pragmatics and only relatively rarely becomes fully conventionalised. *Kettle* in (4) and *house* in (5) and (6) are standard examples in English.

(4)   The kettle is boiling.
(5)   This is on the house.
(6)   The whole house was singing with the band.

Notice that *house* in (5) activates only OWNERS OF HOUSE, not all its patrons (i.e. not its whole 'content'), while in (6) it stands for WHOLE AUDIENCE. Other metonymic senses of *house* are 'an important family, especially a royal family', as in *The House of Windsor*, and, in the expression *this House* (in parliament) to mean 'all those who are voting in a formal debate'.

It should also be observed that in those examples of true lexical metonymy the source expressions are not simply reduced partitives, which can be expanded to form 'literal' noun phrases with *of*-phrases denoting the content. So sentences (7)–(9) sound rather odd and require paraphrases in which the containers function as locatives, as in (10)–(12).

(7)   ??The kettle of water is boiling.
(8)   ??This is on the house of the owner.
(9)   ??The whole house of audience was singing with the band.
(10)   The water in the kettle is boiling.
(11)   This is on the owner of the house.
(12)   The whole audience in the house was singing with the band.

Thus it may be concluded that there is a difference between those more conceptual CONTAINER FOR CONTENT metonymies and very regular formal metonymies whereby the phrase specifying the content is ellipsed, as in these English and Polish sentences:

(13)   Bill had two glasses (of whiskey).
(14)   Oni wypili już dwie butelki (wódki).
         [They've already drunk two bottles (of vodka)].

The same kind of ellipsis, and thus formal metonymy, is involved in expressions in which the unit of volume stands for the specified quantity of a pragmatically determined content, for example *a pint (of beer), a gallon (of petrol)* or *a quarter (of a dollar)*. Therefore, we may conclude that metonymy CONTAINER FOR CONTENT can be realised in two ways:

–   Through formal metonymy: CONTAINER/UNIT FOR CONTAINER/UNIT OF CONTENT, e.g., *bottle* – 'bottle of vodka'
–   Through conceptual metonymy: CONTAINER FOR CONTENT IN/FROM THE CONTAINER, e.g., *kettle* – 'water in kettle'.

In Polish, lexicalised CONTAINER FOR CONTENT metonymy may be illustrated with *dom* (house), which also developed the sense 'an important family, dynasty', *sala* (concert hall) in the sense of 'audience', as in the famous Polish hit *Cała sala śpiewa z nami* (the whole concert hall is singing with us), *kasa* (cash-box) meaning 'money', and *fajka* (pipe) in the expression *palić fajkę* (to smoke a pipe) 'smoking the tobacco in the pipe'.[7]

Finally, we might also note that metonymies may constitute parts of metonymic chains. For instance, *the bottle* in *take to the bottle* in English designates not only 'alcoholic beverage' but also 'heavy drinking'.

(j)   TIME FOR EVENT, for example in Polish *wigilia* (Christmas Eve) has also the sense of 'special supper eaten on the Christmas Eve', *podwieczorek* (lexicalised from *pod wieczór* = 'close to evening' = tea, as 'a light meal eaten in the late afternoon'), *wieczór przy świecach* (an evening by candles) is not just an expression of time but also 'a meeting of people where poets read their poems (often) to the accompaniment of classical or very quiet music', and *Sylwester* (first name), which first developed the sense 'New Year's Eve', and in time acquired the sense 'New Year's Eve party'.

(k)   AGENT FOR INSTRUMENT USED TO PERFORM FUNCTION OF AGENT, for example *printer, mixer, calculator, cutter*. Details of this mapping are discussed in Chapter 3. In Polish this metonymy is less common, since there is a general lexical tendency to distinguish agentive and instrumental nouns formally, for example by means of different gender, as in *drukarz* (printer – person, masc.), *drukarka* (printer – instrument, fem.), *betoniarz* (concrete maker – person, masc.), *betoniarka* (concrete mixer – instrument, fem.).

(l) BODY PART FOR ABILITY TO USE IT OR MANNER/ACTIVITY OF USING, for example in English **head** as 'ability to think, understand' in *keep/ lose one's head, get something into one's head, get one's head around something, be off one's head*; 'activity of thinking' in *use your head, get/put something out of one's head*; **eye** as 'ability to see' (see Hilpert 2006) in *have a good eye for something, have eyes in the back of one's head, have eyes like a hawk, set/lay eyes on something*; 'activity of looking' in *keep an eye on somebody or something, have one/half an eye on somebody or something, make eyes at somebody, run/cast one's eyes over something*; **ear** as 'ability to hear well' in *to have a good/no ear for music*; 'activity of listening' in *to be all ears, lend a sympathetic ear, turn a deaf ear*. Different parts of the face may stand for various aspects of speaking (see Pauwels and Simon-Vandenbergen 1995) such as *jaw* as 'activity of talking, chat' and 'manner of speaking, impudent talk' in *I don't have to take any of his jaw*, **lip** as 'manner of speaking, impudent talk', **chin** as 'manner of speaking, enjoyable conversation' in *chinwag*, **mouth** as 'manner of speaking' as in *have a loud, crude mouth*. The metonymies also work in Polish: **głowa** (head) in *rusz głową* (move your head, 'use your head'), *bez głowy* (without head, 'mindlessly'), *upaść na głowę* (fall on head, 'be crazy'), *w głowie się komuś pomieszało* (be confused in the head, be crazy); **oko** (eye) in *mieć sokole oko* (have a falcon's eye, 'to see very well'), *mieć dobre oko* (have a good eye) meaning 'ability to see well' and 'ability to aim well and hit the target', *mieć na kogoś oko* (have/keep an eye on somebody, 'have an eye for somebody'), *rzucić na coś okiem* (cast an eye at something, 'look'), *przymknąć na coś oko* (close an eye on something, 'turn a blind eye to something'); **ucho** (ear) in *mieć dobre ucho* (have a good ear), *słoń komuś na ucho nadepnął* (elephant has stepped on somebody's ear, 'have no ear for music').

(m) PART OF THE BODY FOR PART OF ARTICLE OF CLOTHING CONTIGUOUS WITH THIS PART OF BODY: *neck, elbow, heel, leg, sole, fingers* (in gloves), *waist*. This metonymy should probably be made a little more general since it extends to other artifacts too, for example *head* and *foot* of the bed (cf. Cruse 2000: 111), *back* of a chair, *arm* of an armchair, etc. In Polish this metonymy is less common than in English, although it does occur in *podeszwa* ('sole'), *palec* ('finger') and *talia* ('waist'). In other cases, the sense of clothing is represented either by independent lexemes, as in *pięta* (the curved back part of foot) and *obcas* (the raised part of the bottom of a shoe), or derived morphologically from the body part, for example *rękaw* (*ręka* 'hand' – 'sleeve') and *nogawka* (*noga* 'leg' – 'leg of trousers').

(n) CLOTHES FOR PEOPLE WEARING THEM, for example *redcap* discussed in Chapter 3, *white* and *blue collars, black belt*, and a whole family of synonyms of *woman*, such as *strap, murrey-kersey, skirt, smock, petticoat* and *placket*, discussed by Kleparski (2000). We should mention also a tendency to refer to players in collective sports using a double metonymy PROPERTY OF CLOTHES (JERSEYS) FOR CLOTHES FOR PLAYERS. The most commonly selected property is the colour, hence the players of Liverpool are referred to as *the Reds*, Chelsea as *the Blues*, etc. Likewise, the Polish national football team is called *biało-czerwoni* (white-red), players of the football team Ruch Chorzów are called *niebiescy* (the blues), and the Italian national football team are referred to as *gli Azzurri* (the azures or 'light blues').

The patterns presented above show that metonymy indeed exhibits considerable systematicity, similar both in number and in kind to the high-level referential and propositional metonymies (discussed in Chapter 4). This should come as no surprise since what we find in semantics is the same metonymies entrenched and lexicalised.

5.2.1.5 From proper names to categories: eponymy as metonymy

As already discussed in Chapter 1, proper names may develop non-unique senses, whereby they stand for whole categories, for example *Mozart* may be re-categorised as a category of extremely musically talented people, and the same is true of other culturally salient, outstanding artists, scientists, philosophers, politicians, inventors or athletes (see Chapter 1). Those paragons (cf. Lakoff, 1987) can also function as conceptual points of reference for the whole category. A slightly different conceptual mechanism is involved in eponymy, where names are used to stand for non-personal categories. Since eponyms involve change of reference, motivated by relations between human agents, their activities and various results of these activities, it makes sense to distinguish a separate category of metonymy, which I will call 'eponymous metonymy' or e-metonymy. It should be stressed, however, that although I will discuss this as a semantic phenomenon, e-metonymy clearly stems from pragmatic referential metonymy, whereby the name of the author is used to refer to the product of his work, as in the Picasso and Shakespeare examples discussed in Chapter 4. The difference is that while in the case of artists, unique individuals create equally unique artistic output, in e-metonymies the result is usually a perfectly replicable unit or a new category.[8] Since the new unit or category has no other name, e-metonymy is usually catachretic. Here are some of the most common patterns:

A. NAME OF RESEARCHER/INVENTOR FOR A UNIT OF ENTITY
André-Marie Ampère – *ampère*, 'unit of electric current'
Daniel Gabriel Fahrenheit – *fahrenheit*, 'unit of temperature'
Heinrich Rudolf Hertz – *hertz*, 'unit of frequency of sound waves'
Isaac Newton – *newton*, 'unit of force'
Georg Ohm – *ohm*, 'unit of electrical resistance'
Alessandro Volta – *volt*, 'unit of force of an electric current'
James Watt – *watt*, 'unit of electrical power'

B. NAME OF INVENTOR FOR INVENTION
Samuel Colt – Colt, 'a revolver'
Joseph-Ignace Guillotin – guillotine
Mikhail Kalashnikov – Kalashnikov, 'automatic rifle'
Charles Mackintosh – mackintosh, 'the waterproof coat'

C. DISCOVERER OF DISEASE FOR DISEASE
Alois Alzheimer – Alzheimer's Disease – Alzheimer[9]
Jakob Heine, Carl Oskar Medin – Heine-Medin Disease – Heine-Medin
John Langdon-Down – Down's syndrome – Down
James Parkinson – Parkinson's disease – Parkinson

In the case of names of diseases semantics often goes hand in hand with pragmatics. Thus, if *Alzheimer* or *Parkinson* have become established as names of diseases, they are often felicitously used as ways of referring to the patients suffering from those diseases, for example *The Parkinson's we examined yesterday should be released from hospital.* The two metonymies involved in the chain are: DISCOVERER OF DISEASE FOR DISEASE FOR BEARER OF DISEASE.

D. FOUNDER OF COMPANY FOR COMPANY FOR PRODUCTS OF COMPANY
Adam Opel – Opel AG – Opel
André Citroën – Citroën – Citroën
Lars Magnus Ericsson – Ericsson – Ericsson
Enzo Ferrari – Ferrari – Ferrari
Henry Ford – Ford Motor Company – Ford
King C. Gillette – Global Gillette – Gillette
William Hewlett and David Packard – Hewlett-Packard – Hewlett-Packard – hp
Sōichiro Honda – Honda – Honda
Shozo Kawasaki – Kawasaki Heavy Industries – Kawasaki
Levi Strauss – Levi Strauss and Co. – Levis (jeans)
Hugon Junkers – Junkers and Co. Warmwasser-Apparatefabrik – Junkers[10]

General patterns do not preclude unpredictable developments or unique metonymic chains. For instance, *braille*, named after its inventor Louis Braille, is a form of printing for blind people not the machine for such printing, while *diesel*, named after a German engineer Rudolf Diesel, may mean 'a kind of engine' (through formal metonymy based on *Diesel engine*), 'heavy oil used as fuel in diesel engines', as well as 'a vehicle that uses diesel as fuel'. There are also various kinds of formal e-metonymy, whereby a part of a proper name is used in the name of a related category. Here are some representative examples:

> Adi Dassler – Adidas – a blend of first name and part of the surname
> Tadao Kashio – Casio — homophonous spelling
> Corel – a complex acronym based on the founder's name Dr Michael Cowpland and the name of the company **CO**wpland **RE**search **L**aboratory
> IKEA – an acronym derived from the initials of the founder Ingvar Kamprad, his family farm called Elmtaryd, and the name of the nearby village of Agunnaryd
> Tesco – a formal blend of TES (from T. E. Stockwell) and CO (from Jack Cohen)

In conclusion, what this brief discussion of the most common kinds of metonymic patterns involved in eponymy shows can be summarised in three points:

1. E-metonymies are not fully predictable, but like other kinds of metonymy, they exploit the established conceptual links between human agents and various aspects of their activities.
2. The particular productivity of e-metonymy probably results from the salience of human agents in the human world, making them, thereby, particularly good vehicles of metonymies. The productivity manifests itself not only in the sheer number of e-metonymies but also the ease with which they become chained.
3. Conceptual e-metonymies are often combined with formal metonymies.

5.2.2 Predicative metonymy conventionalised: polysemy of verbs

Metaphor aside, most verbs extend their meaning by means of synecdoche and metonymy. As in the nominal categories, synecdochic extensions may involve autohyponymy or autosuperordination. For instance, if we follow Langacker (1990: 267) and assume that the prototypical meaning of *run* involves 'rapid two-legged locomotion', then the sense 'rapid n-legged locomotion', which renders it applicable to animal running, could be considered as autosuperordination. The same is true of many other verbs used to designate animal and human activities, which acquire a general sense which abstracts away from the obvious differences in the way these activities are performed by humans and various species of animals (e.g. *swim, walk, sit, lie, stand, eat, drink, sing*). On the other hand, the same verbs may acquire much more specialised meanings, e.g. *run, swim* and *walk* may designate competitive sports activities, *drink* may designate excessive drinking of alcohol, etc., in which case the development should be considered as autohyponymic. An excellent case study of the verb *paint* moving along the schematic-specific scale was presented by Tuggy (1993), who showed how common and important these synecdochic extensions are. However, since our main focus is metonymy, in the remaining part of this section I will try to discuss a number of the most typical ways in which meanings of verbs are extended metonymically.

5.2.2.1 Part for whole *in* walk, fly *and* see

The meanings of verbs are extended by means of different metonymic patterns from those that are typical of nominal extensions. The most pervasive general pattern, however, is similar: PART FOR WHOLE or PART FOR PART. The main difference lies in the nature of the relevant ICMs, which are usually scripts involving processes and activities associated in time. Here are some examples:

(15)   John and Ed walked in silence for a while.
       walk – 'move forward by putting one leg in front of the other in a
       regular way' (COBUILD)
(16)   She walked me to my car.

Unlike in (15), in sentence (16) walking is only part of the whole event involving at least two participants walking to a particular destination at which they part.

(17)   The bird flew away.
(18)   Ed flew from New York to Los Angeles.
(19)   Ed flew a small plane.

In example (17), *fly* means 'move through the air', in (18) it denotes 'an activity performed by the aircraft in which the subject (Ed) is travelling', while example (19) involves a systematic intransitive-transitive alternation, which is discussed in greater detail below (see §5.2.2.2).

In the numerous metonymically extended senses of the verb *see*, illustrated below, the act of seeing is usually a central component of a much more complex event:

(20)   We are going to see Hamlet tonight.
       – seeing as PART OF WATCHING FOR WATCHING

(21) I'm seeing the doctor tomorrow afternoon.
      - seeing as PART OF VISIT FOR VISITING
(22) Tom is seeing a client.
      - seeing as PART OF MEETING FOR MEETING
(23) They've been seeing a lot of each other.
      - seeing as PART OF SPENDING TIME WITH SOMEONE FOR SPENDING TIME WITH THAT PERSON
(24) Mary is seeing John now.
      - seeing as PART OF HAVING A ROMANTIC RELATIONSHIP FOR HAVING A ROMANTIC RELATIONSHIP
(25) It's up to you to see that the job's done properly.
      - seeing as PART OF CHECKING AND CONTROLLING FOR CHECKING AND CONTROLLING

As is often the case in language, although the extensions are motivated, they are seldom fully predictable. Since metonymy is based on larger conceptual structures, such as frames, spaces and scripts, ultimately it is the construal of those structures that determines the choice of the vehicle and the target. For instance, Blank (1999a) discusses two different routes taken by the Latin verb *plicare*, whose basic meaning was 'to fold'. In Romanian, the verb acquired the sense 'to leave', while in Spanish the opposite 'to arrive'. Blank argues that we can account for the difference if we take into consideration the fact that in the Romanian shepherd society folding was associated with the folding of the tents and leaving, while in a marine country like Spain folding was associated with the folding of the sails and arriving. Thus the two target senses of *plicare* developed differently because of the cultural contrasts and the different scripts in which its basic meaning was salient.

5.2.2.2 Intransitive-transitive conversions

There is no doubt that frequent intransitive-transitive conversions in English (cf. ch. 3), called also 'ergative-transitive contrasts' or 'causative alternations', involve conceptual EFFECT FOR CAUSE-EFFECT metonymy. Consider for instance the verb *swing* in these examples:

(26) The sail of the boat swung from one side to the other.
(27) Ed was swinging a bottle of beer by its neck.

In sentence (26), the verb *swing* is used intransitively in the sense 'to move regularly from one side to another', while in sentence (27) it is used transitively in the causative sense 'cause X to move regularly from one side to another'. If it is assumed that the intransitive sense is conceptually basic, then the transitive sense may be considered as conceptually derived through EFFECT FOR CAUSE-EFFECT metonymy. If, on the other hand, it is the causative transitive sense that is considered basic, the relevant metonymy is CAUSE-EFFECT FOR EFFECT. The proper analysis of the group of verbs in question becomes clearer when two basic groups of verbs exhibiting causative alternations are considered. According to Levin (1993), the two groups are verbs of causative/inchoative alternation (represented by *swing*) and verbs of induced action (represented by *run*), illustrated below in (28) and (29) (borrowed from Levin 1993: 31), in which the verb is additionally accompanied by a directional phrase.

(28)   The rats ran through the maze.
(29)   The scientists ran the rats through the maze.

The main difference between *swing* in (26) and *run* in (28) is that *swing* is an unaccusative verb, while *run* is an unergative verb.[11] As a tentative suggestion, to be tested and verified by future research, I propose that at least some unaccusative verbs are conceptually derived from ordinary transitives by means of CAUSE-EFFECT FOR EFFECT metonymy, that is a specific instance of WHOLE-FOR-PART, while the causative transitive senses of unergative verbs are derived by means of ACTIVITY FOR CAUSE-ACTIVITY metonymy, that is a specific instance of PART-FOR-WHOLE.[12] One piece of evidence that two different metonymies are at work comes from a cross-linguistic observation that in Polish the unaccusatives are quite regularly derived from transitive verbs and retain a formal 'trace' of their conceptual transitive source in the form of a pseudo-reflexive *się*, as in *X otworzył Y* (X opened Y), *Y otworzyło się* (Y opened),[13] while unergatives either resist the causative alternation altogether or use some sort of morphological modification, as in *śpiewać* (to sing) and *rozśpiewać* X (cause X to sing).

5.2.2.3 Human sound verbs

A number of what Goossens (1990) calls 'human sound verbs' have developed secondary speech-act senses. The verbs in question are *applaud, giggle, snigger, wheeze, moan, groan, scream* and the like. As Goossens observes, the extended senses have a clear metonymic basis in the sound which is used to stand for the whole speech act of which it is a part. Thus the verb *moan* in (30) designates only the sound, while in (31) it is used to designate the whole complex act consisting of both the non-verbal sound and the act of speaking.

(30)   When my son was younger, he used to moan a lot in his sleep. [HUMAN SOUND]
(31)   'My head,' he moaned. 'You've hurt my head.' [HUMAN SOUND + SPEAKING]

Goossens also argues that these verbs can actually become completely metaphorised and thus designate only speech acts. He proposes calling such cases 'metaphor from metonymy'. Riemer (2003) has shown, however, that they are unlike ordinary metaphors and would be better classified as post-metonymies. Furthermore, it should be pointed out that, while such partial domain separations may be possible for some human sound verbs (e.g. *moan* and *groan* in the sense of 'complain'), it is unlikely that the verb *scream* can be used with reference to a speech act which involves no degree of 'loud, high-pitched voice' (Cobuild EDAL). Consequently, while the metonymic extensions are rather straightforward, the metaphoric ones, if they apply to such cases at all, are subject to more constraints, which again indicates that metonymy is cognitively more natural and basic than metaphor.

5.2.2.4 Verbs of perception

Prototypical perceptual concepts have at least two verbal senses and one nominal sense in English. The nominal sense denotes the sensation, while the two verbal senses denote a perception and activity leading to perception. The three senses are illustrated with the lexeme *smell* in sentences (32)–(34):

(32)   I liked the smell of the soup, but I did not really like its taste. [nominal – SENSATION]
(33)   The soup smelled fantastic. [verbal – PERCEPTION]
(34)   I smelled the soup and I think it is fresh. [verbal – ACTIVITY]

If the concept related to PERCEPTION is considered as basic, then the mappings are PERCEPTION FOR SENSATION, PERCEPTION FOR ACTIVITY LEADING TO PERCEPTION (a special case of EFFECT FOR CAUSE-EFFECT). The metonymies represented by the verb *smell* are also exhibited by *taste* and *look*. As the examples below show, *feel* as a verb of tactile perception has also developed three senses, although the activity sense is usually conveyed by the verb *touch*, and in the domain of auditory perception *sound* has developed only the sensation sense, the activity leading to perception sense being taken over by the verb *listen*.

(35)   I like the feel of this cloth.
(36)   Her hands felt rough.
(37)   The doctor felt his forehead.
(38)   She felt in her bag for a pencil.
(39)   We could hear the sound of voices.
(40)   Her breathing sounded very loud.[14]

5.3 Idiosyncratic metonymic chains – the case of *tongue*

In spite of a number of regularities and high-level metonymies governing the process of metonymic semantic extension, there are also numerous idiosyncratic nominal metonymies. An example of this kind of metonymy is the noun *tongue* in the sense of 'language' in English. The uniqueness of *tongue* lies in the polysemy of the word *language* itself, which may designate not only the 'ability' and actual 'use of written or spoken words to communicate', but also 'a system of rules and regularities which make such communication possible' and it is the latter sense of *tongue* that is unique. Apart from this unique more-abstract sense, *tongue* shares with other words denoting bodily organs, some of which were discussed in Section 5.2.1.3 above, the sense of 'ability to use the organ in its prototypical function or the actual use in its prototypical function'.[15] This is not really surprising. As Hilpert (2007) shows, in a large number of languages the names for organs extend their meaning first to their function. In (41)–(44) different organs are used in this sense:

(41)   Eve has a sharp tongue – can speak 'sharply'.
(42)   Bill has a good ear for music – can hear musical distinctions well.
(43)   My grandma still has very good eyes – can see well.
(44)   John has incredibly fast feet – can run very fast.

Needless to say, the metonymy (often as motivation for metaphor) is also employed in numerous idioms. Here is a short list:

*   Ear – *have somebody's ear, keep an ear to the ground, somebody's ears are flapping*
*   Eye – *only have eyes for somebody, have eyes in the back of one's head, have eyes bigger than one's belly, keep somebody's eyes glued to something, keep an eye on somebody*
*   Hand – *keep one's hand in something, try one's hand at something*
*   Finger – *have sticky fingers, pull one's finger out, lay a finger on somebody, be light-fingered*
*   Tongue – *not be able to get one's tongue round a word or phrase, hold one's tongue, be tongue-tied.*

Predictably, the polysemy of *tongue* shows up also in its idioms and collocations. Accordingly, in the idiom *not be able to get one's tongue round a word or phrase,* as well as in the compound *tongue-twister, tongue* stands for 'ability to pronounce linguistic units', while in *hold one's tongue, be tongue-tied* and in such expressions as *have a nasty/sweet* etc., *tongue* stands for 'content of what is said or written'. However, since *tongue* has also developed the sense of 'a system of rules and regularities relating human sounds and meanings', it can be characterised as *difficult* or *easy*, as well as *regular* or *irregular,* *complicated*, etc. Other bodily organs have not developed such abstract senses; consequently, they cannot be described by such adjectives, for example **difficult eyes, *easy ear, *regular fingers*.

Summing up, the polysemous structure of *tongue* seems to involve a metonymic chain, which may be represented as follows:

> ORGAN OF BODY > ABILITY TO USE THIS ORGAN TO PRONOUNCE MEANINGFUL SOUNDS > ACTUAL ACT OF USING THIS ORGAN TO CONVEY MEANING > MEANING OF WHAT ONE CONVEYS USING THIS ORGAN > THE SYSTEM OF COGNITIVE AND BEHAVIOURAL ROUTINES MAKING THE CONVEYING OF MEANING BY MEANS OF THIS ORGAN POSSIBLE.

5.4 Metonymy generators

Even a rather casual survey of semantic structures of lexemes in different languages shows that cross-linguistically some lexemes in different languages are more productive as vehicles of metonymies and metaphors than others. Consequently, in Bierwiaczonek (2007c) I proposed that each language has its own favourite sense-generators (s-generators), that is those lexical items which exhibit particularly rich polysemies. The importance of s-generators lies in the fact that they are well-entrenched, high-frequency items, which are likely to be used more often than other items in categorising new cognitive entities/conceptualisations. I suggested that four basic kinds of s-generators should be distinguished:

(a) s-generators based on elaboration (e-generators), that is words which have a rather abstract, schematic central meaning and a number of other senses which are elaborations of this abstract central sense. A good example of an e-generator in Polish is the word *płyta*, whose central meaning seems to be 'flat piece of solid material' and whose elaborations involve various materials, which may be rendered in English as *sheet, plate, board, slab, panel, record, surface, apron, plaque, stone,* or *board*. In Cruse's (2000) terms, e-generators involve particularly productive cases of autohyponymy.

(b) s-generators based on feature modification (fm-generators), that is words which form their polysemous semantic structure by means of what Langacker calls 'extension', which "implies some conflict in specification between the basic and extended value" (1990: 266). In Langacker's example of the word *run*, feature modification involves the number of legs of the running people and animals. A good example of the fm-generator is the noun *dial* in English discussed in Bierwiaczonek (2007c). Others that might be adduced are *box, bag, frame*. Since feature modification results in various senses which are very close to each other extensionally (belonging to the same super-ordinate category) and exhibit considerable conceptual overlap inten-sionally, in the present framework they should be called synecdochic metonymies (cf. Chapter 1.8).

(c) s-generators based on metonymy (my-generators), that is lexemes whose rich polysemous semantic structure is a result of metonymic extensions. Since my-generators differ from language to language, a single my-generator in L1 may have a number of different equivalents in L2. A good example of the my-generator in English is the lexeme *paper*. In Table 5.1 the column on the right shows the words in Polish needed to translate various senses of *paper*.[16]

Table 5.1 The word *paper* as a metonymy-generator in English (based on Bierwiaczonek 2007c).

Various senses of lexeme paper *in English*	*Polish equivalents*
1. material in the form of thin sheets used for writing on or wrapping things	*papier*
2. a newspaper	*gazeta*
3. a formal piece of writing about an academic subject[17]	*artykuł, referat*
4. an essay written by a student	*esej, praca (semestralna)*
5. part of a written examination	*egzamin pisemny*
6. report on a question or a set of proposals for changes in law	*raport, referat*
7. cigarette paper	*bibułka*
8. wallpaper	*tapeta*
9. pl. documents	*dokumenty, papiery*

Clearly, all senses 2 through 9 have developed through different metonymic extensions from prototypical sense 1, but two lines of extension following two basic metonymic patterns can easily be discerned: one is MATERIAL FOR OBJECTS MADE OF THIS MATERIAL (senses 7 and 8) and the other is MATERIAL FOR TEXTS WRITTEN ON THIS MATERIAL. In senses 2 and, arguably, 9, which involve dot objects, the two metonymies co-occur. It is enough to consider the complex metonymic extensions of such 'material' concepts as GLASS, IRON and SILVER to see that the metonymy MATERIAL FOR OBJECTS MADE OF THIS MATERIAL is extremely common in English and thus most of the words denoting materials are candidates for being my-generators.

(d) s-generators based on metaphor (mr-generators), that is lexemes whose rich polysemous semantic structure is a result of metaphoric extensions or domain mappings in the sense of Lakoff (1993), Croft (1993) and Barcelona (2002). As an illustration, Table 5.2 shows the main metaphoric extensions of the noun *body* in English and their Polish equivalents.

Table 5.2 The word *body* as a metaphor-generator in English (based on Bierwiaczonek 2007c).

Various senses of lexeme body *in English*	*Polish equivalents*
1. your physical parts	*ciało*
2. main part of your body	*tułów*
3. group of people	*grono, ogół, organ*
4. the largest part of building	*korpus*
5. the main part of a car, plane, etc.	*karoseria, nadwozie, kadłub*
6. the main part (of an army)	*trzon*
7. a large area of water	*akwen*
8. a large amount (of information)	*materiał*
9. strong flavour (of drinks)	*bukiet*
10. (heavenly) natural object in space	*ciało (niebieskie)*
11. = body suit	*trykot*

Note that not all ten senses of *body* extended from the prototypical first sense are metaphoric: senses 2 and 11 are clearly metonymic. However, since all the other senses are metaphoric, we may safely call *body* a metaphor generator in English. Other equally productive mr-generators in English are *face, mouth* (cf. Cruse 1986: 72), *head* (cf. Krzeszowski 1994), *straight* (cf. Cienki 1998), *bed, chip, wing, table, skirt, ring*.

Apart from the more or less clear cases of s-generators, Bierwiaczonek (2007c) also proposed a hybrid category of metonymy-metaphor generators (mm-generators), that is the lexical items which have extended their semantic structure more-or-less evenly through metonymy and metaphor. A good example of an mm-generator in English is the word *cup*, discussed by Dirven (1985). If the everyday use of *cup* as 'a small round container which is used to drink tea, coffee, etc.' is regarded as prototypical, and the senses in the sacred use (synonymous with *chalice*), *eggcup* and *prize cup* as extensions based on feature modification, then we can distinguish eight (underlined) metonymic senses[18] and thirteen metaphoric senses. This shows that *cup* represents a rich mix of metonymic and metaphoric senses. I present this list with their Polish equivalents in Table 5.3. As can be seen, the prototypical sense of *cup* is usually translated into Polish as *filiżanka*. The other senses call for very different equivalents. In sense 24 I have been unable to find a Polish equivalent at all.

Table 5.3

Various senses of lexeme cup *in English*	*Polish equivalents*
1. Everyday use – a small round container which is used to drink tea, coffee, etc.	*filiżanka*
2. Sacred use – 'chalice'	*kielich*
3. <u>Bowl of a cup</u>	*czasza (< czaszka* 'skull'*)*
4. <u>Cupful (quantity)</u>	*szklanka (PWN Oxford)*
5. <u>Wine of communion</u>	*kielich*
6. <u>Bitter experience</u>	*kielich (*not specified in *PWN Oxford)*
7. <u>Mixed beverage</u>	*koktail, pucharek*
8. Eggcup	*kieliszek (=* dim. of *kielich)*
9. Prize cup	*puchar*
10. <u>Sports event – final</u>	*puchar*
11. <u>Sports event (football tournament)</u>	*puchar*
12. Acorn cup	*miseczka (*dim. of *miska* 'bowl'*)*
13. Buttercup	*jaskier*
14. Hip-joint	*staw biodrowy (SLAP)*
15. Heavier part of foliage	*kielich*
16. Socket for capstan	*gniazdo (*'nest'*)*
17. Receptacle for bleeding	*bańka (=* dim. of *bania =* bubble, SLAP*)*
18. Resin receptacle	*bańka*
19. Hollow ('lower part of the ground')	*zagłębienie*
20. Hole (in golf)	*dołek (=* dim. of *dół =* hole in the ground*)*
21. <u>Metal container in hole</u>	*kieszonka (=* dim. of *kieszeń =* pocket*)*
22. Bra cup	*miseczka*
23. Knee protection	*ochraniacz na kolana*
24. Part of glove	No Polish equivalent found

Dictionaries of technology add even more possibilities, for example:

25. cup (in founding) – *skorupa* (shell)
26. socket cup – *łyżka* (spoon) *czerpakowa*
27. cup capacitor – *kondensator kolpaczkowy*
28. cup fructure – *przełom stożkowy* (adj. derived from *stożek* – cone)
29. cup greaser – *smarownica kapturowa* (adj. derived from *kaptur* – hood)
30. cup-head rivet – *nit z łbem półkolistym*

Summing up, apart from *filiżanka*, the most common Polish equivalents of *cup* are: *kielich* – 'chalice', *kieliszek* – 'glass' (as in wineglass), *puchar*

– 'metal container for liquids', and *miseczka* – diminutive of 'bowl'; others include *bańka* – 'bubble', *łyżka* – 'spoon', *dołek* – diminutive of 'hole in the ground', *stożek* – (geometrical) 'cone', *kaptur* – 'hood'. Clearly, there is a large number of different lexemes used in Polish for various senses of *cup*. It should be noted, however, that most of the relevant senses of the Polish words are also metaphorical extensions of other, more basic senses. Besides, most of them seem to be conventionalised (dead) metaphors based on original image metaphors involving shape and function as a container. Therefore, they can all be said to be motivated (cf. Panther and Radden 2004), having conceptual sources related to them by perceptual analogy. However, there is no single lexical item among them which has even a fraction of the metaphorising potential of the English *cup*. The conclusion is of course that the English word *cup* is an extremely powerful metaphor and metonymy generator.

The list of senses of *cup* presented above does not show the internal relationships between the particular senses. As already observed in Chapter 4 and in Section 5.3, metonymies often come in chains, with various metonymic extensions providing bases for further extensions. In the case of *cup* several such chains can be detected. For instance, there seems to be a clear sequential development from sense 1 through 2 through 3 through 5 to 6, that is from everyday use through synecdochic 'sacred use' through PART FOR WHOLE 'bowl of a cup' through CONTAINER FOR CONTENT 'wine of communion' to SALIENT ENTITY FOR EVENT 'bitter experience'. Another chain that should be proposed links sense 1 with sense 11 through senses 9 and 10, although the development from 1 to 9 should probably be classified as feature modification. Thus the chain looks as follows: 'everyday use' > 'prize cup' > 'sports event – final' > 'sports event' (e.g. football tournament).

The *cup* example is also theoretically interesting and important for one more reason. As Barcelona (2000) suggested, it is no accident that chronologically the metonymic extensions precede the metaphoric extensions because metaphors are metonymically motivated insomuch as each metaphor uses only some particular aspect of the source concept (the one that is highlighted or perspectivised in the mapping, in the sense intended by Lakoff and Johnson 1980). For instance, Barcelona argues that in the sense 'acorn cup', it is only the overall shape of the prototypical cup that is perspectivised, at the cost of its function as a container for drinking. We may add that in the sense of 'receptacle for bleeding' neither the shape nor the function for drinking is perspectivised; instead, it is the function of collecting and holding the liquid. The moral of these observations is that certain lexemes become mm-generators because they have a complex cognitive representation of their prototype, which allows for various metonymically extended senses, which in turn may become sources for different further metonymic or metaphoric mappings. It seems then that mm-generators do not have a single meaning focus, in the sense of Kövecses (2000), but rather a number of more-or-less equipotent meaning foci, each of which may serve as an independent source of metaphors. Whether this is the principle governing the extensions of other mm-generators as well remains to be seen.

5.5 Metonymy vs. semantic relations

If metonymy is defined in terms of concepts and conceptual structures which exhibit substantial overlap or association, then it should come as no surprise that it operates not only on the level of lexical polysemy, but also on the level of semantic relations between different lexemes. In Bierwiaczonek (2005) I tried to show that in fact different kinds of metonymy may be distinguished precisely on the basis of the conceptual structures which determine various kinds of semantic relations. As we have already seen in Cruse's account of automeronymy and autoholonymy, some meaning extensions have the same conceptual basis as meronymy. The metonymic pattern is the same when the meronym or holonym are realised by different lexical items: the meronym may stand for the holonym in PART-FOR-WHOLE metonymy, while the holonym may stand for a part in WHOLE-FOR-PART metonymy. In what follows I summarise briefly the main kinds of conceptual structures that motivate semantic relations and are used in metonymy as well. First, though, we shall try to divide all semantic relations into those that may produce metonymy and those which may not.

As I have pointed out in Bierwiaczonek (2005), a similar distinction into metonymic and non-metonymic semantic relations was made by Seto (1999), who, in his discussion of metonymy and synecdoche, distinguished two basic kinds of transfer of meaning: C(ategory)-related transfer and E(ntity)-related transfer. Seto argues that C-related transfer is based on the semantic inclusion between a more comprehensive and a less comprehensive category, while E-related transfer is based on the spatio-temporal contiguity as conceived by the speaker between one entity and another in the (real) world. In other words, synecdoche is defined as being based on taxonomies, which are "concerned with mental (re)classifications of categories", whereas metonymy is defined as being based on partonomy, which involves "real-world constitutive relations" (Seto 1999: 94). Importantly, however, Seto claims that "partonomy is just one of several contiguous relations" (*ibid.*: 95).; such as in the example *the kettle is boiling*, the water is not part of the kettle, but is just in contact with it.[19] In general, the same point is made by Koch (2001), who, however, defends the tradition of calling the PART-WHOLE relation 'synecdoche' and, in addition, suggests that instead of E-relations, we should consider whole frames and their elements as instances of 'engynomic' relations. Thus Koch claims that

"PART-WHOLE 'synecdoches' should be sharply separated from taxonomic processes and definitely assigned to the category of metonymy" (2001: 217). If we ignore the terminological quibble, both researchers agree that there is a crucial difference between the non-metonymic taxonomic relations and metonymy-generating 'engynomic' relations.

Cruse's notion of endonymy, defined as "the incorporation of the meaning of one lexical item in the meaning of another" (Cruse 1986: 123) is useful for characterising various non-metonymic relations referred to below. We should distinguish the endonym, that is the predication conceptually and semantically included in another predication from the exonym (i.e. the more general including predication). What is surprising is that Cruse exemplifies the relation of endonymy with such pairs as *animal* vs. *horse* and *horse* vs. *mare*, which are clear cases of intensional inclusion owing to hyponymy, alongside such pairs as *hand* vs. *finger*, which is a clear case of meronymy, and *horse* vs. *stable*, *hand* vs. *glove*, and *foot* vs. *kick*, which form a rather incongruous set of frame-based contiguities. Therefore, in what follows, we shall restrict the relation of endonymy to C-relations with their familiar logical manifestations in the form of entailment and necessary co-activation on the conceptual and, possibly, neural level.

5.5.1 Voßhagen (1999) on metonymy and opposition

Voßhagen rightly observes that, from the cognitive point of view, the two basic relations of opposition – antonymy (viewed as gradable contrariness, cf. Murphy 2003: ch.5) and complementarity – should be considered as conceptual relations holding within one domain. If the two concepts involved in these relations designate conceptually close regions, it is hardly surprising that the relation may lead to metonymy. Voßhagen discusses two kinds of such metonymy. The first kind of metonymy based on antonymic opposition involves ironic uses of predicates, whereby the target meaning is the opposite of the expression used in the utterance, as in the sentence *X is a fine friend* uttered by Y, who has been cheated by her friend X. The second kind of opposition-based metonymy involves a relatively permanent historical change of meaning. A predicate acquires a new meaning which is the opposite of the meaning it used to have, as in the case of the slang usage of the adjective *bad*, which now means 'eminently suitable or appropriate; excellent, wonderful', or the development of the evaluative meaning of *terrific*, which has changed from the negative to positive.[20]

Although Voßhagen makes this point rather indirectly, it is important to observe that the target meaning is never vague. The expression always designates only one region on the scale, i.e. good or bad, in the case of evaluative predications, and either above or below the standard in the case of descriptive predications, such as *big* vs. *small*, discussed by Voßhagen (see Bierwiaczonek 1990 on 'evaluative' and 'descriptive' predications). There is, however, one significant exception. In most cases of descriptive scales, in questions and certain nominalisations, it is the positive region that metonymically stands for the whole scale, which is evidenced by the neutrality of questions such as *How old, How big* ... and nominalisations such as neutral *length* vs. marked *shortness*, neutral *width* vs. marked *narrowness*, etc. The fact that one part of the whole dimension can stand for the whole dimension lends further support to the claim that antonyms are cognitively contiguous.

The contiguity and hence the extremely strong association of complementaries such as *single – married, alive – dead* is even more obvious in their logical properties since they divide the relevant domain into two regions and one may be accessed simply by negating the other. Thus *not married* entails and thus activates the conceptual structure of *single*, while *not single* entails and activates *married*. Interestingly, Voßhagen shows that even non-complementary evaluative spaces can also be construed as complementary. Although, from the logical and semantic point of view, most domains of values have three 'evaluative regions' – positive, neutral and negative – the metonymic evaluation is based on Hayakawa's 'two-valued orientation'; *bad* can only mean 'good', not 'neutral' (cf. Hayakawa 1949).

5.5.2 Bierwiaczonek on hyperbole, litotes, and synonymy

Although hyperbole and litotes are not semantic relations, the analysis of semantic relations and metonymy in terms of conceptual structures put forward here may help to explain these typically pragmatic phenomena in a way compatible with the analysis of traditional semantic relations. Such analysis shows that the conceptual basis of both semantic and pragmatic relations is the same. They can all be reduced to the five fundamental co-activation processes proposed in Chapter 1 – those involving unassociated separation, associated separation, small partial overlap, large partial overlap and inclusion.

In Bierwiaczonek (2001) I tried to account for the positive hyperbole in (45) and negative hyperbole in (46) in terms of implicatures based on the metonymies with target meanings specified in (45˅), (45˅˅) and (46˅), (46˅˅), respectively:

(45) Everybody knows that Sue is having an affair with the boss.

Target meanings

   (45˘) 'everybody in the office knows that Susan is having an affair with the
      boss'
   (45˘˘) 'most people in the office know that Susan is having an affair with
      the boss'

(46)   Nobody noticed that the actor forgot his lines.

Target meanings

   (46˘) 'nobody in the audience noticed that the actor forgot his lines'
   (46˘˘) 'few people in the audience noticed that the actor forgot his lines,
      the majority didn't'

Although in Bierwiaczonek (2005) I withdrew from the metonymic account
of hyperboles illustrated in (45) and (46), in view of the analysis put forward
here, and the account of collections put forward by Peirsman and Geeraerts
(2006), discussed in Chapter 1, the original proposal made in Bierwiaczonek
(2001) may be maintained at least for the target meanings (45˘˘) and (46˘˘)
since whether a given entity is a member of a particular collection is a
contingent, not a necessary, fact, that is it is an E(ntity) relation. Therefore
I suggest, in accordance with Bierwiaczonek (2005), that the conversational
implicatures indicated in (45˘) and (46˘) should be regarded as cases of
non-metonymic inclusion: *everybody knows* in (45) entails *everybody in the
office knows*, that is a more inclusive expression, or endonym,[21] *everybody*
is used for an extensionally less inclusive expression or exonym *everybody
in the office*. In (46) *nobody noticed* entails *nobody in the audience noticed*:
again a more inclusive expression *nobody* (in the sense that the negation
applies to everybody) is used for an extensionally less inclusive expression
nobody in the audience (in the sense that the negation applies to everybody in
the audience). In contrast, the hyperbolic sense in (45˘˘) should be regarded
as WHOLE (COLLECTION) FOR LARGE GROUP OF ITS MEMBERS metonymy, while the
target sense (46˘˘) of the litotes (46) should be considered as an example
of metonymy NEGATED WHOLE (COLLECTION) FOR NEGATED LARGE GROUP OF ITS
MEMBERS FOR A SMALL GROUP OF ITS MEMBERS metonymy, though in general
both metonymies may be considered as instances of MORE FOR LESS. In fact the
latter metonymy works in more prototypical cases of litotes as well. Consider,
for instance, the case of *not warm* with the target meaning 'cold': the region
of the scale designated by *not warm* is greater than the region of *cold* for it
includes the regions of *chilly* and *lukewarm* as well and it is this larger region
that activates the smaller region of *cold*. Here, again, metonymy conforms to
Hayakawa's 'two-valued orientation'.

   The relation of inclusion and the notions of endonym and exonym are
also relevant to at least some kinds of synonymy (cf. §5.5.3.3 and §5.5.4.5

below).[22] As shown in Bierwiaczonek (2002b), given complex categories like LOVE, most synonyms designate concepts which themselves constitute parts of the overall representation of LOVE, such as AFFECTION, FONDNESS, ATTACHMENT, PASSION. To the extent that these concepts are indeed co-activated each time the predicate *love* is used (at least in its EROTIC sense), they may be treated as exonyms of LOVE (i.e. LOVE is 'a kind of' AFFECTION, FONDNESS). Given, however, that some conceptual components are more likely to be co-activated (or activated more strongly than others), we may have to propose a scale of synonymy ranging from exonymic synonyms (which are activated as a matter of semantic structure and thus do not produce metonymy) to meronymic, and thus metonymic synonyms, which are based on the PART-WHOLE relation holding between a concept construed as a part contiguous with other parts of the ICM, and the ICM itself. In the case of the EROTIC LOVE-ICM, the concept of JEALOUSY could have such a status.[23] Therefore, B's answer in (47) may be taken as a metonymic declaration of love, albeit rather indirect:

(47)   A: Do you love me?
         B: I could kill anybody who would like to touch you.

If the above analysis of synonymy based on the notion of co-activation is accepted, then some kinds of synonymy would share important characteristics with both hyponymy and meronymy. Unilateral entailment resulting from inclusion would make it look like hyponymy: LOVE entails AFFECTION but AFFECTION does not necessarily entail LOVE. On the other hand, AFFECTION may be construed as a rather important but in itself insufficient component of LOVE, rather like an engine is considered to be important, but insufficient, for a car. The following parallelisms bear out these relations between this kind of synonymy, on the one hand, and hyponymy and meronymy, on the other:

Hyponymy
   (48)   a. A rose is a kind of flower / *A flower is a kind of rose
            b. *A rose is a part of a flower / * A flower is a part of a rose

Meronymy
   (49)   a. *A car is a kind of engine / *The engine is a kind of car
            b. *A car is a part of an engine / The engine is a part of a car

Synonymy
   (50)   a. Love is a kind of affection / *Affection is a kind of love
            b. *Love is a part of affection / Affection is a part of love

Clearly, apart from cases of 'absolute synonymy', we might expect synonyms to be more or less hyponymic or more or less meronymic, which brings us back to the more general problem of the conceptual bases of metonymy.

5.5.3 Non-metonymic semantic relations

As noted earlier, there are a number of endonymic semantic relations which result from the necessary co-activation of the conceptual and possibly also neural structures, owing to the fact that one is intrinsically included in the other. These relations are hyponymy, plesionymy, conversion and a number of cases of synonymy. Let us consider them in turn.

5.5.3.1 Hyponymy

The clearest case of necessary co-activation is the relationship between a hyperonym and its hyponyms. The reason is that each time a hyponym is used, the conceptual structure of its hyperonym is also activated, since the scope of the semantic representation of the latter is properly included in the scope of the semantic representation of the former.[24] As we have already seen in Chapter 1, reference by means of expressions representing different levels of generality (or, alternatively, specificity) is typical of synecdoche. In cognitive linguistic terms this inclusion is captured by describing the relationship between the hyperonym (or type) and hyponym (or subtype) in terms of schematicity. The representation of the hyperonym is inherent in the representation of the hyponym, which makes it possible to categorise the lower term in the taxonomic hierarchy by evoking the higher, more inclusive term on any arbitrary level of schematicity. Thus it is perfectly possible, for example, to categorise *Clawee* as a cat or a mammal or just an animal, while it is impossible to do so in meronymic hierarchies: as *soldier Louis* cannot be categorised as a squadron, a company, a battalion, or any higher military unit (cf. Górska 1999: ch. 2; and see below). I have already discussed the reasons why this kind of reference should not be considered as metonymic (Section 1.8).

5.5.3.2 Converses

Ever since Fillmore's classic studies (cf. Fillmore 1982, 1985) converses are known to evoke the whole frame (e.g. both *buy* and *sell* evoke the same frame of COMMERCIAL EXCHANGE). In this sense they may be said to activate the same regions in the conceptual space, although each member of the set of converses represents a different construal of the same frame. Typically, however, converses activate the same elements, although they do so with varying degrees of strength and salience. This is true even of what Cruse refers to as 'indirect converses', such as *take, relinquish/yield/give up,* and *dispossess* (cf. Cruse 1986: 234). The crucial difference between converses on the one hand and hyponyms and plesionyms on the other is that, since converses activate the whole frame, it is impossible to determine which concept should be considered as the endonym and which should be considered as the exonym. The only reasonable candidate for the exonym is the word for the frame itself, in which case it has the form of holonym, since various components of a frame can be regarded as its interdependent constitutive parts. From the logical point of view, this interdependence of converses manifests itself in the form of bilateral entailment, which renders converseness similar to absolute synonymy.

5.5.3.3 Non-metonymic synonymy

Without going into details, it seems rather uncontroversial that most cases of synonymy of predications P1 and P2 involve some overlap of the scope of the conceptual representations of P1 and P2 or the inclusion of the scope of the conceptual representation of one predication in the other. The nice but extremely rare ideal, reconciling the two criteria, is total identity of scopes – what Lyons (1995: ch. 2) calls 'absolute synonymy', which in our terms is tantamount to mutual inclusion – and the resultant bilateral entailment and total substitutability. Most synonyms, however, are either partial synonyms, that is they involve the inclusion of one semantic region in the other, for example *big* vs. *large* (cf. Lyons 1995: 61), *punish* vs. *chastise, correct, discipline, castigate*, and *penalise* (cf. Murphy (2003: ch. 4), or near-synonyms, which differ in their descriptive and/or expressive meaning, such as *homosexual* vs. *gay* vs. *queer, politician* vs. *statesman, thrifty* vs. *mean, skilful* vs. *crafty*. The difficulty with these examples is that, although there is a considerable descriptive overlap, the predications occupy contiguous regions in the axiological domain and thus cannot be regarded as endonymic. This explains why they can be used metonymically in irony (e.g. *thrifty* for 'mean') in the same way as antonyms (see below).

Another kind of synonymy based on inclusion is plesionymy. Plesionyms are like hyponyms in that they involve unilateral entailment (cf. Cruse 1986: 285), for example *thrash* entails *beat, beautiful* entails *pretty, idiot* entails *stupid* but not the other way round. What makes them different from hyponyms is that they do differ not in scope but in intensity. They are thus inherently scalar – the same scales are activated but the exonym is further on the scale than the endonym. This is shown diagrammatically in Figure 5.1.

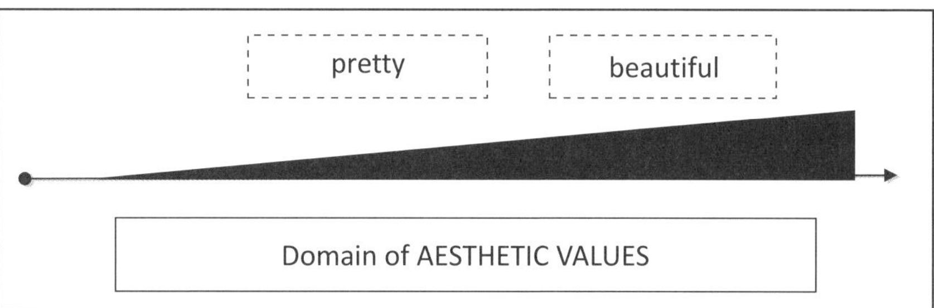

Figure 5.1 Plesionymy of ***pretty*** and ***beautiful*** as a relation based on inclusion in the same domain of AESTHETIC VALUES.

Because of entailment relations, such plesionymic scales, as well as purely quantitative scales, may constitute the conceptual basis of hyperbole: the exonym may be used for the endonym.

The most extreme form of synonymy is tautology, for example *boys will be boys* or *motor oil is motor oil* (cf. Gibbs 1999). Gibbs argues that such tautologies are metonymic because "the speaker refers to the general category (e.g. boys) to refer to specific salient parts or attributes of that category (e.g. unruly behavior)" (1999: 73). However, according to our criteria, tautologies should not be regarded as metonymic but rather as an extreme form of synecdoche, since they are based on mutual inclusion and necessary co-activation, that is the subcategory of NAUGHTY BOYS is just a prototypical subset of the category of BOYS.

In Bierwiaczonek (2007d) I referred to the synonymy based on overlap and inclusion as Synonymy A. Apart from Synonymy A, I also distinguished Synonymy B and C. Synonymy B is based on associations that underlie some typical kinds of metonymy (discussed below in §5.5.4.5). The synonyms of the C type are expressions based on metaphor, such as *reduce – cut, support – stand by – back up, understand – grasp – catch, period – space – stretch, haggard – worn – withered, hand – paw, area – pocket*. These synonyms differ from the other two types in that they are based on a relationship between two predications whose prototypical conceptual regions are separated from each other. This is typical of metaphor.

5.5.4 Typology of metonymy based on semantic relations

The crucial second category of semantic relations relevant to our discussion is the relations which give rise to various kinds of metonymy. In what follows I propose that metonymies can be subcategorised depending on the semantic relationships they are based on.

5.5.4.1 Meronymy-based metonymy

Meronymy by definition implies contiguity (cf. Lakoff 1987: 273), and thus association; however, holonym X can be still categorised as X even though some of its parts are missing, for example a car can still be categorised as a car even if its engine, wheels, or body have been removed. So, the relationship between the holonym and meronyms is not only contiguous but also contingent. Depending on the kind of holonym and its parts, we may distinguish a number of different kinds of meronymy, which correspond to different models of the PART-WHOLE relationship (discussed at length by Górska 1999): functional-part meronymy, segmented-part meronymy, member-collection meronymy and script meronymy, where subevents (or various stages of an event) are arranged on the scale of time which is conceptualised as a temporal whole,[25] and what I shall call 'frame meronymy'. The difference between the frame meronymy and the other kinds of meronymy lies in the fact that frame meronymy involves knowledge structures, which may also be called 'propositional models', associated with a given category (e.g. the fact that cars are usually driven by drivers). A particularly convincing case of frame-meronymy, and the metonymies based on it, is discussed by Koch (1999), who shows that different languages employ different parts of the frame of MARRIAGE to designate either the institution itself, e.g., Latin *matrimonium* meaning 'motherhood' was the source of the Italian and Spanish word for marriage *matrimonio*, or some other salient part of the frame, e.g., Latin *vota*, meaning 'vows' became *boda* in Spanish, meaning 'wedding'; similarly Polish *ślub*, meaning 'vow', has also acquired the meaning of 'wedding'.

In her discussion of PART-WHOLE relations, Górska (1999) points out that one of the crucial factors distinguishing the four kinds of PART-WHOLE relations she has analysed is the degree to which the whole functions as the natural or optional reference point for the conception of its parts. She shows that while the functional, segmented parts and parts of scripts are naturally dependent on their wholes, the member-collection parts are relatively independent (i.e. conceptually autonomous of their wholes). As we shall see below, this fact has interesting consequences for the availability of this kind of PART-WHOLE relation for metonymy. However, we must consider to what extent the whole frame functions as the reference point for its parts. Although the question merits a separate study, it seems that frames, being usually rather complex conceptual structures, can consist of parts that are dependent on the conception of the whole of the frame to different degrees. For instance, in the MARRIAGE frame mentioned above, it seems that concepts such as BRIDE, BRIDEGROOM, WEDDING, HUSBAND, WIFE, and HONEYMOON are totally dependent on the frame of marriage, while concepts such as MOTHERHOOD, SETTING-UP-A-HOUSE, and PRAYER are much more loosely linked with the frame.[26] In conceptual and neural terms this would indicate varying strengths (or weights) of associations connecting the neural networks supporting the conceptual structure of the holonym and its meronyms.

Taking into account the observations made above, four different meronymy-based metonymies can be distinguished:

(a) Functional part-based metonymy. This metonymy works both ways: the functional part may stand for the whole (e.g. *a set of wheels* for 'car'),[27] and the whole may stand for its parts (e.g. *That's my car* referring only to the body of the car in a garage). It seems that the functional factor is crucial: the more the whole depends on the part, the more likely it is that the part and the whole will stand in the metonymic relationship.

(b) Segmented-part-based metonymy. Since the parts in the segmented-part meronymy are totally dependent on the whole (and in addition, having no identifiable Gestalt characteristics, are not denoted by autonomous expressions but by partitives), this relation strongly favours WHOLE-FOR-PART metonymies, as in *Here's your cake*, where cake stands for 'a piece of cake'. There might be, however, marginal cases of PART-FOR-WHOLE, as in *He's a bit of a rascal*. This asymmetry is probably due to the GOOD GESTALT OVER POOR GESTALT principle, suggested by Kövecses and Radden (1998), discussed in Chapter 1.4.

(c) Script-based metonymy, for example *I just stuck out my thumb* in response to the question *How did you get to the party?* as an instance of the metonymy EMBARKATION FOR THE WHOLE JOURNEY (cf. Lakoff 1987: 79). A number of such metonymies are discussed in Chapter 4.2.

(d) Frame-based metonymy, based on the knowledge, that is the propositional models, of the relationships between and among various elements of the frame(s), such as the metonymy EMOTION FOR ITS CAUSE (e.g. *She's my pride*); AUTHOR FOR PRODUCT (e.g. *I've got two Renoirs*); CONTROLLED FOR CONTROLLER (e.g. *The Mercedes has arrived*) (cf. Radden and Kövecses 1998).[28]

Finally we should observe that the moment a meronymy-based metonym becomes sufficiently well-entrenched in the conceptual system, it begins to function as a synonym of the target, for example *a set of wheels* is cited as a synonym of *car*, *frown on* as a synonym of *disapprove*, *love* as a synonym of *the loved-one*.

5.5.4.2 Antonymy- and complementarity-based metonymy[29]

As already discussed in Section 5.5.1 above, antonymy, or gradable contrariness, and complementarity should be considered as conceptual relations holding within one domain, and since antonyms and complementaries designate conceptually close, that is closely associated, regions, both relations provide the natural conceptual basis for metonymy. This is precisely what happens in the phenomenon known as 'enantiodromia', where words change into their opposites (cf. Murphy 2003: 209). Thus, English *sycophant* changed its meaning from 'denouncer' to 'flatterer', *bad* may be used to mean 'good', or *female* may ironically denote 'male'. Furthermore, owing to the two-valued construal of most scalar domains (on which antonyms are based), the metonymic vehicle accesses the target region easily and unequivocally. This should be emphasised since it is precisely the indeterminacy of the target in sets of incompatibles (Cruse 1986) that precludes most metonymies based on incompatibility. Thus *cotton* could not normally stand for another kind of fabric simply because there are too many possible targets.

5.5.4.3 Reversion-based metonymy

Although reversives, for example *rise – fall, ascend – descend, enter – leave* (cf. Cruse 1986: ch. 10), might seem similar to converses in that they also evoke the same frame, they are also crucially different in that they are not endonymous at all, and hence they do not entail each other. However, as opposites sharing the same frame, which makes them at least partly conceptually overlapping and possibly contiguous (as two different kinds of vertical movement), they are available for ironic metonymy, typical of other opposites as well, for example *That was a hell of a rise*, *rise* may be used to target the conceptual structure of *fall*.

5.5.4.4 Synaesthesia-based metonymy

The co-activation of seemingly unrelated sensory domains involved in synaesthesia seems to be a neural fact (see Cytowic 1995; Ramachandran and Hubbard 2003), in which case we should also distinguish synaesthesia-based metonymies. It will be recalled that, while considering such cases of synaesthesia as *loud colour* and *sweet music*, Barcelona (2000b) analysed them as metaphors metonymically motivated. Barcelona argues that both the target domain (COLOUR and MUSIC respectively) and the source domain (SOUND and TASTE respectively) are construed metonymically in terms of their subdomains. Deviant (i.e. high-intensity) sounds are mapped on deviant (i.e. attracting involuntary attention) colours (in *loud colour*), while the pleasurable aspect of sweet food is mapped onto the domain of MUSIC metonymically construed in terms of the positive effect of pleasure and well-being on the hearer (in *sweet music*). Barcelona's account certainly makes sense and may well grasp an important aspect of synaesthesia. However, the psychological and neurological studies of synaesthesia (discussed in greater detail in Chapter 6) strongly suggest that such cross-modular transfers of meaning should be regarded as metonymic as they are based on neuronal associations.

5.5.4.5 Synonymy based on metonymy

The relationship between synonymy and metonymy is special in that synonymy is not based on a single conceptual configuration. As we have already seen, it is possible for synonyms to be based on semantic inclusion and overlap, typical of hyponymy or metaphor. However, probably the most productive way of creating synonyms is metonymy. As already noted in Bierwiaczonek (2007d), this kind of synonymy is referred to as synonymy B, defined as a relation based on the PART-WHOLE relationship, typical of the relation of meronymy, where the PART has considerable conceptual autonomy and thus activates different and often fewer domains than the WHOLE, for example the expression *a set of wheels* activates different and probably fewer domains than the word *car*. Similarly, the conceptual region of *care* forms a subregion which is largely co-extensive with *love* but is considerably smaller and involves fewer domains than those of *love;* for example its script, if there is one, is much less elaborate and less culturally fixed than that of *love* (see Bierwiaczonek 2002b for details). It follows that Synonymy B is intransitive: X typically strongly activates Y, but Y does not necessarily activate X, for example the word *car* typically activates the concept of A SET OF WHEELS (in its PART-WHOLE domain), whereas *a set of wheels* need not strongly activate the concept of a CAR (at least for those speakers who have not yet conventionalised this particular meaning).[30] Similarly, *love* typically activates CARE but is not necessarily activated by it. What is important about this kind of synonymy is that while one term X of the relation may be regarded as basic, the other, in the sense synonymous with X, is formed by means of metonymy (e.g. *love* is basic while *care* meaning 'love' is conceptually derived). Similarly, *car* is basic while the 'car'-sense of *a set of wheels* is derived through metonymy. Therefore, it may be said that Y is a synonym of X, but X is not a synonym of Z, for example *a set of wheels* is a synonym of *car*, but *car* is not a synonym of *a set of wheels*; and *care* is a synonym of *love* but *love* is not a synonym of *care*. It will be remembered that *love* has also a metonymically derived sense of 'loved person', in which case it may be said that *love* is a synonym of *darling* or *beloved*, but *darling* and *beloved* are not synonyms of *love* (in the sense of a loved person). The metonymic extension of the meaning of *care* is indicated in Figure 5.2 by the bold arrow, where L stands for LOVER and OL stands for OBJECT OF LOVE.

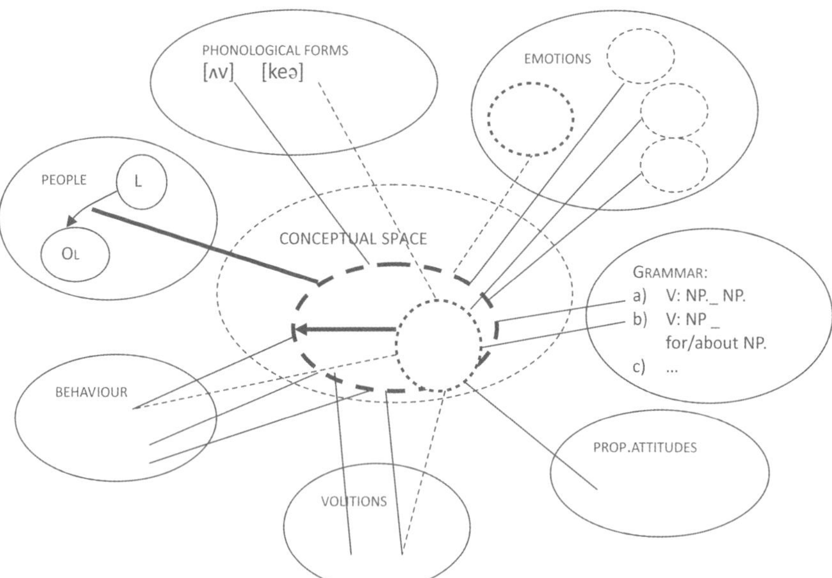

Figure 5.2 Synonymy of *love* and *care*. The arrow in the conceptual space suggests that *care* may be used to access the whole representation of *love*.

Similarly, *chair* may be a synonym of *chairperson*, but *chairman* is not a synonym of *chair*. It is, therefore, felicitous to say *You have to talk to the chair before your presentation*, but it is odd to say *If you get tired, you may sit down on the chairman*.

The above discussion suggests that Synonymy B, based on conceptual and, probably, neural contiguity, has the same conceptual and possibly neural basis as certain types of meronymy. Consequently, it may be concluded that in most well-established cases, the notions of Synonymy B and meronymy-based metonymies (cf. Bierwiaczonek 2005) are in fact equivalent. Here is a short list of other B-Synonyms: *shift – hours, shelter – cover, magazine – paper, few – handful, haggard – hollow-cheeked, help – lend a hand, nearby – at hand, generous – open-handed, gain – capture, gamble – bet – put money on*, etc. As already discussed in Section 5.2.1.5 above, in the history of English various articles of women's clothing, such as *strap, murrey-kersey, skirt, smock, petticoat* and *placket* were used as synonyms of *woman*.

A note on Murphy's pragmatic concept of synonymy
In her well-known study of semantic relations based on the pragmatic principle of the Relation by Contrast, Murphy defines synonymy as "Relation by Contrast – Synonymy (RC-S) A synonym set includes only word concepts that have all the same contextually relevant properties, but differ in form" (2003: 134). The principle elegantly accounts for the examples discussed by Murphy, which were either entrenched lexical synonyms like *punish* vs. *chastise, correct, discipline, castigate*, and *penalise* or ad hoc synonyms like *a renaissance person* vs. *eclectic*, which are all based on semantic overlap or inclusion, and thus represent Synonymy A. As for well-established Synonyms B (e.g. *shift – hours, shelter – cover*) and Synonyms C, for example *reduce – cut, period – space – stretch, haggard – worn – withered*, RC-S may be saved by arguing that the 'contextually relevant properties' of the synonyms are just their relevant senses. However, RC-S fails in the cases of ad hoc Synonymies B and C. As for Synonymy B (based on non-semantic associations within the image space representing the setting of the speech event of the *pork-chop* type), the metonymic synonyms (in this case *pork chop* and *the customer who has ordered pork chop*) simply do not share 'all the relevant properties but differ in form'. On the contrary, they share nothing except a strong association, including the form. As for Synonymy C, based on similarity, for example *man* and *tiger* in *Your tiger is coming*, the metaphoric synonyms share nothing except a single property (e.g. ferocity).

5.5.4.5 Metaphor-based metonymy and synecdoche
Generally, if metonymy is defined in terms of the co-activation of associated conceptual entities and if association is defined in terms of the strengths (i.e heavy weights of synaptic connections between the neural circuits and the

resultant conceptual regions), then even conceptual metaphor may be given a metonymic interpretation.[31] Consequently, so-called 'dead' metaphors can be defined as metonymies, where the target concept is accessed by means of a vehicle which is conceptually remote but strongly associated with it. This is particularly true of the conceptual mappings considered to be synchronic metaphors based on primary scenes (cf. Grady 1997) and conflation (cf. Grady and Johnson 2000), such as KNOWING IS SEEING, ACTION IS SELF-PROPELLED MOTION, CONTROL IS UP, INTIMACY IS CLOSENESS (discussed by Lakoff and Johnson 1999). The associative link between these pairs of domains is so strong that their co-activation is as easy and natural as in other cases of metonymy.

Modifying slightly what I said in Bierwiaczonek (2002b), it may be concluded that metonymy is mainly the principle of activation, while metaphor is the principle of conceptualisation, and hence representation. Thus, while it is certainly true that some (or all) metaphors are motivated metonymically (cf. Barcelona 2000), it is also true that some metaphors may have become so deeply entrenched and so 'obvious' in our conceptual system that they are processed in the same way as metonymies or even synecdoches. This is perhaps what Pinker had in mind when he commented on the ubiquity of the spatial and force-dynamic metaphors in our conceptual system: "Models of space and force don't act like figures of speech intended to convey new insights; they seem closer to the medium of thought itself. I suspect that parts of our mental equipment for time, animate beings, minds, and social relations were copied and modified in the course of our evolution from the module for intuitive physics that we partly share with chimpanzees" (Pinker 1997: 357). In our terms this would mean that some sources and targets of metaphoric concepts are so strongly connected on the neural level that they might be considered contiguous or even, as Pinker seems to suggest, intrinsic.[32]

5.6 Metonymy and grammaticalisation

Although the first observations on grammaticalisation, also called 'grammaticisation', date back to the work of Meillet (1958 [1912]) and even some linguists before him (see Brinton and Traugott 2005), it was much later in the twentieth century that it was studied in greater detail and more systematically. As for the term itself, Kuryłowicz defined it as "the increase of the range of a morpheme advancing from a lexical to a grammatical or from a less grammatical to more grammatical status, e.g. from a derivative formant to an inflectional one" (1975 [1965]: 52). Much in the same vein, Lehmann defines it as "a process which turns lexemes into grammatical formatives and makes grammatical formatives still more grammatical" (1985: 303). The most often cited examples of grammaticalisation are the rise of French future inflections such as *chanterai* fut. 1sg.

(I will sing) from the Latin future construction consisting of the infinitive of the main verb followed by the verb of possession in the present tense indicative, such as *cantare habeo* (Hopper and Traugott 2003: ch. 3) and the rise of English modal verbs from lexical verbs. Hopper and Traugott (2003: ch. 4) also discuss the development of the English *go*-future from *be going to* (V) 'motion verb + purposive clause' to *be gonna* (auxiliary).

If the process as such has been rather uncontroversial, the nature of grammaticalisation has been a subject of heated debates. In particular, some linguists, such as Heine, Claudi and Hünnemayer (1991) saw grammaticalisation as a process driven by metaphor with typical shifts of domains (e.g. PERSON > OBJECT > SPACE > TIME > QUALITY), while others, such as Traugott and König (1991) argued that the process is essentially metonymic, whereby the most common and typical implicatures of lexical items may be semanticised and acquire a more general grammatical status, for example the implied future of the progressive 'motion' *go* has become the central meaning of the *be gonna* construction. Thus, as Brinton and Traugott point out, "While the result of grammaticalisation is often synchronically metaphorical, textual evidence for the development of many grammatical formatives out of lexical and constructional material is metonymic in the sense that it is highly context-bound and arises out of implicatures in the speaker-hearer communicative situation" (2005: 28). One such case of grammaticalised metonymy is the various patterns of encoding possession discussed by Heine (2004). At least three of the patterns are based on spatial contiguity and, hence, the implied possession: ACTION SCHEMA expressed by the formula 'X takes/gets/holds Y'; LOCATION SCHEMA expressed by the formula 'Y is located at X'; and COMPANION SCHEMA expressed by the formula 'X is with Y'. The high-level metonymy which may be proposed for all these cases is SPATIAL PROXIMITY STANDS FOR POSSESSION.

Other cases of grammaticalisation are metonymic as well. For instance, Heine (2004) shows that the systems of numerals in most languages of the world are motivated by the number of digits in human hands and feet. Accordingly, the numeral systems having 5, 10 or 20 as their numeral base are statistically dominant, and the word for HAND is often used in the numerals for 5 and 10. It may be added that until recently numerous languages used various body parts as units of length, for example Polish *łokieć* (elbow) and English *foot*. At times the bodily motivation is less direct, for example *mile* comes from W.Gmc. **milja,* from L. *milia* 'thousands', pl. of *mille* 'a thousand', ellipsed from 'a thousand double paces (one step with each foot)'.

Other closed-set categories often have metonymic sources as well. For instance, Hilpert (2007) shows how, through chaining, body parts have developed into prepositions in a large number of languages. The most frequent changes are shown in Table 5.5 (the number in brackets indicates the number of languages).

Table 5.5 Based on Hilpert (2007: 91)

Body part	*Prepositional meaning*
Back	behind (32), after (12)
Belly	inside (8)
Buttocks	behind (5)
Face	in front of (8)
Forehead	in front of (3), before (2)

Hilpert's data suggest that the grammaticalisation patterns based on the human body may be motivated by either metonymy or metaphor. For instance, body parts such as the face and back are contiguous with a certain space, which is then metonymically denoted by this body part. Of course, this use of body parts would be at first relative to the orientation of a person constituting the point of reference, and only later generalised to other categories of objects. On the other hand, the belly is itself an internal organ (although it is a container in its own right too), so it seems that it might have developed its prepositional sense via an ontological metaphoric mapping, whereby various non-animate objects are conceptualised as bodies.

5.7 Conclusions

In this chapter I have delineated the extent and importance of metonymy for lexical semantics, arguing that metonymy should be distinguished from various meaning extensions based on elaboration/schematisation and metaphor. What is particularly important is the systematicity of metonymy, which, however, does not preclude highly idiosyncratic developments of meaning through various kinds of chaining. The importance of referential metonomy is particularly striking in the development of polysemies of nominal expressions, while predicative metonymy is crucial in the development of polysemies of verbal expressions. In extreme cases, some lexical items can become metonymy generators, that is lexical items which develop a particularly rich polysemous structure based on metonymic extensions.

In the area of semantic and lexical relations, we have demonstrated that metonymy uses some of the same conceptual configurations that support such traditional sense relationships as meronymy, hyponymy, antonymy and complementarity, reversives, and a large number of synonyms. Thus we have been able to discuss metonymy in the same conceptual terms in which both lexical semantics and the semantics of lexical relations must be discussed in the age of cognitive science. Finally, perhaps the furthest-reaching impact of metonymy can be seen in studies of grammaticalisation, which show that some metonymic senses are so conceptually useful that they become grammaticalised and thus become part of the grammatical resources of languages.

Notes

1   Nerlich (2003) discusses the history of the term 'polysemy' and the development of ideas that have led to the modern theories of meaning extension.
2   See Ziomek (1990) and Nerlich (2003) for brilliant surveys of the past theories.
3   Note the same development of German *Rad*.
4   Part of the reason why Cruse (2000) regards both hyponymic and meronymic relations as instances of specialisation and generalisation is that he misleadingly represents them graphically in a similar way, cf. his diagram representing the taxonomic hierarchy of silverware (p. 177) and the formally identical diagram representing the meronymic hierarchy of the human body (p. 181).
5   Admittedly, *I have an earache* is a borderline case allowing both for metonymic and active-zone interpretations.
6   In fact *prick* represents a rather interesting metaphor-metonymy chain. According to *Online Etymological Dictionary*, it first acquired the nominal sense as 'pointed weapon, dagger', first attested in 1552, which was later metaphorically extended to 'penis', first recorded in 1592. The next step was metonymic; as the *ODE* says: "*My prick* was used in 16c.-17c. as a term of endearment by 'immodest maids' for their boyfriends. As a term of abuse, it is attested from 1929".
7   Needless to say, the same metonymy is involved in the English expression *smoke a pipe*.
8   Of course even the unique artistic output can be relatively easily changed into a small category, as *Sisley* and *Monet* in *My friend has two Sisleys and three Monets*.
9   In this and the other metonymic names of diseases, the lexicalisation is a matter of degree and register. Thus in formal and professional English either the full name *Alzheimer's* (or *Alzheimer*) *disease* or its abbreviated form *AD* is usually used; the metonymic *Alzheimer* being more common in informal spoken English. The same tendency can be observed in Polish.
10   In Polish *junkers* has undergone autosuperordination and now is often used in the general sense 'a gas hot-water heater'.
11   See Levin and Rappaport Hovav (1996) for a general introduction to the so-called Unaccusative Hypothesis.
12   Compare Ruiz de Mendoza's (2007) analysis of middle constructions and the 'characteristic property of instrument construction' along similar lines. His formulation of PROCESS FOR ACTION metonymy is similar to my ACTIVITY FOR CAUSE-ACTIVITY but does not explicate the causative relation, which is crucial in my examples.
13   This does not mean that all unaccusative verbs in Polish are conceptually derived from causatives, for example alongside *X złamał Y* (X broke Y), *Y złamało się*

(Y broke), there are verbs like *pęknąć* (to crack), with no corresponding lexical causative and no *się,* and verbs like *rozpadać się* (to fall apart) or *bać się* (to fear), which have *się* but no lexical causative.

14 Of course the verb *sound* does have the active sense of 'pronounce', as in *The 's' in 'island' is not sounded.* Notice, however, that the activity has the effect of others having the acoustic sensation, rather than the Agent (i.e. the producer of the sound). In this respect, *sound* is parallel to *show* in the domain of visual perception.

15 As we saw in Chapter 4, the metonymy POTENTIALITY FOR ACTUALITY is independently motivated (Radden and Kövecses 1998; Panther and Thornburg 1999).

16 Ullmann (1972 [1962]: 162) mentions one more meaning of *paper* still used by Shakespeare, namely 'a note fastened on the back of a criminal, specifying his offence'. In Table 5.1 this meaning has been ignored, but its metonymic nature is obvious.

17 Hilpert (2007) argues that the meanings of *paper* are chained in the following way: material>>writing>>ideas. What he needs to show, however, is that 'writing' and 'ideas' in this case are two different senses or, rather, two facets of the same dot object.

18 I consider the relation between senses (19) and (20) as based on specialization, i.e. sense (20) denotes a more specific category than sense (19). If this is accepted, then the extension should be classified as synecdochic.

19 Two equivalent terms are used for PART-WHOLE relations on the semantic level: 'partonomy' and 'meronymy'. As we have seen, Seto uses the term 'partonomy'. The term 'meronymy' is used by Cruse in his studies of semantic relations and in what follows we shall use his terminology.

20 Of course, a great number of such lexical changes are just pragmatically strengthened and entrenched ironic uses.

21 The terms 'exonym' and 'endonym' are used here in a rather special sense of Cruse, who defines the relation of endonymy as "the incorporation of the meaning of one lexical item in the meaning of another" (1986: 123). Consequently, endonym is "the term whose meaning is included in this way" and exonym is "the containing term" (e.g. in the pair *animal* vs. *horse* animal is the endonym and horse is the exonym). Importantly, the terms are intended also for meronymic pairs like *hand* (endonym) and *finger* (exonym). (Cruse 1986: 123)

22 The same point is made in Murphy (2003: ch. 4) in her discussion of the synonyms of *punish* (e.g. *chastise, correct, discipline, castigate,* and *penalise*, which are all co-hyponyms of *punish*).

23 Cf. Croft and Cruse (2004: 143) who also claim that "sense relations do not hold between words as such but between specific construals of words".

24 As Croft and Cruse (2004: ch. 6) point out, hyponymy is not any kind of inclusion. In particular, the hyperonym and hyponym must have the same 'focal orientation', that is either the same main profile or alternatively the same 'core', which the hyponym further specifies.

25 Górska's discussion is partly based on the typology of meronymy first proposed by Chaffin and Herrmann (1984), who distinguish seven types of PART-WHOLE

relations in addition to 'case relations' (e.g. AGENT-INSTRUMENT, AGENT-ACTION), which are subsumed under the frame meronymy in my account. The typology was subsequently refined and reduced to six types of meronymy in Winston et al. (1987): 1. COMPONENT-INTEGRAL OBJECT (e.g. *pedal-bike*), 2. MEMBER-COLLECTION (e.g. *ship-fleet*), 3. PORTION-MASS (e.g. *slice-pie*), 4. STUFF-OBJECT (e.g. *steel-car*), 5. FEATURE-ACTIVITY (e.g. *paying-shopping*), and 6. PLACE-AREA (e.g. *Everglades-Florida*). A much less elaborate typology is used in the WordNet framework, which distinguishes only three kinds of meronymy, namely COMPONENT-PART-OF-WHOLE (e.g. *leg-body*), MEMBER-OF-WHOLE (e.g. *relative-family*) and STUFF-THAT-WHOLE-IS-MADE-OF (e.g. *flesh-body*) (cf. Miller 1998). See Murphy (2003: ch. 3) for discussion and critique of both approaches.

26 Arguably, the distinction drawn here corresponds to Cruse's notions of 'integral parts' and 'attachments'.

27 This construal of metonymy is based on the original interpretation of the concept of contiguity in purely spatial terms (cf. Koch 1999).

28 Most conversational implicatures are simply frame-based metonymies, though, owing to their dynamic, on-line nature, one might prefer to call them 'space-based' ('space' in the sense of Fauconnier 1985; Turner and Fauconnier 1995). Consider, for example, the classic exchange:
    A (to a passer-by): I've just run out of petrol.
    B: Oh; there's a garage just round the corner. (cf. Levinson 1983: 104)
Radden makes essentially the same point, although he does not refer to frames or spaces and construes the whole relationship slightly differently: "the conceptual relationships between a named and an implicated entity are based on contiguity, or metonymy" (2000: 98).

29 The relationship between metonymy and complementarity is discussed briefly by Radden (2000). However, Radden's construal of complementarity is much broader than the strictly semantic relation I'm considering here, so the two analyses can hardly be equated. Nevertheless, the crucial point Radden makes about the role of complementarity in metonymy is the same as mine: "complementary parts of a situation are often exploited metonymically" (2000: 97).

30 Similarly, Murphy (2003: ch. 4.3.) shows that most cases of synonymy are neither symmetrical nor transitive.

31 This view is not entirely new. The same intuition seems to have underlain Leech's comment that if metonymy is interpreted in terms of association, then it "covers all rules of transference, including that of metaphor, since similarity is a form of association" (Leech 1969: 152).

32 Another possibility is that due to evolutionary history, on some unconscious cognitive level some of the abstract concepts are hyponyms of basic spatial and force-dynamic concepts; e.g. mind is really categorised as a kind of container and love (or at least desire) is really categorised as a force. If this was the case, the co-activation would be based on inclusion, not contiguity, and could not be considered metonymic. Of course, the fact that these concepts are often metaphorically construed in other, quite different ways argues against this possibility.

6 Metonymy in the embodied mind

There seems to be agreement between an increasingly large number of cognitive linguists that linguistic theories should be compatible with the findings of modern cognitive science and that linguists should look for convergent evidence from cognitive science to support their theoretical proposals. Thus, other things being equal, the theory that is better supported by such convergent evidence from other, experimental cognitive fields should be considered superior to a theory that is not supported by such evidence to the same extent. The data discussed in this chapter provide such convergent evidence for the analyses put forward in this study and indicate strongly that metonymy should be considered as one of the crucial aspects of the embodiment of human cognition and language.[1]

I will attempt to show that metonymy is embodied in the sense of having a neuro-physiological basis and thus, in principle, should be able to be described in terms of neuro-computational modelling (cf. Rohrer 2007) or one of several versions of Artificial Neural Networks (cf. Ahlsén 2006). This empirically grounded and neuro-physiologically constrained approach has long been advocated by Lakoff (cf. Lakoff and Johnson 1999; Dodge and Lakoff 2005) and it has been voiced also by Dąbrowska (2004) and Bierwiaczonek (2006a, 2006b, 2007b). This chapter discusses the Neural Theory of Metonymy and the empirical evidence from other fields of research that support it.

6.1 Neural theory of metonymy (NTM)

NTM's basic claim is that metonymy is a cognitive counterpart of neural processes whereby the activation of one group of neurons (neuronal circuit) causes the activation of another group of neurons (neuronal circuit). It follows from NTM that ICMs and frames have neural substrates in the form of neuronal circuits strongly linking various neural regions or other, smaller circuits. It also follows from NTM that metonymy is as common as the neural processes of co-activation or, at least since most of the co-activations are unconscious, it must be defined as a subset of all co-activation processes of which we are phenomenologically aware. And it follows from NTM that certain kinds of metaphor may be considered as metonymies based on a pattern of strong synaptic connections linking two domains belonging to two different cortical modalities, for example KNOWING IS SEEING, STATES ARE LOCATIONS, PROCESSES

ARE ACTIONS. (See Chapter 5.) This form of 'metonymic metaphor' occurs when there is an experiential 'binding' of conceptually distinct domains.

As we have seen in the previous chapters, the essence of metonymy is association, substitution (or mental co-accessibility based on co-activation) and change in the relative salience of elements of frames or ICMs, which may be called highlighting. If NTM is tenable, we must show that there are neural substrates of association, substitution (mental co-accessibility) and highlighting. It must be emphasised, however, that these three properties of metonymy do not have the same status: it is association which conditions both co-activation and highlighting. In other words, the elements that undergo metonymic substitution or highlighting must be associated. Therefore, we must consider association first.

6.1.1 Association

Association in neural terms boils down to synaptic connections: through their axons all neurons reach out to other neurons, which through their axons reach out to other neurons and so on. As LeDoux points out "much of what the brain does involves electrical-to-chemical-to-electrical coding of experience. As hard as it may seem to imagine, electrochemical conversations between neurons make possible all of the wondrous (and sometimes dreadful) accomplishments of human minds" (2002: 47). One important aspect of these 'electrochemical conversations' is that they do not pass without a trace. As Donald Hebb observed in the 1950s "Neurons that fire together, bind together". Thus the more often certain entities co-occur in experience, the stronger the associations between them become, and the more likely it is for them to be co-activated. Another important aspect of 'conversations' between neurons and their circuits is that they are distributed and hierarchical. For instance, in the visual cortex, at first different neurons respond to different physical properties of an object – such as its size, shape, colour and texture – only to be 'bound' into a complete representation of the visual aspects of the object in the inferior temporal cortex. This is not the end of associations, however. First, a more complete multimodal representation is formed. Thus the visual representation is often integrated with other perceptual modalities (e.g. acoustic, tactile or olfactory modalities). This probably happens in another convergence zone, probably somewhere in the amygdala. A more-or-less complete sensory representation in the amygdala is important because it is there that the emotional response to the perceived stimulus is generated. Thus this is the 'what' circuit, which identifies the object (the 'where' circuit is different). The representation may be finer or coarser. A coarser representation is processed by what LeDoux calls a 'quick and dirty' low road linking the sensory thalamus directly with the amygdala, enabling fast responses to intense stimuli. A finer representation of the object becomes available to what LeDoux (2002: 122ff) calls the 'high road' of the emotional processing, which is connected with higher centres in the neocortex and thus enables the subject to respond to the stimulus more adequately (cf. Figure 6.3). In evolutionary terms, it is probably this connection that distinguishes what Damasio called "secondary emotions, which occur once we begin experiencing feelings and forming *systematic connections between categories of objects and situations, on the one hand, and primary emotions, on the other*" (1994: 134, original emphasis).

All in all, those networks of neural connections enable the brain to first divide the perception of a given object into its perceptual modalities and later to integrate it again and, subsequently, connect it with 'higher centres', such as emotionality, motor responses and representation in memory. Apparently, the mind has at least some access to this processing because, as we shall see below, this disintegration-integration process is reflected in metonymy.

Figure 6.1 (based on Figure 11.2 in LeDoux 2002: 309) shows how different brain systems process and store information about different aspects of a single stimulus. In the example at hand, the systems may neurally distinguish, process and store such aspects of an evergreen tree as its appearance (colour and contour) and its tactile attributes (probably split into separate tactile perceptions of the needles and the bark).

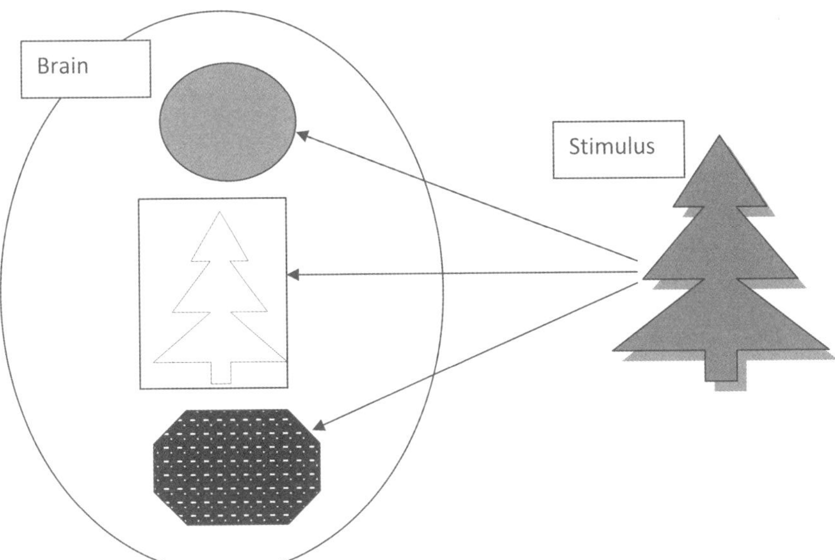

Figure 6.1 Processing of common input (an evergreen tree) by unique brain systems, which in this case may represent the colour and contour of the visual system and tactile system.

Figure 6.2 represents the next stage of processing, called 'binding', whereby the information from different brain systems is bound together to represent a coherent single stimulus in higher brain regions called 'convergence zones'. One of the most interesting aspects of this process is that it is ordered, but bi-directional, which means that once the whole stimulus is integrated, it may in turn affect the way particular perceptual modalities are represented (the dotted arrows). Thus, on the one hand, convergence zones integrate processing in separate perceptual systems, and on the other hand, they often influence processing in those systems (Figure 6.2 is a synthetic and slightly enriched representation of LeDoux's two diagrams in his Figure 11.5 (LeDoux 2002: 316)). We might note in passing that Jackendoff (2002: ch. 11) used a somewhat similar representation of the relationship between perception and concepts. In Jackendoff's account, however, what might be called a perceptual-conceptual representation is divided into a conceptual structure CS (comprising typical 'semantic' components, such as features, functions and predicate-argument structure) and a spatial structure SpS, which represents perceptual, non-propositional properties of categories. An

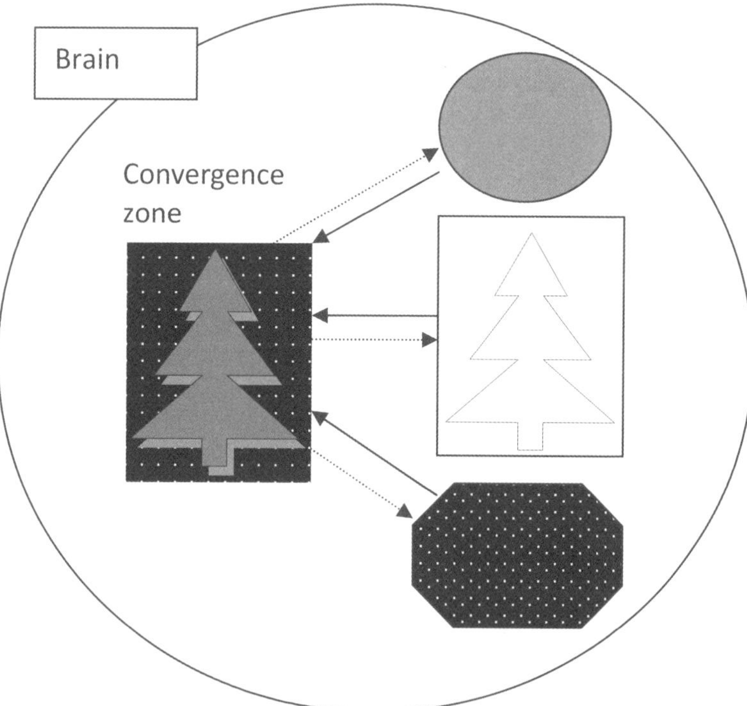

Figure 6.2 Convergence zones both integrate and influence processing in independent systems.

important inadequacy of Jackendoff's proposal is that he links SpS directly with the 'action system' (cf. Figure 11.1: 348). As we have already seen, the link is not direct, and actions are usually mediated by the emotional system and the 'higher' regions of the neocortex. It seems likely that it is through these systems that actions and their subjective results may also influence CSs, for example typical transferring interactions may result in ditransitive syntax, whereby Goals or Beneficiaries are conceptualised and syntactically represented as Recipients.

The crucial importance of the emotion centres for cognition, in general, is presented in Figure 6.3, which shows how an integrated representation of a stimulus activates other systems, in this case the emotional centre in the amygdala. This in turn affects other systems, in particular the frontal neocortex (for rational decision making), bodily responses (for adequate bodily response) and the hippocampus (i.e. the memory system).[2]

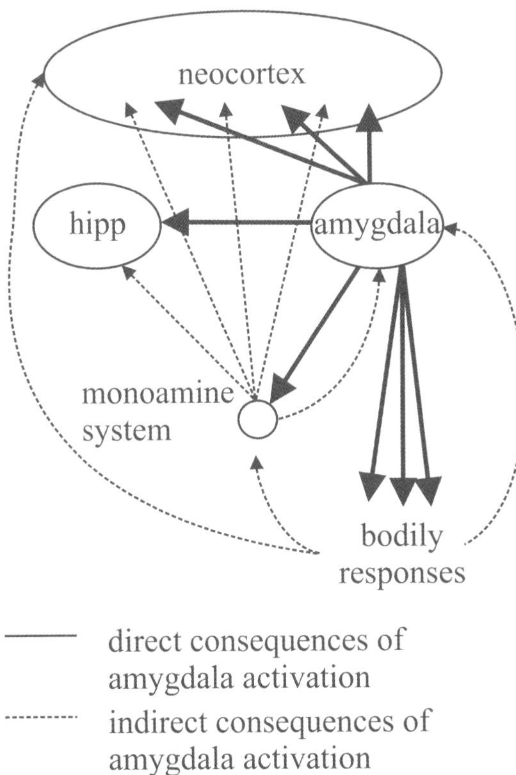

Figure 6.3 Emotional amygdala activation has direct consequences for bodily responses as well as hippocampus and neocortex (scanned from LeDoux 2002: 321, with permission of the author). The strong links are often exploited in PHYSIOLOGICAL RESPONSE FOR EMOTION metonymies.

The direct strong link between the emotional response in the amygdala and bodily responses, which is typical of Damasio's primary emotions, explains why it is so common to describe emotions by using expressions for behavioural reactions, for example *to have cold feet* for FEAR, *to frown on somebody or something* for DISAPPROVE, *jump at something* for ENTHUSIASM.

The common associations between emotional states and their bodily responses are further enhanced by the mirroring mechanisms involved in the perception of the expression of emotions. Wicker et al. (2003) scanned normal subjects both during their own experiences of disgust and while they were watching other people express disgust facially. The participants of the experiment were scanned first while they themselves were inhaling pleasant or disgusting odorants, and then while they were viewing films showing individuals smelling the contents of a glass and forming spontaneous facial expressions in response to those smells. The smells ranged from pleasant through neutral to disgusting. The researchers found that the same brain areas (i.e. the left anterior insula and the right anterior cingulate cortex) were preferentially activated both during the direct experience of disgusting smells and during the observation of other individuals' disgust-expressive faces. Jackson et al. (2004) demonstrated a similar mirroring process for pain. Since emotional and, more generally, internal experiences are neurally communicated through behavioural manifestations, it is hardly surprising that descriptions of these manifestations are used as descriptions of emotions, with verbs such as *flinch, wince, recoil, spring back*, and Ekman's (1972) pictures of faces showing the basic emotions were recognised all over the world.

If some forms of behaviour are neurally connected with emotions, others are strongly associated with body parts. Hauk, Johnsrude and Pulvermüller (2004) carried out an fMRI study which demonstrated that words denoting activities, such as *smile, punch, kick,* differentially activate, respectively, face, arm/hand and leg regions in the somatomotor neural maps. This association explains why activities (real or potential) can be metonymically accessed through the body parts involved in those activities, for example in conversions such as *hand >> to hand* and in idioms such as *one's hands are tied, keep/take one's hands off something, show one's hand, force one's hand.* (See §5.2.1.4 for a discussion of other examples of metonymy based on this kind of association.)

A strong link between a place and an event is crucial for the speed of metonymic processing of PLACE-FOR-INSTITUTION and PLACE-FOR-EVENT metonymies studied on the basis of people's eye-movements by Frisson and Pickering (1999) and discussed by Gibbs (2007). Frisson and Pickering found that sentences with familiar PLACE-FOR-INSTITUTION metonymies (e.g. *That blasphemous woman had to answer to the convent*) are processed much faster than sentences involving less familiar associations (e.g. *That blasphemous woman had to answer to the stadium*). Similarly, if the link between a place and event is strong, as between Vietnam and the Vietnam War, a sentence like *A lot of Americans protested during Vietnam* is processed as fast as a corresponding literal sentence, while a similar sentence involving an unfamiliar relation (e.g. *A lot of Americans protested during Finland*) takes considerably longer.

One particularly telling case of neural connections that have direct linguistic consequences is synaesthesia, discussed briefly in Chapter 5. Let us recall that Barcelona (2000) analysed linguistic synaesthesias like *loud colour* or *sweet music* as metaphors metonymically motivated. His analysis must be rejected on empirical grounds, however, since neural studies (cf. Cytowic 1995; Ramachandran and Hubbard 2003) show quite convincingly that the co-activation of seemingly unrelated sensory domains involved in synaesthesia is a neural fact, which means that (at least for some people) synaesthesia may not be metaphorical at all. If there are real, permanent neural links between sensory domains constituting the semantic matrix of certain predications, which, as a result, become co-activated and conceptually accessible, these domains must be regarded as strongly associated, and thus accessing one by means of another should be regarded as metonymy. What is particularly intriguing is that synaesthesia studies strongly indicate that the links may in fact occur at various stages of processing (i.e. not necessarily at the level of convergence zones). Some connections seem to be sensitive to mere visual representations of numbers (early stage of processing) while others link areas lying at the end of the processing line (TPO – the junction of the temporal, parietal and occipital lobes, including the angular gyrus), where numerical concepts are represented (cf. Ramachandran and Hubbard 2003). The studies also show that if the actual neural basis of the link is damaged, metonymic links on the linguistic level also suffer, e.g. the otherwise normal association between the phonological representation and visual perception in the *bouba-kiki* effect[3] stops occurring in patients with angular gyrus lesions.

In conclusion, different elements of representations of external stimuli (mental images) may be synaptically linked with one another and may effectively co-activate one another. Metonymy uses the same basic principle of association and co-activation. For instance, the fact that the stimulus is first broken into various modalities which later converge in the representation of a whole enables us to form metonymies such as property for the whole object on the one hand and the whole object for a property or part on the other. The first case is exemplified by such metonymies as *To be dressed in blue, to be in the red/black, a triangle* (musical instrument). In the metonymies *a pretty face, a paleface* standing for people, the attribute is associated with the representation of the face. Damasio's work on prosopagnosia (face agnosia, cf. Damasio et al. 1990) has shown that the face has special prominence in cognition and is processed to a considerable extent by its own subsystem and thus may successfully activate the representation of the whole person.

The second case of co-activation, whereby the whole activates its aspects or parts is exemplified by such metonymic developments of meaning as *rose* >> 'colour' or 'fragrance'; *dog* >> 'shape' (contour) or 'sound' or 'smell'; *turquoise* > 'colour'. On the linguistic level, the metonymy shows up in the polysemy or different facets of the word *word*, which in the phrase *difficult word* may mean 'sound', 'articulation' or 'meaning' of a word. Here the neural link between various aspects of linguistic items has long been known. The two crucial 'language areas' of the brain, Broca's (left frontal operculum) and Wernicke's (left superior temporal gyrus) areas are joined by the arcuate fasciculus (AF). When the AF is damaged, conduction aphasia occurs and the patient cannot repeat the words she has heard. However, when she sees referents of the words, she can pronounce them (cf. Szeląg 2000), which shows that the circuit joining the semantic and motor (articulatory) representations does not go through the AF.

6.1.2 Substitution (mental accessibility)

6.1.2.1 Co-activation

Substitution or, in neural terms, co-activation is possible both within a single area and between different areas. Figures 6.4 and 6.5 show how LeDoux (2002: 311) represents the two possibilities.

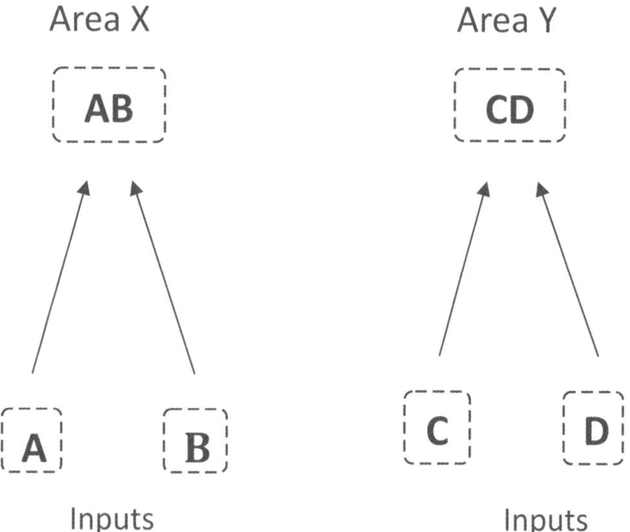

Figure 6.4 Co-active inputs create associations in each area.

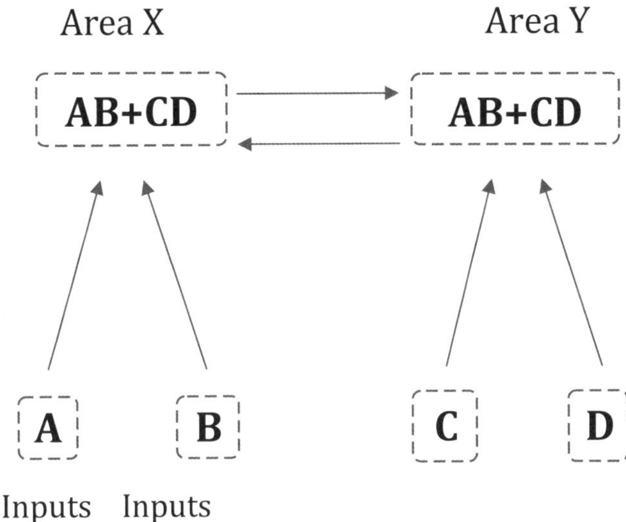

Figure 6.5 Interactions between areas also create associations (both figures based on LeDoux 2002: 311).

Co-activation in single areas is possible because co-active inputs create associations. Thus, for example, the shape and colour of a single object will be bound so that the next time one of those inputs occurs, the other one will be active as well. The same process occurs between networks activated by different objects. When synchronous activation occurs in two different areas, X and Y, through inputs A, B and C, D, respectively, X and Y will become linked, so that whenever one of the networks is activated the other is activated too. As LeDoux puts it "synchrony coordinates parallel plasticity" (*ibid.*: 310) which means that simultaneous and synchronous firing in different regions creates strong links between those regions through parallel plasticity. This principle underlies classical conditioning, where, for example, an otherwise meaningless sound or sight of modest intensity that previously accompanied pain has the same effect as a natural (innate) form of danger (e.g. the sight or smell of a predator). Both innate (genetically 'hardwired') and learned danger signals cause amygdala cells to fire rapidly for a sustained period, and cause the same reactions (LeDoux 2002: 63), and thus may be used as a substitute for the original stimulus. In a similar way, activities may be strongly associated with typical places where they are performed, and thus the place may evoke the activity, hence frequent PLACE FOR ACTIVITY metonymies, for example *to be in the bathroom* for various forms of excreting or *to be in prison* for 'serving time' (See Chapter 4). Since the links are bi-directional, we can just as easily refer to places through activities. The metonymy ACTIVITY FOR PLACE is operative in such expressions as *she's taking a pee* and *she's serving time* as answers to the question *Where is she*? The same or similar mechanism is probably involved in the association of sequences of activities (also discussed in Chapter 4), which enables us to use one activity for another that usually accompanies it within a single integrated act. Recent intersubjectivity studies (cf. Meltzoff and Brooks 2007) suggest that the ability to 'see through' parts of complex scenarios to the whole achieved intended act is displayed by 18-month-old infants and is likely to be innate. This kind of metonymic mapping is particularly common in euphemistic expressions in which conversationally acceptable activities are used to activate scenarios representing various forms of taboo, for example *go to bed* for 'have sex'; *powder one's nose* for 'excrete'; *close one's eyes* for 'die'. Probably the purpose of avoiding taboo expressions explains why this kind of metonymy is not reversible. Thus there is no reason to say that Eve and Bill had sex if one intends to say that they went to bed. Another reason might be that, culturally, going to bed strongly implies having sex, especially if this implicature is primed by the context (e.g. when talking about two more or less adult individuals of opposite sex), while having sex only weakly implies going to bed. Of course the extent to which these connections are formed on the basis of actual experiences is a matter of degree and differs from culture to culture. Nonetheless, the empathetic ability to understand goals, that is Agent's intentions, of complex acts on the basis of partial behavioural signals, discussed by Meltzoff and Brooks (2007), provides a firm ground for the development of more complex inferential patterns we have observed in propositional and speech-act metonymies, where a part of the whole scenario successfully activates the core part of this scenario. Here metonymy uses one of the greatest human evolutionary achievements: the ability to 'read' the complex intentions of others on the basis of the perception of behavioural parts of their acts.

6.1.2.2 *Filling in*

Broadly speaking, the brain-mind has a remarkable capacity of filling in the missing parts of its percepts and concepts. In neuro-psychological literature the term 'filling in' is used in the studies of the scotoma. The scotoma is defined as "a local lesion in the visual field within which nothing can be consciously perceived" (Ramachandran 1993: 56). Despite the neural gap, patients perceive the objects they are looking at normally, because the brain 'fills in' the scotoma with the surrounding colour or pattern. The filling-in process occurs both in acquired, cortical scotomas and artificial ones, as well as in the natural 'blind spots'. For instance, in an experiment devised and carried out by Ramachandran and his associates (Ramachandran 1993) (which everybody can repeat using their own television displaying a snowy screen), a 1-cm-square piece of grey paper located about 7–8 cm from the point of fixation of the gaze vanishes after 5–10 seconds and gets completely replaced by the twinkling 'snow' of the surround. On the linguistic level we have seen this kind of filling in with elements of the surround in various kinds of formal metonymy, for example question tags, reduced comparatives, anaphoric ellipsis, gapping and discourse ellipsis. Thus the predicative part of the second clause in *Bill is at least as tall as Jim* is conceptually filled in with the predicate in the first clause (i.e. *is tall*) and the missing verb in the second clause of the sentence *John ordered meat; and Bill fish* is filled in with the verb from the first clause (i.e. *ordered*) and so on.

However, metonymy does not usually involve filling in the missing parts with the surround (e.g. *a sub* is not *a subsub* but *a submarine*). The gap is not filled by the surrounding material but by what is known and entrenched. So what is the relevance of filling-in studies for the study of conceptual metonymy? The relevance becomes apparent when more results of scotoma research are examined. For instance, in one of the experiments discussed by Ramachandran, two white bar segments (in Figure 6.6 they are black) were presented on either side of the scotoma (indicated by a circle), which got filled in within 4–5 seconds so the bars formed a single straight line (the arrow shows the direction of change). This result could still be explained in terms of the influence of the surround, however; what is crucial is what happens when the two white bars are misaligned (Figure 6.6b). The subjects reported that "the lines moved vividly toward each other until they became collinear" (Ramachandran 1993: 61), that is to say an unfamiliar shape was replaced by a familiar straight line (cf. Cienki 1998). The missing details were also filled in, in accordance with the familiar shapes, when the scotoma interfered with the perception of a circle (**c** in Figure 6.6) or a square (**d** in Figure 6.6).

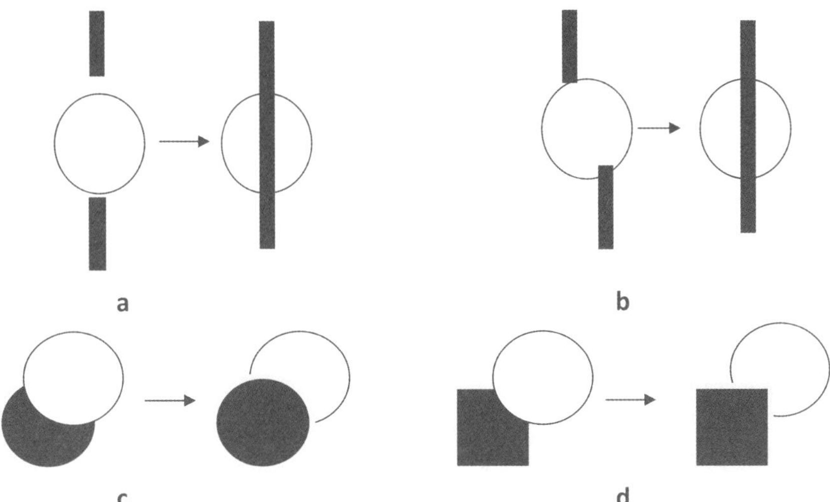

Figure 6.6 The filling-in of scotomas, based on Ramachandran (1993).

The filling-in processes observed in perception have been noted in other areas of cognition as well, particularly in studies of memory, although the most common term for it in cognitive psychology is 'elaboration', defined as "additions to the target information" [which] "relate the target item to other target items or to previously acquired knowledge" (Stillings et al. 1987: 78). In the latter case (i.e. the relationship to previously acquired knowledge) elaborations are performed on the basis of frames, scripts and other forms of dispositional spaces. For instance, in the now classic experimental studies of scripts, Bower et al. (1979) demonstrated that, while recalling stories, people often fill in the details of the stories from the scripts rather than from the actual texts they have read. The finding was confirmed by a recognition memory experiment, where the subjects were presented with a number of sentences which were part of the story or part of the script but not part of the story or just likely episodes representing neither the stories nor the script. Then the subjects were asked to rate how sure they were they had read the sentences in the story. The results showed that the subjects exhibited a significantly greater tendency to falsely recognise unstated sentences belonging to the script than unstated sentences about non-script events.

In another study (Loftus and Palmer 1974), subjects viewed a film showing a car accident and then were asked a series of questions about the accident, for example *Did you see any broken glass? How fast do you think the car was going?* It turned out that the answers to some of the questions depended on the framing of the whole event determined by the verb used in the question. For instance, if the verb used in the question was *smash* (e.g. *About how fast were the cars going when they smashed into each other?*) the subjects gave much higher estimates of speed than when the same question was asked using the verb *hit*. Moreover, the framing of the question affected the memory of the accident as well, since when the two groups were asked more questions a week later, their recall of the accident differed as well. For instance, when they were asked *Did you see any broken glass?* 32% of the *smash* group answered affirmatively, compared to 14% of the *hit* group, although there was no broken glass in the film.

Another process in which filling-in can be proposed as a neural-cognitive basis is stereotyping. For instance, Cantor and Mischel (1979) showed how schematic, stereotypical representations of personality types influence the initial perception and memory of people. Consequently, when subjects read a description of an extrovert with some explicitly mentioned features that were not typical but clearly activated the stereotype of an extrovert, they tended to fill in other, more typical features which were not mentioned. Moreover, in a recognition memory test they cited those highly typical features, although they were not mentioned in the actual description. In my own work on stereotypes (Bierwiaczonek 2004b), I argued as well that stereotyping involves filling in the details of the representation of some member (token) of a stereotyped category with the details from the dispositional representation of this category. Crucially, purely descriptive components of the token of the category usually activate not only other missing descriptive parts but also its evaluative components, leading to quick stereotyped judgments (see Lakoff 1987 and Bierwiaczonek 1990).

Filling-in can be observed very early at the pre-conceptual stage. As Stern (1985, discussed by Johnson and Rohrer 2007) showed, infants acquire 'vitality affect contours', that is modality-independent emotional patterns based on their emotional experiences of (for example) an adrenaline rush, a rush of joy or the rush of a hot-flash. Johnson and Rohrer note that "witnessing even just a portion of the pattern is enough to set our affect contours in motion" (2007: 36). This explains why the infant often calms down when the adult simply begins to reach for the bottle: a part of the pattern (contour) evokes the remaining whole. In general, what Johnson (1987) and Lakoff (1987) called 'preconceptual image schemata', such as CONTAINMENT, LINKAGE, FORCE, UP-DOWN, as well as geometrical schemata STRAIGHT (cf. Cienki 1998) and CIRCLE (cf. Bierwiaczonek 2004b) afford pattern filling-in completions. Arguably, Zlatev's 'mimetic schemas' (see §6.2) may provide the basis for such completions as well.

6.1.2.3 Mirroring

A rather special case of substitution is represented by mirror neurons in the motor cortex which fire even though the subject only sees the motor activity in another individual: a highly specific visual representation activates an actual motor neural pattern (cf. Arbib and Rizzolatti 1999). Moreover, vision may not be the only modality that makes such mirroring possible. Fadiga and Craighero (2007) discuss evidence that motor circuits may be also activated when subjects hear action-related sounds. Thus, on the neural level, the sight or sound of other people's behaviour substitutes for the subject's own behaviour. A special property of this kind of association is that probably we do not have to learn it – the mirror neurons are part of our evolutionary hardware and they just fire whether we want it or not, making the associations ever stronger. The metonymies where sight or sound targets activities are common in conversions of nouns into verbs. The sight of activities provides the basis for the verbal motion meanings of *zigzag, round, slalom, corner,* and manual activity verbs like *straighten, cross, dot, blot,* whereas the sound of activities motivates the verbal meanings of *thunder, screech, roar,* etc. Another obvious kind of metonymy that results from the workings of the mirroring mechanism is the substitution of visual representations of facial expressions of emotions for emotions (discussed in the previous section; see also Rizzolatti et al. 2006). However, at times substitution takes on more sophisticated forms. Consider, for instance, mothers describing their children's behaviour in the first person pronoun, for example *And now I'm throwing the ball back to Mum, I'm eating this spoonful*, where a visual child becomes the motor I, even if the whole act is only intended.

6.1.2.4 Rewiring

A particularly striking example of substitution has been found in the cases of phantom limbs, whereby an area responsible for the processing of inputs from the limb is 'invaded' by the inputs from an adjacent area (cf. Ramachandran 1993). Because the hand area in the Penfield homunculus is adjacent to the face and the upper arm,[4] after the amputation of the hand, the hand area starts receiving inputs from the face and from the upper arm. Consequently, the stimulation of the face or upper arm can now substitute for the stimulation of the hand. The new organisation is topographical and modal specific, for example warm water trickling down the patient's face was felt as a sensation of warm water trickling down the phantom hand.

6.1.3 Highlighting

Highlighting seems to be a natural consequence of associations on the neural level which we have discussed briefly above. However, in order to explain how it is actually achieved, let us recall that metonymy usually begins as an ad hoc referential device which sometimes, but by no means always, ends up as lexical polysemy. Therefore the crucial problem that NTM has to account for in neural terms is how metonymies arise in actual contexts where they are created for referential purposes. I suggest that the explanation lies in the way extra-linguistic context is represented neurally in the form of what Damasio dubbed 'image space' and the way image spaces interact with dispositional space in the working memory. Following Damasio, image space may be defined as "the space in which images of all sensory types explicitly occur and which includes the manifest mental contents" (Damasio 1999: 219). Damasio's account of the image space is opposed to his concept of dispositional space – "a space in which dispositional memories contain records of implicit knowledge on the basis of which images can be constructed in recall, movements can be generated, and the processing of images can be facilitated" (Damasio 1999: 219).

It follows that if sufficiently entrenched, representations in image space may become elements of dispositional space. Let us quote Damasio again:

> All of our memory, inherited in evolution and available at birth, or acquired through learning thereafter, in short, all our memory of things, of properties of things, of persons and places, of events and relationships, of skills, of biological

> regulations (…) exist in dispositional form, waiting to become an explicit image or action. Note that dispositions are not words. They are abstract records of potentialities. Words or signs, which can signify any entity or event or relationship, along with the rules with which we put words and signs together also exist as dispositions and come to life as images and action, as in speech and signing. (…)

And, importantly, "… dispositions are held in neuron ensembles called convergence zones" (Damasio 1999: 332f). The crucial region where image spaces and dispositional spaces meet and can be processed together is the seat of the working memory: the frontal and prefrontal cortex (LeDoux 2002: ch. 7). Given image and dispositional neural spaces, I will argue that, paradoxically, PART-FOR-WHOLE/PART metonymies result from the activation of the whole, while WHOLE-FOR-PART metonymies result from the activation of a part.

6.1.3.1 PART-FOR-PART/WHOLE

If image space makes it possible to perceptually construct multisensory representations of the context, then it may be assumed that the representations consist of a variable number of elements in various relations to each other linked by identity relations as they develop in time. Owing to the Gestalt nature of human perception and the ability to preserve identity, some of those elements will be perceived as 'contiguous', others as causal, still others as consecutive, etc. In order for the Conceptualiser/Speaker/Writer to select single entities for the purpose of reference, the entity must be, first, categorised and, second, distinguished from other competing members of the same category. While categorisation usually involves finding a number of conceptual domains and profiles that a given entity shares with other members of the category, the process of setting off one member of a category from others usually involves identification of at least one distinguishing domain and/or profile which the entity does not share with other members of its category. I assume that the context and the roles of the participants in discourse prime for certain domains and profiles which are neurally particularly strongly activated as focus of attention (figure against the ground) and are conceptually particularly relevant, for example in the context of the hospital, the patient may be identified by his disease; in the context of the restaurant, the customer may be identified by her dish; in the context of a research institute, the researcher may be identified by his ability to use his brain (or head) for thinking. The chemical basis of such salience has already been partly established: synaptic connections are controlled by two crucial neurotransmitters: the excitatory glutamate and the inhibitory GABA, which make sure that useful synaptic links are formed and useless ones are blocked (or, rather, filtered away; LeDoux, 2002: 189). In this way the cells which were active before become even more active, while the inactive ones remain inactive.

In discourse, such salient parts serve the same purpose as proper names and definite descriptions, except that they use perceptual contiguity in the image space. Thus, in PART-FOR-WHOLE metonymies, the vehicle of metonymy is provided by the most active part of the representation of the target, which in turn is active in the representation of the context in the image space. As Lakoff (1987: 84) characterised it in his description of the metonymic model: "There is a conceptual structure containing both A [i.e. the target – BB] and another concept B [i.e. the vehicle – BB]. B is either part of A or closely associated with it in that conceptual structure. Typically, a choice of B will uniquely determine A in that conceptual structure." I shall refer to the concept B in such typical situations as the 'distinguisher'. In Figure 6.7, which represents the image space of a waitress in a restaurant with different customers sitting at the tables covered with different tablecloths and eating different dishes, the waitress has at least two ways of referring to the customers, since she may use as distinguishers either the dishes or the tablecloths. The figure actually represents the construal in which the dish of one of the customers is selected as the most salient part of the Gestalt of that customer, giving rise to the well-known metonymy PORK CHOP for CUSTOMER WHO ORDERED PORK CHOP in *The pork chop is waiting for his check*. The figure shows that the metonymy is actually motivated by the perceptual and cognitive salience and activation of the dish in the Gestalt of the customer, which is also salient in the image space of the restaurant and, as such, is being accessed in the emergent meaning.

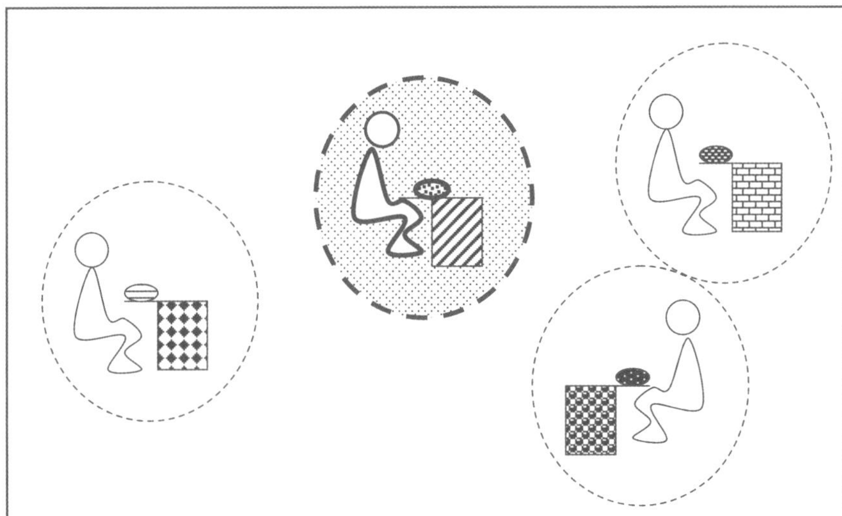

Figure 6.7 A representation of a waitress's image space of her customers in a restaurant. The Gestalt of a customer sitting at a table and eating a pork chop (bold dotted ellipse) is salient and the waitress refers to him as the pork chop, where the pork chop is the customer's distinguisher.

It is perhaps worth pointing out at this juncture that what I have suggested as a representation of the waitress's image space is in fact a result of a complex integrating process on the neural level, which is quite thoroughly described in neuropsychological literature. The integration concerns two aspects of the space in question: the representation of the individual objects (i.e. the customers, their dishes and tables), and the representation of the locations of these objects relative to each other. As Figure 6.8 shows, the 'what' pathway, supporting the representation of objects, leads to the temporal cortex, while the 'where' pathway, supporting the spatial relations between the objects, is processed by the parietal cortex. In the end, however, both pathways meet in a convergence zone in the prefrontal cortex (PFC), where they are integrated into a single space and subjected to various 'executive functions' in the working memory. One important executive function is attention, which in the restaurant scene is focused on the dish paired with the customer.

If other, more abstract objects, for example events and their spatial (and relational) properties, are also supported by different pathways which are

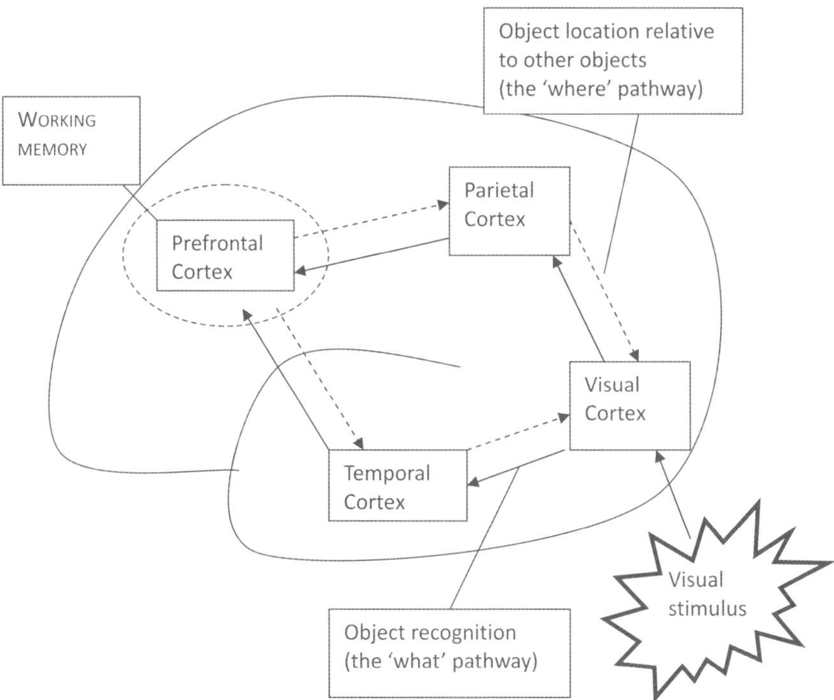

Figure 6.8 'What' and 'where' visual inputs to working memory in the prefrontal cortex (based on LeDoux 2002: 181, Figure 7.2 – with permission of the author). See also Mishkin and Appenzeller (1987), who explain how objects are usually represented along with their locations and other contiguous objects.

integrated in the prefrontal working memory area, then the same general mechanism would be responsible for such metonymies as PLACE FOR EVENT (e.g. *Americans fear that Iraq may become another Vietnam*) or PLACE FOR ACTIVITY (e.g. *John is in the bathroom*).

6.1.3.2 WHOLE-FOR-PART

The situation is rather different in the case of WHOLE-FOR-PART metonymies. What seems to happen in those metonymies is that a salient part PX of an entity x in the image space activates the cognitive representation of the category X, to which x belongs, along with its phonological representation. The process has all the makings of conceptual integration (cf. Turner and Fauconnier 1995; Fauconnier and Turner 1998, 2002), whereby one input space, provided by the perceptual material from the image space, is integrated with another input space which is a dispositional space, activated by the salient part PX in the image space and representing the whole of which the category PX is a part in the dispositional space, although the context itself may significantly prime for the activation of the representation of the whole of X as well. Again the process of integration would take place in the working memory, which has neural connections not only with the perceptual centres, but also with the hippocampus and other cortical areas supporting long-term memory, which makes it possible to retrieve all the stored dispositional spaces representing facts, scripts, schemas, and personal experiences and use them in the coding and decoding of the current utterances. As for the decoding process, as early as 1975 Riesbeck once remarked that "comprehension is a memory process" (quoted by Brown and Yule 1983: 236). Clearly, the above description bears Riebeck's conjecture out: there is no meaning construction or understanding without activating dispositional spaces.

Let us consider two examples, which I first discussed in Bierwiaczonek (2007b). In the first example, two students are watching a parade shown on television. Small groups of representatives of various local institutions are taking part in the parade, amongst them groups of representatives of schools (so schools are already primed). Suddenly, one of the students sees a group of teachers from her school and shouts: *That's our school!* I suggest that what happens is this: the perception of teachers in the image space activates their representations in the dispositional space where they are part of a larger representation of the whole school. In the blend the teachers, as distinguishers, are integrated with the school, activated as a whole, along with its phonological representation, although in the emergent meaning only the teachers will constitute the school. Thus the dispositional space provides the boundary for the group of teachers and the phonological form of the whole expression: the teachers function as a unit by virtue of representing the whole school and, consequently, are referred to as *my school*, as shown in Figure 6.9.

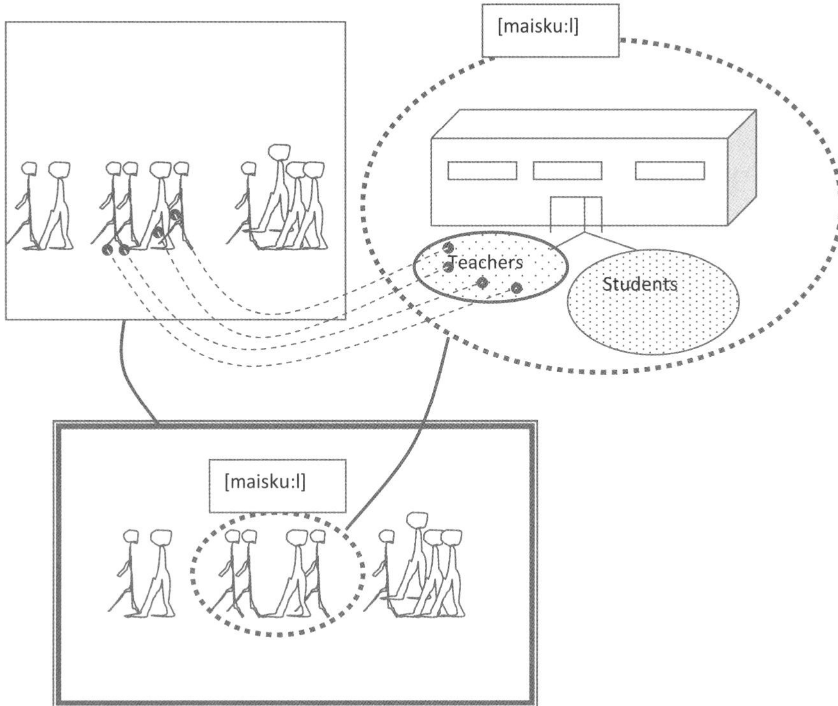

Figure 6.9 The emergent meaning of *my school* (lower rectangle) from two input spaces: the image space of a PARADE (upper left rectangle) and the dispositional space representing the speaker's SCHOOL (upper ellipse).

The other case is an example of the well-known AUTHOR FOR PRODUCT metonymy, in which the proper name *Patrick White* stands for copies of novels written by Patrick White. Again, the object in the image space (i.e. a book by Patrick White) activates the PATRICK WHITE dispositional space, in which he is a writer who has written a few texts and published a few books. The conceptual link enables the conceptualiser/speaker to designate the books by Patrick White (e.g. *This is my Patrick White*). The integration is represented in Figure 6.8.

Both image spaces and dispositional spaces have been recently described quite precisely in neural terms. Damasio (1999: 332f) locates them as follows: The areas of the cerebral cortex located in and around the arrival point of visual, auditory, and other sensory signals – the so-called early sensory cortices – support explicit neural patterns, and so do parts of limbic areas, such as the cingulate, and non-cortical structures, such as the tectum. These neural patterns of maps continuously change under the influence of internal

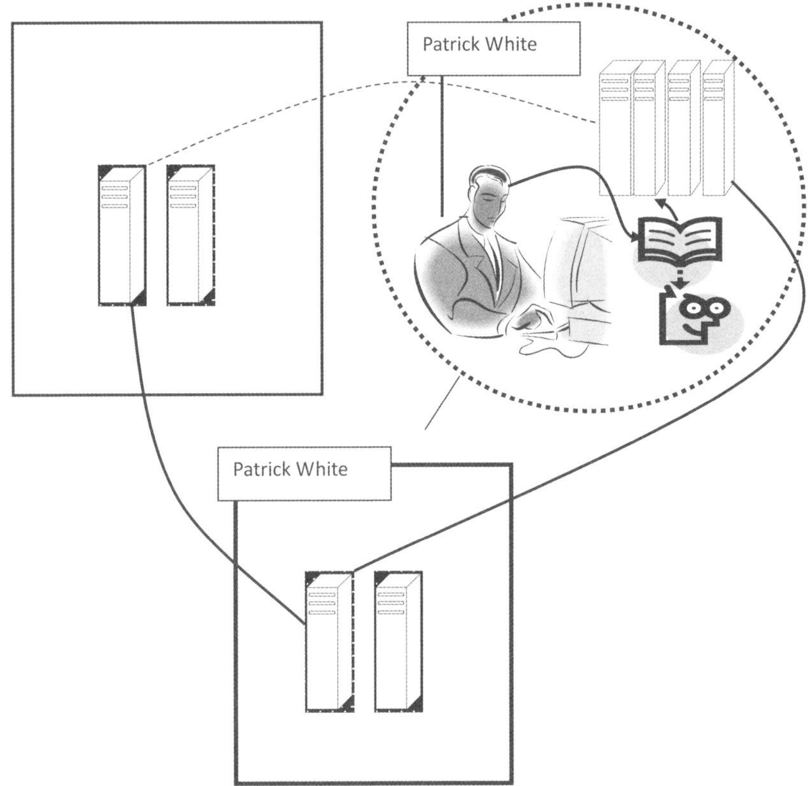

Figure 6.10 The integration of the representation of books by Patrick White in the image space with the dispositional space of Patrick White, producing the metonymic expression *Patrick White* standing for a book written by Patrick White.

and external inputs and are likely to be the basis for images, whose dynamics parallel the neural pattern changes over time.

On the other hand, higher-order cortices (which make up the cerebral cortex around the islands of early sensory cortices and motor cortices), parts of limbic cortices, and numerous subcortical nuclei, from the amygdala to the brain stem, hold dispositions, that is, implicit records of knowledge. When disposition circuits are activated, they signal to other circuits and cause images or actions to be generated from elsewhere in the brain. As we have suggested, the main convergence zone where the circuits from sensory cortices are integrated with the signals from dispositions is the prefrontal cortex. More specifically, the inputs from sensory, memory and emotional systems are received by the middle layers of the prefrontal cortex, whereas the integration work, assisted by neurotransmitters such as dopamine, is probably carried out by the densely interconnected neurons within and between the layers, which explains why those connections are far more numerous than the connections reaching the prefrontal convergence zones from the sensory and other areas (cf. LeDoux 2002: ch. 7).

6.1.3.3 Neural and conceptual constraints on metonymy – the Principle of Correspondence

As we saw in Chapter 1, Kövecses and Radden (1998) suggest a number of cognitive principles governing the choice of vehicles of metonymies. These principles are:

(a) **human experience**
   - human over non-human
   - subjective over objective
   - concrete over abstract
   - bodily over mental
   - interactional over non-interactional
   - functional over non-functional

(b) **perceptual selectivity**
   - immediate over non-immediate
   - occurrent over non-occurrent
   - more over less
   - dominant over less dominant
   - good Gestalt over poor Gestalt
   - bounded over unbounded
   - specific over generic

(c) **cultural preferences**
   - stereotypical over non-stereotypical
   - ideal over non-ideal
   - typical over non-typical
   - central over peripheral
   - initial or final over middle
   - basic over non-basic
   - important over less important

To date it is still impossible to translate all the above principles into their neural substrates. Nevertheless, certain general answers suggest themselves, especially if meaning construction is viewed as a process of integrating image spaces with dispositional spaces. For instance, the principles HUMAN OVER NON-HUMAN, SUBJECTIVE OVER OBJECTIVE, INTERACTIONAL OVER NON-INTERACTIONAL, FUNCTIONAL OVER NON-FUNCTIONAL can be accounted for in terms of neural underpinnings of interpersonal empathy, special circuits for face recognition and processing of facial expressions and better mirroring of human activities.

On the other hand, principles such as CONCRETE OVER ABSTRACT, BODILY OVER MENTAL, IMMEDIATE OVER NON-IMMEDIATE or OCCURRENT OVER NON-OCCURRENT probably result from the principles of human perception and proprioception, which constrain the structure and content of the image space. In addition, in all the above cases, the principles are also, to a large extent, determined by the way our actual perceptual and emotional experiences are stored in memory systems, which is instrumental in the representation of the dispositional space. For instance, the principles INITIAL OR FINAL OVER MIDDLE and IMPORTANT OVER LESS IMPORTANT have to do not only with the representation of the current event in the image space but also with the way this event is memorised and contributes to the emergence of a new dispositional space or modification of an already existing dispositional space.

As well as Kövecses and Radden's cognitive principles, we have also discussed Ruiz de Mendoza and Mairal Usón's (2007) three principles regulating and constraining the choice of metonymic vehicles and interpretations, namely the Extended Invariance Principle, the Correlation Principle, and the Mapping Enforcement Principle, as well as Croft's suggestion that "the dependent predication can induce domain highlighting in the autonomous one, and the autonomous predication can induce domain mapping in the dependent one" (1993: 359).[5] We have observed, however, that Croft's principle is not really reliable as in fact either the autonomous or dependent predication in a grammatical unit can have its domain adjusted, via metaphor or metonymy. It seems that, given the theory of meaning-construction based on the blending of dispositional and image spaces, both Ruiz de Mendoza and Mairal Usón's principles and Croft's proposal can be given a more general formulation in the form of a single principle which I suggest should be called the Principle of Correspondence. The Principle of Correspondence (PC) may be formulated as follows:

> Make your dispositional space (the conceptual-lexical vehicle) fit your image space (target conceptualisation) as closely as possible.

In particular:

(a) preserve the image schematic structure of the image space
(b) preserve the conceptual structure of the image space in terms of its participants, their relations and their relative salience
(c) preserve the axiological value of the image space.

I believe that PC subsumes three of Grice's Maxims of Conversations: the Maxim of Quality, the Maxim of Quantity and the Maxim of Relevance in the following way:

- the Maxim of Quality – the image space represents what the Speaker/ Writer (S/W) really wants to communicate and what s/he believes to be true, including its epistemic status (i.e. to what extent S/W believes it to be true) and S/W's true axiological evaluation, so the symbolic units s/he draws from the dispositional space fit those intentions, beliefs and evaluations as closely as possible
- the Maxim of Quantity – the image space represents the exact amount of information for the current stage of the verbal exchange, so the symbolic units s/he draws from the dispositional space fit this amount of information as closely as possible
- the Maxim of Relevance – the conceptualisation represented by the image space reflects various degrees of salience. By definition: what is salient in S/W's image space is relevant (hence Kövecses and Radden's principle IMPORTANT OVER LESS IMPORTANT), so the symbolic units s/he draws from the dispositional space fit the conceptualisation represented by the image space as closely as possible by preserving the relative salience, and hence relevance, of its components.

In order to account for the formal properties of the symbolic units (i.e. expressions used in actual utterances) used in verbal communication, PC must be supplemented with a version of the Maxim of Manner (suggested in §1.4.3) which I have called the Principle of Verbal Economy (PVE):

> Be brief. Don't say what your addressee(s) already know from their experience and context and make maximal use of their ability to form conceptual associations and construct relevant meaning on the basis of the words they hear, their perception of context, and their knowledge of the world.

Needless to say, PVE describes a general tendency. Conceptual space construction and blending are governed by a number of more specific principles such as compression, topology, pattern completion (cf. Fauconnier and Turner 2002). In most cases, metaphors and metonymies as well as various floutings of the Maxims of Conversation are practical manifestations of PVE and more specific principles of conceptual integration.

A detailed justification, illustration and defence of the workings of PC and PVE would require a separate study, so here we shall focus only on their relevance and explanatory power in the analysis of the phenomena discussed in the previous chapters. To begin with, PC subsumes Ruiz de Mendoza and Mairal Usón's Extended Invariance Hypothesis in that it requires that all the relevant (salient) aspects of the image space IS be preserved in the utterance U expressing the dispositional space DS and designating IS. It also subsumes the Correlation Principle since it preserves the inter- and intra-domain relations between the elements of the image space, for example it explains why the most salient property in the restaurant space is chosen as the vehicle to access the customer. Finally, PC also explains the cases covered by the Mapping Enforcement Principle. The example *He gave John a kick* is acceptable as it denotes a conceptualisation in which kicking indeed involves three participants: the KICKER, the KICKEE and the KICK construed metonymically as the EFFECT OF KICKING in an unspecified active zone.

Secondly, PC explains why "either the autonomous or dependent predication in a grammatical unit can have its domain adjusted, via domain mapping [i.e. via metaphor – BB] or domain highlighting [i.e. via metonymy – BB]" (Croft 1993: 362), since according to PC these adjustments simply reflect different conceptualisations. In particular, PC ensures that the emergent meaning must be coherent, in the traditional sense of the discourse analysis (cf. Brown and Yule 1983), to the extent that the image space is coherent. For instance, the utterance *the pork chop is waiting for his check* may be licensed either by the familiar restaurant situation or by a cartoon scene or a commercial in which various dishes are literally doing shopping, in which there is no metonymic transfer from the dish to the customer because the target meaning must be coherent with the image space. In addition, PC can help to account for a large number of other phenomena we discussed in the previous chapters. Here are some examples:

(a) The ubiquity of active-zone phenomena (discussed in Chapter 1). There is often no good fit between the conceptualised region in the image space and the corresponding expression (symbolic unit) in the dispositional space, hence the expression for the WHOLE is the best way to access the target part or region.

(b) The conceptual mechanism behind the Principle of Omission under Low Discourse Prominence (discussed in Chapter 2.5) allowing the omission of objects with transitive verbs: if the object is maximally demoted (i.e. has extremely low salience in the image space) and the target activity is best designated by a transitive verb, the verb is used intransitively.

(c) The motivation for using particular parts for wholes: the whole, for example a person, is accessed through the most salient part in the image space, such as the head, in the image space involving intellectual activity, or a hand, in the image space involving manual work.

(d) The process of pragmatic strengthening and the emergence of generalised conventional implicatures from invited conversational implicatures in Traugott and Dasher's Invited Inferencing Theory of Semantic Change (discussed in Chapter 4) can now be described as the process of an image space linked with some particular expression becoming a symbolic unit in the dispositional space.

6.1.4 Where in the brain? A note on the lateralisation of metonymy

There is little doubt that language as such and speaking in particular cannot be restricted to a single language module or a single "language faculty" (see Dąbrowska 2004; Ahlsén 2006). As we have seen, metonymy as a cognitive process involves a whole range of various aspects of language from the level of linguistic forms to the level of pragmatic inferencing, and thus it is impossible to locate it in one brain area or region. The most sophisticated kinds of metonymies, involving conceptual blending, are probably processed in the working memory areas of the prefrontal cortex. However, the inputs to the blending may come from different non-language areas (e.g. different perceptual centres, memory and emotional systems). So each kind of metonymic integration should probably be studied separately and its neural basis might well be unique. Though this may be so in particular cases, there are indications that, in general, metonymy is processed in the left hemisphere as opposed to metaphor, which seems to be supported by the right hemisphere. Here are the reasons why.

Ever since the experiments in the 1970s involving patients who had undergone a surgical procedure of splitting the brain called cerebral 'commissurotomy', it has been known that each hemisphere has "a mind of its own" (see Kurcz 2000: 52ff). For instance, Sperry (1982) found that when split-brain patients could only feel unseen objects and then were asked to name them, they were much more successful when they touched the objects with their right hand, which suggested that the objects' names were more readily available to the left hemisphere, which controls the right hand. On the other hand, the right hemisphere performed better in picking out the right objects on the basis of touch, when the patients were shown the pictures of those objects. Experiments also showed that the two hemispheres make different kinds of associations. In particular, Levy and Trevarthen (1976) demonstrated that the left hemisphere associated the objects it could see on the basis of their functional properties, for example a cake was associated with a fork and spoon, a pair of scissors was associated with pins and thread, while the right hemisphere associated objects on the basis of their physical similarity, for example a cake on a plate was associated with a hat, a pair of scissors was associated with a crossed spoon and fork. These functional associations suggest that it is the left hemisphere that is responsible for metonymic thinking and speaking, while the metaphoric mappings are carried out in the right hemisphere. This conjecture is further supported by the evidence suggesting that it is the left hemisphere that analyses and represents objects as integrated wholes consisting of specified parts. Pinker discusses a patient, who, having suffered a left-hemisphere stroke, complained:

> When I try to imagine a plant, an animal, an object, I can recall but one part. My inner vision is fleeting, fragmented; if I'm asked to imagine the head of a cow, I know it has ears and horns, but I can't revisualise their places.
>
> (Pinker 1997: 271)

Moreover, the left hemisphere does not only represent parts of physical objects, it is also instrumental in perceiving and representing narrative wholes in terms of parts. Gazzaninga (1992/1997) discusses experiments where split-brain patients were shown stories in the form of pictures depicting various stages of the story. The right hemisphere could remember and later recognise the pictures but when it saw a new picture it could not relate it to others, although it fitted well into the plot of the story. It seems that it is precisely this left hemisphere ability that is crucial for the emergence of propositional metonymies (discussed in Chapter 4), in which a single part of a script activates another part or the whole script. As we saw in Chapter 3, the PART-FOR-WHOLE metonymy also works on syntactic structures, normally localised in the left hemisphere. All this strongly suggests that metonymy is produced in the left hemisphere, a view explicitly expressed by Lofting (1997).

6.1.5 Neural motivation

The previous discussion suggests that metonymy is an 'embodied' mental process occurring naturally and unconsciously as a result of the synaptic links in the parts of the brain supporting mental and linguistic activities. In this sense it may be said that most metonymies, particularly the pragmatic ones, are neurally motivated. Thus, in addition to the motivations for metonymy (discussed briefly in the final section of Chapter 1), we may now view metonymy as a natural manifestation of the embodiment of language. However, as has been known at least since the publication of de Saussure's *Course of General Linguistics* (1915), the notion of motivation has its own special place in linguistics. For instance, in a recent paper, Heine (2004) suggests that two different kinds of motivation should be distinguished: structural motivation and genetic motivation. Following Lyons, Heine defines structural motivation as "any non-arbitrary form-meaning or meaning-meaning relationship that can be shown to be based on some general principle" (Lyons 1977: 105). Until recently it was assumed that language structures were essentially arbitrary, and hence it was the motivated structures that needed explaining. It seems that one of the merits of the present study, and indeed of most cognitive linguistic research, is that it gradually reduces the area of arbitrariness of language by revealing cognitive as well as (in the present account) possible neural motivations for the linguistic forms and meanings. In contrast, the genetic view of motivation is characterised as follows:

> Human behavior is not arbitrary but is driven by motivations. Language structure, being one of the products of behavior, therefore must also be motivated. If we find "arbitrary" language structures then these are in need of explanation. (Heine 2004: 105).

Heine's contention is of course true but it is one thing to say that language must be behaviourally motivated and it is another thing to show how the motivation actually works. One of the aims of this study has been to elucidate at least some aspects of this motivation. I believe that it is precisely the relationship between the embodied cognition (involving also cultural mimetic schemas) and language that points to the most promising directions of future research.

6.1.6 Summary

In their recent paper on motivation in language, Radden and Panther have suggested that "motivational processes (...) pertain to semiotic relations within the linguistic unit and/or across linguistic units" (2004: 14) and thus they can be represented in terms of five kinds of motivating relationships between content and form within a single unit and across units: (unmotivated) arbitrary semiotic relationship between content and form within one unit; content motivating form within one unit; form motivating content within one unit; content of one unit$_1$ motivating content of another unit$_2$; form of one unit$_1$ motivating form of another unit$_2$.

In addition, Radden and Panther consider language-independent factors of motivation. These include ecological motivation, genetic motivation, experiential motivation, perceptual motivation, cognitive motivation and communicative motivation. Radden and Panther also point out that there might be "other motivations", such as "biological and neurological determinants, which, however, are not yet sufficiently known" (2004: 31).

This chapter shows that, although we are far from knowing everything about the neural underpinnings of language and metonymy in particular, enough is known about the relationship between the neural, the mental and the linguistic phenomena to start formulating the first hypotheses. In particular, I have tried to show that Kövecses and Radden's (1998) definition of metonymy as a cognitive process whereby one conceptual entity provides mental access to another conceptual entity within the same domain, can be reinterpreted in neural terms. We have seen that the crucial aspects of metonymy, namely association, substitution and highlighting, all have well-established substrates in the workings of the central nervous system. These observations confirm the main thesis of the Neural Theory of Metonymy that, in general, metonymy is a cognitive manifestation of neural processes whereby the activation of one group (circuit) of neurons causes the activation of another group (circuit) of neurons. The co-activations take place both within particular neural pathways, enabling single modalities of an object to represent the whole object, as well as between various pathways representing relational aspects of objects integrated in cortical convergence zones such as the prefrontal lobes. Such pragmatic metonymies as AUTHORS FOR THEIR WORKS would be impossible without the neural mechanisms enabling the integration of image spaces and dispositional spaces. Although some of the proposals made above, particularly the ones concerning the neural substrates of metonymies based on the connections between activities, events and places, are rather speculative at this stage, I hope that future research in neuroscience will shed more light on those links and show to what extent such metonymies are motivated by the processes on the neural level. Finally, it should be observed that the dependence of specific kinds of metonymy on specific neural regions and circuits as well as the processes of their co-activation is a further strong argument in favour of the thesis of the embodiment of language, which is one of the pillars of cognitive linguistics (cf. Lakoff and Johnson 1999; Rohrer 2007). The data discussed above show that metonymy is the product of the most basic neural processes underlying human cognition; therefore it should be studied not as a rare figure of speech but as a basic mechanism of linguistic organisation. These neurological findings are further supported by what we know about the evolution and acquisition of language.

6.2 Metonymy in the origin and acquisition of language

If conceptual metonymy is indeed based on the most fundamental principles of neural mechanisms of cognition, which are also crucial for language and communication, the legitimate question arises about the evolutionary history of metonymy. In particular, I shall consider three questions:

1. Is it possible to detect earlier stages of 'metonymic capacity' in the evolutionary history of cognition? In other words, can we identify the pre-conceptual predecessors of conceptual metonymy?
2. What were the evolutionary beginnings of conceptual metonymy and what role did it play in the evolution of language?
3. Are there still traces of what happened thousands of years ago that are governed by the same metonymic principles?

6.2.1 Metonymy in perception

Kwiatkowska observes:

> Life would be really difficult if we had not developed mental strategies to overcome our perceptual limitations and to recover the whole from parts on the basis of our experience and memory; the ability to do so is one of the most basic human cognitive skills. It is not restricted to humans either. A dog will also know that a body part sticking out from under a blanket belongs to a larger whole. He is quite capable, too, of recognising an individual as a representative of a category (CAT or HUMAN). Like people, animals could not function if they did not have access to the PART-WHOLE schema. (2007: 298f)

Thus the first, most basic kind of metonymy might well have been perceptual. The chances of survival of our animal predecessors increased if they could identify their foods and their enemies earlier than others. This 'perceptual metonymy' gave them precisely this advantage: instead of perceiving the whole of a deer, it was enough for the wolf to see its rear or head, or hear it run. The principle was clearly metonymic: a perceived part or aspect enables the organism to identify the whole. However, the particular associative links did not appear indiscriminately all at once. As Zlatev (2003) points out, the mechanism is selective and species-specific (e.g. pigeons associate food with sight but not with smell or sound, rats can associate shock with size but not taste).

On the other hand, the whole can 'stand' for its parts too: the predator hardly ever eats the whole of its prey. In fact, he chases the whole in order to get the tastiest parts. Perceptually, however, the identification of the whole makes it possible to access the perceptual parts, which is the true reason why the predator starts its chase. As Kwiatkowska quite rightly points out, the evolutionary development of perceptual metonymy could have arisen only in conjunction with an even more basic ability to categorise: for it is the types that have a real survival value, not the individual tokens (i.e. the wolf instinctively 'knows' that it is the whole extension of the category DEER that provides it with food, not only some particular individual). This in turn suggests that the emergence of perceptual metonymy was conditioned by the prior emergence of the categorising capacity and the fact the categories were represented in the brain. Since the first representations were probably perceptual, the first metonymies were perceptual as well. Nonetheless, more complex cognitive representations in the form of teleological causality associating the stimulus, response and the expected result probably followed shortly afterwards (cf. Zlatev 2003).

The perceptual mechanisms enabling humans to categorise 'wholes' on the basis of the perception of parts has been well known at least since the publication of the studies of perception conducted by German Gestalt psychologists. These mechanisms, known as laws of perception, include the laws of proximity, similarity, continuity, closure, symmetry and local attitude (cf. Wertheimer 1923; discussed also by Jackendoff 1983; Crick 1997: ch. 4; Maruszewski 2001). In addition Jackendoff (1983: ch. 3) argues that the viewer's internal state also contributes to perception. The internal factors may include the viewer's intention or need, as well as the knowledge (familiarity) of the perceived objects. In Bierwiaczonek (2005) I pointed out that such shapes as straight, circle and square may function as perceptual image schemas which are particularly 'familiar' and various arrangements of dots in psychological experiments are usually filled in (see §6.1.2.2) and thus made continuous wholes according to those schemas.

Consequently, this metonymic capacity might have constituted an important element of what Bates (1994) called 'cognitive infrastructure' on the basis of which conceptual metonymy could develop. On the other hand, however, in evolutionary terms it is the same capacity that was probably necessary for the emergence of language itself. Dąbrowska (2004: 62) suggests that there are at least four kinds of pre-adaptations necessary in order for natural language to develop. These are:

1. proto-phonological capacities, such as the ability to produce and recognise sounds and to coordinate complex motor routines involving the articulators
2. proto-semantic capacities, such as the ability to categorise percepts and to construct complex concepts (as well as some elementary concepts and/or feature detectors)
3. the capacity to form cross-modal associations (necessary to learn form-meaning pairings)
4. the ability to store and restore such pairings when required.

It seems that what we now know about metonymy enables us to slightly modify the above formulation. For it is not only the capacities to form, store and restore the cross-modal, cross-conceptual and form-meaning associations that are necessary for language. What is crucial is the metonymic ability to access particular parts or wholes of those associations through their other parts or wholes. In terms of Zlatev's theory of meaning (Zlatev 2003), this metonymic ability emerged and developed gradually as an important aspect of associational and mimetic meaning systems and was only possible because of the increasingly important role of what Piaget called 'symbols' and what Zlatev (2007) calls 'internalized imitations' or 'mimetic schemas'. Since these schemas were the first representations, the organism could now detach itself from the presence of its referent. It was through the capacity for co-activation of and within those first representations that the first holophrases probably emerged as meaningful units, to be further constrained by two-word sequences and telegraphic speech. And it was probably after this stage that another non-language-specific ability, namely the ability to package sequences of movements and incorporate them into more elaborate actions (cf. Dąbrowska 2004: 65ff) was exapted as the basic mechanism of syntax.

6.2.2 From perceptions to concepts, to protolanguage

It is not clear how adaptive perceptual metonymy could have extended to concepts and developed into full-fledged conceptual and verbal metonymy typical of humans. Zlatev (2007) is probably right when he insists that it must have been mediated by bodily mimesis, with its concomitant first representations and 'communicative sign function'. However, it must also have been associated with the evolution of long-term memory and the increasingly sophisticated ability to categorise, one of the hallmarks and driving forces of the fast-evolving hominids. Long-term memory enabled them to store increasingly more memories of individuals and events, probably based on mimetic schemas, while the categorising capacity made it possible for them to form categories and hence concepts on perceptual but also non-perceptual grounds. The first links of this kind were inherited from our animal ancestors. These were the first signals in the form of the most basic life-sustaining and life-threatening calls. In this way, most species informed other species-members of their readiness to procreate or of imminent danger. Animal signals are characterised by a fixed association of STIMULUS (internal state, object or occasion) > RESPONSE′ (call) > RESPONSE″ (the 'addressee's' behaviour). As Cheney and Seyfarth (1990) have shown in their study of vervet monkey communication, there is a different danger signal used when a snake is around (something like CHUTTER) and another (RRAUP) when an eagle is in sight, each provoking different behaviours (RESPONSE). Although we might legitimately ask if these signals have prototype structure (i.e. if they apply to more-or-less obvious danger situations), they certainly cannot be used metonymically, for example they cannot be used to mean 'Have you just seen a snake?' or 'If the snake comes along we can kill it and have a great feast'. Or, as Jackendoff puts it, "a leopard alarm call can report the sighting of a leopard, but cannot be used to ask if anyone has seen a leopard lately" (Jackendoff 2002: 239).

However, probably rather early, it also transpired that the more you could communicate, the higher your chances of survival, hence the communicative neural adaptations (or exaptations) of the evolving brain, particularly its pre-frontal cortex, made it possible to gradually (or perhaps suddenly) develop more complex neural networks, which enabled the organism to communicate more meanings. For instance, the perceptual properties of a piece of stone (colour, hardness) might have been supplemented by its functional properties, such as its usefulness in fighting. This was the dawn of the conceptual-metonymic mind and metonymic proto-language. Those first conceptual links made it possible for the hominids to use the original holoforms of the original protolanguage in non-situation-specific senses. The first of those was "the voluntary use of discrete symbolic vocalisations (or other signals such as gestures" (Jackendoff 2002: 239). Those, as Jackendoff names them, "single-symbol utterances" differ from primate calls in that they are non-situation-specific. In other words, now *leopard* can be used to ask if anyone has seen a leopard lately.

Once this conceptual-metonymic mechanism developed, it provided the speakers of protolanguage with considerable expressive power, certainly much greater than that of animal calls, but also different from language as we know it. The main problem with this new expressiveness was that it was too powerful: without the constraints of the context, a single proto-word could mean virtually anything – virtually because it was probably constrained by the existing mimetic schemas. What was needed was a way of narrowing down the range of metonymic interpretations to those that the speaker was trying to convey without necessarily resorting to context. Thus, the first metonymic step was followed by two more steps. The first was also metonymic and led directly to what is sometimes called "protolanguage" (Bickerton 1990) or "The Basic Variety" (Klein and Perdue 1997). It consisted in simply concatenating two or more symbols, which, compared to single words, reduced the number of possible meanings of utterances to those which involved both participants or a single participant and his, her or its activity or property, for example *Mary beautiful* could still mean a lot of things, like 'Mary is beautiful' or 'Mary is making herself beautiful' or 'Mary is dancing beautifully' or even 'Mary has made something beautiful', but it could not mean 'Mary is hungry' or 'Mary has found a big bone' or 'Mary is badly hurt', which could all be communicated by *Mary* alone. Studies of animal communication suggest that primates have this concatenating ability to some extent. For instance, the famous Nim Chimpsky was able to convey quite complex meanings using up to three signs, for example *yogurt Nim eat* or *more eat Nim* (cf. Aitchison 1996). Another well-known example is the bonobo Kanzi, which was taught to use logograms and also learnt to put them together to convey meanings involving a combination of concepts.

The proposal that purely metonymic meaning-construction preceded the emergence of syntax is also supported by the examples of speakers who, for some reason, cannot rely on their syntactic competence, as in the case of speakers of pidgin and agrammatic aphasics (cf. Bickerton 1990). Finally, it should be mentioned that basic, pre-syntactic communication has by no means been superseded by syntax, even in fully developed 'modern' languages. As Jackendoff (2002: 240) has pointed out, there are still "fossils" of the non-grammatic proto-words in most languages (such as pure expressives in English like *ouch, dammit, wow*), lexicalised but still basically metonymic conversions (cf. Dirven 1999) and grammatical processes still relying on pure concatenation, whose meanings are almost open-ended and determined more by pragmatics than by syntactic constraints, such as the English N-N compounds discussed in Chapter 3 (see also Jackendoff 2002: 249ff and Sweetser 1999 for illuminating discussion). In fact, one can still see the two tendencies in meaning-construction that we have discussed, which were so essential in the evolution of language. On the one hand, there are hundreds of examples of the type illustrated by the famous *The pork chop has left without paying*, and, on the other hand, there are grammatical or morphological mechanisms put in place that constrain the range of interpretations such as diminutive suffixes in Polish which indicate a metonymic shift – BODY PART FOR DISH MADE OF THIS BODY PART, as in *nóżki* (little legs), *płucka* (little lungs), *skrzydełka* (little wings) and syntax in general (cf. Brdar 2007).

Although those formal ways of constraining this basically metonymic open-ended mechanism of meaning-construction later developed into modern languages, it has not disappeared as an effective means of communication. For instance, in a context when a farmer's family are worried about their crops because of a drought, it is enough for one of them to say *Rain,* on getting up, to make everybody wake up and communicate the whole propositional structure "It's raining". Consider also the following short exchanges:

(1) A: How did you spend the weekend?
     B: Nothing special; just beer and TV.
(2) A: Oh, my God. I had no idea Bill was dead. Do you know what happened?
     B: Heart attack.

In both examples B's answers are perfectly informative because the nominal expressions *beer and TV* and *heart attack,* that B uses metonymically, evoke the dispositional spaces of the complex events which A expects as answers to her questions. A similar metonymic strategy of meaning-construction is amply used by journalists when they form headlines of their stories, writers when they look for titles of their novels, stories, poems or songs, and almost anybody putting a note on the noticeboard of a well-defined institution such as a university (see Brown and Yule 1983).

6.2.3 Metonymy in first language acquisition

The plausibility of the suggestion that concatenated symbols were direct predecessors of grammar is also supported by acquisition studies. As is well known, most studies of first language acquisition distinguish several stages of the process (Kurcz 2000: ch. 7). Usually, after the pre-linguistic stage of babbling and cooing, children enter the stage of one-word communication, followed by the two-word stage, followed by the stage of multiword (telegraphic) communication with a lot of meaning and little syntax, which gradually gives way to the acquisition of syntax. Thus it seems that, as usual, the phylogenic origins of language are reiterated in ontogenesis. In particular, the one-word, two-word and telegraphic stages would be impossible without the metonymic capacity of the child's brain. However, this metonymic basis of acquisition has been usually ignored. For instance, Clark (1993) in her classic study of the acquisition of first language lexicon focuses mainly on 'over-inclusions' and 'analogical over-extensions'. However, the metonymic extensions seem to be at least as important. For instance, Nerlich et al. (1999) have demonstrated that the metonymic capacity manifests itself in two different ways in first language acquisition: in 'compelled over-extension' and 'creative metonymical shrinking'. The compelled over-extension has to do with the more general strategies the child uses in order to compensate for her limited vocabulary. It takes on three different forms. The first form is referred to as 'synecdochical overextensions', that is Clarke's 'over-inclusions', based on conceptual contiguity inside a taxonomy, for example *papa* used for father, grandfather, mother or any man. The second type are 'metaphorical over-extensions' (equivalent to Clarke's 'analogical over-extensions', based on perceptual similarity), for example *milk bottle* used for a bottle containing white tooth powder. Finally, Nerlich et al. also distinguish "compelled metonymical over-extensions", which are "based on perceptual, spatio-temporal and functional contiguity" (1999: 367). Thus the word *wheel* can be used to denote or refer to a wheelbarrow, a toy wagon or a ring, while *choo-choo* may be used to mean a train, airplane, streetcar, wheelbarrow, in other words anything that produces a sound resembling [tʃuː tʃuː]. Surprisingly, the data discussed by Nerlich et al. represent a lot of the most common 'adult' metonymies. Consider a few examples and the high-level mappings they represent:

(a) *want pocket* – CONTAINER (*pocket*) FOR CONTENT ('sweets')
(b) *here more book* – INSTRUMENT (*book*) FOR ACTION ('reading')
(c) *all gone blow* – ACTION (*blow*) FOR INSTRUMENT ('match')
(d) *that hello* – WORDS (*hello*) FOR OBJECT ('telephone')

Note that these utterances are also meant to have a metonymically determined illocutionary force: (a) and (b) are requests, while (c) and (d) are comments.

Compelled metonymic extensions are typical of the early period of language acquisition (approximately till the age of 2.5) and gradually, at about the age of 5.0, give way to what Nerlich et al. call 'creative metonymical shrinking', because, they argue, they are metonymies "usually produced in order to communicate new ideas with the least verbal effort" (1999: 370). These metonymies are already fully integrated with the well-developed syntax. They are thus reduced to single conceptual mappings, the exact relations and speech-act properties being taken over by syntax. Here are three examples with the researchers' emphases and comments:

(3) Matthew was wearing a pullover that went down to his knees – we laughed and said it was a mini-dress, whereupon he pretended to be a girl and started to curtsey. As he was not very good at it, he practised all afternoon. At bedtime he pulled off the pullover and said "*I have enough of it, I have been wearing this **curtsey** all day.*"

(4) Matthew was playing with his Playmobil operating theater. He was asked by a doctor-friend "*Do you want to become a doctor in an operating theater, that is a surgeon like me?*" – "*No,*" he said, "*I don't like the **breathing-in-stuff** (anesthesiologist), I would rather be a **listen-to-your-heart-doctor**"* (physician).

(5) While eating cheese on biscuits, Matthew said: "*I'm eating a **bone-sandwich**.*" – Why? – "*Because cheese is good for your bones*".

In Example 3 Matthew uses the conceptual metonymy ACTIVITY-FOR-OBJECT-INVOLVED-IN-THIS-ACTIVITY (the activity of curtseying for 'pullover'). This metonymy was also at work in the conversion of the verb *cheat* to denote an object involved in cheating (e.g. *That liquidiser was a cheat – it broke down completely only two days after I'd bought it*). Other examples are not hard to find. Consider for example *the support, a press, a write-off, a rip-off,* as well as *the breathing-in-stuff* (in Example 4) although this is further extended to 'anesthesiologist' through OBJECT FOR USER. The relevant metonymy in the second expression in Example 4, namely *listen-to-your-heart doctor*, seems to be CHARACTERISTIC ACTIVITY FOR PROPERTY OR DISTINCTIVE FEATURE (or WHAT YOU DO FOR WHAT YOU'RE LIKE), motivating, among others, the attributing meaning of present participles, as in *loving husband, interesting book, hard-working guy, living animals*, and infinitival N-premodifiers, for example *a cry-baby, a die-hard supporter, a turn-the-other-cheek Catholic, well-to-do citizens*, or personal nouns converted from action-verbs such as *a tearaway, a creep, an easy lay*.

In Example 5 Matthew is using the full expressive metonymic potential of English N-N compounds, which blend the mental spaces metonymically activated by both components of the compound. In the case of *bone-sandwich* the relevant spaces are those of the human body (whole activated by part: *bone*), and eating with its nourishing consequences, activated by *sandwich* (see Turner and Fauconnier 1995 and Benczes 2006 for other examples).

In summary, if we compare the findings we have presented in this chapter with the facts discussed in Chapters 2 to 5, the situation seems paradoxical. On the one hand, metonymy, defined as a process of co-activation and highlighting based on association, is shown to be productive but on the whole contingent in the domains of linguistic forms and meanings on all levels of linguistic organisation. On the other hand, however, metonymy can also be viewed as a pre-linguistic principle of meaning-construction, which was (and continues to be) fundamental and necessary in the phylogenic and ontogenetic development of language.

I am not sure if we are genetically equipped with 'language instinct', but we are certainly born with the need to communicate, and metonymy is no doubt one of the most effective cognitive tools that can make communication happen, the tool which, along with a few others, like mimesis, has ultimately led and, in the case of our own short stories of language acquisition, leads to the emergence of language.

Notes

1 Large parts of the present chapter have already been discussed in Bierwiaczonek (2007b).
2 Which may explain why *Forget it* means 'It is not important' and hence 'Don't do anything about it'. It is as if denying one part of a complex representation implies the denial of other parts as well.
3 The effect is based on the consistent association of drawings showing an inkblot and a jagged piece of shattered glass with sounds *bouba* and *kiki*, respectively, independently of the language of the speakers.
4 Penfield homunculus (also known as 'cortical homunculus') is a pictorial representation of the primary motor cortex and the primary somatosensory cortex, which was created in the 1950s by the Canadian neurologist Wilder Penfield.
5 Other principles of verbal communication suggested in the literature are discussed in Turner (2009).

7 Summary and prospects for future research

7.1 Summary

What we have presented in this book can be summarised in nine main points:

1. Metonymy is a process of transfer of meaning based on the co-activation of two relatively strongly associated concepts or conceptual structures (such as the propositional parts of scripts) which are part of a single coherent conceptualisation. The metonymic process involves co-activation of the target concept or target conceptual structure by means of a vehicle which is conceptually highlighted. In general, metonymy is contingent, except for lexicalised catachretic metonymy when the target concept or conceptual structure has no independent lexical representation.

2. There are three basic kinds of metonymy, depending on the structural relationship between the vehicle and the target concept or conceptual structure: WHOLE X FOR PART OF X, PART OF X FOR WHOLE X and PART(Y) OF X FOR PART(Z) OF X. In general, the more independent and conceptually entrenched the vehicle and the target, the more prototypical the metonymy. In synecdochic metonymy, the vehicle and the target are both on the sub-basic level of categorisation and share a substantial part of their semantic representation.

3. The targets of metonymic mappings are well conceptualised and easily verbalised in non-metonymic ways; therefore active-zone phenomena, which involve non-conceptualised and hard-to-verbalise targets, are excluded from the scope of metonymy. Reference to objects belonging to categories involving facets may be metonymic or non-metonymic, depending on the co-activation or inhibition of the activation of facets. Only the latter case is considered metonymic.

4. From the point of view of the ontological domains of the vehicle and the target, metonymic expressions may be divided into formal, referential, propositional and illocutionary. Formal metonymy motivates a large number of morphological and syntactic phenomena, referential metonymy leads to extensions of lexical semantic structures, propositional metonymy often motivates the meaning of idioms and

implicatures, while illocutionary metonymy underlies the use of indirect speech acts.

5. Depending on the conceptual relation between the vehicle and the target concept or conceptual structure we may distinguish meronymy-, antonymy-, reversiveness- and synaesthesia-based metonymy.

6. Metonymy is an extremely productive way of extending the meanings of individual lexemes. The new metonymic senses are either catachretic, i.e. filling the lexical gaps of a language, or rhetorical, i.e. synonymous with other lexical items. Languages have their own particularly productive metonymy-generators (lexical items which have developed particularly rich polysemous structures through, often chained, metonymic extensions).

7. In evolutionary terms, the metonymic principle of co-activation of associated concepts and conceptual structures precedes the emergence of language. However, since the same metonymic principle makes it possible for single words, or two or more concatenated words, to evoke complex propositional structures, metonymy became one of the fundamental principles of proto-linguistic communication, which finally gave rise to language. This process is still reflected in first language acquisition as well as in spoken communication, breaking the phrase structure and clause structure rules of language.

8. Metonymic meaning in context is an emergent result of the blending of the image space (the target conceptualisation) with the dispositional space (conceptual-lexical vehicle) constrained by the Principle of Correspondence, which requires that the dispositional space match the current image space as closely as possible.

9. Metonymy is a conceptual and linguistic manifestation of the basic neural mechanisms of cognition typical of the left hemisphere of the human brain.

7.2 As for the future …

As for future research related to the issues discussed in this study, the most interesting lines of investigation seem to be the following:

1. Further research into the role of metonymy in the origin of language, pidgins, first and second language acquisition.

2. Further research into the role of metonymy in discourse, with special emphasis on formal, propositional and illocutionary metonymy (along the lines of Panther and Thornburg (1998, 1999, 2000, 2003b), Traugott and Dasher (2002), Brinton and Traugott (2005) among others), as

well as non-grammaticalised forms of expression (e.g. one-word and two-word communication).

3. The role of formal, propositional and illocutionary metonymy in the emergence of grammatical constructions from typological perspective, along the lines of Panther and Thornburg (1999), Hernandez (2007) and Brdar-Szabó (2007).

4. Verification, on the basis of neural studies, of the proposal made here that WHOLE-FOR-PART metonymy and active-zone phenomena are two distinct processes.

5. Verification and refinement of the neural basis of different kinds of concepts and conceptual relations on which the theory of metonymy and semantic relations presented here is based. In particular, answers should be sought to such questions as: What is the neural substrate of the term 'coherent conceptualisation'? What neurological sense does it make to say that two or more concepts are strongly or weakly associated, or that two concepts overlap or are included in one another? Do synonymous concepts indeed involve necessary co-activation of some part of the neural circuits that support them? Are there processing and neural differences between WHOLE-FOR-PART, PART-FOR-PART and PART-FOR-WHOLE metonymies?

6. In light of the theory of blending, based on the integration of dispositional and image spaces (Damasio 1999), it is extremely important to investigate the role of different memory systems, in particular short-term and long-term memory and how they interact in working memory, as well as the way metonymic expressions are represented in declarative and procedural memory systems (cf. Ullman 2004). In particular, it would be interesting to check if the metonymic patterns evident in ad hoc referential and propositional metonymies are part of procedural memory. Longitudinal studies could also show if there is any discernible change from declarative to procedural memory systems accompanying various forms of grammaticalisation, including their neural substrates.

7. Verification of various constraints on metonymy and research into the implications of The Principle of Correspondence.

8. Identification of the most important cortical and subcortical convergence zones for metonymy.

9. Further studies into the influence of intersubjectivity and mimetic (mirroring) processes in the brain on cognition in general and metonymy in particular.

References

Ahlsén, E. (2006) *Introduction to Neurolinguistics*. Amsterdam/Philadelphia: John Benjamins Publishing Company.

Aitchison, J. (1996) *The Seeds of Speech. Language Origin and Evolution*. Cambridge: Cambridge University Press.

Allan, K. and Burridge, K. (1991) *Euphemism and Dysphemism. Language Used as Shield and Weapon*. New York, Oxford: Oxford University Press.

Al-Sharafi, A. G. M. (2004) *Textual Metonymy. A Semiotic Approach*. New York: Palgrave Macmillan.

Arbib, A.M. and Rizzolatti, G. (1999) Neural expectations: a possible evolutionary path from manual skills to language. In P. Van Loocke (ed.) *The Nature of Concepts. Evolution, Structure and Representation,* 128–154. London and New York: Routledge.

Aristotle. *Rhetoric* and *Poetics*, translated into Polish by H. Podbielski (1988). Warsaw: Państwowe Wydawnictwo Naukowe.

Bach, A. (1952) *Deutsche Namenkunde*. Bd. I: Die deutschen Personannamen. 2nd edition. Heidelberg: Winter.

Bach, E. (1974) *Syntactic Theory*. New York: Holt, Rinehart and Winston.

Balteiro, I. (2007) *A Contribution to the Study of Conversion in English*. Münster/ New York/ München/ Berlin: Waxmann.

Barber, C. (1993) *The English Language. A Historical Introduction*. (7th printing). Cambridge: Cambridge University Press.

Barcelona, A. (2000) On the plausibility of claiming a metonymic motivation for conceptual metaphor. In A. Barcelona (ed.) *Metaphor and Metonymy at the Crossroads,* 31–58. Berlin, New York: Mouton de Gruyter.

Barcelona, A. (2003 [1998]) Clarifying and applying metaphor and metonymy. In R. Dirven and R. Pörings (eds) *Metaphor and Metonymy in Comparison and Contrast,* 207–277. Berlin, New York: Mouton de Gruyter.

Barcelona, A. (2004) Metonymy behind grammar: the motivation for the seemingly 'irregular' grammatical behavior of English paragon names. In G. Radden and K-U. Panther (eds) *Studies in Linguistic Motivation,* 357–374. Berlin, New York: Mouton de Gruyter.

Barcelona, A. (2005) The multilevel operations of metonymy in grammar and discourse, with particular attention to metonymic chains. In F. Ruiz de Mendoza and S. Peña Cervel (eds) *Cognitive Linguistics: Internal Dynamics and Interdisciplinary Interaction,* 313–352. Berlin: Mouton de Gruyter.

Barcelona, A. (2007) The multi-level role of metonymy in grammar and discourse: a case study. In K. Kosecki (2007a), 103–131.

Barnden, J. A. (2010) Metaphor and metonymy: making their connections more slippery. *Cognitive Linguistics* 21 (1): 1–34.

Bates, E. (1994) Modularity, domain specificity and the development of language. *Discussions in Neuroscience* 10: 136–49.

Bauer, L. (1983) *English Word-formation.* Cambridge: Cambridge University Press.

Bauer, L. (2005) Conversion and the notion of lexical category. In L. Bauer and S. Varela (eds) *Approaches to Conversion/Zero Derivation,* 19–30. Münster/New York/München/Berlin: Waxmann.

Bauer, L. (2009) Typology of compounds. In R. Lieber and P. Štekauer (eds) *The Oxford Handbook of Compounding,* 343–356. Oxford: Oxford University Press.

Benczes, R. (2006) *Creative Compounding in English. The Semantics of Metaphorical and Metonymical Noun-Noun Combinations.* Amsterdam/Philadelphia: John Benjamins Publishing Company.

Bergen, B. (2004) The psychological reality of phonaesthemes. *Language* 80: 290–311.

Berk, L. (1999) *English Syntax: From Word to Discourse.* Oxford: Oxford University Press.

Bickerton, D. (1990) *Language and Species.* Chicago: University of Chicago Press.

Bierwiaczonek, B. (1990) 'A Cognitive Study of Axiological Aspects of Language'. Unpublished doctoral dissertation, University of Gdańsk.

Bierwiaczonek, B. (2000) Metonymies of love. In B. Rozwadowska (ed.) *Proceedings of the 8th Annual Conference of the Polish Association for the Study of English,* 53–60. Wrocław: Aksel s.c.

Bierwiaczonek, B. (2001) Implikatury jako metonimie, czyli o poznawczych podstawach pragmatyki. In W. Kubiński and D. Stanulewicz (eds) *Językoznawstwo kognitywne II. Zjawiska pragmatyczne,* 95–115. Gdańsk: Wydawnictwo Uniwersytetu Gdańskiego.

Bierwiaczonek, B. (2002a) Implicatures and metonymies. In J. Burzyńska and D. Stanulewicz (eds) *Proceedings of the 9th Annual Conference of the Polish Association for the Study of English,* 78–90. Gdańsk: Wydawnictwo Uniwersytetu Gdańskiego.

Bierwiaczonek, B. (2002b) *A Cognitive Study of the Concept of Love in English.* Katowice: Wydawnictwo Uniwersytetu Śląskiego.

Bierwiaczonek, B. (2004a) Geometry in perception, thought and language. In B. Lewandowska-Tomaszczyk and A. Kwiatkowska (eds) *Imagery in Language. Festschrift in Honor of Professor Ronald W. Langacker,* 321–341. Frankfurt am Main: Peter Lang.

Bierwiaczonek, B. (2004b) I metonymize therefore I stereotype. In A. Barker (ed.) *The Power and Persistence of Stereotypes,* 33–49. Aveiro: University of Aveiro Press.

Bierwiaczonek, B. (2005) On the neural and conceptual basis of semantic relations and metonymy. In E. Górska and G. Radden (eds) *Metonymy-Metaphor Collage,* 11–36. Warsaw: Warsaw University Press.

Bierwiaczonek, B. (2006a) O języku ucieleśnionym. In O. Sokołowska and D. Stanulewicz (eds) *Językoznawstwo kognitywne III. Kognitywizm w świetle innych teorii,* 444–479. Gdańsk: Wydawnictwo Uniwersytetu Gdańskiego.

Bierwiaczonek, B. (2006b) Teorie metonimii – historia, dzień dzisiejszy i perspektywy. In O. Sokołowska and D. Stanulewicz (eds) *Językoznawstwo kognitywne III. Kognitywizm w świetle innych teorii,* 227–245. Gdańsk: Wydawnictwo Uniwersytetu Gdańskiego.

Bierwiaczonek, B. (2007a) On formal metonymy. In K. Kosecki (2007a), 43–67.

Bierwiaczonek, B. (2007b) Toward a neural theory of metonymy. In B. Bierwiaczonek and C. Humphries (eds) *Studies in English Culture, Literature and Linguistics.* Vol. 1. 17–36. Bielsko-Biala: Wydawnictwo Akademii Techniczno-Humanistycznej.

Bierwiaczonek, B. (2007c) On sense generators in translation. In A. Baicchi (ed.) *Rassegna Italiana di Linguistica Applicata. Voices on Translation. Linguistic, Multimedia and Cognitive Perspectives,* 277–293. Rome: Bulzoni Editore.

Bierwiaczonek, B. (2007d) Synonymy reactivated. *Linguistica Silesiana* 28: 7–21.

Bierwiaczonek, B. (2010) Active zones revisited and revised. In B. Bierwiaczonek and A. Turula (eds) *Studies in Cognitive Semantics,* 6–27. Czestochowa: Wydawnictwo WSL.

Black, M. (1993) More about metaphor. In A. Ortony (ed.) *Metaphor and Thought,* 2nd edition, 19–41. Cambridge: Cambridge University Press.

Blank, A. (1999a) Why do new meanings occur? In A. Blank and P. Koch (eds) *Historical Semantics and Cognition,* 61–89. Berlin, New York: Mouton de Gruyter.

Blank, A. (1999b) Co-presence and succession. A cognitive typology of metonymy. In K-U. Panther and G. Radden (eds) *Metonymy in Language and Thought,* 169–191. Amsterdam/Philadelphia: John Benjamins Publishing Company.

Blank, A. (2003) Polysemy in the lexicon and in discourse. In B. Nerlich, Z. Todd, V. Herman and D. D. Clarke (eds) *Polysemy. Flexible Patterns of Meaning in Mind and Language,* 267–293. Berlin, New York: Mouton de Gruyter.

Bloomfield, L. (1933) *Language.* New York: Henry Holt and Company.

Bower, G. H., Black, J. B. and Turner, T. J. (1979) Scripts in memory for texts. *Cognitive Psychology* 11: 177–220.

Bråten, S. (ed.) *On Being Moved. From Mirror Neurons to Empathy.* Amsterdam/ Philadelphia: John Benjamins Publishing Company.

Brdar, M. (2007) Where have all the metonymies gone? In K. Kosecki (2007a), 69–86.

Brdar, M. and Brdar-Shabó, R. (2003) Metonymic coding of linguistic action. In K-U. Panther and L. Thornburg (eds) *Metonymy in Pragmatic Inferencing,* 241–266. Amsterdam/Philadelphia: John Benjamins Publishing Company.

Brdar, M. and Brdar-Shabó, R. (2007) When Zidane is not simply Zidane, and Bill Gates is not just Bill Gates. Some thoughts on the construction of metaphtonymic meanings of proper names. In G. Radden, K-M. Köpke, T. Berg and P. Siemund (eds) *Aspects of Meaning Construction,* 125–142. Amsterdam/Philadelphia: John Benjamins Publishing Company.

Brdar-Szabó, R. (2007) The role of metonymy in motivating cross-linguistic differences in the exploitation of stand-alone conditionals in indirect directives. In K. Kosecki (2007a), 175–197.

Brinton, L. and Traugott, E. C. (2005) *Lexicalization and Language Change.* Cambridge: Cambridge University Press.

Brown, G. and Yule, G. (1983) *Discourse Analysis.* Cambridge: Cambridge University Press.

Burkhardt, A. (1996) Zwischen Poesie und Ökonomie. Die Metonymie als semantisches Prinzip. *Zeitschrift für germanistische Linguistik* 24 (2): 175–194.

Cantor, N. and Mischel, W. (1979) Prototypes in person perception. In L. Berkowitz (ed.) *Advances in Experimental Social Psychology.* Vol. 12. 3–52. New York: Academic Press.

Carter, R. and McCarthy, M. (2006) *Cambridge Grammar of English. A Comprehensive Guide.* Cambridge: Cambridge University Press.

Cetnarowska, B. (1993) *The Syntax, Semantics and Derivation of Bare Nominalisations in English.* Katowice: Wydawnictwo Uniwersytetu Śląskiego.

Chaffin, R. and Herrmann, D. J. (1984) The similarity and diversity of semantic relations. *Memory and Cognition* 12: 134–41.

Cheney, D. and Seyfarth, R. (1990) *How Monkeys See the World.* Chicago: University of Chicago Press.

Cienki, A. (1998) STRAIGHT: An image schema and its metaphorical extensions. *Cognitive Linguistics* 9 (2): 107–150.

Clark, E. (1993) *The Lexicon in Acquisition.* Cambridge: Cambridge University Press.

Clausner, T. and Croft, W. (1999) Domains and image schemas. *Cognitive Linguistics* 10 (1): 1–31.

Crick, F. (1997) Zdumiewająca hipoteza, czyli nauka w poszukiwaniu duszy. Trans. B. Chęcińska-Abrahamowicz and M. Abrahamowicz. Warsaw: Prószyński i S-ka.

Croft, W. (1993) The role of domains in the interpretation of metaphors and metonymies. *Cognitive Linguistics* 4 (4): 335–370.

Croft, W. (2006) On explaining metonymy: Comment on Peirsman and Geeraerts, "Metonymy as a prototypical category". *Cognitive Linguistics* 17 (3): 317–326.

Croft, W. and Cruse, A. (2004) *Cognitive Linguistics.* Cambridge: Cambridge University Press.

Cruse, A. (1986) *Lexical Semantics.* Cambridge: Cambridge University Press.

Cruse, A. (1995) Between polysemy and monosemy: senses, facets and qualia roles. In H. Kardela and G. Persson (eds) *New Trends in Semantics and Lexicography,* 25–34. Umeå: Acta Universitatis Umensis.

Cruse, A. (2000) *Meaning in Language. An Introduction to Semantics and Pragmatics.* 2nd edition. Oxford: Oxford University Press.

Culicover, P. and Jackendoff, R. (2005) *Simpler Syntax.* Oxford: Oxford University Press.

Cytowic, R. E. (1995) Synesthesia: phenomenology and neuropsychology. A review of current knowledge. *Psyche* 2 (10).

Dąbrowska, E. (2004) *Language, Mind and Brain. Some Psychological and Neurological Constraints on Theories of Grammar.* Edinburgh: Edinburgh University Press.

Damasio, A. (1994) *Decartes' Error. Emotion, Reason and the Human Brain.* New York: Grosset/Putnam.

Damasio, A. (1999) *The Feeling of What Happens. Body and Emotion in the Making of Consciousness.* San Diego, New York, London: Harcourt Inc.

Damasio, A., Tranel, D. and Damasio, H. (1990) Face agnosia and the neural substrates of memory. *Annual Review of Neuroscience* 13: 89–109.

Damasio, H. (1999) Words and concepts in the brain. In J. Branquinho (ed.) *The Foundations of Cognitive Science,* 107–120. Oxford: Clarendon Press.

Dancygier, B. (1980) Non-typical cases of plural nouns in English and Polish. *Papers and Studies in Contrastive Linguistics* XI: 75–94.

Dancygier, B. and Sweetser, E. (2005) *Mental Spaces in Grammar. Conditional Constructions*. Cambridge: Cambridge University Press.

Dirven, R. (1985) Metaphor as a basic means of extending the lexicon. In W. Paprotté and R. Dirven (eds) *The Ubiquity of Metaphor. Metaphor in Language and Thought*, 85–120. Amsterdam/Philadelphia: John Benjamins.

Dirven, R. (1999) Conversion as a conceptual metonymy of event schemata. In K-U. Panther and G. Radden (eds) *Metonymy in Language and Thought*, 275–287. Amsterdam/Philadelphia: John Benjamins Publishing Company.

Dirven, R. (2003) Metonymy and metaphor: Different strategies of conceptualization. In R. Dirven and R. Pörings (eds) *Metaphor and Metonymy in Comparison and Contrast*, 75–111. Berlin, New York: Mouton de Gruyter.

Dirven, R. and Verspoor, M. (1998) *Cognitive Exploration of Language and Linguistics*. Amsterdam/Philadelphia: John Benjamins Publishing Company.

Dirven, R. and Pörings, R. (2003) (eds) *Metaphor and Metonymy in Comparison and Contrast*. Berlin, New York: Mouton de Gruyter.

Dodge, E. and Lakoff, G. (2005) Image schemas: From linguistic analysis to neural grounding. In B. Hampe (ed.) *From Perception to Meaning. Image Schemas in Cognitive Linguistics*, 57–91. Amsterdam/Philadelphia: John Benjamins Publishing Company.

Ekman, P. (1972) Universals and cultural differences in facial expressions of emotion. In J. Cole (ed.) *Nebraska Symposium on Motivation*, 207–283. Lincoln: University of Nebraska Press.

Esnault, G. (1925) *L'Imagination Populaire: Métaphores Occidentals*. Paris: Presses Universitaires de France.

Fabiszak, M. (2001) Kognitywne ujęcie aktów mowy na podstawie Koriolana Szekspira w tłumaczeniu Stanisława Barańczaka. In W. Kubiński and D. Stanulewicz (eds) *Językoznawstwo kognitywne II. Zjawiska pragmatyczne*, 159–169. Gdańsk: Wydawnictwo Uniwersytetu Gdańskiego.

Fadiga, L. and Craighero, L. (2007) Cues on the origin of language: From electrophysiological data on mirror neurons and motor representations. In S. Bråten (ed.) *On Being Moved. From Mirror Neurons to Empathy*, 101–110. Amsterdam/Philadelphia: John Benjamins Publishing Company.

Fauconnier, G. (1985) *Mental Spaces*. Cambridge, MA.: MIT Press.

Fauconnier, G. and Turner, M. (1998) Conceptual Integration Networks. *Cognitive Science* 22(2): 133–187. Reprinted in Geeraerts (ed.) (2006), 303–371.

Fauconnier, G. and Turner, M. (2002) *The Way We Think. Conceptual Blending and the Mind's Hidden Complexities*. New York: Basic Books.

Feyaerts, K. (1999) Metonymic hierarchies. The conceptualization of stupidity in German idiomatic expressions. In K-U. Panther and G. Radden (eds) *Metonymy in Language and Thought*, 309–332. Amsterdam/Philadelphia: John Benjamins Publishing Company.

Fillmore, C. (1982) Frame semantics. In The Linguistic Society of Korea (ed.) *Linguistics in the Morning Calm*, 111–137. Seoul: Hanshin Publishing Co.

Fillmore, C. (1985) Frames and the semantics of understanding. *Quaderni di Semantica* 6 (2): 222–253.

Fillmore, C. J., Kay, P. and O'Connor, M. K. (1988) Regularity and idiomaticity in grammatical constructions: the case of let alone. *Language* 64: 501–38.

Fischbach, G. (1992/4) Mind and brain. A *Scientific American* Special Report. *Scientific American*. (offprint)

Fleischman, S. (1982) *The Future in Thought and Language. Diachronic Evidence from Romance.* Cambridge: Cambridge University Press.

Fried, M. and Östman, J-O. (2004) Construction grammar – a thumbnail sketch. In M. Fried and J-O. Östman (eds) *Construction Grammar in Cross-Language Perspective,* 11–86. Amsterdam/Philadelphia: John Benjamins Publishing Company.

Frisson, S. and Pickering, M. (1999) The processing of metonymy: evidence from eye-movements. *Journal of Experimental Psychology: Learning, Memory and Cognition* 25: 1366–1383.

Gazzaninga, M. (1992/1997) *O tajemnicach ludzkiego umysłu.* Transl. A. Szczuka. Warsaw: Książka i Wiedza.

Geeraerts, D. (2003) The interaction of metaphor and metonymy in composite expressions. In R. Dirven and R. Pörings (eds) *Metaphor and Metonymy in Comparison and Contrast,* 435–465. Berlin, New York: Mouton de Gruyter.

Geeraerts, D. (ed.) (2006) *Cognitive Linguistics: Basic Readings.* Berlin/New York: Mouton de Gruyter.

Gibbs, R. W. Jr. (1999) Speaking and thinking with metonymy. In K-U. Panther and G. Radden (eds) *Metonymy in Language and Thought,* 61–76. Amsterdam/ Philadelphia: John Benjamins Publishing Company.

Gibbs, R. W. Jr. (2007) Experimental tests of figurative meaning construction. In G. Radden, K-M. Köpke, T. Berg and P. Siemund (eds) *Aspects of Meaning Construction,* 19–32. Amsterdam/Philadelphia: John Benjamins Publishing Company.

Głowiński, M., Kostkiewiczowa, T., Okopień-Sławińska, A. and Sławiński, J. (1988) *Słownik terminów literackich.* Wrocław: Ossolineum.

Glynn, D. (2007) Concept delimitation, frame semantics, and pragmatic implicature: issues for the usage-based study of metonymy. In K. Kosecki (2007a), 157–173.

Goldberg, A. (1995) *Constructions: A Construction Grammar Approach to Argument Structure.* Chicago: University of Chicago Press.

Goldberg, A. (2005) Argument realization: the role of constructions, lexical semantics and discourse factors. In J-O. Östman and M. Fried (eds) *Construction Grammars. Cognitive Grounding and Theoretical Extensions,* 17–43. Amsterdam/Philadelphia: John Benjamins Publishing Company.

Goldman, A. I. (2009) Mirroring, simulating and mindreading. *Mind & Language* 24 (2): 235–252.

Goossens, L. (1990) Metaphtonymy: the interaction of metaphor and metonymy in expressions for linguistic action. *Cognitive Linguistics* 1 (3): 323–340.

Górska, E. (ed.) (1993) *Images from the Cognitive Scene.* Kraków: Universitas.

Górska, E. (1999) *On Parts and Wholes. A Cognitive Study of English Schematic Part Terms.* Warsaw: Warsaw University Press.

Górska, E. and Radden, G. (eds) (2005) *Metonymy-Metaphor Collage.* Warsaw: Wydawnictwo Uniwersytetu Warszawskiego.

Grady, J. (1997) 'Foundations of Meaning: Primary Metaphors and Primary Scenes'. Ph.D. dissertation at the University of Berkeley.

Grady, J. (1999) A typology of motivation for conceptual metaphor. In R. Gibbs and G. Steen (eds) *Metaphor in Cognitive Linguistics,* 79–100. Amsterdam/Philadelphia: John Benjamins Publishing Company.

Grady, J. and Johnson, C. (2000) Converging evidence for the notions of 'subscene' and 'primary scene'. *Proceedings of the 23rd Annual Meeting of the Berkeley Linguistic Society*, 123–136. Berkeley: Berkeley Linguistic Society.

Grice, H. P. (1975) Logic and conversation. In P. Cole and J. Morgan (eds) *Syntax and Semantics.* Vol. 3: Speech Acts, 113–127. New York: Academic Press.

Grygiel, M. (2007) Metonymic projection as a major factor in the rise of English historical synonyms of 'man' and 'woman'. In K. Kosecki (2007a), 227–240.

Grzegorczykowa, R. (1984) *Zarys słowotwórstwa polskiego.* Warsaw: Państwowe Wydawnictwo Naukowe.

Grzegorczykowa, R. and Pajdzińska, A. (eds) (1996) *Językowa kategoryzacja świata.* Lublin: Wydawnictwo UMCS.

Grzegorczykowa, R. and Puzynina, J. (1984) Słowotwórstwo rzeczowników. In R. Grzegorczykowa, R. Laskowski and H. Wróbel (eds) (1984) *Gramatyka współczesnego języka polskiego: Morfologia,* 332–407. Warsaw: PWN.

Hampe, B. (ed.) (2005) *From Perception to Meaning. Image Schemas in Cognitive Linguistics.* Amsterdam/Philadelphia: John Benjamins Publishing Company.

Halliday, M. A. K. (1994 [1985]) *An Introduction to Functional Grammar.* 2nd edition. London, New York, Sydney, Auckland: Edward Arnold.

Hauk, O., Johnsrude, I. and Pulvermüller, F. (2004) Somatotopic representation of action words in human motor and premotor cortex. *Neuron* 41: 301–307.

Hayakawa, S. I. (1949) *Language in Thought and Action.* New York: Harcourt, Brace, Jovanovich, Inc.

Heine, B. (2004) On genetic motivation in grammar. In G. Radden and K-U. Panther (eds) *Studies in Linguistic Motivation,* 103–120. Berlin, New York: Mouton de Gruyter.

Heine, B., Claudi, U. and Hünnemeyer, F. (1991) *Grammaticalization: A Conceptual Framework.* Chicago/London: University of Chicago Press.

Hernández, L. (2007) High-level metonymies in the understanding of modality: a cross-linguistic analysis. In K. Kosecki (2007a), 133–146.

Heyvaert, L. (2009) Compounding in cognitive linguistics. In R. Lieber and P. Štekauer, P. (eds) *The Oxford Handbook of Compounding,* 233–254. Oxford: Oxford University Press.

Hilpert, M. (2006) Keeping an eye on the data: metonymies and their patterns. In A. Stefanowitsch and S. Th. Gries (eds) *Corpus-Based Approaches to Metaphor and Metonymy,* 123–151. Berlin, New York: Mouton de Gruyter.

Hilpert, M. (2007) Chained metonymies in lexicon and grammar. In G. Radden, K-M. Köpke, T. Berg and P. Siemund (eds) *Aspects of Meaning Construction*, 77–98. Amsterdam/Philadelphia: John Benjamins Publishing Company.

Hockett, C. F. (1958) *A Course in Modern Linguistics.* New York: The Macmillan Company.

Hopper, P. J. and Thompson, S.A. (1984) The discourse basis for lexical categories in universal grammar. *Language* 60: 703–752.

Hopper, P. J. and Thompson, S. A. (1985) The iconicity of the universal categories 'noun' and 'verbs'. In J. Haiman (ed.) *Iconicity in Syntax,* 151–186. Amsterdam: John Benjamins Publishing Company.

Hopper, P. J. and Traugott, E. (eds) (2003) *Grammaticalization,* 2nd edition. Cambridge: Cambridge University Press.

Ingarden, R. (1960) *O dziele literackim.* Warsaw: Państwowe Wydawnictwo Naukowe.

Jackendoff, R. (1983) *Semantics and Cognition.* Cambridge, MA: MIT Press.

Jackendoff, R. (2002) *Foundations of Language. Brain, Meaning, Grammar, Evolution.* Oxford: Oxford University Press.

Jackendoff, R. (2009) Compounding in the parallel architecture and conceptual semantics. In R. Lieber and P. Štekauer, *The Oxford Handbook of Compounding,* 105–128. Oxford: Oxford University Press.

Jackson, P. L., Meltzoff, A. N. and Decety, J. (2004) How do we perceive the pain of others? A window into the neural processes involved in empathy. *NeuroImage* 24: 771–779.

Jäkel, O. (1999) Metonymy in onomastics. In K-U. Panther and G. Radden (eds) *Metonymy in Language and Thought,* 211–229. Amsterdam/Philadelphia: John Benjamins Publishing Company.

Jakobson, R. and Halle, M. (1956/64) *Podstawy języka.* Wrocław: Ossolineum.

Johnson, M. (1987) *The Body in the Mind: The Bodily Basis of Meaning, Imagination, and Reason.* Chicago: University of Chicago Press.

Johnson, M. and Rohrer, T. (2007) We are live creatures: embodiment, American pragmatism and the cognitive organism. In T. Ziemke, J. Zlatev and R. M. Frank (eds) *Body, Language and Mind.* Vol. 1: Embodiment, 17–54. Berlin, New York: Mouton de Gruyter.

Kalisz, R. (1983) On so-called 'beheaded noun phrases' in English and Polish. *PSiCL* 16: 43–51.

Kalisz, R. (1993) *Pragmatyka językowa.* Gdańsk: Wydawnictwo Uniwersytetu Gdańskiego.

Kalisz, R. (1998) Profilowanie, perspektywa i strefy aktywne. In J. Bartmiński and R. Tokarski (eds) *Profilowanie w języku i w tekście,* 53–61. Lublin: Wydawnictwo UMCS.

Kalisz, R. and Kubiński, W. (1993) Speech act as a radial category. In E. Górska (ed.) *Images from the Cognitive Scene,* 73–85. Kraków: Universitas.

Kardela, H. (ed.) (1994) *Podstawy gramatyki kognitywnej.* Warsaw: Polskie Towarzystwo Semiotyczne.

Kardela, H. (1996) Płynność kategorii w opozycjach policzalny/niepoliczalny i dokonany/niedokonany. In R. Grzegorczykowa and A. Pajdzińska (eds) *Językowa kategoryzacja świata,* 297–331. Lublin: Wydawnictwo UMCS.

Kardela, H. (2000) *Dimensions and Parameters in Grammar. Studies on A/D Asymmetries and Subjectivity Relations in Polish.* Lublin: Wydawnictwo UMCS.

Kay, P. and Fillmore, C. (1999) Grammatical constructions and linguistic generalizations: the what's x doing y? construction. *Language* 75 (1): 1–33.

Kleiber, G. and Tamba, I. (1990) L'hyponimie revisitée: inclusion et hiérarchie. *Language* 98: 7–32.

Klein, W. and Perdue, C. (1997) The basic variety, or: couldn't language be much simpler? *Second Language Research* 13: 301–347.

Kleparski, G. (2000) Metonymy and the growth of lexical categories related to the conceptual category FEMALE HUMAN BEING. In G. Kleparski (ed) *Studia Anglica Resoviensia* 1: 17–27. Zeszyty Naukowe Wyższej Szkoły Pedagogicznej w Rzeszowie, Seria Filologiczna, Zeszyt 38, Wydawnictwo Wyższej Szkoły Pedagogicznej w Rzeszowie.

Koch, P. (1999) Frame and contiguity: on the cognitive bases of metonymy and certain types of word formation. In K-U. Panther and G. Radden (eds) *Metonymy in Language and Thought*, 139–168. Amsterdam/Philadelphia: John Benjamins Publishing Company.

Koch, P. (2001) Metonymy. Unity in diversity. *Journal of Historical Pragmatics* 2 (2): 201–244.

Köhler, W. (1975[1947]) *Gestalt Psychology.* New York and Scarborough: A Mentor Book.

Kosecki, K. (2005) *On the Part-Whole Configuration and Multiple Construals of Salience within a Simple Lexeme.* Łódź: Wydawnictwo Uniwersytetu Łódzkiego.

Kosecki, K. (ed.) (2007a) *Perspectives on Metonymy.* Proceedings of the International Conference "Perspectives on Metonymy", held in Łódź, Poland, May 6–7, 2005. Frankfurt am Main: Peter Lang.

Kosecki, K. (2007b) Some remarks on metonymy in compounding. In K. Kosecki (2007a), 241–251.

Kövecses, Z. (1986) *Metaphors of Anger, Pride, and Love: A Lexical Approach to the Structure of Concepts.* Amsterdam: John Benjamins Publishing Company.

Kövecses, Z. (1988) *The Language of Love. The Semantics of Passion in Conversational English.* Lewisburg, PA: Bucknell University Press

Kövecses, Z. (1989) *Emotion Concepts.* New York, Berlin, Heidelberg: Springer–Verlag.

Kövecses, Z. (2000) The scope of metaphor. In A. Barcelona (ed.) *Metaphor and Metonymy at the Crossroads*, 79–92. Berlin, New York: Mouton de Gruyter.

Kövecses, Z. and Radden, G. (1998) Metonymy: developing a cognitive linguistic view. *Cognitive Linguistics* 9 (1): 37–77.

Kowalik-Kaleta, Z. (2007) *Historia nazwisk polskich na tle społecznym i obyczajowym* (XII-XV wiek), t.1. część 1. Warsaw: Wyd. Instytut Slawistyki PAN, Fundacja Slawistyczna.

Królak, E. (2005) The hyphen construction as an instance of metonymy. In E. Górska and G. Radden (eds) *Metonymy-Metaphor Collage,* 197–204. Warsaw: Wydawnictwo Uniwersytetu Warszawskiego.

Krzeszowski, T. (1994) Konotacja i denotacja. In H. Kardela (ed.) *Podstawy gramatyki kognitywnej,* 85–95. Warsaw: Polskie Towarzystwo Semiotyczne.

Kubiński, W. (1982) Polish *się* constructions and their English counterparts. *PSiCL* 15: 55–65.

Kurcz, I. (2000) *Psychologia języka i komunikacji*. Warsaw: Wydawnictwo Naukowe „Scholar".

Kuryłowicz, J. (1975 [1965]) Metaphor and metonymy in linguistics. In J. Kuryłowicz *Esquisses linguistiques*. Vol. II, 88–92. Munich: Wilhelm Fink.

Kwiatkowska, A. (2007) Pre-linguistic and non-linguistic metonymy. In K. Kosecki (2007a), 297–307.

Lakoff, G. (1987) *Women, Fire and Dangerous Things: What Categories Reveal About the Mind*. Chicago: University of Chicago Press.

Lakoff, G. (1990) The invariance hypothesis: is abstract reason based on image-schemas? *Cognitive Linguistics* 1: 39–74.

Lakoff, G. (1993) The contemporary theory of metaphor. In A. Ortony (ed.) *Metaphor and Thought*, 2nd edition, 202–251. Cambridge: Cambridge University Press.

Lakoff, G. and Johnson, M. (1980) *Metaphors We Live By*. Chicago: University of Chicago Press.

Lakoff, G. and Johnson, M. (1999) *Philosophy in the Flesh*. New York: Basic Books.

Lakoff, G. and Kövecses, Z. (1987) The cognitive model of anger inherent in American English. In D. Holland and N. Quinn (eds) *Cultural Models in Language and Thought,* 195–221. Cambridge: Cambridge University Press.

Lakoff, G. and Turner, M. (1989) *More Than Cool Reason: A Field Guide to Poetic Metaphor.* Chicago: University of Chicago Press.

Langacker, R. (1987) *Foundations of Cognitive Grammar.* Vol. 1. Stanford: Stanford University Press.

Langacker, R. (1990) *Concept, Image, and Symbol. The Cognitive Basis of Grammar.* Berlin: Mouton de Gruyter.

Langacker, R. (1991) *Foundations of Cognitive Grammar*, vol. 2: Descriptive Application. Stanford: Stanford University Press.

Langacker, R. (1993) Reference-point constructions. *Cognitive Linguistics* 4, 1–38.

Langacker, R. (2000) *Grammar and Conceptualization.* Berlin, New York: Mouton de Gruyter.

Langacker, R. (2010) Metonymic grammar. In K-U. Panther, L. Thornburg and A. Barcelona (eds), *Metonymy and Metaphor in Grammar,* 45–71. Amsterdam/Philadelphia: John Benjamins Publishing Company.

Langendoen, T. (1970) *Essentials of English Grammar*. New York: Holt, Rinehart and Winston.

Lass, R. (1994) *Old English. A Historical Linguistic Companion.* Cambridge: Cambridge University Press.

LeDoux, J. (2002) *Synaptic Self. How Our Brains Become Who We Are.* New York: Penguin Books.

Lee, D. (2004 [2001]) *Cognitive Linguistics. An Introduction.* Oxford/New York: Oxford University Press.

Leech, G. (1969) *Toward a Semantic Description of English*. London: Longmans.

Leech, G. (1974) *Semantics*. London: Penguin Books.

Lehmann, C. (1985) Grammaticalization: Synchronic variation and diachronic change. *Lingua e Stile* 20: 303–18.

Lehrer, A. (2003) Polysemy in derivational affixes. In B. Nerlich, Z. Todd, V. Herman and D. D. Clarke (eds) *Polysemy. Flexible Patterns of Meaning in Mind and Language*, 217–232. Berlin, New York: Mouton de Gruyter.

Leino, J. (2005) Frames, profiles and constructions: Two collaborating CG's meet the Finnish permissive construction. In J-O. Östman and M. Fried (eds) *Construction Grammars. Cognitive grounding and theoretical extensions*, 89–120. Amsterdam/Philadelphia: John Benjamins Publishing Company.

Levin, B. (1993) *English Verb Classes and Alternations. A Preliminary Investigation.* Chicago and London: The University of Chicago Press.

Levin, B. and Rappaport Hovav, M. (1996) Lexical semantics and syntactic structure. In S. Lappin (ed.) *The Handbook of Contemporary Semantic Theory*, 487–507. Oxford: Blackwell.

Levinson, S. (1983) *Pragmatics*. Cambridge; Cambridge University Press.

Levinson, S. (1995) Three levels of meaning. In F. R. Palmer (ed.) *Grammar and Meaning. Essays in Honour of Sir John Lyons*, 90–115. Cambridge: Cambridge University Press.

Levy, J. and Trevarten, C. (1976) Metacontrol of hemispheric functions in human split-brain patients. *Journal of Experimental Psychology: Human Perception and Performance* 2: 299–312.

Lofting, C. J. (1997) A summary of left and right hemisphere functions and their affect on our mappings of reality. http://members.ozemail.com.au/~ddiamond/hemis.html.

Loftus, E. F. and Palmer, J. C. (1974) Reconstruction of automobile destruction. An example of the interaction between language and memory. *Journal of Verbal Learning and Verbal Behavior* 13: 585–589.

Łuria, A. R. (1976) *Problemy neuropsychologii i neurolingwistyki.* Warsaw: Państwowe Wydawnictwo Naukowe.

Lyons, J. (1977) *Semantics*. Cambridge: Cambridge University Press.

Lyons, J. (1995) *Linguistic Semantics. An Introduction.* Cambridge: Cambridge University Press.

Malec, M. (1996) *O imionach i nazwiskach w Polsce. Tradycja i współczesność.* Kraków: Biblioteczka Towarzystwa Miłośników Języka Polskiego Nr 23.

Maruszewski, T. (2001) *Psychologia poznania.* Gdańsk: Gdańskie Wydawnictwo Psychologiczne.

Meillet, A. (1958 [1912]) L'évolution des formes grammaticales. In A. Meillet *Linguistique historique et linguistique generale,* 130–148. Paris: Champion.

Meltzoff, A. N. and Brooks, R. (2007) Intersubjectivity before language. Three windows on preverbal sharing. In S. Bråten (ed.) *On Being Moved. From Mirror Neurons to Empathy,* 149–174. Amsterdam/Philadelphia: John Benjamins Publishing Company.

Milewski, T. (1959) O pochodzeniu słowiańskich imion złożonych. I Międzynarodowa Slawistyczna Konferencja Onomastyczna, Kraków, 1959 (1961), 235–247. Reprinted in T. Milewski (1993) *Teoria, typologia i historia języka*, 226–237. Kraków: Universitas.

Miller, G. (1998) Nouns in WordNet. In C. Fellbaum (ed.) *WordNet: An Electronic Lexical Database,* 23–46. Cambridge, MA: MIT Press.

Minsky, M. (1977) Frame-System theory. In P. Wason and P. Johnson Laird (eds) *Thinking: Readings in Cognitive Science,* 355–376. Cambridge: Cambridge University Press.

Mishkin, M. and Appenzeller, T. (1987) The anatomy of memory. A Scientific American Special Report. *Scientific American.* (offprint)

Murphy, M. L. (2003) *Semantic Relations and the Lexicon.* Cambridge: Cambridge University Press.

Nerlich, B. (2003) Polysemy: past and present. In B. Nerlich, Z. Todd, V. Herman and D. D. Clarke (eds) *Polysemy. Flexible Patterns of Meaning in Mind and Language,* 49–76. Berlin, New York: Mouton de Gruyter.

Nerlich, B. and Clarke, D. D. (1999) Synecdoche as a cognitive and communicative strategy. In A. Blank and P. Koch (eds) *Historical Semantics and Cognition,* 197–213. Berlin, New York: Mouton de Gruyter.

Nerlich, B., Clarke, D. D. and Todd, Z. (1999) "Mummy, I'd like to be a sandwich": metonymy in language acquisition. In K-U. Panther and G. Radden (eds) *Metonymy in Language and Thought,* 361–383. Amsterdam/Philadelphia: John Benjamins Publishing Company.

Niemczak, A. (2008) 'Metonymic Patterns in English and Polish Onomastics'. M.A. thesis: Czestochowa, Wyższa Szkoła Lingwistyczna.

Norlander, J. (2007) The metonymic element in Krio conceptualization: the cases of bif and bush. In K. Kosecki (2007a), 271–287.

Norrick, N. R. (1981) *Semiotic Principles in Semantic Theory.* Amsterdam: John Benjamins Publishing Company.

Nowakowska-Kempna, I. (2000) Język ciała i ciało w umyśle, czyli o metaforyce uczuć. In I. Nowakowska-Kempna, A. Dąbrowska and J. Anusiewicz (eds) *Uczucia w języku i tekście,* 25–58. Wrocław: Wydawnictwo Uniwersytetu Wrocławskiego.

Nunberg, G. (1978) *The Pragmatics of Reference.* Indiana University Linguistics.

Nunberg, G. (1995) Transfers of meaning. *Journal of Semantics* 12: 109–132.

Nunberg, G., Sag, I. E. and Wasow, T. (1994) Idioms. *Language* 70: 491–538.

Ogden, C. K. and Richards, I. A. (1985 [1923]) *The Meaning of Meaning.* London: Ark.

Östman, J-O. and Fried, M. (eds) (2005) *Construction Grammars. Cognitive grounding and theoretical extensions.* Amsterdam/Philadelphia: John Benjamins Publishing Company.

Panther, K-U. and Radden, G. (eds) (1999) *Metonymy in Language and Thought.* Amsterdam/Philadelphia: John Benjamins Publishing Company.

Panther, K-U. and Thornburg, L. (1996) *Metonymic and Indexical Inferencing in Conversation.* Paper presented at the 5th International Pragmatics Conference, Mexico City, July 4–9, 1996.

Panther, K-U. and Thornburg, L. (1998) A cognitive approach to inferencing in conversation. *Journal of Pragmatics* 30: 755–769.

Panther, K-U. and Thornburg, L. (1999) The potentiality for actuality metonymy in English and Hungarian. In K-U. Panther and G. Radden (eds) *Metonymy in Language and Thought,* 303–332. Amsterdam/Philadelphia: John Benjamins Publishing Company.

Panther, K-U. and Thornburg, L. (2000) The effect for cause metonymy in English grammar. In A. Barcelona (ed) *Metaphor and Metonymy at the Crossroads*, 215–231. Berlin, New York: Mouton de Gruyter.

Panther, K-U. and Thornburg, L. (2003a) Introduction: On the nature of conceptual metonymy. In K-U. Panther and L. Thornburg (eds) *Metonymy in Pragmatic Inferencing*, 1–20. Amsterdam/Philadelphia: John Benjamins Publishing Company.

Panther, K-U. and Thornburg, L. (2003b) Metonymies as natural inference and activation schemas: the case of dependent clauses as independent speech acts. In K-U. Panther and L. Thornburg (eds) *Metonymy in Pragmatic Inferencing*, 127–147. Amsterdam/Philadelphia: John Benjamins Publishing Company.

Panther, K-U. and Thornburg, L. (2003c) The roles of metaphor and metonymy in English -er nominals. In R. Dirven and R. Pörings (eds) *Metaphor and Metonymy in Comparison and Contrast*, 279–319. Berlin, New York: Mouton de Gruyter.

Panther, K-U. and Thornburg, L. (2005) Inference in the construction of meaning: The role of conceptual metonymy. In E. Górska and G. Radden (eds) *Metonymy-Metaphor Collage*, 37–57. Warsaw: Wydawnictwo Uniwersytetu Warszawskiego.

Panther, K-U. and Thornburg, L. (2007) Metonymy. In D. Geeraerts and H. Cuyckens (eds) *The Oxford Handbook of Cognitive Linguistics*, 236–263. Oxford: Oxford University Press.

Panther, K-U., Thornburg, L. and Barcelona, A. (eds) (2010) *Metonymy and Metaphor in Grammar.* Amsterdam/Philadelphia: John Benjamins Publishing Company.

Pauwels, P. and Simon-Vandenbergen, A-M. (1995) Body parts in linguistic action. In L. Goossens, P. Pauwels, B. Rudzka-Ostyn, A-M. Simon-Vandenbergen and J. Vanparys (eds), *By Word of Mouth. Metaphor, Metonymy and Linguistic Action in a Cognitive Perspective,* 35–69. Amsterdam/Philadelphia: John Benjamins Publishing Company.

Peirsman, Y. and Geeraerts, D. (2006) Metonymy as a prototypical category. *Cognitive Linguistics* 17 (3): 269–316.

Pinker, S. (1997) *How the Mind Works.* London: Penguin Books.

Plag, I. (2003) *Word-Formation in English.* Cambridge: Cambridge University Press.

Płuciennik, J. (2007) Princess Antonomasia, individualism, and the Quixotism of culture: a case of *Tristram Shandy* by Laurence Sterne. In K. Kosecki (2007a), 349–366.

Polański, K. (ed.) (1993) *Encyklopedia Językoznawstwa Ogólnego.* Wrocław: Ossolineum.

Pustejovsky, J. (1995) *The Generative Lexicon.* Cambridge, MA: MIT Press.

Quirk, R. and Greenbaum, S. (1990) *A University Grammar of English.* London: Longman.

Quirk, R., Greenbaum, S., Leech, G. and Svartvik, J. (1972) *A Grammar of Contemporary English.* London: Longman.

Quirk, R., Greenbaum, S., Leech, G. and Svartvik, J. (1985) *A Comprehensive Grammar of the English Language.* London: Longman.

Radden, G. (2000) How metonymic are metaphors? In A. Barcelona (ed.) *Metaphor and Metonymy at the Crossroads*, 93–108. Berlin, New York: Mouton de Gruyte.

Radden, G. and Dirven, D. (2007) *Cognitive English Grammar.* Amsterdam/Philadelphia: John Benjamins Publishing Company.

Radden, G., Köpke, K-M., Berg, T. and Siemund, P. (eds) (2007) *Aspects of Meaning Construction*. Amsterdam/Philadelphia: John Benjamins Publishing Company.

Radden, G. and Kövecses, Z. (1999) Towards a theory of metonymy. In K-U. Panther and G. Radden (eds) *Metonymy in Language and Thought*, 17–59. Amsterdam/Philadelphia: John Benjamins Publishing Company.

Radden, G. and Panther, K-U. (eds) (2004) *Studies in Linguistic Motivation*. Berlin, New York: Mouton de Gruyter.

Radden, G. and Seto, K. (2003) Metonymic construals of shopping requests in have- and be- languages. In K-U. Panther and L. Thornburg (eds) *Metonymy in Pragmatic Inferencing*, 223–239. Amsterdam/Philadelphia: John Benjamins Publishing Company.

Ramachandran, V. S. (1993) Filling in gaps in perception: Part II. Scotomas and phantom limbs. *Current Directions in Psychological Science,* Vol. II (2): 56–65.

Ramachandran, V. S. and Hubbard, E. (2003) Hearing colors, tasting shapes. *Scientific American.com,* April 15.

Redford, A., Atkinson, M., Britain, D., Clahsen, H. and Spencer, A. (1999) *Linguistics. An Introduction*. Cambridge: Cambridge University Press.

Riemer, N. (2003) When is a metonymy no longer a metonymy? In R. Dirven and R. Pörings (eds) *Metaphor and Metonymy in Comparison and Contrast,* 379–406. Berlin, New York: Mouton de Gruyter.

Rizzolatti, G., Fogassi, L. and Gallese, V. (2006) Zwierciadła umysłu. *Świat Nauki* 12: 38–45.

Rohrer, T. (2007) The body in space: dimensions of embodiment. In T. Ziemke, J. Zlatev, R. M. Frank (eds) *Body, Language and Mind.* Vol. 1: Embodiment, 339–377. Berlin, New York: Mouton de Gruyter.

Rosch, E. (1973) Natural categories. *Cognitive Psychology* 4: 328–50.

Rosch, E. (1977) Classification of real-world objects: origins and representations in cognition. In P. C. Wason and P. N. Johnson-Laird (eds) *Thinking: Readings in Cognitive Science*, 212–222. Cambridge: Cambridge University Press.

Rosch, E. (1978) Principles of categorization. In E. Rosch and B. Lloyd (eds) *Cognition and Categorization*, 27–48. Hillsdale, NJ: Lawrence Erlbaum Associates.

Rozwadowski, J. (1921) O dwuczłonowości wyrazów. *Język Polski* 6: 129–139.

Ruiz de Mendoza, F. (2000) The role of mappings and domains in understanding metonymy. In A. Barcelona (ed.) *Metaphor and Metonymy at the Crossroads*, 109–132. Berlin, New York: Mouton de Gruyter.

Ruiz de Mendoza, F. J. (2007) High-level cognitive models: in search of a unified framework for inferential and grammatical behavior. In K. Kosecki (2007a), 11–30.

Ruiz de Mendoza, F. J. and Pérez Hernández, L. (2003) Cognitive operations and pragmatic implication. In K-U. Panther and L. Thornburg (eds) *Metonymy in Pragmatic Inferencing*, 23–49. Amsterdam/Philadelphia: John Benjamins Publishing Company.

Ruiz de Mendoza, F. J. and Mairal Usón, R. (2007) High-level metaphor and metonymy in meaning construction. In G. Radden, K-M. Köpke, T. Berg and P. Siemund (eds) *Aspects of Meaning Construction*, 33–49. Amsterdam/Philadelphia: John Benjamins Publishing Company.

Scalise, S. and Bisetto, A. (2009) The classification of compounds. In R. Lieber and P. Štekauer (eds) *The Oxford Handbook of Compounding*, 34–53. Oxford: Oxford University Press.

Schönefeld, D. (2005) Zero derivation – functional change – metonymy. In L. Bauer and S. Varela (eds) *Approaches to Conversion/Zero Derivation*, 131–57. Münster/New York/München/Berlin: Waxmann.

Searle, J. (1975) Indirect speech acts. In P. Cole and J. L. Morgan (eds) *Syntax and Semantics*, 59–82. Vol. 3: Speech Acts. New York: Academic Press.

Seto, K. (1999) Distinguishing metonymy from synecdoche. In K-U. Panther and G. Radden (eds) *Metonymy in Language and Thought*, 91–120. Amsterdam/Philadelphia: John Benjamins Publishing Company.

Seto, K. (2003) Metonymic polysemy and its place in meaning extension. In B. Nerlich, Z. Todd, V. Herman and D. D. Clarke (eds) *Polysemy. Flexible Patterns of Meaning in Mind and Language*, 195–214. Berlin, New York: Mouton de Gruyter.

Sokołowska, O. (2001) Akty mowy – ujęcie kognitywne. In W. Kubiński and D. Stanulewicz (eds) *Językoznawstwo kognitywne II. Zjawiska pragmatyczne*, 148–58. Gdańsk: Wydawnictwo Uniwersytetu Gdańskiego.

Sperry, R. W. (1982) Some effects of disconnecting the cerebral hemispheres. *Science* 217: 1223–1226.

Štekauer, P. (1996) *A Theory of Conversion in English*. Frankfurt am Main: Peter Lang.

Stern, D. (1985) *The Interpersonal World of the Infant*. New York: Basic Books.

Stillings, N. A., Feinstein, M., Garfield, J., Rissland, E. L., Rosenbaum, D. A., Weisler, S. and Baker-Ward, L. (1987) *Cognitive Science: An Introduction*. Cambridge MA: The MIT Press.

Swan, M. (1995) *Practical English Usage*. Oxford: Oxford University Press.

Sweetser, E. (1999) Compositionality and blending: Semantic composition in a cognitively realistic framework. In T. Janssen and G. Redeker (eds) *Cognitive Linguistics: Foundations, Scope and Methodology*, 129–162. Berlin, New York: Mouton de Gruyter.

Szawerna, M. (2007) Deverbal nominalization as a type of metonymic extension from processes to things. In K. Kosecki (2007a), 147–155.

Szeląg, E. (2000) Neoropsychologiczne podłoże mowy. In T. Górska, A. Grabowska and J. Zagrodzka (ed.) *Mózg a zachowanie*, 429–459. Warsaw: Wydawnictwo Naukowe PWN.

Szober, S. (1966) *Gramatyka języka polskiego. Wydanie siódme*. Warsaw: PWN.

Szwedek, A. (2002) Objectification: from object perception to metaphor creation. In B. Lewandowska-Tomaszczyk and K. Turewicz (eds) *Cognitive Linguistics To-day*, 159–75. Frankfurt am Main: Peter Lang.

Szymanek, B. (1998) *Introduction to Morphological Analysis*. Warsaw: Wydawnictwo Naukowe PWN.

Taylor, J. (1995) *Linguistic Categorization. Prototypes in Linguistic Theory*, 2nd revised edition. Oxford: Clarendon Press.

Taylor, J. (1999) Cognitive semantics and structuralist semantics. In A. Blank and P. Koch (eds) *Historical Semantics and Cognition*, 17–48. Berlin, New York: Mouton de Gruyter.

Taylor, J. (2002) *Cognitive Grammar.* Oxford: Oxford University Press.

Taylor, J. (2004) The ecology of constructions. In G. Radden and K-U. Panther (eds) *Studies in Linguistic Motivation,* 49–73. Berlin, New York: Mouton de Gruyter.

Traugott, E. (1988) Pragmatic strengthening and grammaticalization. In S. Axmaker, A. Jaisser and H. Signmaster (eds) *Proceedings of the Fourteenth Annual Meeting of the Berkeley Linguistic Society*, 406–416. Berkeley: Berkeley Linguistic Society.

Traugott, E. and Dasher, R. (2002) *Regularity in Semantic Change.* Cambridge: Cambridge University Press.

Traugott, E. and König, E. (1991) The semantics-pragmatics of grammaticalization revisited. In E. C. Traugott and B. Heine (eds) *Approaches to Grammaticalization,* 189–218. Amsterdam: Benjamins Publishing Company.

Tuggy, D. (1987) Scarecrow nouns, generalizations, and cognitive grammar. *Pacific Linguistics Conference* 3: 307–320. Available on the Internet: www.sil.org/~tyggyd/scarecrow/scarecro.htm.

Tuggy, D. (1993) Ambiguity, polysemy, and vagueness. *Cognitive Linguistics* 4 (3): 273–290.

Turner, K. (2009) Semantics vs. pragmatics. In F. Brisard, J-O. Östman and J. Verschueren (eds) *Grammar, Meaning and Pragmatics*, 250–267. Amsterdam/ Philadelphia: John Benjamins Publishing Company.

Turner, M. and Fauconnier, G. (1995) Conceptual integration and formal expression. *Journal of Metaphor and Symbolic Activity* 10 (3): 183–203.

Turner, M. and Fauconnier, G. (2000) Metaphor, metonymy, and binding. In A. Barcelona (ed.) *Metaphor and Metonymy at the Crossroads*, 133–145. Berlin, New York: Mouton de Gruyter.

Ullman, M. (2004) Contributions of memory circuits to language: the declarative/ procedural model. *Cognition* 92: 231–270.

Ullmann, S. (1972 [1962]) *Semantics. An Introduction to the Science of Meaning.* Oxford: Basil Blackwell.

Voßhagen, C. (1999) Opposition as a metonymic principle. In K-U. Panther and G. Radden (eds) *Metonymy in Language and Thought,* 289–308. Amsterdam/ Philadelphia: John Benjamins Publishing Company.

Warren, B. (1999) Laws of thought, knowledge and lexical change. In A. Blank and P. Koch (eds) *Historical Semantics and Cognition*, 215–229. Berlin, New York: Mouton de Gruyter.

Warren, B. (2003) An alternative account of the interpretation of referential metonymy and metaphor. In R. Dirven and R. Pörings (eds) *Metaphor and Metonymy in Comparison and Contrast,* 75–130. Berlin, New York: Mouton de Gruyter.

Waszakowa, K. (1998) Słowotwórczy aspekt procesów profilowania. In J. Bartmiński and R. Tokarski (eds) *Profilowanie w języku i w tekście*, 105–116. Lublin: Wydawnictwo UMCS.

Wells, R. S. (1977) Metonymy and misunderstanding: an aspect of language change. In Cole, R. W. (ed.) *Current Issues in Linguistic Theory,* 195–214. Bloomington/ London: Indiana University Press.

Wertheimer, M. (1923) Laws of organization in perceptual forms. Reprinted in W. D. Ellis (ed.) (1938) *The Source Book of Gestalt Psychology*, 71–88. London: Routledge and Kegan Paul.

Wicker, B., Keysers, C., Plailly, J., Royet, J-P., Gallese, V. and Rizzolatti, G. (2003) Both of us disgusted in my peninsula: the common neural basis of seeing and feeling disgust. *Neuron* 40: 655–664.

Winston, M. E., Chaffin, R. and Herrmann, D. (1987) A taxonomy of part-whole relations. *Cognitive Science* 11: 417–44.

Wróbel, H. (1984) Słowotwórstwo czasowników. In R. Grzegorczykowa, R. Laskowski and H. Wróbel (eds) *Gramatyka współczesnego języka polskiego. Morfologia*, 467–512. Warsaw: PWN.

Wróbel, H. (2001) *Gramatyka języka polskiego.* Kraków: Spółka Wydawnicza 'OD NOWA'.

Ziomek, J. (1990) *Retoryka opisowa.* Wrocław, Warsaw, Kraków: Ossolineum.

Zlatev, J. (2003) Meaning = Life (+ Culture) An outline of a unified biocultural theory of meaning. *Evolution of Communication* 4 (2): 253–296.

Zlatev, J. (2007) Embodiment, language and mimesis. In T. Ziemke, J. Zlatev and R. M. Frank (eds) *Body, Language and Mind.* Vol. 1: Embodiment, 297–337. Berlin, New York: Mouton de Gruyter.

Index

acronym 61, 66–70, 115, 200
active zones 20, 41–8, 50–1, 59, 85–90,
  94, 121, 127, 227, 254, 267, 269
alphabetism 61, 65–8
anthroponymy 142–3, 147
antonomasia 60, 145, 151
antonymy 22, 37, 39, 189, 212–13, 217,
  220, 226, 268
association 15, 28–33, 37–9, 43, 45, 49,
  58, 178, 194, 211–13, 218–19, 221,
  229, 232, 236–40, 243–4, 255, 257,
  260–1, 266
    conceptual 18, 114, 253
    neuronal 221
    strong 37, 52–4, 105, 169, 189,
      192, 213, 223–4, 236–9, 267
    weak 99, 269
autoholonymy 190–3
autohyponymy 190–1, 200–1, 206
automeronymy 190–1, 211
autosuperordination 190–1, 200–1, 227

basic level 34–5, 38–9, 51, 58, 267
blending 19, 55, 126–9, 141, 146, 173,
  252–3, 255, 268–9

catachresis 188, 198, 267–8
clips 61, 70, 88, 115, 143–4, 151
cognitive model 157, 184
    idealized cognitive model (ICM)
      14–15, 24–5, 34, 37, 57, 61,
      64–5, 72, 105, 112, 156, 185,
      201, 215, 231–2
complementarity 39, 212–13, 220, 226,
  229
compounds 20, 22, 71–3, 113, 115,
  125–44, 146–51, 205, 263, 265
    endocentric 126, 135–41, 146,
      149–51
    exocentric 22, 126, 136–41, 143

construction grammar 74, 90, 107–8
constructions 1, 52, 70, 73, 75, 80, 86,
  94–7, 100, 107, 127, 140–1, 147, 151,
  158, 163–5, 169, 176, 179, 269
    be-gonna construction 225
    can construction 169
    comparative construction 81–3,
      108
    conditional construction 173–7
    Deprofiled Object Construction
      103
    futurity construction 179, 225
    hyphen construction 135
    if-only construction 97–100, 175
    independent *if*-clause construction
      96–7
    independent subordinate clause
      construction 96
    (in)transitive construction 101–2
    meaning construction 1, 52, 184,
      248, 251–2, 262–3, 266
    metonymic construction 79, 81
    modifier-head construction 115
    name–surname construction 145–6
    phrasal construction 74–5
    raising construction 47, 79, 85–6,
      88–94
    sentential construction 22, 79, 84,
      96, 140
    tag question construction 80
    target construction 75, 82, 96
    the-ADJ construction 75–6
    że-też construction 96
    żeby-tylko construction 96
constructional schema 107, 127–31,
  149
contiguity 5, 7, 11, 15, 19, 22–3, 32–3,
  45, 59, 74, 188, 192, 197, 211–13,
  215–18, 221, 223–6, 229, 245–7
    conceptual 4, 40, 264

spatial 28, 30, 225
  temporal 211
convergence zones 232–4, 237, 245,
  247, 250–1, 258, 269
conversion 46, 74–7, 107, 113–24, 130,
  138, 140–4, 147, 149–51, 187, 195,
  202, 216, 236, 243, 263–5

ellipsis 27, 61, 71–2, 74–6, 79–81,
  83–5, 90, 98, 100–4, 108
endonymy 212, 214, 216–18, 221, 228
eponymy 56, 122, 198–200
euphemism 9, 55, 62, 70, 79, 159, 240
evolution 2, 224, 229, 233, 240, 243–4,
  258–63, 268

facets 39, 41, 48–51, 60, 112, 191, 228,
  238, 267

gapping 79, 84, 241
grammaticalisation 81, 224–7, 269

hyperbole 48, 56–7, 59, 213–14, 218
hyponymy 31, 38–9, 190–1, 200, 206,
  212, 215–16, 221, 226, 228

Idealized Cognitive Models (ICM), *see*
  cognitive models
implicature 23, 25, 153, 157–9, 171,
  180, 184–5, 213–14, 225, 229, 240,
  254, 268
initialism 61, 66

language acquisition 127, 258, 263–6,
  268
litotes 57, 59, 213–14

meronymy 37, 39, 190–1, 211–12,
  215–16, 218–23, 226–9, 268
metaphor 1, 3–5, 7, 11, 18–23, 30–1,
  33–40, 43–4, 54–5, 105, 109–13,
  126–7, 133, 136, 138–9, 141–2,
  147–8, 150, 157, 159, 185, 187–8,
  200, 204–11, 218, 223–7, 229, 231–2,
  237, 252–5, 264
    conceptual metaphor 37, 134,
      193, 224

metaphoric mapping 19, 30, 43,
  210, 226, 255
  ontological metaphor 32–8, 121,
    193, 226
metaphor generator 208
metonymic chain 6, 66, 112, 154–6,
  168, 196, 200, 205–6
metonymy
  constructional metonymy 73–4,
    79, 108
  discourse metonymy 100
  eponymous metonymy
    (e-metonymy) 198, 200
  formal metonymy 2, 6–7, 27,
    61–108, 115–17, 140, 143–5,
    151, 173–5, 190, 196, 200, 241,
    267
  illocutionary metonymy 26–7,
    268–9
  morphological metonymy 71
  phrasal metonymy 74–5
  pragmatic metonymy 101
  predicative metonymy 21, 26,
    200, 226
  propositional metonymy 6, 24–7,
    156–7, 168, 267
  propositional sentential metonymy
    26, 27
  referential metonymy 6, 24, 27,
    119–20, 163, 189, 198, 267
  sentential metonymy 79, 85
  speech-sound metonymy 70
  synecdochic metonymy 23, 40–1,
    54, 267
  writing metonymy 65–6
metonymy generators 206–7, 210, 226,
  268
mirroring 236, 243, 251, 269
morphology 1, 23, 27, 109, 120, 122,
  142, 149
motivation 8, 17, 62–3, 77, 81, 88, 97,
  134, 140, 144, 146, 151, 156, 169–74,
  185, 205, 225, 254, 256–7

Neural Theory of Metonymy (NTM)
  231–2, 244, 258

neurons 2, 10, 19, 30, 38, 59, 184, 212,
    216, 219–24, 231–52, 255–8, 268–9

onomastics 117, 142, 152

partonomy 31, 211, 228
perspectivisation 41, 48–51, 127
plesionymy 38, 216–17
polysemy 85, 88–9, 96, 109, 111–14,
    118, 187–94, 200, 205–7, 211, 226–7,
    238, 244, 268
post-metonymy 194
pragmatic strengthening 156–7, 254
pragmatics 1–2, 23, 25, 63, 73–5,
    79–80, 85, 94–101, 103, 153–85,
    255–6, 258, 263
principles
    cognitive principles 16–17, 104,
        188, 251–3
    communicative principles 16–18
    Correlation Principle 18, 252–3
    Extended Invariance Principle 18,
        252
    Mapping Enforcement Principle
        19, 252, 254
    metonymic principles 57, 73, 142,
        150, 165, 258–9
    Principle of Correspondence
        251–2, 268
    Principle of Minimal and Maximal
        Overlap 34, 51, 56
    Principle of Omission under Low
        Discourse Prominence 103, 254
    Principle of the Relation by
        Contrast 223
    Principle of Verbal Economy 18,
        253
    semiotic principles 8, 10
profile 20–2, 35, 41, 44–7, 50, 59,
    85, 88–9, 92, 105, 113–14, 118–21,
    123–4, 127, 132–4, 228, 245
proper names 41, 51–5, 58, 60, 117, 122,
    145, 147, 151, 198, 200, 246, 249
protolanguage 261–2

raising 27, 61, 71–6, 79–85, 90, 98,
    100–4, 108

reversives 37, 221, 226, 268
rhyming slang 73

scenario 13, 22, 25–6, 58, 96–7, 108,
    135–6, 156–8, 180, 184–5, 240
    Basic Shopping Scenario 182–4
    Obligation Scenario 180
    Reasoning Scenario 97–9, 175
    Regret Scenario 175–6
    Request Scenario 169–74, 180
    State-of-Affairs Scenario (SAS)
        156, 163, 167–8
semantics 1, 2, 19, 21, 23, 34, 76, 90,
    95, 109, 121, 127, 150, 178, 187–8,
    198–9, 226
sense generator (s-generator) 206–8
sense relations 189, 226, 228
space 37, 58, 202, 247
    blended space 174
    conditional space 173
    dispositional space 19, 242,
        244–5, 248–54, 258, 263, 268–9
    generic space 38
    hypothetical space 97
    image space 14–15, 19, 58,
        244–54, 258, 268–9
    input space 130, 133, 248–9
    mental space 37, 97, 112, 127,
        129–33, 173, 184, 213, 229, 265
    physical space 20, 29–30, 32, 216,
        224–46
    reality space 97
speech acts 1, 96, 103, 108, 136, 165–6,
    171, 179–80, 183–5, 203–4, 240
    indirect 23, 26, 166, 169, 172,
        268
synaesthesia 221, 237, 268
synecdoche 4, 22–3, 32–3, 38, 40, 44,
    189–90, 194, 200, 211–12, 216, 218,
    223–4
synonymy 3, 37–9, 49, 55, 161, 165,
    179, 185, 188–9, 193, 198, 208,
    213–23, 226, 228–9, 268–9
syntax 1, 2, 27, 60–1, 73–4, 95, 104,
    107, 235, 261–5

toponymy 147–9, 152